Faith and Reason
through Christian History

Faith and Reason
through Christian History
A Theological Essay

Grant Kaplan

The Catholic University of America Press
Washington, D.C.

Cataloging-in-Publication data available from the Library of Congress.
ISBN: 978-0-8132-3583-7
eISBN: 978-0-8132-3584-4

Table of Contents

Acknowledgments

This dedication begins where it began—in the classroom. I am thankful for the undergraduate students in my "THEO 259: Faith and Reason" courses offered during the 2014–15 academic year. The initial stages of the project were propelled by the excellent conversations generated in those classes. Numerous interruptions delayed the completion of this book, some of which were joyful—the birth of two children and the opportunity to relocate to Germany on two different occasions.

I was aided by multiple graduate assistants. Three stand out: Joshua Schendel, Stephen Lawson, and Mitchell Stevens. They read drafts with keen eyes and attended to more mundane tasks like tracking down books and articles. The book also benefited from the charitable readings and conversations of many colleagues former and present: William O'Brien, SJ, Mary Dunn, Jay Hammond, Atria Larson, Randy Rosenberg, Jeffrey Wickes, and Julie Rubio. From afar, Beth Beshear Toft read the entire manuscript and improved the wobbly prose and sometimes flaccid arguments. I cannot thank her sufficiently for the care and skill that surely surpassed all but the most seasoned professional editors.

Thanks are also owed to the team at CUA, especially John Martino, who encouraged the project at its most fragile moment, and Laureen Gleason, who steadily and swiftly guided it through production. In addition, I owe a debt of gratitude to Travis Myers, my most recent graduate assistant, for help in the final stages.

I was supported by Saint Louis University in numerous ways. Most noteworthy was a 2018 Summer Research Award and the Steber Chair in Theological Studies, which gave me additional research funds toward the end of the project. I also thank the National Institute of Newman Studies, which awarded me an Experienced Scholar Grant and permitted me to republish part of my article "Locating Newman: Faith and Reason in Newman and Johannes Kuhn," *Newman Studies Journal* 16, no. 2 (Winter 2019): 5–27, portions of which are incorporated into chapter 6.

Outside the academy, I thank my parish, Saint Margaret of Scotland. Through the course of walking in the faith with that parish community, I tried to keep in mind the need to reach a wider audience. I also owe thanks to the staff at MoKaBe's for keeping me happily caffeinated and fed over the years, before and through the pandemic.

Within the academy, but outside of my institution, I have been sustained by a number of friendships, both ecclesial and academic. I like to think that this book contributes to a larger project of theological renewal. The most proximate model of this renewal is Frederick Lawrence, my former professor whose student I will never stop being. Those who have particularly embodied this project and enlivened it with many memorable conversations deserve mention: Brian Robinette, Trent Pomplun, Ryan Marr, Kevin Hughes, James Alison, Anna Bonta Moreland, Leonhard Hell, Jeremy Wilkins, Stephen Lawson, Jennifer Newsome Martin, Jonathan King, Ryan Duns, Mark Miller, Aaron Pidel, Tim O'Malley, Elisabeth Kincaid, Jordan Wood, and John Betz (*frater inter fratrum*). It would be hard for me to imagine what I am trying to do and say without them.

This book is dedicated to my mother, Carol Kaplan. She provided an early model of faith seeking understanding, and without her influence and encouragement, my tenuous inhabitation of the intellectual or religious virtues would be in a far shabbier state than at present.

Preface

I.

For part of almost every summer, from sixth through tenth grade, I attended a Presbyterian camp in the Sierra Nevada mountain range with my best friend. His faith was more fervent than mine. The camp's activities mostly involved swimming, sports, songs, and some flirting in the later years. It was also a place of faith formation that my Catholic parish did not provide. The lively after-dinner sermons delivered by young charismatic preachers presented a stark contrast to the more somber and considerably shorter sermons I had been raised on. Through this camp I began to grasp that being a Christian rested on a personal decision, not just the circumstances of one's upbringing.

Around the same time that I began to reflect on what Christianity entailed, a bright camper raised questions about whether an intelligent, informed person could believe in a personal God. Our small group leader, still just a teenager, mentioned that the work of C. S. Lewis contained many of the answers to these and other important questions. The advice stuck with me, and a few weeks after coming down from the Sierra Nevada mountains I began to read C. S. Lewis's *Mere Christianity*. It was my first encounter with written theology, and I remember feeling the onrush of excitement when I encountered his apology for the existence of God and for Christianity. I had entered a world in which argumentation and logic could supplement the gift of faith I had received as a child, when I never questioned that God existed and could hear my prayers.

I had no notion that this seemingly spontaneous attempt at *faith seeking understanding* would begin a long search that would ultimately lead to my professional vocation. What was obvious, however, was that my identifying as Christian would depend on the discovery and affirmation of faith's intelligibility.

II.

In one sense this book began at that camp and grew roots when I began to read the non-fiction of Lewis. What follows, however, is not an apology along the lines of *Mere Christianity*, but rather an historical essay. First and foremost, this book is an "essay" in the older sense of an attempt or an effort. It is not a summa of the question, and does not claim or even attempt a comprehensive overview of the history of the question. Nor does it provide a theological reconciliation of faith and reason.[1] Its aim is more modest: It traces some of the key conversations, events, disputes, and figures that have propelled the conversation throughout the two-thousand-year history of Christianity. Compared to more sweeping overviews, it is joyfully parochial. It tells a story, and it tells it historically, as opposed to a typological telling in the spirit of Avery Dulles's "models."

A book of this length cannot hope to present each of the time periods in a way that attends to the nuances and diversity that accompany any period of historical Christianity. This book consciously chooses quality over quantity. By engaging a smaller range of figures, it permits these figures to speak for themselves and even to stretch their lungs a bit. Their voices are not stifled by an author seeking to summarize. They speak, sometimes loudly and a bit discordantly, in the pages below.

III.

The book begins with the scriptural attempts to address questions that arose as biblical monotheism encountered surrounding religious cultures. It ends with contemporary, twenty-first century challenges and the initial responses to these challenges by leading theologians, including Pope Benedict XVI's well-known "Regensburg Address." The intervening chapters trace important crises and responses that have shaped the relationship between faith and reason in the history of Christian theology. The decision to focus on mainstream, well-known theologians is justified based on the impact of these figures. Their thought, for better or worse, played a large part in determining the state of the question for their own, as well as for subsequent periods of theology.

One could argue that there is an imperative to recover figures lost to history in order to demonstrate how much broader and more

---

1. Such efforts are numerous and many of them quite good, although no attempt is made here to review them.

diverse the tradition is than the impression so often given. Such an argument has real merit. I would only respond by noting that almost all of Christian history is becoming forgotten. The conversation is open and I hope the book spurs more to join it.

As an essay, the book points to, and even claims normativity for, a certain recurring Christian grammar about faith and reason. It is a *theological* essay, meaning that it allows the grammatical structure of Christian speech about God to guide it through the past twenty centuries. In doing so it moves toward answering a set of questions: Why did different syntheses between faith and reason, achieved by Latin and Greek Church Fathers, and reconceived by the towering figures of medieval scholasticism, come to be seen as unrealizable in the modern period? What caused faith and reason to be seen as irreconcilable? To answer these questions requires tilting the focus toward the modern period. As modernity occasioned many of the problems that beset attempts to reconcile faith and reason, it was also the period in history when the question heated up.

Besides devoting six of nine chapters to the modern period, the book also takes up a more primary challenge: to show the rationality of faith in light of the extremes that this search can engender. These extremes are often identified by the terms *fideism* and *rationalism*, both of which dissolve one order of knowing into another. Fideism asserts that faith alone provides what is necessary for knowledge of God and Christ. Reason only corrupts and pollutes what is known by faith. On the cusp of the third century, Tertullian, a North African bishop, wrote the "Prescription Against Heretics," where he bellowed:

> What indeed has Athens to do with Jerusalem? What concord is there between the Academy and the Church? . . . Away with attempts to produce a mottled Christianity of Stoic, Platonic, and dialectical compensation! We want no curious disputation after possessing Christ Jesus, no inquisition after enjoying the gospel! With our faith we desire no further belief.[2]

2. Tertullian, "The Prescription Against Heretics," in *Ante-Nicene Fathers,* eds. Roberts and Donaldson, vol. 3, *Latin Christianity: Its Founder, Tertullian* (Peabody, MA: Hendrickson, 1994), 246.

Tertullian's revulsion toward "mottled Christianity" would be echoed and reformulated by many theologians, either in spirit or in letter, in subsequent centuries.

Rationalism, by contrast, dissolves the knowledge gained from faith into truths attainable by reason alone. As a corollary, any revealed truth not also demonstrable to reason lacks the proper status of truth. A leading figure of the Enlightenment, Gotthold Lessing, declared, "Revelation . . . gives the human race nothing which human reason, left to itself, could not also arrive at."[3] According to Lessing, all religious or theological truths, regardless of whether they were given by God, can be discerned by the power of reason. Commitment to human progress almost demands that we seek a purely rational means and explanation for all truths, including those purportedly given from above. Rationalism did not first appear in the modern period, but it proved most compelling in the time of Lessing. These rationalizing tendencies pushed almost all of the traditional disciplines—theology, philosophy, classical studies, history—to follow the same methods as modern science in order to prove their legitimacy in the modern university.

Although the book is arranged historically and displays a definite caesura between modern and premodern theology, it is not genealogical. One kind of genealogy attempts to show how whatever is being said has prior origins. Another, more popular kind identifies a fall, which explains the subsequent decline. For the latter genealogists, medieval thought and culture, especially from the thirteenth century forward, committed the sins that paved the way for an eventual separation of faith and reason in modernity. Humpty Dumpty fell off his wall and could not be put back together again. Granted, all historical approaches must endeavor to illuminate contrasts between one period and another so as to move historical investigation beyond positivism. In the process of making contrasts, blame or praise can be assigned. But the chapters below do not present a neat and tidy narrative that solves the mystery of faith and reason—it was not the Scotist, in the

3. Lessing, "The Education of the Human Race," in *Philosophical and Theological Writings*, ed. and trans. H. B. Nisbet (Cambridge: Cambridge University Press, 2005), 218.

billiard room, with the lead pipe. *Faith and Reason through Christian History: A Theological Essay* examines its subjects closely and dispassionately, hoping to engender the same habits in the reader. Genealogies, by contrast, too often invite the reader to dismiss the subjects deemed no longer worthy of attention.

The attempt to show how a selection of leading figures from different historical periods understood the relationship between faith and reason presents an immediate challenge. To demonstrate a relationship between two stationary objects requires identifying first and foremost the location of these objects. If "faith" and "reason" had stable meanings, chronicling their relationship would perhaps merit an essay in the more contemporary sense. This stability, however, does not exist, which also makes a typological analysis only marginally helpful. In his important historical overview of faith, Avery Dulles concludes that typological analysis has:

> limited value because the authors do not share a common understanding of the meaning of either faith or reason. [...] It makes considerable difference whether faith is seen, for example, as an assent to doctrine, a unitive experience, a heartfelt trust in Christ, or a commitment to a certain style of action.[4]

Given that the meaning of faith and reason shifted between historical eras or even among theologians of the same era, illustrating the rationality of faith will always need to be performed anew. Only after acknowledging this state of affairs can one compare eras with the aim of finding a pattern.

IV.

The historical proximity between modernity and the Protestant Reformation has proven very tempting to some Catholic genealogists. Brad Gregory's *The Unintended Reformation* (2012) represents the most significant recent yielding to this temptation. In the book, Gregory draws a direct line between the Protestant Reformation and the rise of

---

4. Avery Dulles, *Assurance of Things Hoped For: A Theology of Christian Faith* (New York: Oxford University Press, 1994), 207.

modern secularism.[5] These attempts often coincide with efforts to portray Catholicism as the great synthesizer of faith and reason, while Protestantism, due to its "totally depraved" view of nature, mistrusts reason and opts for dialectic rather than analogy. Although written by a Catholic, this book is not an apologetic against a Protestant "rupture" of faith and reason that a Catholic synthesis corrects. My justification for avoiding such an apologetic does not stem from any desire for forced irenicism, but instead from a familiarity with Protestant theology. Yes, Luther made disparaging comments about reason, even calling it "the devil's whore."[6] Scholars of Luther have long recognized that such statements, shocking as they may sound, misrepresent Luther's theology of reason. Luther's *Disputatio de homine* (1536), for instance, declares that reason is "the most important and the highest in rank among all things and, in comparison with other things of his life, the best and something divine."[7] In reconciling this statement with Luther's more fideist pronouncements, Denis Janz notes, "[Reason's] proper jurisdiction and competence extend to all human affairs. When it claims supremacy in matters of faith, however, it becomes 'the Devil's whore,' for these things transcend reason."[8] Luther will be given fuller attention below. For now, it suffices to note that in this book Protestantism will not serve as a metonym for fideism. Whatever inclinations inhere in the modern Western denominations, both Catholic and Protestant, these traditions are too diverse and theologically complex to reduce to stereotypes. That having been said, the urgency to relate faith to reason seems most keenly felt by Catholic theologians, and their voices are given greater attention, especially in part III.

V.

To write a work not overly long and to proceed in the manner I have chosen, much has been passed over. One could almost just as easily

---

5. Brad Gregory, *The Unintended Reformation: How a Religious Revolution Secularized Society* (Cambridge: Belknap Press, 2012).

6. See Luther, *Luther's Works*, 40:175; 51:374.

7. *Luther's Works*, 34:137.

8. Denis Janz, "Whore or Handmaid? Luther and Aquinas on the Function of Reason in Theology," in *The Devil's Whore: Reason and Philosophy in the Lutheran Tradition*, ed. Jennifer Hockenberry Dragseth (Minneapolis: Fortress Press, 2011), 50.

substitute different voices for many of the figures below. A word about those omissions. Once the essay passes the fourth century, the riches of Eastern theology are wholly ignored. Likewise, many theologians from the fringes of mainstream Western academic theology are passed over without mention. Key mainstream theologians have been likewise elided. In order to keep the book from growing to a length that would rule out its purpose—to introduce newcomers to a theological topic—such decisions were made, not always to the liking of the author. It is hoped that those figures passed over in silence can, with the help of their staunchest advocates, be brought into conversation with the figures contained herein.

One could, of course, have written less about certain theologians in order to include others. Some might even find this book morally deficient for failing to do so. My decision to let the reader sit for a bit with Newman, or Aquinas, or to hear the words of Hugh of St. Victor for perhaps the first time, was also an ethical decision, and one that I hope pays dividends, even if it lends credence to the claim that traditionally under-represented voices have not been allowed to speak.

VI.

This essay unfolds in three parts. The first covers premodern theology, beginning with the Scriptures and ending in the late-medieval period. The second covers the arc of modernity from the eve of the Reformation through the great nineteenth-century figures of Newman and Kierkegaard. The final part treats "the long twentieth century," stretching from the rise of neo-scholasticism to the "Regensburg Address" of Pope Benedict in 2005. Each part contains three chapters, creating a triptych within a triptych. The chapters put into conversation multiple authors and movements with an aim of incarnating, so to speak, the conversational nature of the discipline of theology.

If the book comes off as conversational, it is because the history of theology is conversational. Not conversational in the pedestrian sense of two people sitting on a bench and talking about whatever happens to float through one's mind, but conversational in the sense of *con-verso*, to turn with. The history of theology, like the history of any field of discourse, takes a number of turns. Some turns lead to an opening hitherto unseen. Other turns lead to the need for a *re-versal*, or what Bernard Lonergan calls an inverse insight. Every tradition engages in the process of handing down a selective summation of what it considers most essential. This process of handing down inevitably involves and even demands a forgetting, thus stimulating, at some point, the need to *re-member*, to stitch together what has been dis-membered. In the ebb and flow of forgetting and remembering the collection of communities that call themselves Christian measure themselves against, distance themselves from, and pledge themselves to the collective life, spread out over time, called the body of Christ.

PART I

Premodern Christianity

Chapter 1

Christian Origins
Setting the Stage for Faith
and Reason

The most famous definition of theology comes from Anselm, who declared that faith seeks understanding. What, however, is the faith that one seeks to understand, to lend intelligibility to? Faith is both the content of things believed—the oneness of God, the Incarnation of the Son, that this incarnate Word was raised on the third day—and the mode of knowing by which one acquires this knowledge. The Bible captures this when it declares that "we walk by faith and not by sight" (2 Cor 5:7).[1] The matter of reconciling faith and reason involves taking up both the content of faith, the things believed, and the mode by which one knows these things. In the Old Testament, faith is attributed to God in the sense that God is faithful to Israel. Faith, or belief, also denotes a trust in God. Abraham, as the father of faith, exhibits an existential faith in the sense of placing his trust in God, and this faith "was reckoned to him as righteousness" (Rom 4:22). As the prototype of God's covenant with Israel, later scriptural authors recollect Abraham's faithfulness (Sir 44:19–20; Rom 4; Heb: 11:8–22).[2] While both Testaments emphasize the truthfulness of the message revealed to Israel and to the believing community, there is almost no effort given to relating faith to reason, or of showing the rationality of faith.

Like its Hebrew precursor, the New Testament noun *pistis*, meaning faith, and the root of the verb for "believe" (*pisteuein*) most often mean faith on a personal level, as trust or confidence.[3] Sometimes it

---

1. Throughout, biblical citations are from the Revised Standard Version (RSV).

2. For a basic overview of biblical faith, see Dulles, *The Assurance of Things Hoped For*, 7–19.

3. In their chapter "Faith in the Bible," Francesca Aran Murphy, Balazs M. Mezei, and Kenneth Oakes write, "The Hebrew root '*mn* is used in various forms in the Old

associates faith with salvation, as when Jesus declares, "Your faith has healed you" (Mark 5:34, Matthew 9:22; see also Mark 10:52, Luke 8:48, 8:50, 17:19, and 18:42). In such instances faith seems closer to trust than to a set of doctrines or teachings with an objective content. This meaning also appears in other biblical writings, especially in the Pauline corpus. Paul writes in Romans: "For one believes (*pisteuetai*) with the heart and so is justified" (10:10). Despite the strong correlation between belief and trust, the New Testament also emphasizes content. Although the creeds recited in many Christian churches today date only to the fourth century, the New Testament already contains proto-creeds. Paul writes to the Corinthians: "Christ died for our sins in accordance with the scriptures, [. . .] he was buried, and [. . .] raised on the third day in accordance with the scriptures" (1 Cor 15:3–4). A similar proto-creed appears in Acts: "I believe that Jesus Christ is the Son of God" (8:37).[4] The New Testament presents both the act of believing and the content of belief as central to the life of the community.

Reason is a concept almost totally missing from the biblical texts. The Greek word for reason, *logos*, also means speech, and perhaps most closely equates to *order*. John's Gospel famously opens with its *logos*-Christology—"In the beginning was the Word, and the Word was with God, and the Word was God. He was in the beginning with God" (1:1–2). Only rarely does it function in the rest of the New Testament as John employs it in his prologue. *Logos* can also be rendered as "saying" or "phrase." In some places it functions like "word," as in "I can put in a good word for you." Even when it denotes "reason" it does not always imply an abstract, intellective faculty, but something like "on what basis" (Acts 10:29).

From this brief lexical review, it seems that one can simply omit the New Testament texts from an overview of the relationship between faith and reason in the history of Christianity. This would be a mistake, for certain passages have served as signposts for the attempts by Chris-

---

Testament. [. . .] When used of human beings it signifies confidence, trust, loyalty and faithfulness (Gen 15.6 and Hab 2.4)." See their helpful introductory text: *Illuminating Faith: An Invitation to Theology* (New York: Bloomsbury, 2015), 3. Later they write, "The Septuagint translated all words with the root '*mn* into Greek words with the root *pist*" (Murphy, Mezei, Oakes, *Illuminating Faith,* 4).

4. Many commentators argue that this verse is a later insertion.

tians to find the best way to think about this relationship. Statements like 1 Peter 3:15—"Be prepared to give an account of the hope that is in you"—gave license to subsequent theologians to reconcile faith and reason, and to engage in the kind of high-wire project of uniting Jerusalem to Athens. It is therefore essential to review a few of these passages in order to anticipate a trajectory.

THE PAULINE APPROACH

No biblical passage has provided greater fuel to anti-intellectual tendencies in Christianity than the first two chapters of Paul's First Epistle to the Corinthians. Paul writes to a community in the midst of a schism based on a misguided allegiance to the person or group who baptized the fledgling Corinthian community (1:11–12). Paul warns against the "wisdom of words" (*sophia logou*)[5] that run the risk of emptying meaning from the "cross of Christ" (1:17). This is the first of many instances where Paul appears to contrast the gospel message with human ways of knowing. In the following verses, recalling a saying from Isaiah— "The wisdom of the wise men shall perish" (Is 29:14)—Paul contrasts God's ways with the ways of the world. He sets foolishness against wisdom, not faith against reason. Verse 25 summarizes his line of argument: "For the foolishness of God is wiser than human wisdom, and the weakness of God is stronger than human strength" (1:25).[6]

In the remaining verses of chapter 1, as well as chapter 2, Paul contrasts human and divine ways of knowing. He uses the adjective "wise," the noun "wisdom," or some variant thereof, twenty different times in chapters 1 and 2. Sometimes Paul employs wisdom, *sophia*, as an attribute of God—"we speak of God's wisdom" (2:7)—that Christ shares—"who became for us wisdom from God" (1:30). Thus wisdom is not bad, even though Paul juxtaposes it with a foolishness that saves. In chapter 2 he contrasts the wisdom of the age with a true wisdom: "Yet we do speak a wisdom to those who are mature, but not a wisdom

---

5. Here I have used the KJV, whose translation of this phrase is more literal than many more recent translations (the NAB translates *logou* as "human eloquence").

6. It is possible that Paul is intentionally referencing Isaiah here: "As high as the heavens are above the earth, so high are my ways above your ways and my thoughts above your thoughts" (55:9).

of this age" (2:6). This contrast is helpful to keep in mind in recalling the most frequently cited verse from these chapters: "For Jews demand signs and Greeks look for wisdom, but we proclaim Christ crucified, a stumbling block to Jews and foolishness to Gentiles" (1:22–23). Here Paul associates wisdom with pagan, Greek thought.

Paul writes to the Corinthians in an effort to respond to community divisions that resulted from overemphasizing the role of the baptizer. Throughout the opening chapters Paul argues that the gospel message of "Christ crucified" has confounded the wisdom, or common sense, of the powerful, who considered such a phrase an oxymoron. To believe in Jesus, therefore, meant already thinking about things counter-intuitive to worldly logic. But creating hierarchy in the Corinthian community based on the "status" of one's baptizer meant clinging to the old way of thinking that would not be able to imagine how a savior could suffer the humiliating fate of crucifixion.

Paul's visceral language and gripping metaphors make him a powerful evangelizer. Yet it would be a mistake to read Paul's stance in 1 Corinthians as an endorsement of fideism. Despite the contrast of wisdom to foolishness, in which Christianity aligns with foolishness, Paul does not regard the Christian worldview as opposed to a rational or scientific worldview. It would be more accurate to say that Paul presents two contrasting "orders of reasoning"—one that assumed might made right, and another that could find truth in the witness of the marginalized. It is the latter position that grasps things as they really are and thus enables the correct judgment about the most important things. After contrasting two kinds of wisdom in 2:6–7. Paul notes that, "if the rulers of this age had known [God's wisdom], they would not have crucified the Lord of glory" (2:8). This statement underlines how Christian wisdom is superior to the wisdom of the world.

Despite this analysis, there is no doubt that subsequent readers justified drawing the greatest possible contrast between faith and reason on the basis of Paul's words. When read carefully and in context, however, Paul offers a richer and subtler image of how faith and reason—understood in the broadest possible way—interact. Paul's position, even when calling Christianity foolish, does not call for Christians to abandon the intellectual life and replace it with blind trust in authority or another's testimony. Paul and John, so often contrasted in terms of their theological emphases, may be closer together on this question than often assumed.

ADDITIONAL NEW TESTAMENT REFLECTIONS

In a famous passage from Johann Wolfgang Goethe's *Faust*, the lead character sits in his study and seeks the highest truths of the world by attempting to translate the first verses from John's Gospel from Greek into German. He begins by translating *logos* as "word" but then laments: *Ich kann das Wort so hoch unmöglich schätzen, / Ich muß es anders übersetzen* ("I cannot value the word so impossibly high / I must translate it somehow else" [lines 1226–27]). Faust then tries on a number of alternatives: *meaning, power, act* (lines 1229–37). Goethe's play captures the difficulty in finding a suitable translation for *logos* in the preface to John's Gospel.

Some recent commentators on the Gospel of John have emphasized how the prologue attempts to bridge the Jewish biblical worldview of personal experience and encounter, on the one hand, with Greek philosophy, on the other. The prologue does this by identifying the *logos*—an abstract term connoting logic or order—with Jesus, understood in Jewish metaphor as Son of God. It would stretch credulity to read John's prologue, especially the opening verse, as cobbling together a synthesis between Jerusalem and Athens.[7] The first words— *en arche, in the beginning*—clearly reference the opening of Genesis. John's opening reads, "In the beginning was the Word, and the Word was with God, and the Word was God." Later in the prologue, John connects the *logos* and the human being, Jesus Christ: "The Word became flesh, and made his dwelling among us, and we saw his glory, the glory as of the Father's only Son" (1:14). John uses the same opening phrase as Genesis in order to link Jesus of Nazareth with the creator-God, who brought the universe into existence. John even defines

7. Regarding the link between John's use of *logos* and Greek philosophy, Pheme Perkins concludes, "Suggestions that part of John's unique perspective was shaped by philosophy, even of a popular sort, are unlikely." See Pheme Perkins, "The Gospel According to John," in *The New Jerome Biblical Commentary*, eds. Raymond E. Brown, Joseph A. Fitzmyer, and Roland E. Murphy (Englewood Cliffs, NJ: Prentice Hall, 1990), 944.

God as *logos*—"the Word was God." John deems the creative process described in Genesis as orderly and intentional, part of a plan that will come to include the Word becoming flesh, and revealing divine glory.

The rest of the Gospel offers little trace of the identity between Jesus and *logos*. Yet John's opening salvo made a lasting impact on subsequent efforts to apply the highest standards of rational thought to Christian discourse. If Paul's letters to the Corinthians gave permission for subsequent believers to ignore the standards of secular intellectuals, John's Gospel permitted believers to apply secular science and philosophy to biblical revelation. Part of this project involved showing the compatibility, even identity, between the natural law that ordered the cosmos and the divine will that created and sustained all things.

John's prologue is not the only scriptural text that inspired later efforts to reconcile biblical revelation with rational discourse. The third chapter of First Peter contains the cornerstone verse for later Christian apologetics: "Always be ready to make your defense (*apologian*) to anyone who demands from you a reason (*logon*) for the hope that is in you" (3:15). Whereas 1 Corinthians emphasized the contrast between worldly and divine ways of knowing, 1 Peter indicates recourse to a common language for issuing a defense of faith. The text casts this advice in the imperative, capped with "always," thus implying a duty to be able to defend "the hope that is in you," a metonym for the content of Christian belief. Many have taken this passage to mean that Christians should be ready and able to defend their beliefs with the use of reason. This imperative seems, like John's prologue, to stand in tension with Paul's advice, especially 1 Cor 1:17: "For Christ did not send me to baptize but to proclaim the gospel, and not with wisdom of words (*sophia logou*), so that the cross of Christ might not be emptied of its power." More than any other verse, 1 Peter 3:15 has inspired those engaged in the branch of theology called "fundamental theology," which employs arguments from philosophy or other extra-theological disciplines in order to strengthen claims for the credibility of the act of faith.

The biblical texts occupy an exalted place for Christians, yet a brief perusal of these texts unveils a tension concerning how to relate faith to reason. It is not surprising to learn that subsequent attempts to relate these terms led many Christian authors to turn to the Bible for inspiration, yet few of these attempts produced a solution. Part of the basis for the long and seemingly irresolvable argument about how to relate the two is rooted in the lack of a uniform biblical teaching. One must engage the history of theology for a more satisfactory answer to the question of how faith reconciles itself to reason.

JUSTIN MARTYR

The movement toward a clearly defined Christianity, with a canon and a creed, proved an untidy and arduous process. Early Christianity did not live in a bubble or breathe pure oxygen unsullied by the messiness of particularity and place. The first generations of Christians did not inhabit a self-contained world of Second Temple Judaism. Hellenistic influences had already altered the course of Judaism. Additionally, Israel was under Roman occupation. The Jewish people had for centuries been subject to a diaspora, beginning with the sixth-century exile imposed by the Babylonian captivity. By the time of Paul's missionary work, Jews found themselves spread throughout different parts of the Middle East, Northern Africa, Mediterranean Europe, and Asia Minor (modern-day Turkey). The Acts of the Apostles relate that Paul first went to the Jewish communities on his missions. Not long into these travels, Paul (as well as Peter, as reported in Acts 10), began to realize that the gospel proclamation could find a receptive audience among not only Jews, but among Gentiles as well. By following the risen Lord's command at the end of Matthew, to preach the gospel to the ends of the earth, early Christians, sometimes by means of painful deliberation, came to understand this command to mean preaching not just to exiled Jews, but to Gentiles as well.

No matter what early Christians thought of this shift in mission, all would have agreed that it required a different strategy. One sees this already in the way Paul preaches at the Acropolis in Athens (Acts 17), compared to his pleas in different synagogues.[8] Gentiles did not accept the authority of the Hebrew Scriptures, so the kind of arguments that showed how Jesus fulfilled what the Jewish prophets had

---

8. For compelling research on the nature of Paul's arguments, see Matthew Thiessen, *Paul and the Gentile Problem* (Oxford: Oxford University Press, 2016).

foretold did not prove as effective. The sporadic and short-lived Jewish persecution of Christians, witnessed to in Acts and alluded to in John, preceded and coincided with Roman persecution of Christianity. This political reality also shaped the nature of the apologetic arguments called for in 1 Peter 3:15. One of the most important second-century apologists, Justin Martyr, wrote in the context of this persecution.

A Samaritan by birth, Justin became immersed in Greek culture and thought. In his *Dialogue with Trypho* Justin recalls his intellectual odyssey. This journey began with his encounter with the Stoics, who taught him "nothing new about God," before he passed through the Peripatetics, Pythagoreans, and Platonists.[9] At a point of despair, Justin found himself walking along a path near the sea. Here he came into conversation with a "respectable old man" who teased out of Justin, in the course of a Socratic back and forth, the conclusion that philosophy, even the Platonic variety, had not answered his deepest questions.[10] Unable to respond adequately to the old man's queries, Justin asked him for advice, and he recommended the prophets, who "made known Christ."[11] Justin describes his conversion thusly: "My spirit was immediately set on fire, and an affection for the prophets, and for those who are friends of Christ, took hold of me; while pondering on his words, I discovered that his was the only sure and useful philosophy."[12] In Justin's account, a true seeker of wisdom will eventually settle on Christianity, whose truths are higher than those of any other philosophy or religion.[13] Justin's embrace of Christianity eventually led to his being martyred, most likely in 167 AD.

---

9. Justin Martyr, *Dialogue with Trypho*, chapter 2. I have consulted the following translation: St. Justin Martyr, *Dialogue with Trypho*, trans. Thomas B. Falls (Washington, DC: The Catholic University of America Press, 2003).

10. Justin, *Dialogue with Trypho*, 3.

11. Justin, *Dialogue with Trypho*, 7. It is noteworthy that the old man does not recommend the Gospels, most likely because they were not yet widely dispersed.

12. Justin, *Dialogue with Trypho*, 8.

13. Here it is worth mentioning briefly the persuasive but under-read work of Pierre Hadot, who argues that classical philosophy functioned much more like religion—as a way of life with ascetical practices—than we recognize. See Pierre Hadot, *Philosophy as a Way of Life: Spiritual Exercises from Socrates to Foucault*, ed. Arnold I. Davidson, trans. Michael Chase (Oxford: Blackwell, 1995); *What is Ancient Philosophy?*, trans. Michael Chase (Cambridge, MA: Harvard University Press, 2002). An attentive reading of Justin lends further evidence to Hadot's thesis that no gulf separated philosophy and religion in the ancient world.

Besides the *Dialogue with Trypho*, Justin is best known for his two apologies, both dated between 150 and 160 AD. Justin's main thesis in the *First Apology*—the longer and more influential of the two—is that Christianity is the one, true philosophy. After his introduction, he states, "Reason (*logos*) dictates that those who are truly pious and philosophers should honor and love only the truth, declining to follow the opinions of the ancients if they are worthless."[14] Justin does not appeal to faith, or to the authority of sacred or ancient texts, but to the truth and to the love of wisdom (*philo-sophia*). Justin addresses his appeal to the Emperor Titus, and to his son as well as Lucius, both philosophers. Justin makes a plea for a fair judgment against Christianity, based on sound reason rather than irrational impulse, or "unreasoning passion" (*alogo pathei*).[15]

In making his appeal to the authorities—the Roman emperor and his key advisors, who decide whether professing Christianity should be a crime punishable by death—Justin references the trial of Socrates. Just as the courts in Socrates's Athens made an irrational choice, so too do those who persecute Christians. They will be judged by Christ, reason personified. He writes, "For these errors were not only condemned among the Greeks by reason, through Socrates, but among the barbarians, by Reason (*Logos*) himself, who took form and became man and was called Jesus Christ."[16] This reference to John's prologue exemplifies the kind of retrieval that happened at the very beginning of Christian theology. In order to make an argument suitable to the situation, Justin appeals to the most fitting scriptural passage. His fate, and the fate of other Christians awaiting their sentence in Rome, lay in the hands of a philosopher-prince. His immediate goal was to secure their release.

---

14. Justin Martyr, *The First Apology*, 2. The apology by standard convention is divided into 67 paragraphs. I will cite by paragraph number. I have consulted the following edition: *St. Justin Martyr: The First and Second Apologies*, trans. Leslie William Barnard (New York: Paulist Press, 1997).

15. Justin, *The First Apology*, 5. Here one can also note that Clement of Alexandria, the teacher of Origen, argued that, just as the Old Testament prepared Jews to receive the gospel, so did philosophy prepare Greeks to receive it. Justin embodied this idea. See Clement of Alexandria, *Stromateis* Book I. v. 20. For a modern edition, see Clement of Alexandria, *Stromateis Books One to Three*, trans. John Ferguson (Washington, DC: The Catholic University of America Press, 1991).

16. Justin, *The First Apology*, 5.

Justin's appeal centers not just on the compatibility between Christian belief and reason, but specifically on the overlap between the two. Reasoning, according to Justin and to Platonism, did not constitute a purely human activity, self-enclosed and separated from God; instead, reasoning participated in the divine. The gift of being created in God's "image and likeness" entailed the capacity to reason and to make ethical decisions that constituted human activity, properly speaking. According to the underlying logic of Justin's apologetic, true or proper reasoning, whenever and wherever it occurs, brings its practitioners closer to the gospel. Justin makes an astounding claim: "We have been taught that Christ is the First-begotten of God and have previously testified that he is the Reason of which every race of man partakes. Those who live in accordance with Reason are Christians, even though they were called godless. [. . .] So also those who lived without Reason were ungracious and enemies to Christ, and murderers of those who lived by Reason. But those who lived by Reason, and those who so live now, are Christians, fearless and unperturbed."[17] Justin draws a continuity between the death of Christ and of subsequent Christians, and the death of Socrates, the most admired philosopher in the classical world. Just as the truth lay with Socrates, not his accusers, so the truth aligns with Christians, not the Romans who persecute them.

In one of his more controversial (and also misunderstood) theological positions, Karl Rahner, perhaps the most influential Catholic theologian of the twentieth century, used the term "anonymous Christian" to describe those who could qualify as Christian without professing it explicitly.[18] Writing roughly 1800 years before Rahner, Justin seems to believe the same thing. Living by reason, for Justin, does not meaning living without God, but rather with and in God. Since Plato's writings so closely approximate biblical revelation, Justin posits that Plato must have borrowed them from Moses.[19]

17. Justin, *The First Apology*, 46.
18. Rahner treats the theme of anonymous Christianity in a variety of essays collected in his multi-volume *Theological Investigations*. For a concise summary of his position, see the chapter by Stephen J. Duffy, "Experience of Grace," in *The Cambridge Companion to Karl Rahner*, eds. Declan Marmion and Mary Hines (Cambridge: Cambridge University Press, 2005), 43–62, esp. 52–55, and 60–61n20.
19. He states, "When Plato said, 'The blame belongs to him who chooses, and God is free from blame,' he took this from the prophet Moses. For Moses was earlier than

His second and much shorter apology takes on the same tenor as the first. Here too Justin appeals to reason, understood not as calculating or instrumental reason, but as insight into the very order of things, through which rational creatures come to know what is right and just ("right reason," a phrase borrowed from Stoic philosophy). Here Justin uses a different metaphor to explain the overlap between Christianity and the best of the classical philosophical tradition. Justin attributes this overlap to the "seed of reason" (*sperma tou logou*)[20] that has been given to all of humanity. Justin bases the implicit justification on the Word that was from the very beginning. Earlier philosophers and prophets participated in this *logos*, but Christians live "by the knowledge and contemplation of the whole logos, who is Christ."[21] Christians, metaphorically, bathe in the *logos* into which earlier philosophers merely dipped their toes.

Justin's argument recalls the Johannine connection between Jesus and *logos* outlined above: "In the beginning was the word." Earlier traditions had access to this *logos*: "Whatever either lawgivers or philosophers uttered well, they elaborated according to their share of *logos* by invention and contemplation."[22] Prior actions can also anticipate the saving deed revealed in Christ's passion. The death of Socrates foretells the death of Christ in that Socrates, because he told the truth and thus aroused the anger of the demons, was brought to death before a tribunal. Christ dies a better death than Socrates, on account of the fact that Christ's followers came from a more diverse social milieu, and these followers willingly died undignified deaths.

Justin has been rightly lauded as the first Christian apologist. His own path to Christ wandered through the different philosophical schools. Whatever is good in these pre-Christian teachings can be understood as consistent with Christianity: "whatever things were rightly said among all people are the property of us Christians. For next to God, we worship and love the *logos* who is from the unbe-

Plato and all the Greek writers" (*First Apology*, 44). The citation comes from Plato's *Republic*, 617e.

    20. Justin, *The Second Apology*, 8.
    21. Justin, *The Second Apology*, 8.
    22. Justin, *The Second Apology*, 10.

gotten and ineffable God."[23] Justin did not experience the surrounding culture as friendly and did not see the solution for Christianity in a bland "openness to cultures." He succeeded, however, in shedding light on how classical philosophy could also be subversive of dominant cultural and political forms. He drew continuity between classical philosophy and Christian doctrine, and his writings inaugurated a long tradition of Christian openness to science, while expressing serious reservations about the surrounding cultural and political milieu.

IRENAEUS OF LYONS

Next to Origen, Irenaeus (c. 130–200) can be considered perhaps the greatest Christian mind before the Council of Nicaea in 325.[24] His theology continues to draw interest. Especially through the work of Hans Urs von Balthasar, Irenaeus's critiques of Gnosticism have served as a model for modern Christianity's critique of secularism.[25] One can surmise that he was an established ecclesiastical figure by 177, when he wrote a letter about Roman persecutions.[26] Irenaeus also mentions his personal acquaintance with Polycarp, who was martyred in 155. Born in Smyrna, a city in Asia Minor (modern-day Turkey) not far from Ephesus, Irenaeus made his way to Rome, where he possibly studied under Justin Martyr and read Justin's works. He eventually settled in Lyons, in modern-day France. Although many imagine a life north of the Alps cut off from the classical Mediterranean world, second-cen-

---

23. Justin, *The Second Apology*, 13.

24. Robert Grant writes, "Irenaeus of Lyons was the most important Christian controversialist and theologian between the apostles and the third-century genius Origen." See Robert Grant, "The Life of Irenaeus," in *Irenaeus of Lyons* (New York: Routledge, 1997), 1.

25. Balthasar published a selection of Irenaeus's famous text against the Gnostics. The English title reads: *The Scandal of the Incarnation: Irenaeus Against the Heresies*, selected and introduced by Hans Urs von Balthasar (San Francisco: Ignatius, 1990). For a study of Irenaeus's influence on von Balthasar, see Kevin Mongrain, *The Systematic Thought of Hans Urs von Balthasar: An Irenaean Retrieval* (New York: Crossroad/Herder, 2002). For the connection between ancient and modern Gnosticism, as viewed through "Irenaean lenses," see Cyril O'Regan, *Gnostic Return in Modernity* (New York: SUNY Press, 2001). Editors of an important selection of early Christian texts write of Irenaeus, "No Christian writer of the age before Augustine has been so frequently called to enter directly into our modern controversies" (*Early Christian Fathers*, ed. Cyril C. Richardson et al. (New York: Simon & Schuster, 1996), 343.

26. I have gleaned the bibliographical information from the "Introduction" to his writings in *Early Christian Fathers*, 343–54.

tury Lyons served as an important imperial center in the Gallic region of the Roman Empire. When Irenaeus arrived, he engaged in missionary work as presbyter and eventually bishop.

Like Justin, Irenaeus migrated from the Greek East to the Latin west, but still wrote in Greek, which was considered the language of learning and culture until the fifth century. His most famous text, *On the Detection and Refutation of the Knowledge Falsely So Called* (often referred to as *Against the Heresies*), comes to us via a Latin translation, in which Irenaeus defends Christianity against the heretical movement called Gnosticism. Modern scholars have rightly cautioned against using the term Gnosticism, an umbrella term encompassing a variety of teachings and movements. Much like "liberalism," which in one century denoted a belief in free-market economics and in another century leftist progressivism, so Gnosticism did not carry a stable meaning. In Irenaeus's century, Marcion led a movement of Christians who denied the connection between the Old and New Testaments and rejected the goodness of the physical world, leading to a skepticism about the Incarnation and the bodily resurrection. Valentinus, a contemporary of Marcion, left a group of followers whose doctrines Irenaeus sought to refute in *Against the Heresies*.

Here we must shift the syntax of the chapter away from *pistis/logos* and toward *gnosis/paradosis* (tradition), two key terms for Irenaeus. Irenaeus's arguments against the Valentinians extend into soteriology, protology, and Trinitarian theology, but for our purposes we will focus on one aspect, Irenaeus's appeal to authority. Before doing so, it will prove helpful to remember Gnosticism as the first major *internal* threat to Christianity. Balthasar's vivid introduction to his selection of *On the Detection and Refutation* makes this point rather dramatically:

> Then, like a vampire, the parasite took hold of the youthful bloom and vigour of Christianity. What made it so insidious was the fact that the Gnostics very often did not want to leave the Church. Instead, they claimed to be offering a superior and more authentic exposition of Holy Scripture, though, of course, this was only for the "superior souls" ("the spiritual," "the pneumatic"); the common folk ("the psychic") were left to get on with their crude practices. It

is not hard to see how this kind of compartmentalizing of the Church's members [. . .] inevitably encouraged [. . .] an almost unbounded arrogance in those who had moved from mere "faith" to real, enlightened "knowledge."[27]

Gnostics thought salvation came through a knowledge (*gnosis*), and that superior, spiritual types had special access to this knowledge. In order to bring out Irenaeus's contribution to faith and reason, it will be helpful to focus on his theology of tradition.

Unlike Justin, just a generation before him, Irenaeus had much greater access to the books of the New Testament, which he quoted liberally in his corpus. Yet the Marcionites and Valentinians did as well. The question naturally arose: Who had the authority to interpret the Scriptures? The Gnostics located their authority in the special powers of their elite members. In Irenaeus's mind, tradition trumped charism. He offers genealogies of the leadership of the churches in Rome and in his hometown of Smyrna, where he heard the preaching and teaching of Polycarp. Irenaeus recalls, "We ourselves saw him in our early youth, for he lived long [. . .] He always taught the doctrine he had learned from the apostles, which he delivered to the church, and it alone is true."[28] Irenaeus traces the authentic teaching back through Polycarp to the original circle of John the Evangelist's disciples. This communal tradition, in Irenaeus's account, provides "housing" for answers to the questions that subsequently emerge: "If some question of minor importance should arise, would it not be best to turn to the most ancient churches, those in which the apostles lived?"[29] The Gnostics, by contrast, cannot trace their doctrines through any analogous tradition, let alone one that goes all the way back to the apostles: "Before Valentinus there were no disciples of Valentinus; before Marcion there were no disciples of Marcion."[30]

Irenaeus brings to the conversation a fundamentally conservative presupposition. The older, more original doctrine must be the better one. Additionally, differences can be adjudicated through appeal to

27. Balthasar, "Introduction," in *The Scandal of the Incarnation*, 1.
28. Irenaeus, *On the Detection and Refutation*, III, 3.4; Grant, *Irenaeus of Lyons*, 126.
29. Irenaeus, *On the Detection and Refutation*, III, 4.1; Grant, *Irenaeus of Lyons*, 127.
30. Irenaeus, *On the Detection and Refutation*, III, 4.3; Grant, *Irenaeus of Lyons*, 127.

authority. He writes of his appeal, "This is a complete proof that the life-giving faith is one and the same, preserved and transmitted in truth in the church from the apostles up till now."[31] As a consequence of his battle with the Gnostics, Irenaeus exposits a tradition-centered, conservative mentality: What has been taught should continue being taught; an authentic manifestation of Christianity traces its roots to the apostolic source. Cyril Richardson explains, "He was, to be sure, a man of tradition, *paradosis*. To him, however, what was handed down was [. . .] a means of living contact with the sources of life, indeed with the Life himself."[32] Christianity was primarily something to be lived and only secondarily to be contemplated. The most authentic form of connection to the original teaching of Jesus was organic, not speculative, and the means of this encounter was sacramental—mediated through rituals like baptism and Eucharistic celebration—not theoretical.

Irenaeus frames his answer to the Gnostic crisis within a grammar of tradition. He highlights the contrast between the Scriptures and the doctrinal tradition on one side, and Gnostic innovation on the other. Unlike Justin, concerned mainly with dialoguing with non-believers, Irenaeus faces an intramural challenge. If John's prologue inspired Justin, John's first epistle may have done the same for Irenaeus: "What was from the beginning, what we have heard, what we have seen with our eyes, what we looked upon and touched with our hands concerns the Word of life" (1 John 1:1). Here the author of the epistle appeals to a personal encounter, which trumps any appeal to intellectual innovation or discovery. The goodness of the Lord is to be tasted and seen (Psalm 34:9), not abstractly known. The crisis brought about by the Gnostic challenge compelled Christians to answer questions not just about what counted as authentic, revelatory texts, but also what inspired these texts. Was the Christianity of the following centuries capable of appealing not merely to authority, but to a reasonable method for interpreting the authoritative texts—the Old and New Testaments—so as to forestall attempts to hijack the basic teaching of Christianity? Nobody rose to the task with greater force than Origen of Alexandria (c. 185–253).

---

31. Irenaeus, *On the Detection and Refutation*, III, 3.2; Grant, *Irenaeus of Lyons*, 125.
32. Richardson, "Introduction," in *Early Christian Fathers*, 350.

ORIGEN OF ALEXANDRIA

Origen's *Peri Archon*, or *On First Principles*, anticipates later attempts at devising a theological system or systematic theology, however anachronistic such a comparison may be.[33] Arranged in four books, *On First Principles* offers a comprehensive, interconnected account of cosmology, Christology, salvific economy, and scriptural interpretation.[34] The Alexandria of Origen's time was a leading intellectual center, and Origen, like his father, served as a catechist for initiates. His contributions were vast, even if many of them have been lost. Perhaps his most impressive work was the oversight he gave to the first "critical edition" of the Bible, the *Hexapla*, which arranged six different translations and editions side by side to aid in comparison and thus advance understanding of the biblical text. Although he was condemned posthumously at the Council of Constantinople in 553,[35] which led to the destruction of a number of his writings, Origen still left a rich corpus, including many scriptural commentaries and mystical writings. The leading *ressourcement* theologians of the twentieth century—Henri de Lubac, Hans Urs von Balthasar, and Jean Daniélou—took great effort in restoring Origen's reputation by researching some of the problematic ways in which later insertions by opponents of Origen made their way into his texts and thus negatively colored the reception of his thought, especially in the Christian West.

33. See, for one example, Francis Schüssler Fiorenza, "Systematic Theology: Tasks and Methods," in *Systematic Theology: Roman Catholic Perspectives*, 2nd ed., eds. Francis Schüssler Fiorenza and John P. Galvin (Minneapolis: Fortress, 2011), where he writes, under the subheading "Beginning of Systematic Theology in the Greek Church," "[Origen] gave a systematic presentation of theology that indeed has earned him the label of the first systematic theologian" (Fiorenza, Galvin, *Systematic Theology*, 7). Sarah Coakley writes that Origen's *On First Principles*, "has often been read in the modern period as his attempt to do 'systematic theology.'" See Coakley, *God, Sexuality, and the Self: An Essay 'On the Trinity'* (Cambridge: Cambridge University Press, 2013), 37.

34. For a helpful introduction both to his life and to the theology of *On First Principles*, see John Behr, "Introduction," to *Origen: On First Principles: A Reader's Edition*, trans. John Behr (Oxford, Oxford University Press, 2019), xiii–lxxxviii.

35. For the connection between Origen's condemnation and his place in the "Hellenization" of Christianity, see Peter W. Martens, "Embodiment, Heresy, and the Hellenization of Christianity: The Descent of the Soul in Plato and Origen," *Harvard Theological Review* 108:4 (2015), 594–620, at 596.

Written around 229/230, *On First Principles* provides the clearest example of Origen's understanding of how faith relates to reason. His opening paragraph gestures toward John's prologue: "By the words of Christ we mean not only those which he spoke when he became human and dwelt in the flesh; for even before this, Christ, the Word of God, was in Moses and the prophets. For without the Word of God how could they have been able to prophesy of Christ?"[36] In part due to his very Platonic argument for the pre-existence of souls, casual acquaintance with Origen can lead to casting him as a speculative, philosophical theologian. Yet later in the same preface he echoes Irenaeus regarding the crisis of Christian churches in conflict: "One must guard the ecclesiastical preaching, handed down from the apostles through the order of succession and remaining in the churches to the present: that alone is to be believed to be the truth which differs in no way from the ecclesiastical and apostolic tradition."[37] Origen, the paradigmatic figure of "Alexandrian," that is, philosophical, Hellenistic Christianity, like Irenaeus, grounded his thought in tradition.

Before turning to his hermeneutical theory, it is helpful to recall that, like Irenaeus, Origen polemicized against dissenters, in his case the pagan critic Celsus. In *True Doctrine*, Celsus accused Christians of disregarding reason and replacing it with blind faith. He complained, "Some Christians do not even want to give or to receive a reason for what they believe, and use expressions such as 'Do not ask questions, just believe' and 'Your faith will save you.'"[38] Origen addressed Celsus's critique in *Contra Celsum* by showing that Christianity could be respectable to Platonists, in order to refute Celsus's claim that no self-respecting Platonist could ever take Christianity seriously.[39] Origen was willing to take on his critic on the critic's terms.

36. Although many readers are more familiar with the older edition translated by G. W. Butterworth, I have chosen to cite from the new translation by John Behr: *Origin: On First Principles*, 5 (Preface).

37. Origen, *On First Principles*, 6 (Preface).

38. We do not have Celsus's text, but the fragments that remain in Origen's response, *Contra Celsus*. For this passage, see *Contra Celsus*, I.9. I have cited it from Robert Louis Wilken, *The Spirit of Early Christian Thought: Seeking the Face of God* (New Haven, CT: Yale University Press, 2003), 162.

39. For an English translation see Origen, *Contra Celsum*, trans. Henry Chadwick (Cambridge: Cambridge University, 1953).

As Robert Wilken notes, "No one can read Celsus's *True Doctrine* and Origen's *Contra Celsum* and come away thinking that Celsus, a pagan philosopher, appealed to reason and argument and Origen relied solely on authority and faith."[40] In addition, Origen also revisits claims made earlier about the proper way to interpret the Bible, which he lays out succinctly in the fourth book of *On First Principles.*

To understand what was at stake in the matter of biblical interpretation, it is necessary to step back and assess the type of religion Christianity claims to be. Unlike a purely natural religion, to which one would have access by natural reason, Christianity is a historical religion, meaning that its deepest truths rest on historical claims. Consider, for example, the claims made in Christianity's most universal creed—born of the Virgin Mary, crucified under Pontius Pilate, rose again on the third day—these are claims about historical events. In addition to grand metaphysical claims—true God from true God, one in being with the Father—the Nicene-Constantinople creed also makes definitive historical claims, upon which the faith of the church rests. As Nicholas Lash explains, "What the Scriptures say at length, the creed says briefly."[41] Although not all Christian churches would equate the word of God with the Old and New Testaments, all Christian churches agree that Scripture accurately and faithfully reflects God's word, and thus has an ongoing, undeniable authority for Christians. Scripture also had authority for Gnostics, and, in the case of the Jews, the Old Testament was *their* sacred text first. Yet these three groups read these texts in ways that led them to very different conclusions about key questions, like whether the Son of God was identical with Jesus of Nazareth. If Origen was not the first to realize the implications of this dilemma, he was the first to understand the dire consequences, and to attempt to offer a solution that would anticipate future problems.

A text, even a sacred text, can never transmit meaning by itself. It requires a reader. And the reader engages in an activity—interpreta-

---

40. Wilken, *The Spirit of Early Christian Thought,* 163.

41. See Nicholas Lash, *Believing Three Ways in One God. A Reading of the Apostles' Creed* (Notre Dame: University of Notre Dame Press, 1992), 8. The gist of this laconic statement is fleshed out in this delightful commentary on the Creed.

tion—that is less passive than appears at first glance. Origin discusses three groups of people—Jews, heretics, and "simple believers"—all of whom reach the wrong conclusions about God and Jesus. The cause of their erroneous conclusions lies in their failure to interpret the Bible according to its spiritual sense: "Now, the reason for the false apprehension of all these points by those whom we have mentioned above is nothing other than this, that Holy Scripture is not understood by them according to its spiritual sense, but according to the sound of the letter."[42] The problem does not have to do with these groups not accepting the validity of the sacred text, but instead with the way they were reading the text. The "heretics," who would have followed Marcion, took the images of an angry God of the Old Testament too literally and thus thought that the God of the Old Testament was a different, inferior God. The Jews did not interpret the prophesies in their scriptures according to the spiritual sense, so they were not able to conceive how Jesus fulfilled them. The "simple," a precursor to current-day fundamentalists, read every arbitrary or violent act attributed to God literally. If interpreted in this way, then the Bible demanded that believers obey and worship a God who was neither good nor just, but merely omnipotent.

How should the Bible be interpreted and what kind of text is it? Origen notes that much in the writings of Paul and Revelation could qualify as mystical and thus not easily understood. He notes,

> And who, on reading the revelations made to John, would not be struck with amazement at the obscurity of the unspeakable mysteries, evident even to one who does not understand what is written? And to whom of those skilled in investigating words would the epistles of the apostles seem to be plain and easily understood, since there are in them thousands of passages providing as if through a lattice a narrow opening to the greatest and deepest thoughts?[43]

These passages demand a sophisticated method. Yet so do the more banal passages, for instance, which portray a brutal God, or defy basic logic, like the creation according to "days" which precede the creation

42. Origen, *On First Principles*, 248 (IV.2.2).
43. Origin, *On First Principles*, 251 (IV.2.3).

of the sun, as in Genesis. The plain absurdity or moral horror inspired by a literal, or what Origen calls a "bodily," interpretation indicates the need to look for a spiritual or allegorical meaning. Origen explains, "But since there are certain passages which do not at all contain the bodily sense at all [. . .] there are places where it is necessary to seek only the soul and the spirit, as it were, of the Scriptures."[44] Origen recommends a method foretold in Proverbs (22:20):

> It is necessary to register in one's own soul the senses of the sacred writings thrice: so that the simple may be edified from the *flesh*, as it were, of Scripture, for so we designate the obvious interpretation; while one who has ascended a certain measure may be edified by the *soul*, as it were; and the person who is perfect [. . .] may be edified from the *spiritual* law. [. . .] Just as the human being consists of body and soul and spirit, in the same way so also does Scripture.[45]

Not all believers have the education and the spiritual maturity to decode the different layers of scriptural meaning. Although this may sound snobbish or elitist to modern ears, this judgment can be softened by comparing it to watching a sport like baseball. The simple can understand and can cheer for home runs, or strikeouts, and indeed these results often generate the greatest applause. Only those more advanced fans can appreciate the strategy of an intentional walk, or a seemingly abrupt pitching change. The wise, meanwhile, enjoy the game at the other levels, also appreciating the subtle shifts before a pitch is thrown, the subterfuge of middle infielders against base runners, and the intricate ways in which a manager strategizes to win in the short term but also steers the team over a six-month season.

Origen's method anchors itself not only in Scripture but in classical anthropology. Just as the human being consisted in a complex, interwoven nature of flesh (*sarx*), soul or life (*psyche*), and spirit (*pneuma*), so the Scriptures, analogously, consist in these three "layers" of meaning. Origen found allusion to this threefold structure in Scripture itself. Second Corinthians 3:6 provided his most direct confirma-

---

44. Origin, *On First Principles*, 255 (IV.2.5).
45. Origin, *On First Principles*, 252–53 (IV.2.4), emphasis mine.

tion—"the letter kills but the spirit gives life." Origen's employment of this method, especially the allegorical method, had precedent in authors who sought to unify Homeric texts with Greek philosophy. Meanwhile Philo of Alexandria, the epitome of Hellenized Judaism, employed similar methods to interpret the Hebrew Bible. Origen uses these methods to great effect. Readers of his biblical commentaries note both a creative brilliance and also a profoundly prayerful, faith-filled mind at work, fully convinced that every word of every biblical verse is "God-breathed" (2 Tim 3:16).[46]

The task at hand does not permit surveying Origen's exegetical brilliance. It is necessary, however, to pause for a minute to understand the extent to which Origen's hermeneutical method reflects an important moment in understanding the relationship between faith and reason. At first glance it might seem that, by appealing to authority—Scripture, tradition, or both—Christianity suppresses rational inquiry. By placing so much authority in a text, one might assume that Christianity could not help but do this. Origen's argument in book IV of *On First Principles* illustrates how belief in a text's authority need not reduce the believer's rational powers. Even Origen's simple believers reach potentially damaging conclusions by failing to consider the revealed text in the correct light.

More than almost any figure in Christian history, Origen manifests how affinity for Greek learning does not undermine devotion to biblical faith. Secular learning helps Origen derive the maximum insight out of the biblical text. Some fundamental claims in classical thought may remain at odds with the biblical narrative and its faith claims, but it does not follow that one cannot understand the former as helping to deepen understanding and appreciation of the latter. For this reason, Origen has inspired subsequent students of the Bible and theology, seeking greater understanding of the faith handed down to them.

---

46. For a compelling account of Origen as exegete, see Peter W Martens, *Origen and Scripture: The Contours of the Exegetical Life* (Oxford: Oxford University Press, 2012).

ATHANASIUS

It is a great leap from the middle of the third century to the middle of
the fourth century, when Athanasius of Alexandria (c. 295–373) wrote
his biography of Antony, the legendary Egyptian monk. Between the
death of Origen and the *Life of Antony*, which Athanasius wrote during
his third exile from Alexandria (356–62), much had changed for
Christians. The emperor Constantine's conversion to Christianity led
to the Edict of Milan, a decree that removed the proscription against
Christianity in 312. In the previous two centuries, many Christians
had been martyred or had lived under the threat of martyrdom. Now
the tables, it would seem, had been turned. Constantine in 325 convened a council in Nicaea, which addressed pressing questions about
the metaphysical relationship between Jesus and God. The council
produced a creed that many present-day Christians believe to have
settled the matter, as it is still recited in churches today. Nicaea,
however, did not quell objections raised originally by Arius and
renewed by Eunomius, among others. Eventually it took another great
council, the Council of Constantinople in 381, to clarify the Nicene
creed in the hopes of quelling the disputes that dominated much of
the theological discourse between Nicaea and Constantinople.[47]

Between these two councils no figure dominated the course of
Christianity more than Athanasius during his long reign (328–73) as
bishop of Alexandria. Like so many of the great theologians from early
Christianity, Athanasius was born into a well-to-do pagan family and
benefitted from the classical education he received.[48] At an early age
he came under the tutelage of Alexander, then the bishop of Alexandria (312–28), who condemned Arius for insisting upon a distinction
in rank between the Son and the Father. Athanasius as bishop considered it his mission to uphold the legacy of Alexander, and of the Council of Nicaea, when he took over for his mentor in 328. Due to his

47. What most Christians learn as the "Nicene creed" is really the creed formulated
at Nicaea, but further amended at Constantinople.
48. According to one biography, Athanasius wrote in a "powerful and evocative"
style, but "he [did] not appear to have shared the extensive training in classical literature
and rhetoric of some of his contemporaries. See David Gwynn, *Athanasius of Alexandria:
Bishop, Theologian, Ascetic, Father* (Oxford: Oxford University Press, 2012), 3–4.

unwillingness to brook any compromise, Athanasius was exiled six times, sometimes for many years, until the ecclesial and political winds shifted. This made him a model for later episcopal resistance to political forces, especially in nineteenth-century Germany.[49]

One of Athanasius's most influential writings is his *Life of Antony*. Though not the first desert monk, Antony, through Athanasius's vivid account, came to embody the virtues of desert monasticism—wisdom, orthodoxy, and holiness. The *Life of Anthony* constitutes one of the first and best efforts in the genre of hagiography, the translation of the life of a holy person into a text. The life of a saint came to constitute an authority in itself. For Christians like Athanasius, committed to creedal claims and to the scriptural canon (indeed it is from Athanasius that we have our first complete New Testament canon),[50] it became important to show how Antony aligned with what Athanasius understood as the orthodox position.[51] Hagiographic literature suggests that the life of a person, through whom God illumines his saving power, comprises its own argument. Such arguments aim more at persuading the imagination, rather than leading the intellect through logic or demonstration.

It has been shown above how leading representatives of early Christianity, like Justin and Origen, exhibit favorable attitudes toward classical learning. Athanasius gives us a contrasting portrait in his *Life of Antony*. He presents the child Antony as having a pure fire for God, so pure in fact that "he refused to learn to read and write," and he did not even like sweets.[52] Antony's parents passed

---

49. Joseph Görres, for instance, compared the Archbishop of Cologne, who was imprisoned in 1837 for refusing to comply with government policy on mixed marriages, to Athanasius. See Joseph Görres, *Athanasius* (Regensburg: Joseph Manz, 1838).

50. This canon appears in his thirty-ninth *Festal Letter* (Gwynn, *Athanasius of Alexandria*, 16).

51. George Herring writes, "The Antony that speaks to us in the *Life* is very much one moulded, one might almost say manipulated, by Athanasius into his view of the ideal monk, simple and guileless, relatively uneducated, but firmly orthodox (in Athanasius's view of that concept), and hence staunchly anti-Arian, but touchingly obedient to his clerical superiors." See George Herring, *Introduction to the History of Christianity* (New York: New York University, 2006), 76.

52. Athanasius, *Life of Antony*, 1. The traditional numeration of the text consists in 94 sections. In what follows, I cite according to these sections with the translation provided in *Early Christian Lives*, trans. Carolinne White (New York: Penguin Books, 1998), 7–70.

away when he was on the brink of adulthood. Rather than continuing to live in the comfort to which he had grown accustomed, Antony sold his parents' possessions, giving most of the proceedings to the poor, and the rest to his sister. At the beginning of his life as a monk, Antony "listened attentively to the Scriptures so that nothing should slip from his mind. He preserved all the Lord's commandments, keeping them safe in his memory rather than in books."[53] These details might give the appearance that Athanasius connects the pure form of Christianity with anti-intellectualism: refusal to learn to read and a disdain toward books. Does Athanasius intend to present the greatest representative of early Christian monasticism as antipodal to the intellectually open, receptive Christianity of other leading figures of the first four centuries?

It would be misguided to identify Athanasius's suspicion toward reading and written texts with anti-intellectualism. Though written texts had existed in the region for perhaps a millennium or more, late-antique Mediterranean culture was still primarily oral. And as the great communication theorist Walter Ong emphasizes, oral cultures differ dramatically from written cultures in regard to how one acquires knowledge and passes it down. Ong explains that subjects in oral cultures

> Do not "study." [. . .] They learn by apprenticeship—hunting with experienced hunters, for example—by discipleship, which is a kind of apprenticeship, by listening, by repeating what they hear, by mastering proverbs and ways of combining and recombining them, by assimilating other formulary materials, by participation in a kind of corporate retrospection—not by study in the strict sense.[54]

For the person shaped in an oral culture, the idea of learning from a written text violated the conscience in a manner analogous to the initial resistance among the intellectual class to Wikipedia and other sources of knowledge stored in electronic media. There is a difference between knowing something and having to look it up! Plato's dialogue *Phaedrus* expressed skepticism about writing, "as a mechanical, inhuman way of processing knowledge, unresponsive to questions and

---

53. Athanasius, *Life of Antony*, 3.
54. Walter J. Ong, *Orality and Literacy* (New York: Routledge, [1982] 2002), 9.

destructive of memory."[55] If one has to rely on a written text (or a screen) to recall a beloved Shakespeare sonnet, then the knowledge of the sonnet is not really yours. Socrates explains, "those who learn [to read and write] will not practice using their memory because they will put their trust in writing, which is external and depends on signs that belongs to others, instead of trying to remember from the inside, completely on their own. [. . .] You provide your students with the appearance of wisdom, not with its reality."[56] Perhaps thinking of the safety of his own employment (foretelling professors' suspicion about online courses), Socrates further complains about the capacity of texts to teach. If a reader has a question, the written text cannot respond and thus contains a danger of misleading the reading public.[57] By presenting Antony as somebody who relied on memory rather than written text, Athanasius sought to locate Antony within a wisdom tradition stretching back to Plato. Athanasius's Antony may not have been learned, but he was wise.

Like Jesus in the desert, Antony faced demonic temptation during his desert isolation, which came in all forms, including attacks from simulacra of vicious animals and beautiful women. After twenty years, Antony did not return to the world; the world came to him. Visitors interrupted his isolation, including would-be disciples seeking union with God, and ordinary believers in need of healing, for which Antony possessed a charism. Speaking to his novices, Antony implored: "I beg you not to fear the word 'virtue' as if it were something unattainable. [. . .] Let the Greeks pursue their studies across the seas and go in search of teachers of useless literature in foreign lands. We however feel no compulsion to travel or cross the waves for the kingdom of heaven is to be found everywhere on earth."[58] The implication here is that, to attain holiness, one need not bother with what we might today call "secular learning." One can hear in his exhortation a distant echo of Paul's warning: "Knowledge puffs up, love builds up" (1 Cor 11:1).

---

55. Ong, *Orality and Literacy*, 24.
56. Plato, *Phaedrus*, 275a.
57. Plato, *Phaedrus*, 275e.
58. Athanasius, *Life of Antony*, 3.

In Athanasius's portrait, the unlearned Antony still holds the proper theological opinions. Antony unequivocally refutes the Arians before a group of bishops in Alexandria, after the Arians had claimed him for their cause.[59] Despite the emphasis on interior holiness and virtue, one finds no precursor to later quietist movements that downplayed the need for doctrines and theological distinctions. Athanasius recalls how Antony outwitted a pair of pagan philosophers on account of his wisdom: "Considering that he had no education (*paideia*), it was amazing how very clever and shrewd he was."[60] Yet when it comes to relating faith to reason, the former trumps the latter, and by a wide margin. Compared to earlier authors, Athanasius displays a tepidity, not toward reason *per se*, but toward mainstream Greek educational culture. His fundamental priority as bishop is to care for and grow his flock; this means, when necessary (which happened frequently), engaging in very high-level Christological disputes with fourth-century Arians. He understands that the model of a holy life and the portrayal of Jesus's *life* has more persuasive power than any philosophy: "As to Greek wisdom, however, and the philosophers' noisy talk, I really think no one requires argument from us; for the amazing fact is patent to all that, for all that they had written so much, the Greeks failed to convince even a few from their own neighborhood in regard to the immortality and the virtuous ordering of life."[61] Though Nietzsche would later dismiss Christianity as "Platonism for the people," Athanasius places great weight on how Christianity is the first movement, at least known to him, that promotes an ascetic ideal as something not solely for elite disciples, but for entire groups of people. And in this respect, it challenges the legitimacy of exclusivist and elitist philosophy as a way of life.

Like Tertullian before him, Athanasius, especially in the *Life of Antony*, gives witness to tensions among early Christian leaders and theologians about how to relate faith to reason. More was under consideration than simply showing the intellectual legitimacy of Christianity in a manner that would satisfy pagan concerns. Both Tertullian

---

59. Athanasius, *Life of Antony*, 69.
60. Athanasius, *Life of Antony*, 72.
61. Athanasius, *On the Incarnation*, 46, cited from Athanasius, *On the Incarnation*, trans. John Behr (Crestwood, New York: St. Vladimir's Seminary Press, 1977).

and Athanasius appeared, at least in their most inflammatory passages, to scoff at secular learning and education. These tensions would crystallize at the end of the fourth and the beginning of the fifth century in the person of Augustine.

AUGUSTINE

Perhaps the greatest thinker in the history of Christianity, Augustine of Hippo (354–430) made an inestimable contribution to the Christian understanding of how faith relates to reason. His voluminous writings reflect a profound meditation on the key points highlighted earlier in this chapter: the relationship between Greek philosophy to *logos*-Christology, the question of how to interpret the Bible, and the refutation of heresy, especially Gnostic offshoots. His pre-Christian formation centered on rhetoric, but the young north-African, like Justin Martyr before him, passed through a variety of philosophical traditions. He employed his rhetorical gifts and philosophical—especially neo-Platonic—syntax to produce a truly astounding theological achievement. To this day he continues to dazzle, confound, and convince his readers.

Turning now to Augustine means passing over some very rich theological contributions, especially those of the Cappadocians: Gregory of Nyssa, Basil of Caesarea, and Gregory of Nazianzus. The fourth century represents, along with the thirteenth century, a golden century of theological breakthrough, and it is thus particularly difficult to justify these and other omissions. Nevertheless, the treatment of Augustine serves as the most appropriate way to conclude this chapter, for in Augustine one finds not only a culmination of the Church's diverse reflections on the topic, but also the most formative seedbed for the eventual development of the medieval, scholastic theology that would dominate the Latin West for a half-millennium.

Perhaps more than any major figure in Christian theology, Augustine's theological outlook retains the scent of his biographical experiences.[62] Born into a family with a pagan father and a Christian mother,

---

62. Or as John Peter Kenney puts it, "The theoretical was the personal for Augustine." See John Peter Kenney, "Faith and Reason," in *The Cambridge Companion to Augustine*, 2nd ed., eds. David Vincent Meconi and Eleonore Stump (Cambridge: Cambridge University Press, 2014), 275–91, at 276.

deeply swayed by Manicheanism for most of his twenties, Augustine found himself liberated through an encounter with neo-Platonism, which paved the way for his Christian baptism. This baptism launched a remarkable ascendency: Within a decade of his initiation into the Church, Augustine was appointed as bishop in Hippo. Three events contributed to the shape of Augustine's activity and writings as a bishop: the controversy with the Donatists, the sack of Rome in 410, and the dispute with Pelagius about grace and free will. Augustine wrote long treatises like *The City of God*, polemics against such opponents as the Donatists and Pelagians, sermons, scriptural commentaries, dialogues, pastoral letters meant for publication, as well as texts like *Confessions*, considered the world's first autobiography, and *On Christian Doctrine*, a handbook for interpreting Scripture.

More than one commentator suggests that Augustine's encounter with, and subsequent rejection of, the Manicheans provides the biographical anchor for understanding how Augustine conceived the relationship between faith and reason.[63] The Manichean dismissal of textual authority in favor of a kind of rationalist naturalism appealed to Augustine as a young student.[64] Augustine's *Confessions*, however, later reveal how the Manichean could not stand up against the highest expressions of Greek philosophy. He writes,

> I compared these [philosophical writings] with the sayings of Mani who wrote much on these matters very copiously and foolishly. I did not notice any rational account of solstices and equinoxes or eclipses of luminaries nor anything resembling what I had learnt in the books of secular wisdom. Yet I was ordered to believe Mani. But he was not in agreement with the rational explanations which I had verified by calculation and had observed with my own eyes.[65]

63. See Kenney, "Faith and Reason," 276–78; Wilken, *The Spirit of Early Christian Thought*, 166–70.

64. This may seem strange for those familiar with Augustine's *Confessions*, in which he paints an arbitrary and superstitious portrait of the Manicheans. One could point to Scientology as a modern analogue. Their cosmology seems fanciful, yet they clothe many of their arguments and treatises in modern scientific jargon. So too with the Manicheans, at least as Augustine encountered them.

65. Augustine, *Confessions*, book V, iii. Here and below I cite from the Chadwick translation (New York: Oxford University Press, 1991), 75.

Through the neo-Platonists, Augustine came to understand the short-comings of Manichean dualism, which maintained that the material world was tainted from its very inception, and the path to salvation meant escape from this world. Neo-Platonism helped Augustine understand evil as a privation and also to reconceive God as the ground of being, rather than *a being*.[66] Augustine underwent an intellectual conversion, which enabled him to abandon the Manicheans for good. It also led him only to the brink of baptism and conversion to Christianity, but not to the waters.

In *Confessions*, book VII, Augustine interweaves his own tepidity toward the gospel and the key shortcoming of the Platonists around a single theme: humility. Augustine recalls reading Marius Victorinus's Latin translations of Plotinus and Porphyry, two leading Platonists. These texts loosely paraphrased John's prologue, which identified God with the word that leaves its mark on the created order. Yet the neo-Platonists had no corresponding theory of the Incarnation: "But that 'the word was made flesh and dwelt among us' (John 1:13–14), I did not read there."[67] Nothing in these texts matched the expression of *kenosis*, or self-emptying, expressed so succinctly in Philippians 2:6–8. The idea that the *logos* could become flesh, that God would not only let himself be sullied by entering history, but die on a cross, seemed scandalous to Platonic philosophy, despite all that it shared in common with Christian metaphysics. Augustine connects his own lack of humility with the proud metaphysics of Platonism: "To possess by God the humble Jesus, I was not yet humble enough. I did not know what his weakness was meant to teach."[68] Becoming humble could not happen through Augustine's sheer power of intelligence; it required an affective change, something difficult to accept for such a towering intellect.

It may help to linger with this point a bit. Suppose one has spent one's entire life thinking that the best places to learn and to inhabit are exclusive centers of excellence and privilege, like Eton, Harvard,

---

66. Although many rightly associate the term "ground of being" with Paul Tillich, it seems a more fitting phrase to describe neo-Platonic theology than "Being." Augustine clearly articulates this understanding of God in *Confessions*, VII.xv.

67. Augustine, *Confessions*, VII.ix.

68. Augustine, *Confessions*, VII.xx.

or the Aspen Institute. Holding such a viewpoint systematically excludes the possibility that the truly wise person could be located at an American public school or university or could be giving a free seminar at the public library. Yet imagine that today's anonymous Socrates was offering courses at a local community college, providing exactly the kind of analysis or wisdom that one was seeking. Bias or snobbery might prevent a receptivity to that source of wisdom. It is possible to apply this situation to the question of where to hear the best music or try the best food. So it was with Augustine, whose pursuit of truth and the virtuous life, in good pagan form, excluded humility. Christianity had introduced the virtue of humility to a Greco-Roman landscape that had developed a sophisticated virtue theory, especially through Aristotle's *Nicomachean Ethics*, but had omitted humility from this theory. In the *Confessions*, Augustine recalls the way he came to understand that he needed to become humbler in order to receive the teachings of the Church. This humility would not be acquired through reading the Platonic books, which otherwise had provided succor against the Manicheans.

It is important to recall that Platonism was not philosophy, in the sense of an academic pursuit broken into topics like epistemology, ethics, and metaphysics. Taking philosophy seriously meant engaging in ascetic and contemplative practices.[69] Augustine describes a Platonic mystical experience within the very same chapter that he chronicles Platonism's shortcomings:

> By the Platonic books I was admonished to return into myself. With you as my guide I entered into my innermost citadel. [. . .] I entered and with my soul's eye, such as it was, saw above that same eye of my soul the immutable light higher than my mind—not the light of every day, obvious to anyone, nor a larger version of the same kind. [. . .] It was not that light, but a different thing, utterly different from all our kinds of light. It transcended my mind, not in the way that oil floats on water, nor as heaven is above earth. It was superior because it made me, and I was inferior because I was made by it.[70]

69. For this argument, see Hadot, *Philosophy as a Way of Life*.
70. Augustine, *Confessions*, VII.x.

Later, in book VII of the *Confessions*, Augustine describes a knowledge of the forms gained through a kind of contemplative ratiocination.[71] John Kenney describes it as "an unmediated form of intellection in which the knower achieves a non-symbolic, non-discursive knowledge of God."[72] Augustine accepted and even exalted the use of reason in order to experience God as Being. Yet he realized that this experience in itself, lofty as it was, did not make him a Christian.

In his own struggles to commit himself to living a Christian life—specifically, to give up his illicit romantic relationships—Augustine came to experience an inability to bring his appetitive desires into alignment with what his intellect knew to be the good life. In reflecting on his own incapacity in light of biblical and salvation history, Augustine describes how he came to believe that the fall of Adam has affected the state of his own soul. In the course of this analysis, he interpreted Paul's discourse on Adam and Christ (Romans 5 and 7) as giving biblical evidence for the idea that we inherit original sin from our ancestors through propagation. The development in Augustine's thought on original sin corresponded to his theology of grace. Pride, the sense that one can do it on one's own without the help of God, explains not only Adam's fall, but our own unwillingness to hear the saving message of the gospel. Joined to this recognition of the human sinful condition was an increased appreciation for faith as grace. Paul writes to the Corinthians: "What do you have that you did not receive?" (1 Cor 4:7). Augustine took this to heart: To receive the most important, saving knowledge as a gift requires acknowledging that one's salvation comes gratuitously, not through merit.

Before moving on to Augustine's short treatise, *De Utilitate Credendi* (*On the Benefit of Believing*, composed in 391), it is important to remember that in Augustine's view the need for grace—indeed, he later became known as *doctor gratiae*, the "doctor of grace"—does not apply solely to faith. God's gift infuses all of our intellectual activities. Augustine does not regard reason as functioning autonomously in the way moderns imagine it, as a capacity distinct from faith. As Wayne Hankey notes, "Within the Christian religion reason, faith, and under-

71. Augustine, *Confessions*, VII.xvii.
72. Kenney, "Faith and Reason," 283.

standing were different modes of apprehending a single truth."[73] As the citation above from *Confessions*, book VII indicates, Platonic reason participates in the mind of God. Filtered through a Christian framework, this participation means that no moment of authentic truth-seeking occurs without divine initiative.

These matters helped Augustine refine his theology of faith and reason in the short treatise mentioned above. Here Augustine points to the relationship between reason and authority that lies at the root of the tension between the Manicheans and the Christians: "You know, Honoratus, that I fell among these people [Manicheans] for no other reason than that they declared that they would put aside all overawing authority, and by pure and simple reason would bring to God those who were willing to listen to them."[74] In his letter to the Romans, Paul declares: "faith comes from hearing" (10:17). Augustine takes this to mean that we believe on authority. The issue for Augustine in this treatise concerns a meta-question about faith and reason. In his response to Honoratus he moves beyond the meaning of faith and reason to ask whether the act of believing is rational. Augustine's response is commonsensical. Although the Manicheans considered naive those who believed based on authority by trusting, for example, the testimony of a priest or bishop, Augustine counters that in many ordinary life circumstances one starts with trust, which is later verified by other means: "I do not see how anyone who accepts that as true can ever have a friend. For if to believe anything is base, either it is base to believe a friend, or without such belief I cannot see how anyone can go on speaking about friendship."[75] Friendship involves a level of trust in claims that cannot initially be verified. Analogously, Christianity demands assent to the sacredness of its Scriptures and to the veracity of certain historical events, and one must somehow judge these things true before they can be verified by a simple act of understanding. On one level, Augustine understood that the act of believing involves a

---

73. Wayne Hankey, "*Ratio*, Reason, Rationalism," in *Augustine through the Ages: An Encyclopedia*, ed. Allan D. Fitzgerald (Grand Rapids, MI: Eerdmans), 696–702, at 696.

74. Augustine, *De Utilitate Credendi*, 2. Cited from Augustine, *Earlier Writings*, ed. J. H. S. Burleigh (Louisville: Westminster John Knox, [1953] 2006), 292. Here and below I cite by Arabic numeral, which runs to 36 in this text.

75. Augustine, *De Utilitate Credendi*, 23.

movement of the will. Yet he sees that faith also involves an intellectual assent, and it is fair to ask whether this assent is in accord with reason. Augustine asks, "If nothing which is not known is to be believed, how will children serve their parents and love them with mutual dutifulness if they do not believe that they are their parents? That cannot be known by reason. [. . .] But we believe, and that without hesitation, what we confess we do not know."[76] Without a certain level of credulity, in other words, it is impossible to have even a basic level of order in one's life. Augustine concludes, "I could bring many instances to show that nothing would remain stable in human society if we determined to believe nothing that we could not scientifically establish."[77]

Augustine's commonsense response helps to refute a Manichean criticism of the fact that core Christian teachings like the Incarnation can only be accepted on the authority of teachers and texts. This manner of believing did not differ in kind from the level of belief exercised by non-Christians. Ordinary activities often entail trust in the authority of another. In the diverse world of late fourth-century North Africa, a variety of religious schools and doctrines purported to have authoritative teachers. This reality brings to life a paradox: How can one find a truly wise teacher if one is not truly wise? Augustine and the recipient of his letter, Honoratus, lived this experience. Before becoming a Christian, Augustine scoffed at Christianity and placed his hope in the wisdom of Faustus, the Manichean with a clever tongue. In *De Utilitate Credendi* Augustine, no longer a Manichee, pleads with Honoratus to reconsider his earlier dismissal of Christianity. The road to higher wisdom, for Augustine, means that one must allow one's faith to heal the mind: "I judge that believing before reasoning, if you are not able to follow reasoning, and cultivating the mind by faith in order to be ready to receive the seeds of truth, is not only most wholesome, but is indeed the only way by which health can return to sick minds."[78] In allowing the intellect to wane, and to receive the gifts of faith, it permits the possibility for the intellect to grasp more deeply truths, and an order of knowing, that it would otherwise dismiss out of hand.

76. Augustine, *De Utilitate Credendi*, 26.
77. Augustine, *De Utilitate Credendi*, 26.
78. Augustine, *De Utilitate Credendi*, 31.

Not all purported authorities are in fact authoritative, but Augustine intuits no other way into the truth of Christianity without some trust in authority: "Many want to appear wise, and it is not easy to discern whether they are not in reality fools."[79] Yet if one seeks beatitude, Augustine insists that the surest way is by trusting through faith what the church affirms.[80] After all, one cannot even know that Christ existed without some trust in authority:

> I myself did not see Christ as it was his will to be seen by men. [. . .] From whom did I derive my faith in him, so that I may come to you duly prepared by faith? I see that I owe my faith to opinion and reports widely spread and firmly established among the peoples and nations of the earth, and that these peoples everywhere observe the mysteries of the Catholic Church. Why, then, should I not rather ask most diligently of them what Christ taught, seeing that I was brought by their authority to believe that what he taught was profitable?[81]

Of course, the Manicheans did not oppose spiritual truths or even eschew the message of Jesus. But they pursued these truths through what we might call an esoteric framework: Rather than trusting the most popular and basic mode for passing on Christianity's saving truths, they preferred to sidestep authority. Augustine asks whether this mode of pursuing the truth bears the rational shape that it purports to uphold. Is it not more rational, he suggests, to trust accepted authorities, including bishops like Ambrose, rather than charismatic rhetoricians like Faustus? Is it right to malign the simple Christians for being more willing to accept what is told than pursue the route of meditative experience of Being, given that they do not have the time or capability to follow such a pursuit?

In Augustine's world reasoning entails an openness to larger, cosmic forces like a creator God. Many intellectuals in late antiquity

79. Augustine, *De Utilitate Credendi*, 33.

80. Augustine, *De Utilitate Credendi*, 33. Augustine makes the same point in *De Vera Religione* (*Of True Religion*), a treatise from 390, especially sections 45–46, where he writes, "Authority demands belief and prepares man for reason. Reason leads to understanding and knowledge. But reason is not entirely absent from authority, for we have to consider whom we have to believe."

81. Augustine, *De Utilitate Credendi*, 31.

accepted the idea that reason could lead one, at least most of the way, toward the Christian God. Believing, however, had a more contentious standing. Augustine argues, from the standpoint of ordinary life, for the necessity of trusting authorities that cannot be verified, despite the risk entailed. One might be led astray, and one can only do so much to sidestep such a risk. Yet it is even less reasonable to refuse to accept any authority and thus risk missing out on the highest wisdom.

CONCLUSION

Chapter 1 has transported the reader from first-century Corinth to fifth-century North Africa, engaging figures who helped chart the trajectory for thinking about how faith relates to reason. In Augustine's own lifetime, the Western part of the Roman Empire passed from seeming invincibility to collapse. Concurrent with the political collapse, which citizens of the Empire experienced in waves, there occurred a collapse of various institutions, including educational institutions, which left a gaping hole that would not be filled for many centuries. Political and economic instability, especially against the backdrop of an Empire that had lasted for over a millennium, lent a fragility to attempts to foster uniformity, and tradition needed to ensure theological reflection that would match the rich offerings of previous centuries. Pockets of wisdom prevailed, often in monastic enclaves, but these were peripheral, rather than central. Rome could no longer function as the political and cultural center that it once was. Within a few centuries, the rise of Islam in the seventh century and its subsequent expansion destabilized concentrations of Christianity, especially in the Middle East and North Africa. Here we pass from patristic to medieval, scholastic theology. This transition signals a clear break in style and audience, which will be important to note. Just as important, however, will be the effort to trace how certain ideas were handed down and translated, from one era to the next.

Chapter 2

Early Medieval Theology and the Scholastic Achievement

The Middle Ages—*media aetas* in Latin—was first coined in the sixteenth century as a term of contempt for this era. As Josef Pieper relates, this term "signified the 'middle period,' a time of waiting in which nothing of importance happened, an era without qualities of its own, an intermezzo, as opposed to two ages which did have intrinsic qualities: Greco-Roman antiquity and 'Modern Times.'"[1] Although historians of Christianity and of world history now more readily acknowledge the lasting achievements and intellectual breakthroughs of the Middle Ages, and medieval thought is no longer consonant with an intellectual wasteland, there still persists a sense that one can simply pass over a number of centuries on account that nothing of significance happened during them.[2]

No period of Christian history is less understood than the early Middle Ages, commonly referred to as the Dark Ages. This term refers to the period from roughly 500 to 1000 A.D. Some broadly read theologians struggle to name a theologian or controversy during this period, and surveys on the history of Christian theology sometimes presume that no theologian of significance lived between Augustine and Anselm.[3] Even among those disinclined toward the medieval period, there is a begrudging acceptance that the twelfth and thirteenth centuries, marked by the creation of universities, the rise of the Franciscan

---

1. Josef Pieper, *Scholasticism*, trans. Richard and Clara Winston (South Bend, IN: St. Augustine's Press, 2001), 15.

2. Pieper notes that even Hegel considered the Middle Ages unworthy of serious investigation, as conveyed in his *Lectures on the History of Philosophy*. See Pieper, *Scholasticism*, 15–16.

3. For instance, in Murphy, Mezei and Oakes's *Illuminating Faith*, which covers the understanding of faith in Christian history, it does not treat any author between the Council of Orange in 529 and Anselm, who wrote in the late eleventh century.

and Dominican orders, the rediscovery of Aristotle, and such massively influential texts as Lombard's *Sentences* and Aquinas's *Summa*, represent a lasting achievement. Rather than understanding these centuries as the product of advances made in earlier centuries, the tendency has been to deracinate these achievements from prior centuries.

The current chapter, covering the fifth to the twelfth centuries, cannot do justice to the theological richness of the early medieval period. It can only point to a few examples that indicate, despite all of the political and social upheaval felt in the Christian realm, that Christian reflection on the relationship between faith and reason occupied the greatest thinkers of this period. Before doing so, it will be helpful to revisit, ever briefly, some of the political and social circumstances confronting medieval theologians. Muslim invasions dislodged the Middle East and North Africa as cultural and political centers of Christian influence. The center of power and influence in Christianity moved from the Mediterranean—encompassing southern Europe, but also occupying Saharan Africa and the Middle East—to Europe proper. Indeed, in this period, Europe came to be imagined for the first time as a coherent geographical and civilizational entity. This transition took many centuries, mostly due to ongoing battles in its center, as Edward Grant explains:

> The birth of the new Europe was a lengthy process because Germanic tribes—Ostrogoths, Visigoths, Burgundians, Lombards, Franks, and others—from the fourth to the seventh centuries were constantly at war in the northern part of continental Europe, or in process of migration, as imperial Rome weakened and gradually dissolved in Western Europe. Just when it seemed that the Franks under Charlemagne would bring a much greater degree of stability and peace than had hitherto been known in Europe, the death of Charlemagne in 814 brought further disintegration.[4]

The economic and political circumstances in large part circumscribed the intellectual aspirations of the era, just as they do in our own. In popular imagination, the "Dark Ages" imply a willful turning against

---

4. Edward Grant, *God and Reason in the Middle Ages* (Cambridge: Cambridge University Press, 2001), 17.

the light, encouraged by a Christianity now distanced from the classical legacy. Nothing could be further from the truth.

BOETHIUS

No figure overturns this narrative more directly than Anicius Manlius Severinus Boethius (480–525), born four years after the last Roman emperor had been deposed by a Germanic usurper. An aristocrat by birth, Boethius rose to become something like chief of staff for King Theodoric.[5] With good reason, Boethius has been called, "the last of the Romans and the first of the Scholastics."[6] Any reader of the cult classic novel *A Confederacy of Dunces* knows that Boethius's *The Consolations of Philosophy*, with its vivid depiction of Fortuna, is his most famous book and a true classic in the genre of prison literature. For our purposes, it is enough to note Boethius's role in collating what came to be known as the old logic (*logica vetus*) as well as translating a number of Greek works into Latin. These works served as the most important link to the classical intellectual world prior to the influx of Arabic translations many centuries later.[7] Boethius also offered a model for later scholastics to incorporate not just the Greek wisdom tradition, but also the science of logic into theology.[8]

Boethius's *Opuscula Sacra*, or *Theological Tractates*, shed light on how he integrated logic and philosophy into theological questions, thus serving as a precursor for the scholastic character of medieval theology.[9] In the first tractate, *De Trinitate*, Boethius explains to his

5. The references to Boethius's life come from V. E. Watts, "Introduction," to Boethius, *The Consolation of Philosophy*, trans V. E. Watts (London: Penguin, 1969), 7–32.

6. This moniker may have derived from the fifteenth-century humanist, Lorenzo Valla. For this point see Grant, *God and Reason*, 39n30. Pieper writes: "Boethius must be located on the narrow strip of no-man's-land that divides epochs; this historical locus determined his personal destiny. He knew that the world in which he had grown to manhood was doomed; and the world coming into being was not his own" (Pieper, *Scholasticism*, 26).

7. For this point see Grant, *God and Reason*, 39–41.

8. Pieper writes, "Six hundred years after [Boethius's] death we find his name mentioned on almost every page of Abelard's treatises on logic" (Pieper, *Scholasticism*, 30).

9. Boethius, *The Theological Tractates and The Consolation of Philosophy*, trans. H. F. Stewart, E. K. Rand, and S. J. Tester (Cambridge: Harvard University Press, 1978), 2–129. In the subsequent footnotes, I refer to the title and line of the tractate, with the page number from this edition in parentheses.

father-in-law how Christians can believe in the Trinity while believing in God's oneness.[10] In doing so Boethius follows in the footsteps of the great speculative theologians who used reason to explain the Trinity, Augustine being foremost among them.[11] Yet unlike these thinkers, Boethius does not make a single reference to Scripture or to liturgy. By putting philosophy, especially Aristotelian logic, at the center of his treatises, Boethius set the course for later scholastic theology. Previous theologians certainly used these sources, but Boethius marked a new era in the application of reason to faith. Boethius uses reason, exclusively, to explain Christian doctrine. In reading many of the patristic theologians, one gets the impression, especially from the post-Nicene period when access to Scripture was more readily available, that these theologians immersed themselves in the sacred text. Boethius, by comparison, seemed content to bracket Scripture from his discussion.

In *Contra Eutychen et Nestorium* Boethius defends the orthodox position on Christ's humanity by an appeal to definitions of terms like person, nature, and substance. His definitions derive from philosophical treatises, especially the *Categories* of Aristotle. According to one assessment, Boethius's attempt:

> turns out to have been very different from that of the philosophically educated theologians, such as Augustine and Marius Victorinus. [. . .] Boethius defends the orthodox position, and tries to expose the failing of heretical views, by using the language and techniques of the *Categories* [of Aristotle] and the *Isagoge* [of Porphory], with some help from Aristotelian physics.[12]

Rather than pagan philosophy merely serving theology, or theology borrowing some terms and ideas from philosophy, in Boethius one finds a different method: He begins with the truths of faith and sees what reason, at its highest and best, can make of these truths. The

---

10. Boethius, *De Trinitate*, 1–5 (3).
11. Boethius even writes, "You must however examine whether the seeds of argument sown in my mind by St. Augustine's writings have borne fruit" (*De Trinitate*, 31–33 [5]).
12. John Marenbon, *Boethius* (Oxford: Oxford University Press, 2003), 76.

effort may be informed by the Christian faith, but it is not interrupted or curtailed by it, nor need it be, if one understands faith properly. This appears to be Boethius's own assessment at the end of *De Trinitate*: "If, the grace of God helping me, I have furnished some fitting support in argument to an article which stands firmly by itself on the foundation of faith, the joy felt for the finished work will flow back to the source whence its effecting cause came. But if human nature has failed to reach beyond its limits [. . .] my prayers will make it up."[13] The goal is to give an intelligibility to faith made possible through the most rigorous application of reason. If this fails, one can fall back on the articles of faith, but one should make the attempt at a higher understanding without trepidation or fear.

Boethius's efforts to retrieve and preserve classical learning, in a world where East and West grew ever more distant from one another, predated the closing of the Academy in Athens by the emperor Justinian in 529, a date which often marks the end of the classical era.[14] If a revival is to be marked, then one can point to the 789 *Admonitio generalis* (general admonition) of Charlemagne, which "advised that all cathedrals and monasteries were to open schools dedicated to the study of the psalms, musical notation, chant, computistics, and grammar."[15] Charlemagne brought to his court Alcuin of York, who urged Charlemagne to support these schools and also instituted a curriculum based on a fifth-century model. This model entailed a trivium of grammar, rhetoric, and dialectic, and a quadrivium of arithmetic, geometry, music, and astronomy, which would prove the bedrock of European learning for centuries to come. In addition, Alcuin made sure to integrate the texts of Boethius, including his commentaries on classical logic, into the curriculum at Charlemagne's court.[16] The rise of the "Carolingians," which reached its apex with the papal coronation of Charlemagne as Holy Roman Emperor in 800, marked the

---

13. Boethius, *De Trinitate*, VI, 30–35 (31).

14. See for instance, Pieper, *Scholasticism*, 16–17.

15. Deirdre Carabine, *John Scottus Eriugena* (New York: Oxford University Press, 2000), 6; Grant, *God & Reason in the Middle Ages*, 26. As Grant shows, these chapters began to bolster both monasteries and cathedrals, but by the twelfth century, they had become associated almost exclusively with cathedrals (Grant, *God & Reason*, 26).

16. Carabine, *John Scottus Eriugena*, 7.

gradual but seismic shift of Christian culture away from the Mediterranean and toward northern and central Europe.

JOHN SCOTTUS ERIUGENA

Prior to and during the rise of the Carolingians, Ireland's monasteries became centers of cultural and intellectual transmission. Their *scriptoria* preserved fragile Christian texts by copying them. The *Book of Kells*, composed around 800, marks the splendor of this legacy. Around the same time, John Scottus Eriugena (c. 815–c. 880), an Irish monk, joined the court of Charles the Bald, grandson of Charlemagne. Like Boethius, Eriugena engaged deeply with Greek patristic authors. This familiarity made Eriugena something of a unicorn. One biographer notes, "As a translator, Eriugena stood out in the ninth century because so few of his contemporaries could read Greek."[17]

Already in the ninth century one can identify the dialectic of forgetting and remembering that characterizes the history of theology. *Tradition* is never just there for people to hand down or reject; instead, it must continually be presented to the current age, lest it be forgotten. Those who preserve it do so selectively. Two instances of this pattern correspond to the legacy of Eriugena: first, his translation of Pseudo-Dionysius; second, his role in the predestination controversy of the 850s. These texts reflect how, by the ninth century, vast portions of Christendom had forgotten more than they knew. Before examining his contribution, it will be helpful to return to the first century.

Paul's missionary activity in Athens did not constitute a great success; although he was not run out of town, many scoffed at his preaching. A more receptive minority group, however, asked for a follow-up meeting, which led to many conversions to the message of proclamation. Of these converts, Luke mentions only two: a woman named Damaris, and Dionysius, a member of the Court of the Areopagus (Acts 17:32–34). The Areopagus incarnated the Greek philosophical spirit, and the figure of Dionysius the Areopagite came to symbolize rapprochement between Jerusalem and Athens, or faith and reason. The first Church historian, Eusebius, even had Dionysius taking over

---

17. Carabine, *John Scottus Eriugena*, 16.

an episcopal see, although no other historical record confirms this. An anonymous late fifth-century Syrian monk wrote several Platonic-leaning mystical treatises and gave himself the name Dionysius the Areopagite.[18] Nineteenth-century scholars concluded on the basis of the obvious neo-Platonic references that these texts dated much later than the first century. Despite the eventual overturning of their authenticity, the texts had a lasting impact on the development of theology, especially through the translation of Eriugena, who introduced these works into Western Christianity.[19]

Eriugena's was not the first ninth-century effort to render Pseudo-Dionysius into Latin. Already in 838, the abbot Hinduin made an attempt in his monastery outside of Paris. As Leclerq notes, the translation was so incomprehensible that Charles the Bald commissioned Eriugena to produce a fresh one.[20] With his strong philosophical bent, Eriugena likely jumped at the chance to translate the writings of a figure thought to be a contemporary of St. Paul. In the ongoing attempt to make faith intelligible, Eriugena did not understand his task as supplementing the Western Fathers with the Eastern Fathers; instead, he understood himself as bringing a highly philosophical understanding of Christianity to bear on biblical-experiential theology. This translation project, moreover, occurred at the behest of a Carolingian king committed to restoring the educational edifice of Christian faith through the reintegration of an author presumed to be the incarnation of philosophical Christianity.

The writings of Eriugena display the seriousness with which he undertook the integration of faith and reason. His investigation of the Eastern Fathers enabled him to see the need to apply logic and dialectic to theology in order to resolve lingering disputes that were making life more challenging in the court of Charles the Bald. Appeals to

18. For an accessible English translation, see Pseudo-Dionysius, *The Complete Works*, trans. and ed. Colm Luibheid and Paul Rorem (New York: Paulist, 1987).

19. Concerning their impact on the medieval West, see Jean Leclerq, "Influence and Noninfluence of Dionysius in the Western Middle Ages," in Pseudo-Dionysius, *The Complete Works*, 25–32. Concerning the neo-Platonic influence, Carabine notes, "His works display the obvious influence of the late Neoplatonism of Proclus" (Carabine, *John Scottus Eriugena*, 16).

20. Leclerq, "Influence and Noninfluence," 26.

authority in matters of theology would not suffice, as he explains in the *Periphyseon* (*On Divine Nature*):

> Authority proceeds from true reason, but reason certainly does not proceed from authority. For every authority which is not upheld by true reason is seen to be weak. [. . .] For it seems to me that true authority is nothing else but the truth that has been discovered by the power of reason and set down in writing by the Holy Fathers for the use of posterity.[21]

It would be easy to infer from this passage that Eriugena prefigures the modern preference for reason over faith. For Eriugena, however, reason constituted a court of appeal when authority could only reach a split decision.

Although the *Periphyseon* represents the apex of Eriugena's thinking, his treatise on predestination, *De Divina Praedestinatione*, gives the most precise articulation of the relation between faith and reason. Written as a response to Gottschalk's defense of double predestination—for which Gottschalk was imprisoned and beaten—Eriugena's *Treatise on Predestination* displays a profound trust in reason during a period so often dismissed as "dark." In the *Treatise* he suggests that lack of training in the liberal arts, rather than lack of faith, explains the mistaken opinions of Gottschalk and his followers. This "gravest" of errors "had its beginnings from an ignorance of the useful arts [. . .] and on top of that, ignorance also of Greek writings in which the interpretation of predestination generates no mist of ambiguity."[22] Eriugena aimed to untangle these difficult Greek writings, which can soften some of the sharper statements by Augustine on predestination, by using dialectic and logic. The goal was not simply to find a text in Augustine that supported one's position, but to understand Augustine against the horizon of the truths of faith and reason, for Augustine too was both a "pious father of doctrine" and "keenest enquirer into truth [. . . and] most zealous teacher of the liberal arts."[23] Being a good Augustinian meant shar-

---

21. Eriugena, *Periphyseon*, trans. Inglis Patric, Sheldon-Williams, and John O'Meara (WA: Dumbarton Oaks, 1987), 110 (513b–c).

22. John Scottus Eriugena, *Treatise on Divine Predestination*, trans. Mary Brennan (Notre Dame, IN: University of Notre Dame Press, 1998), 117 (ch. 18.1).

23. Eriugena, *Treatise on Divine Predestination*, 120 (ch. 18.6).

ing that zeal for the liberal arts, not stringing together a series of unrelated quotations from a compendium of his thought.

In his opening chapter, Eriugena leans on Augustine's *On True Religion* to bring philosophy and theology into union. He explains:

> If, indeed, as Saint Augustine says, it is believed and taught as the fun-
> damental principle of man's salvation that philosophy [. . .] is not one
> thing and religion another [. . .] what else is the exercise of philosophy
> but the exposition of the rules of true religion by which the supreme
> and principal cause of all things, God, is worshipped with humility
> and rationally searched for? It follows then that true philosophy is
> true religion and conversely that true religion is true philosophy.[24]

Eriugena hoped that, by invoking Augustine's appeal to reason, he
could move the dispute over predestination, generated in large part
by Augustine's own strong statements in favor of predestination from
his later corpus, beyond the realm of an intra-Augustinian dispute.

Subsequent chapters in the *Treatise on Divine Predestination* demonstrate this attempt, most especially chapter 3, "Reason Does Not
Permit of Two Predestinations." Although other writings evidence his
scriptural learning, Eriugena only sparingly cites Scripture to refute
Gottschalk. Instead he offers an exposition of the divine will in order
to show how double predestination would contradict what we know
of God. Eriugena rejects Gottschalk's teaching on the basis of logical
impossibility: "Say then, Gottschalk, where can one find those two
predestinations which you affirm? True reason does not allow for their
existence in God, for the most part because of the force of necessity
which you maintain is within them."[25] Gottschalk's teachings, Eriugena
explains, "are not true since everything that contradicts the truth is
not from the truth."[26]

At the peak of what many consider the Dark Ages, one finds in
Eriugena a brightly lit lamp. The dispute with Gottschalk reveals Eriugena's robust confidence that faith could become intelligible through
a fearless application of reason. One could even say that in Eriugena,

---

24. Eriugena, *Treatise on Divine Predestination*, 7 (ch. 1.1).
25. Eriugena, *Treatise on Divine Predestination*, 15 (ch. 2.6).
26. Eriugena, *Treatise on Divine Predestination*, 18 (ch. 3.1).

like in Boethius, one finds a faith in reason itself. The later attempts to bring the truths of faith into a purer philosophical understanding, undertaken by modern figures like Hegel, have often been dismissed as rationalism, yet it is not unwarranted to see in Boethius and Eriugena a precursor to these attempts. More directly, the confidence in reason illustrated by, but not limited to, these two figures would set the precedent for subsequent attempts in the period of the Middle Ages more familiar to most readers.

ANSELM OF CANTERBURY

The distance between the ninth-century court of Charles the Bald, and twelfth-century Paris—bustling with intellectual innovation—remains vast. In *God & Reason in the Middle Ages*, Edward Grant highlights the importance of logic as a bridge between these periods. He identifies the pioneering role of Gerbert of Aurilac, future Pope Sylvester II (c. 946–1003; fl. 999–1003), the most respected teacher of his day. Writes Grant, "Gerbert regarded logic with special favor. He may have been the first to teach the works of the old logic, including Boethius's commentaries and original treatises."[27] Grant traces a direct line from Gerbert to Abelard, a pioneering figure in the history of theology, who grew to fame as a teacher of logic within the cathedral chapter system. One can already observe the influence of reason and logic on theology one century earlier in the work of Anselm (c. 1033–1109), the patron saint of theology and the inventor of the most influential demonstration for the existence of God. Anselm's achievements matched the splendor of the greatest theologians from the early church. His classic texts, the *Monologion*, *Proslogion*, and *Cur Deus Homo* (*Why God Became Human*) tackled the most vexing questions in theology: the existence of God and the atonement. A review of these texts illuminates how Anselm built on earlier contributions to make definitive breakthroughs in understanding and also illustrating how faith relates to reason.

Written in 1076, the *Monologion*, a "speech made to oneself," was composed during Anselm's time at Bec, the monastery where he became abbot. Under Anselm's rule, Bec gained a reputation for its

27. Grant, *God & Reason*, 46.

vibrant intellectual and spiritual climate, which led to an influx of new monks eager to sit at his feet. This context cannot be forgotten, for Anselm did not set out to prove the existence of God to nonbelievers. Instead, both the *Monologion* and the *Proslogion* present a *meditatio*—a meditation—which had a precise meaning in medieval learning and prayer. Although not a perfect analogy, one can get a sense of what *meditatio* means by recalling Händel's famous "Hallelujah" chorus from his *Messiah*. The chorus resembles a *meditatio* in that it focuses on a specific word, sung every possible way, in order to extract every conceivable ounce of meaning from that word. Anselm wanted his monks to meditate on the being of God, to understand God more deeply as *one*, *true*, and *good*. He writes, "It is in accordance with their wish, rather than with my ability, that they have prescribed such a form for the writing of this meditation; in order that nothing in Scripture should be urged on the authority of Scripture itself."[28] Here Anselm reveals that the monks had requested this form of writing, which makes no reference to the Bible at all. This method made Anselm a revolutionary figure in the history of theology.[29] He describes his mode of proceeding as an "independent investigation," undertaken in an "unadorned style, with common proofs and with a simple argument [. . .] enforced by the cogency of reason."[30] This method led many to condemn Anselm, who pleaded out of fear of misunderstanding that his preface, which announced his intentions and motives, be included in any future edition of the *Monologion*.

Before examining his argument, it will be helpful to recall how Anselm frames his project in the *Proslogion* (1078), his subsequent and more succinct representation of the argument for God. Anselm admits personal dissatisfaction with his earlier book, which the *Proslogion*, in the course of "meditating on the reason of faith" (*meditandi de ratione fidei*), simplifies and even corrects.[31] Thus the relationship

28. Anselm, *Monologion*, preface. Here and below I borrow from the following translation: *Basic Writings*, 2nd ed., trans. S. N. Deane (Chicago: Open Court, 1962), but in what follows only the chapter will be given.

29. For this claim see Grant, *God & Reason*, 56.

30. Anselm, *Monologion*, preface.

31. Here and below I cite from Anselm, *Proslogion with the replies of Gaunilo and Anselm*, trans. Thomas Williams (Indianapolis: Hackett, 1995), prologue. Since no

between faith and reason, or understanding (*intellectus*), lies at the heart of the *Proslogion*. Anselm establishes this point in chapter 1, where he gives a famous rendering of Augustine's gloss of Isaiah 7:9: "Unless I believe, I shall not understand."[32] Anselm modifies and clarifies the statement: "For I do not seek to understand in order to believe; I believe in order to understand." Against an overly rationalizing tendency, which some would say that Anselm's work manifests, Anselm reminds detractors of his earlier work that he gives priority to faith, not reason.

At this point it will be helpful to make a broader point about faith and reason, one frequently forgotten. A commonly accepted modern framework presumes that faith is a supernatural grace, whereas reason, or understanding, is a strictly natural operation. This presumption not only muddles how best to conceive the relationship between faith and reason, but also obscures the modern origin of this dichotomy by projecting it onto premodern authors. Such has too often been the fate of the interpretation of Anselm. Attending to the *Proslogion* reveals the gulf between Anselm and this modern framework. In the *Proslogion*, Anselm makes a prayer to God (indeed, the entire *Proslogion* takes shape as a prayer): "Therefore, Lord, you who grant (*dare*) understanding to faith, grant that, insofar as you know it is useful to me, I may understand that you exist."[33] The understanding arrived at through the rational, cogitative activity takes place on the same graced continuum as faith. Understanding—*intellectus*—does not mean the rational pursuit that humans undertake *on their own*. Premodern authors, *en masse*, did not think about reason this way.

A full exposition of Anselm's proof cannot be offered here. His argument, subsequently known as the "ontological proof," has become

---

standard pagination exists, I will cite by chapter. Occasionally, in consultation with the Latin text, I have modified the translation. For the original, I have consulted *L'oeuvre de S. Anselme de Cantorbéry*, ed. Michel Corbin, vol. 1, *Monologion, Proslogion* (Paris: Cerf, 1986). The above citation is found in Corbin, *L'oeuvre de S. Anselme de Cantorbéry*, 228.

32. Subsequent theologians commented on this gloss with frequency. Augustine's variant of Isaiah 7:9 "came from the (Greek) Septuagint and differed from both the Hebrew and the Vulgate (which have 'Unless you believe you will not be strengthened)." See Giulio D'Onofrio, *History of Theology II: The Middle Ages*, trans. Matthew J. O'Connell (Collegeville, MN: Liturgical, 2008), 2.

33. Anselm, *Proslogion*, 2.

one of the three most famous proofs for the existence of God, along-side the cosmological and teleological proofs. It continues to dazzle and amaze, and has even cast a spell over subsequent philosophers not beholden to traditional Christianity, in particular Leibniz and Hegel.[34] Two preliminary points bear making: first, the argument comes in the form of a prayer; second, the text proceeds with almost no reference to Scripture, save a few Psalms, the most memorable being, "The fool in his heart says there is no God" (Ps 14:1; 53:2).

Like *being, God* cannot *not* be thought. To say: *being is not* or *there is no being* contains a contradiction, for one cannot make this claim without using a form of the word *to be*. For Anselm, thinking through the idea that God is "the greatest of all beings"[35] has radical con-sequences. Unlike creatures, who merely participate in goodness when they are good, or in justice when they are just, God *is* justice and good-ness. Anselm explains: "You are the very life by which you live, the wisdom by which you are wise, the very goodness by which you are good to the good and to the wicked."[36] God relates to these qualities in a wholly other way than do humans, for God is both transcendent and immanent. Anselm explains that God also relates to human beings in a particular manner: "You are wholly present everywhere, and yet I do not see you. 'In you I move and in you I have my being' (Acts 17:28), and yet I cannot approach your presence. You are within me and all around me, and yet I do not perceive you."[37] The way that God is determines our experience of God: not as another being, but as *Being*, not merely as good, just, and merciful, but as the source of goodness, justice, and mercy. This crucial difference impacts how one should meditate on God's existence.

Anselm and the monks at Bec lived a life soaked in Scripture, as would have any medieval monk: at least six times per day these monks recited scriptural passages while praying the daily Office of Readings. Through this process the Psalms would have become a second lan-guage to them. Yet Anselm does not deduce the results of his great

34. For a review of its influence, see *The Ontological Argument: From St. Anselm to Contemporary Philosophers*, ed. Alvin Plantinga (Garden City, NY: Doubleday, 1965).
35. Anselm, *Proslogion*, 5.
36. Anselm, *Proslogion*, 12.
37. Anselm, *Proslogion*, 16.

meditation on the nature of God in the *Monologion* and *Proslogion* from the revealed scriptural data. Instead, the insights come from an *a priori* method. Anselm here offers what we might call the first secular theological discourse, describing God *etsi scriptura non daretur*, as if there were no Scripture. In doing so he prefigures modern secular modes of knowing by methodologically eschewing authority, with the proviso that Anselm does not imagine reason as an autonomous human activity unaided by divine illumination. Anselm postulates what reason can know of God and God's relationship to us by thinking through the claim of God as the ground of being.[38] By doing so he stretches a certain kind of reason as far as it will go, just as we imagine certain "saints" of secular learning to have done (Newton, Darwin, Einstein). When questioned about his method, Anselm gives a brilliant answer: Look at what Augustine did in his masterpiece, *On the Trinity*.[39] In this text Augustine invented various analogies, including the human experience of understanding as memory, intellect, and will, which had no explicit scriptural basis. In like manner, Anselm offers a highly theoretical form of speculation. This mode of doing theology led one commentator to assert that Anselm "lay the foundations for [theology's] conversion to a science by twelfth- and thirteenth-century theologians."[40]

Compared to the two texts on the existence of God, Anselm's preface to *Cur Deus Homo*, his famous text on Christ's atonement, suspends the arguments made on the basis of faith even more explicitly. This choice comes as something of a surprise because the data concerning Christ and the Incarnation arises from revelation. Anselm already shows his hand in the first word of his book: *Cur*—why. He does not take up a "that question," to which only historical authority could provide an answer. Scripture of course wades into the "why question," perhaps in the most noteworthy fashion in John 3:16: "for God so loved the world." Yet the speculative nature of a why question makes it open-ended and discursive. In the preface Anselm explains

38. Of course, there is a scriptural basis in Exodus 3:14 ("I am who I am") for God as being.

39. Anselm, *Monologion*, preface.

40. Grant, *Faith & Reason*, 56. Grant cites Etienne Gilson, *History of Christian Philosophy in the Middle Ages* (London: Sheed and Ward, 1955), 139.

that he wrote the first part of *Cur Deus Homo* for the infidels, that is, those unconvinced by the biblical account. Anselm states his plan to "leave Christ out of view," an astonishing claim for an eleventh-century abbot in a monastery. By so doing he will prove, "by necessary reasons, the impossibility that any human should be saved without him."[41] Anselm, to be clear, does not reject truths of faith known from Scripture and tradition, but instead focuses on the reasons for the divine mission of the Father sending the Son, a question for which the details of that sending—the birth, life, and death of Jesus—can be set aside. If one understands God correctly, Anselm reasons, then one will better understand why God became human.

Anselm amplifies his explanation in chapter 1, when he explains that certain people have written him, asking for "reasons" (*rationes*) for a certain doctrine.[42] He quickly clarifies that these interlocutors do not intend to reason their way into faith: "This they ask, not for the sake of attaining to faith by means of reason (*rationes*), but that they may be delighted by understanding and contemplating on those things which they believe."[43] In addition, they fulfill the biblical injunction of 1 Peter 3:15, giving a rationale for the hope that is in them.[44] Anselm does not intend to set aside the tradition of the Church, which, he adds, "ought to be sufficient" to satisfy queries; instead he wants to amplify this teaching by contributing what God has revealed to him.[45] In what follows, Anselm solves what appears paradoxical to unbelievers: that God as ground of being and highest good in the universe had to subject the Son to a set of circumstances, including crucifixion and death, in order for humans to be reconciled with God. For those within the Christian narrative, it is possible and even easy to forget how striking this paradox is. *Cur Deus Homo* intends to

41. Anselm, *Cur Deus Homo*, preface. As with the *Monologion*, I cite from the Deane translation of the *Basic Writings*. When prudent, I have altered the translation based on my review of the Latin found in *L'oeuvre de S. Anselme de Cantorbéry*, ed. Michel Corbin and Alain Galonnier, vol. 3 (Paris: Cerf, 1988). Above I have rendered *rationibus necessariis* as "necessary" reasons, whereas Deane has "absolute reasons."

42. Here Deane renders this "proofs," a translation that makes it easier for the modern reader to relocate Anselm into a modern framework.

43. Anselm, *Cur Deus Homo*, 1.

44. Anselm, *Cur Deus Homo*, 1.

45. Anselm, *Cur Deus Homo*, 1.

untangle this riddle by using reason to answer questions that the Scriptures and the previous tradition did not ask.

On the basis of this achievement, many rate Anselm as a truly great theologian who advanced the faith. Others, meanwhile, bemoan his unfortunate and unyielding application of the tools of rationality, which resulted in the popularization of the pastorally catastrophic substitutionary penal atonement (Christ served as a substitute for our sins and the penalty that followed from them).[46] This section does not aim either to exonerate or to condemn Anselm, but merely to illustrate the daring and radical nature of his theological project, one that would have lasting impact on Western Christianity.

PETER ABELARD

Before turning to twelfth-century theology, it will be helpful to note the changes that occurred in the century between Anselm and Abelard. Theology left the monastery for what would eventually become the university, and the twelfth century bears the scars of this uneasy transition. Marie-Dominique Chenu notes the twelfth-century overlap between "two types of Christian high culture, each with its own theology: the monastic and the scholastic."[47] The newer, scholastic method, despite the precedent set by a figure like Anselm, still came as a shock; Anselm, after all, was an abbot in a monastery. Meanwhile, as Chenu notes, a growing consciousness of qualification emerged in the twelfth century: the *licentia* became a required "degree" to teach in places like Paris. Although the thirteenth century would come to designate a high point in the understanding of theology as a science, Chenu reminds his readers of the importance of the previous century: "The key developments in the professionalization of theology took

---

46. For a lucid defense of Anselm's atonement theory against later iterations, see David Bentley Hart, "A Gift Exceeding Every Debt: An Eastern Orthodox Appreciation of Anselm's Cur Deus Homo," *Pro Ecclesia* 7, no. 3 (1998): 333–48. My own approach to show the unity between *Cur Deus Homo* and the *Monologion* and *Proslogion* is prefigured in the ground-breaking work of Michel Corbin. See, in particular, *Prière et raison de la foi: introduction à l'ouvre de St Anselme de Cantebory* (Paris: Cerf, 1992).

47. Marie-Dominique Chenu, *Nature, Man, and Society in the 12th Century. Essays on New Theological Perspectives in the Latin West*, ed. and trans. Jerome Taylor and Lester Little (Chicago: University of Chicago Press, 1968), 274.

place in the twelfth century."[48] In this century the *quaestio* and the *summa*, two ways of doing theology forever linked with Thomas Aquinas in the minds of most students of theology, came into vogue. It is helpful to keep these developments in mind while recalling the contributions of three leading theologians of the twelfth century.

Peter Abelard (c. 1079–1142) was the figure most responsible for shaping medieval theology, at least in its scholastic form, into a scientific disciple. He ventured further than Anselm in subjecting theology to logic, which left him subject to charges of rationalism. For Abelard, "Theology was the application of *scientia* to the understanding of the nature of God and of the Christian religion."[49] His daring—some might say foolish—theological adventures, coupled with his anti-authoritarian bent, contributed to him running afoul of authorities, including many former teachers, not least of whom was the powerful Bernard of Clairvaux, who pushed for Abelard's excommunication. His personal life was no less tumultuous: his infamous affair with a student, Heloise, led to his castration. Besides his autobiographical writings—the letters to Heloise and the *Historia Calamitatum* (*History of My Calamities*)— Abelard is perhaps best known for *Sic et Non* (*Yes and No*), a collection of seemingly opposing positions from different theological authorities on a controversial question.[50] Many regard this text as a precursor to Lombard's *Sentences*, a scholastic, medieval fulfillment of the "systematic" theology promised in Origen's *On First Principles*. To his marrow, Abelard was a logician and dialectician, ever ready to engage and debate. This orientation led to a pattern in which he would first learn from a master before setting up a school in competition with that master. One finds this pattern reflected in both *Sic et Non* and the *Dialogue Between a Philosopher, a Jew, and a Christian*.

In "Dialogue 2" of his *Dialogue Between a Philosopher, a Jew, and a Christian*, Abelard constructs a debate with a philosopher dissatis-

---

48. Chenu, *Nature, Man, and Society*, 276, 279.

49. Roger French and Andrew Cunningham, *Before Science: The Invention of the Friars' Natural Philosophy* (Brookfield, VT: Scholar, 1996), 58. Cited in Grant, *God & Reason in the Middle Ages*, 59.

50. For a brief summary, and a helpful introduction to Abelard's thought, see Rik Van Nieuwenhove, *An Introduction to Medieval Theology* (Cambridge: Cambridge University Press, 2012), 99–112.

fied with Gregory the Great's famous comment on the rationality of faith: "Faith for which human reason supplies a test has no merit."[51] Abelard's imagined philosopher is committed to a particular mode of finding truth, and deems this response inadequate—weak "consolation for their incompetence."[52] Both the philosopher and his imagined Christian realize, from the perspective of reason and logic, that arguments from authority do not always carry the power to convince. The Christian notes, "In any battle of disputation, a declared truth of reason is stronger than pointing to an authority."[53] Arguments from scriptural authority, the bedrock of Christian theology, do not convince somebody like his interlocutor, and in these cases, "one must affirm or defend the faith mainly by reasons."[54] In the course of the dialogue the two figures discuss virtue and the good life. The Christian recalls the concern that sophistry can replace proper reasoning, thus leading many to false conclusions about the purported irreconcilability between reason and faith.[55] Abelard's *Dialogue* not only marks an intellectual openness and willingness to apply other disciplines, especially logic, to theology; it also reveals a confidence in the capacity of reason to solve problems unresolved by appeals to authority, a theme that would dominate his most important work.

Abelard marked the growing crisis of authority in medieval theology with *Sic et Non*.[56] In this text Abelard poses 158 statements, which cover a multitude of metaphysical, ethical, and doctrinal topics, including, *that God is three*,[57] *that the Son was generated eternally*,[58] *that a lie is permissible*.[59] In the different statements, Abelard lines up seemingly contradictory statements from different scriptural and

51. Gregory, *Homilies*, 26. Cited in Abelard, *Dialogue* 160. Here and below I cite from Peter Abelard, *Ethical Writings*, trans. Paul Vincent Spade (Indianapolis: Hackett, 1995), 96. While using Spade's translation, I will notate parenthetically the corresponding passage in Luscombe's authoritative Latin edition.

52. Peter Abelard, *Dialogue*, 160.

53. Peter Abelard, *Dialogue*, 171.

54. Peter Abelard, *Dialogue*, 173.

55. Peter Abelard, *Dialogue*, 230–38.

56. For an online version of the Latin, see http://individual.utoronto.ca/pking/resources/abelard/Sic_et_non.txt.

57. Peter Abelard, *Sic et Non*, 6.

58. Peter Abelard, *Sic et Non*, 15.

59. Peter Abelard, *Sic et Non*, 154.

patristic authorities, sometimes even within a single authority, like Augustine. The rhetorical effect of this method is striking: When attempting to answer a contested question, brute appeal to authority does not suffice. One must apply additional skills and methods. Abelard does not give conclusions to each contested thesis, but he does give clues to explain the discrepancy. He lays these out in the book's preface: first, words do not always mean the same thing. One author may mean something different by a term like *procession*, which explains seemingly contradictory statements among authorities about how procession in the Trinity works. Second, one must also take into account the possibility of a slip up by a scribe or a misleading translation of a Greek word, like *physis*, in the Trinitarian theology of a Greek father. Further, a Christian authority, commenting on Aristotle or Plato, could have misunderstood their thought and thus embraced or rejected their teaching based on a fallacious reading.

Abelard was not the first to notice contradictions in authority. Yet Abelard's works exuded great conviction in the power of dialectical thinking. In the words of one commentator: "His confidence in reason to determine the outcome of disagreements and conflicts was great indeed."[60] Abelard pushed far beyond eleventh-century precursors by leaving unanswered so many of *Sic et Non*'s questions. The same commentator adds, "Nothing is exempted from this rigorous inspection except the Bible and those pronouncements that the Church has accepted as true. All other authorities and texts are open to criticism and analysis in an effort to arrive at the truth."[61] With Abelard, one can imagine how scholastic theology came to be viewed pejoratively: These methods were applied in such a way that theology detaches itself from spirituality and prayer, gradually becoming confined to endless logic chopping. Even if Abelard himself did not succumb to rationalism,[62] he exuded nearly unprecedented confidence in the power of reason, generating a sharp backlash. This backlash occurred in Peter's lifetime, most importantly in the push by Bernard of Clairvaux to have Abelard's books condemned in 1140, on the basis that they relied

60. Grant, *God & Reason*, 61.
61. Grant, *God & Reason*, 61.
62. On this point scholars of Abelard are not in agreement.

excessively on reason.[63] Since the history of theology in large part characterizes Abelard as somebody who overstepped the reach of reason in the quest to bring understanding to faith, his role in the shaping of subsequent theology remains underappreciated. One can trace his impact on both of the final two theologians examined in this chapter, despite their efforts to distinguish their method from his.

HUGH OF ST. VICTOR

In the latter books of his magisterial *de Trinitate* (*On the Trinity*), Saint Augustine distinguishes between knowledge, which covers contingent realities, and a wisdom that deals with eternal truths. Wisdom, for Augustine, is the higher truth, and lower truths derive their value from being directed upward. In book XIV of *de Trinitate*, Augustine exclaims, "For this wisdom of man is so called, in that it is also of God. For then it is true wisdom, for if it is human, it is vain."[64] Augustine makes this assertion in the course of answering a question about one of Christianity's greatest mysteries, the Incarnation. If God entered into human history, and truth took shape as an event, then it was not immediately obvious, as it had been to the Platonists, how eternal truths shared a status higher than contingent truths—for the highest truth took the shape of an event. Picking up on this theme, Augustine notes in book XIII of *de Trinitate* that Christ reveals both temporal and eternal truths: "Therefore Christ is our knowledge, and the same Christ is also our wisdom. He Himself implants in us faith concerning temporal things, He Himself shows forth the truth concerning eternal things."[65] From here, Augustine concludes that all truths should point toward the one Truth; any other orientation runs the risk of falling into vain and sinful pride, and of leading to the confusion that Paul recollected in Romans: "For though they knew God, they did not honor him as God or give thanks to him, but they became futile in their thinking,

---

63. Grant, *God & Reason*, 64.

64. Augustine, *de Trinitate*, XIV, xii, 15. I have taken the translation from St. Augustine, *On the Trinity, Doctrinal Treatises, Moral Treatises*, trans. Arthur West Haddan (Peabody, MA: Hendrickson, 1995), 191.

65. Augustine, *de Trinitate*, XIII, xix, 24, 181.

and their senseless minds were darkened. Claiming to be wise, they became fools" (Rom 1:21–22).

Medieval theology's ongoing dialogue with Augustine, the *doctor communis* or common teacher for the Latin West, meant involving itself in a continual remembering and forgetting, de- and re-emphasizing aspects of Augustine's thought. This was true in the time of Eriugena and also for the generation after Peter Abelard, that struggled to integrate new secular modes of learning into the theological disciplines. One manifestation of this struggle, and a significant form of pushback against Abelard's shock treatment of dialectic, came from St. Victor, the famous school near Paris. St. Victor was founded by William of Champeaux, who had taught and later ran afoul of Abelard.[66] The most important member of the "Victorines" was Hugh of St. Victor (c. 1096–1141). Hugh led the abbey during the peak of its influence and taught both Peter Lombard and Richard of St. Victor, two giants of twelfth-century theology. Many consider Hugh's *De Sacramentis Christianae Fidei* the first reliable summary of medieval theology, but perhaps his most influential work was his primer, the *Didascalicon de Studio Legendi*.

Compared to somebody like Bernard of Clairvaux (1090–1153), the Cistercian reformer and vehement opponent of Abelard, Hugh appears as the less obvious juxtaposition to Abelard; after all, Bernard had publicly opposed Abelard and had even managed to get a council convened in 1141 to hear a debate between Abelard and himself. Hugh opposed Abelard more indirectly, but in some ways this added force to his opposition. Hugh's *Didascalicon* demonstrates the necessity of the seven liberal arts for theology, but at key points strongly opposes the twelfth-century trends that Abelard had embraced.

The *Didascalicon* was the twelfth-century version of Mortimer Adler's twentieth-century classic: *How to Read a Book*.[67] In it, Hugh sets out to explain how one can gain knowledge through reading. Hugh aims to answer the three questions that follow from this endeavor: what books to read, in what order to read these books, and

---

66. Nieuwenhove, *An Introduction to Medieval Theology*, 120.

67. Mortimer Adler, *How to Read a Book: The Art of Getting a Liberal Education* (New York: Simon and Schuster, 1940).

in what manner these books should be read.[68] The *Didascalicon* provides an architectonic for understanding how each of the sciences, or arts, relates to the rest of knowledge. It also describes the ideal disposition of the student who aims to read both sacred and secular texts. It is noteworthy how Hugh, in no way rejecting secular learning or the importance of the intellectual life for monks, implants an Augustinian caution on pursuit of the liberal arts and on the place of logic and dialectic in theology. Whereas Abelard had conflated wisdom with rational questioning,[69] Hugh attempted to place the use of reason within a framework provided by wisdom, in which all rational pursuit would be futile absent a corresponding moral gain.

Hugh alludes only briefly to the fall of Adam, but even so his classic text reflects an aura of loss and recovery. At the outset of book 1 he notes, "For the mind, stupefied by bodily sensations and enticed out of itself by sensuous forms, has forgotten what it was. [. . .] But we are restored through instruction, so that we may recognize our nature and learn not to seek outside ourselves what we can find within."[70] Knowing involves not just the raw pursuit of answers, aided by distinctions and the liberal learning that give one the tools to make such distinctions; in addition, it requires avoiding and correcting certain residual tendencies. After dividing the kinds of knowledge into the theoretical, practical, and mechanical, Hugh adds logic as a fourth branch of knowledge, and he subordinates logic to wisdom. Here the text underscores how wisdom involves friendship with God, and "is moderator over all that we do deliberately."[71]

After integrating practical arts with the traditional seven liberal arts—*trivium* and *quadrivium*—in book 2, Hugh outlines in book 3 the ideals to which the student should strive. He emphasizes the good-

68. Hugh of St. Victor, "Preface," in *The Didascalicon of Hugh of St. Victor: A Medieval Guide to the Arts*, trans. Jerome Taylor (New York: Columbia University Press, 1961), 43–45. Henceforth the book will be cited by book and chapter, with the pagination from this translation in parenthesis.

69. Monika Asztalos notes that rational questioning "is according to Abelard the key to wisdom." See Asztalos, "The Faculty of Theology," in *A History of the University in Europe*, ed. Hilde de Ridder-Symoens, vol. 1, *Universities in the Middle Ages* (Cambridge: Cambridge University Press, 1991), 409–41, at 411.

70. Hugh, *Didascalicon*, I, 1 (47).

71. Hugh, *Didascalicon*, I, 2 (48); I, 8 (55).

ness of all learning, offering no hint of suspicion about the dangers of secular learning. It is helpful to imagine the twelfth-century school of St. Victor as a start-up company in the middle of twenty-first century Silicon Valley. Everybody interested in ideas and innovation, who also had the means, gravitated to Paris, which produced and reproduced a certain intellectual culture. Hugh's plea for humility strikes a powerful chord: "Many are deceived by the desire to appear wise before their time. They therefore break out in a certain swollen importance and begin to simulate what they are not and to be ashamed of what they are; and they slip all the farther from wisdom in proportion as they think, not of being wise, but of being thought so."[72] Hugh laments something analogous to a celebrity culture in the Paris of his day. More people were interested in seeming wise than being wise, in a vain attempt to achieve academic celebrity.

It is no great stretch to imagine the kind of academic culture lamented by Hugh. Graduate programs in the humanities are filled with showoffs and charlatans. These behaviors arise partially from students' own insecurities, but they can also be generated through modeling their professors, who value appearance over substance. Twelfth-century academic culture arose out of the monasteries, and thus there was a stronger cultural memory than there is now of the ideal scholar-monk or saint, who seamlessly interwove the intellectual and moral virtues. Hugh's *Didascalicon* aimed to recover that ideal without retreating from the cutting edge of learning. Hugh continues, "The good student, then, ought to be humble and docile, free alike from vain cares and from sensual indulgences [. . .] to consider a matter thoroughly and at length before judging of it, to seek to *be* learned rather than merely to seem so."[73] It is not difficult to identify Abelard as the unspoken anti-model here. After all, as Abelard recalled in his memoirs, he had grown full of sensual appetite and had lacked all humility in the course of his calamitous seduction of Heloise.[74]

In the last three books of the *Didascalicon* Hugh turns to scriptural interpretation, knowledge of which Hugh defends against those

---

72. Hugh, *Didascalicon*, III, 13 (95).
73. Hugh, *Didascalicon*, III, 13 (97).
74. See Abelard, *History of my Calamities*.

too proud to bother with such a simple text: "They wrinkle their noses and purse their lips at lecturers in divinity. [. . .] It is not my advice that you imitate men of this kind."[75] Hugh recommends respect for the scriptural text, not because of its exceptional status, but because no student should scorn learning from any text.[76] Even if Scripture does not pose the same challenges as Boethius's commentaries on logic, one still needs a guide to preserve oneself from error: "This introduction must be sought from learned teachers and men who have wisdom, who are able to produce and unfold the matter to you both through the authorities of the holy fathers and the evidences of the Scriptures, as is needful."[77] Whether studying Scripture or the secular arts, all knowing involves a participation in God,[78] and failing to acknowledge this participation means that one has not yet become wise. This failure can result both from intellectual *and* moral shortcomings, from the student lacking in aptitude and the student lacking in humility. A man like Abelard—and who knows how many Abelards were running around Paris in the 1130s!—may seem to be wise, but if he lacks humility, he is distant from Christ and thus alienated from the true wisdom for which God made us.

PETER LOMBARD

Concerning Peter Lombard's centrality in the history of theology, Philipp Rosemann notes, "The Western tradition of Christianity was ready for a full-blown theological system—one that would render the faith as intelligible as humanly possible through comprehensive coverage of all its major themes in a methodical order and the application of dialectical procedures to several layers of authoritative texts. Peter Lombard was to create such a system."[79] Peter Lombard (c. 1100–1160) wrote perhaps the most influential textbook in the history of theology. His *Sententiae in quatuor libris distinctae*, frequently truncated to the

---

75. Hugh, *Didascalicon*, III, 13 (96–97).
76. Hugh, *Didascalicon*, III, 13 (96): "Hold no learning in contempt, for all learning is good."
77. Hugh, *Didascalicon*, VI, 4 (144).
78. Hugh, *Didascalicon*, VI, 5 (145): "Every nature tells of God."
79. Philipp W. Rosemann, *Peter Lombard* (Oxford: Oxford University Press, 2004), 33.

Sentences, was a theological standard-bearer from the twelfth to the seventeenth century, during which time it was subject to more than 1400 commentaries from theologians as divergent as Thomas Aquinas and Martin Luther.[80] Lombard's *Sentences* not only provided a steadying force in the middle of a tumultuous century, but it also accomplished a long-desired task: to analyze theology through a rational structure in order to make explicit its scientific aspirations.

In medieval thought, a *sententia* designates "an opinion expressed by an authoritative writer."[81] Lombard's *Sentences* express opinions based on scriptural and patristic authorities, with Augustine cited more than all other authorities combined. Lombard designed the *Sentences* to supply a framework for theology in the generation after the upheaval resulting from Abelard's *Sic et Non*. Despite the success of Lombard's work, both in terms of genre breakthrough and longevity, Lombard himself has often been dismissed as a second-rate compiler of theological opinions, lacking the creativity and insight of a great theologian. As a consequence, the *Sentences* have been almost fully supplanted by later medieval efforts, especially Aquinas's *Summa Theologiae*. More recent scholarship has given Lombard his proper due. Marcia Colish, for instance, thinks the *Sentences* represent an important theological breakthrough. Work like hers has generated new interest in Peter Lombard's theology.[82]

Lombard was born into an Italian family of no significance, and became a master at the theological school in Paris and, in the last year of his life, bishop of Paris. His life carries nothing of the intrigue and particularity of Abelard's. The *Sentences* was his one and only *magnum opus*, and in it Lombard, like Abelard, wanted to demonstrate the scientific character of theology and the rationality of faith. To do so Lombard replaced the more traditional form of commentary, or gloss, with a new mode of expression. Glosses had allowed their authors to apply

---

80. Rosemann, *Peter Lombard*, 3. Subsequent material on Lombard's life, unless otherwise noted, comes from this work.

81. Rosemann, *Peter Lombard*, 17.

82. Marcia Colish, *Peter Lombard*, 2 vols. (Leiden: Brill, 1994). The marginalization of Lombard helps explain why it took until 2007 before a complete translation of *The Sentences* appeared in English. See Lombard, *The Sentences*, trans. Giulio Silano (Toronto: Pontifical Institute of Mediaeval Studies, 2007).

logical distinctions and philosophical exposition on a given topic. Lombard found this approach too topical. What the *Sentences* accomplished, on the other hand, was "a system of theology in which every important topic not only receives treatment, but occupies a logical place within a general schema."[83] In short, this ordering gave theology a heuristic to illumine its inherent rationality.

Both Abelard and Lombard took up the task of reconciling authorities. Abelard's manner of doing so, combined with the nature of his personality, has resulted in a mixed legacy for this master theologian. Lombard's reputation, meanwhile, is that of a conservative thinker who steadied the boat. It is helpful to make two points about the *Sentences*. First, unlike Hugh of St. Victor's *de Sacramentis*, the *Sentences* are not arranged according to salvation history, but rather topically. Book 1 treats God and things to be enjoyed; book 2 covers creation, both angelic and material; book 3 discusses Christology and the virtues; book 4 the sacraments.[84] Peter Lombard bases this structure on the use/enjoy distinction employed by Augustine in *On Christian Teaching*. Second, Lombard does not gesture toward the insufficiency of theology itself and the corresponding need for philosophy or logic to save theology from its essential limitations. For the most part, common sense, a steady hand, and a deep knowledge of the sources usually suffice to point toward a satisfactory conclusion of the matter. One sees this in the discussion of faith, in book III, distinction 24.[85] Here Lombard reconciles the different authoritative texts— mostly from Scripture and Augustine—about matters relating to faith and understanding. Does faith always precede understanding? How exactly does faith come "from hearing" (Rom 10:17) if faith is an intellectual assent? Were the biblical figures before Christ saved by faith? Regarding the middle question, Lombard remarks: "And since faith comes from hearing, but in an interior way, and not an exterior one, it cannot concern something of which one is entirely ignorant."[86] Such measured answers suffuse the *Sentences*. Lombard does not supply the

83. Rosemann, *Peter Lombard*, 54.
84. Van Nieuwenhove, *An Introduction to Medieval Theology*, 150.
85. Lombard, *The Sentences. Book 3: On the Incarnation of the Word*, 103–11.
86. Lombard, *The Sentences. Book 3*, 105.

brilliant reflections on key questions that somebody like Anselm provided, but he nonetheless contributes to a greater *rapprochement* between faith and reason.

The prologue to the *Sentences* is a good place to identify what one commentator has called the "middleness," or balanced synthesis that Lombard produces.[87] Lombard declares his intention to protect the faith as well as to "reveal the hidden depths of theological investigations and to convey an understanding of the Church's mysteries."[88] Yet throughout the first two paragraphs Lombard betrays a humility, comparing his offering to the widow's two bits (Luke 21:1–2). He even conveys a sense of terror at the immensity of the task and downplays his own intelligence. He continues in the prologue by outlining the problems that arise in theology on account of impious wills: "Their pursuit consists more in seeking what pleases them than what ought to be taught."[89] In response to this crisis, Lombard presents the *Sentences*: "We have, with God's aid, put together with much labour and sweat a volume from the witnesses of truth established for all eternity, and divided it in four books. [. . .] Here, by the sincere profession of the Lord's faith, we have denounced the falsehood of a poisonous doctrine."[90] Lombard continues and even acknowledges the "middle way" of his method: "Embracing an approach to showing the truth without incurring the danger of professing impiety, we have pursued a moderate middle course between the two. And if in some places our voice has rung out a little loudly, it has not transgressed the bounds set by our forefathers."[91] In spite of undertaking a wildly ambitious task, Lombard recedes from the foreground, like the author of a legal casebook.[92]

In the final paragraph of the prologue, Lombard offers a parallel to Abelard's *Sic et Non*: "In this brief volume, we have brought together the sentences of the Fathers and the testimonies apposite to them, so

---

87. See Giulio Silano, "Introduction," to *The Sentences. Book 1: The Mystery of the Trinity*, vii–l, at xxvii: "The more important reason for its influence is its 'middleness' as it attempts to provide balanced syntheses of theological debates which have preceded it."
88. "Prologue," 1–2 in Lombard, *Sentences. Book 1*, 3. I have changed the translation of "sacramenta" to "mysteries," rather than "sacraments," as Silano renders it.
89. "Prologue," 3 in *Sentences. Book 1*, 4.
90. "Prologue," 4 in *Sentences. Book 1*, 4.
91. "Prologue," 4 in *Sentences. Book 1*, 4.
92. For this comparison, see Silano, "Introduction," xix–xxxi.

that one who seeks them shall find it unnecessary to rifle through numerous books, when this brief collection effortlessly offers him what he seeks."[93] On this note Lombard finishes his prologue and begins his discussion of the Trinity. In light of his own prefatory words, it is easy to understand why many have dismissed Lombard as a second-rate compiler unworthy of deep study. Against such a judgment a few points can be made. Like so many great books, the *Sentences* seems like a book that almost any master in Paris could have written. But Peter's text lasted, and was not surpassed as a textbook for several centuries. This fact alone should make critics pause. It cannot be underestimated how immense a task it must have been (as Lombard himself admits) to organize all of Christian teaching into a coherent topical structure. As Silano notes, the basic Lombardian architecture underlying the *Sentences* "was successfully used in the schools for many generations, to the point that the basic theological course of Faculties of Theology almost into the 1960s would still be marked by the division of topics devised in the *Sentences*."[94] The shift brought about by Lombard required conceiving the truths or mysteries of theology within a different framework from their narrative unfolding. Though salvation history unfolded historically, Lombard made it possible to imagine how these truths could be systematized for the sake of analysis, and apart from how they were revealed. This deeply imaginative task presupposed, and also made possible, the confidence in the compatibility between faith and reason unsettled by Abelard. This confidence became a hallmark of the medieval period, especially the century subsequent to Lombard. In organizing the most important patristic texts in the way that he did, Lombard put his thumb very much on the scale. While relegating his voice to the background, Lombard weighed and judged much of the theological tradition through the order he conceived for analyzing it. Perhaps more than any other medieval figure, he deserves credit for the stunning breakthroughs of the thirteenth century, often remembered as the century which produced the greatest harmony between the aspirations of human reason and the weight of Christian tradition.

93. "Prologue," 5 in *Sentences. Book 1*, 4–5.
94. Silano, "Introduction," xxviii.

CONCLUSION

The period from the "early" to the "middle" Middle Ages saw tremendous growth in theology and new frameworks for conceiving how to conjoin theology to the rest of scientific and secular learning. The story that has been told has been shamefully parochial with its focus on Latin Christianity, at the expense of the vast non-Latin Christian tradition. This overly Western European trajectory is chosen on the basis of subsequent history, and the incredible challenge that the Enlightenment, whose greatest exponents came from this Western European tradition, posed to Christianity, specifically regarding the purported compatibility between faith and reason.

Chapter 3

The High Middle Ages
Aquinas, Bonaventure, and Scotus

UNIVERSITY CLIMATE IN THE 1200s

It is helpful to recall how radically different the climate of Lombard's Paris of the 1150s was from Aquinas and Bonaventure's Paris of the 1250s and 1260s. Lombard's *Sentences* came into prominence at the beginning of the thirteenth century, when Alexander of Hales first used it as a textbook.[1] Although some theologians challenged the authority of the *Sentences*, it acquired near canonical status by 1215, when the Fourth Lateran Council cleared the text of any suspicion. In the same year, Robert of Courçon, then serving as a papal legate, granted official statutes to the "university" of Paris, which gave the teaching masters some protection from episcopal intervention. This meant exchanging one authority for another; freedom from episcopal oversight gave way to an increase in papal influence over what was taught. Both Robert of Courçon, chancellor at the university, and Pope Innocent III had been masters at the university, and it is reasonable to imagine, given their shared experience in formation, that they would have come to similar conclusions about the oversight of theology, even though they represented two different seats of authority, one academic and the other ecclesiastical.[2]

One can also discern the difference between centuries by revisiting the structure of university curricula and their bearing on theology. The nascent university curriculum complemented the earlier curriculum of the cathedral chapters—trivium and quadrivium—with three university disciplines: medicine, law, and theology. These disciplines had long been taught, but they were given new parameters and order

---

1. Grant, *God & Reason*, 210.
2. Asztalos, "The Faculty of Theology," 412–13.

within their university setting. Among universities, Bologna became the epicenter of legal studies, and Oxford and Paris constituted the most important theological centers in the thirteenth and fourteenth centuries. Paris's superior reputation was based largely on the foundation laid by the twelfth-century figures mentioned in the previous chapter. In time, however, the Oxford theologians came to enjoy greater liberty than their counterparts, at least until ecclesial authorities began intervening at Oxford in 1277.[3] The thirteenth century records numerous bans and expulsions of certain teachings and texts. The efficacy of these bans can be questioned, for their repetition indicates a lack of reception. Evidence indicates that universities remained vibrant, and faculty continued to communicate contested ideas that challenged certain doctrines, despite official policies.

Two additional factors complicated and also made possible the flourishing of theology in the thirteenth century. The first was the creation of two extremely successful religious orders: the Franciscans and the Dominicans. Dynamic founders helped both of these orders grow rapidly; the times demanded educated postulants who could combat heresy (especially in the case of the Dominicans) and preach more effectively to a society undergoing massive economic growth and urbanization. These orders set up schools in Paris, Oxford, and other university towns in order to benefit from the proximity of master theologians. Even if their students took courses at their in-house institutions, the border between a Dominican or Franciscan "house of studies" and the adjacent university faculties was porous. Dominicans and Franciscans came to occupy chairs in the theology faculties at places like Oxford, and such renowned figures as Alexander of Hales and Robert Bacon—trained as secular masters—joined these mendicant orders subsequent to their formation.

With such rapid changes territorial conflicts arose, with the secular (in its medieval usage *secular* denotes not belonging to a religious order) faculties sometimes banning members of orders, and the orders forbidding secular students to attend their lectures.[4] The antagonisms created by the growth of these orders—they boasted over ten thousand

---

3. Asztalos, "The Faculty of Theology," 414.
4. Asztalos, "The Faculty of Theology," 415–17.

members by the end of the thirteenth century—both complicated and enriched university culture during this time. In light of their impact on university culture, it is no surprise that the two theologians under survey from this century—Aquinas and Bonaventure—came from the Dominicans and Franciscans.

The second factor that made possible the flourishing of theology in the thirteenth century was the reintroduction of Aristotle's scientific work into the Latin West.[5] This story begins near the end of the eleventh century, when Christian forces won victories over Muslim armies in Spain (1085) and Sicily (1091). Aware that Islamic learning, especially scientific learning, had outpaced Christian efforts to that point, scholars traveled to Spain and Sicily to translate Arabic and Greek texts, lost to Christian Europe in the intervening centuries, into Latin. Boethius's editions of Aristotle's logic had preserved a portion of his corpus. When scholars had discovered, among other treasures, Aristotle's "lost" texts, covering such topics as politics, physics, biology, astronomy, and poetics, they naturally gravitated to these treatises.[6] Edward Grant calls this new literature a "knowledge explosion," adding, "Here was a body of literature that was ready-made to serve as a curriculum for the newly emerging universities."[7] Aristotle's natural philosophy augmented the body of knowledge that had hitherto constituted the quadrivium. Compared to a text like Plato's *Timaeus*, which explained the origins of the world mythically, Aristotle's grounded, methodical approach instituted a paradigm shift in thinking about the natural world. This new approach would form students who needed to complete the required arts curriculum before moving on to theology.

Thirteenth-century Christian intellectuals were faced with the task of deciding how to integrate this new "science" with long accepted Christian assumptions about cosmology, the soul, and other matters. These scholars found precedent in the Arab world, most notably in the figure of Ibn Rushd (1126–98), better known by his Latinized

---

5. The specifics from this paragraph derive largely from Grant, *God & Reason*, 83–114.

6. Stephen Brown, "General Introduction," in *Thomas Aquinas on Faith and Reason*, ed. Stephen F. Brown (Indianapolis: Hackett, 1999), xi.

7. Grant, *God & Reason*, 101.

name, Averroes. Born in Spain, Averroes attempted to synthesize Aristotle's philosophy with Islamic theology. Near the end of his life, authorities banished him to Morocco and burned many of his works. These measures, however, did not prevent the eventual spread of his writings throughout Christian Europe. Averroes gave Christians a model for examining the revealed claims of faith in light of new science. The so-called "Latin Averroists" followed Averroes by designating philosophy and theology to two separate realms, and through this distinction hoped to assuage ecclesiastical authorities. This hope did not come to pass, as Etienne Gilson notes: "In the year 1277, the Bishop of Paris, Etienne Tempier, solemnly condemned 219 propositions either borrowed from Averroistic writings, or expressing current Averroistic opinions."[8] The Latin Averroists and the censorship of their ideas are emblematic of the growing pains in thirteenth-century theology occasioned by the rediscovery of Aristotle's scientific corpus and the rapid ascension of two religious orders that lacked the prestige of long-established ones.

Attempts to ban Aristotle began in the first third of the thirteenth century. The first such occurrence was in 1210 at Paris, when ecclesiastical authorities forbade Aristotle's "natural books."[9] In 1228 Pope Gregory IX accused the Parisian master theologians of transgressing the parameters set by the church fathers in applying philosophical ideas to theological matters, including the interpretation of Scripture. Philosophy, reasoned Pope Gregory, is a handmaiden to theology, not its peer. The spirit of concern also found voice in leading theologians, including John of St. Giles, a Dominican master in Paris. In 1231 he complained, "When they come to theology they can hardly part from their philosophy, as is clear in certain persons, who cannot part from Aristotle in theology, bringing with them brass instead of gold."[10] Oxford had no such ban, and as a result it, along with other less rep-

---

8. Etienne Gilson, *Reason and Revelation in the Middle Ages* (New York: Charles Scribner's Sons, 1938), 64. For a readable introduction to the impact of Averroes and the Latin Averroists, see Gilson, *Reason and Revelation*, 37–66.

9. The specifics for this paragraph derive from Asztalos, "The Faculty of Theology," 420–33.

10. Marie-Madeleine Davy, *Les Sermons universitaires parisiens de 1230–31* (Paris: Vrin, 1931), 292. Cited in Asztalos, "The Faculty of Theology," 422.

utable faculties, surpassed Paris as the leading center of intellectual activity in Europe. As Monika Asztalos notes, the application of Aristotle, even when done outside of acceptable limits in the first decades of the thirteenth century, still took place within an Augustinian framework. By the 1240s, these conditions changed, as notably seen in Albertus Magnus (Albert the Great, c. 1193–1280). A pivotal figure, this Dominican master taught at Paris as well as various Dominican houses of formation in Germany. In 1248 he began commenting on all of Aristotle's works. He became master general of the Dominicans in 1254, and it was in this atmosphere that Thomas Aquinas undertook his studies.

THOMAS AQUINAS, THE ANGELIC DOCTOR

Known as the *doctor angelicus*, Angelic Doctor, Thomas Aquinas (ca. 1225–74) was one of the greatest geniuses in recorded human history. Against the wishes of his family, Aquinas entered the Dominicans, a mendicant order. Being mendicant meant that the order was not supported, as would have been the norm in the older feudal model, on property that would generate income, but instead subsisted on gifts. Much as Dorothy Day sought to form Catholic Worker houses in the mid-twentieth century that existed outside the "capitalist system," so too the mendicant orders wanted to operate outside the normative world of landholding, which would include realities like benefices and sinecures.[11] Such a move by Thomas, the youngest son from a noble family, was not well-received. Aquinas persevered in his desire to become a preaching friar, which led him from Naples to Paris, to Cologne, and back to Paris, where he became a master in theology in 1256. For the next seventeen years, Aquinas taught both in Paris and at several locations in Italy. Before dying in March 1274, Aquinas, not yet fifty, abruptly ceased writing in December 1273, after nearly two decades of composing theology at a breathtaking, frenetic pace.[12]

---

11. This point simply distills what Frederick Bauerschmidt has said. Here, and throughout this section, I rely heavily on his book: *Thomas Aquinas: Faith, Reason, and Following Christ* (Oxford: Oxford University Press, 2013), 15.

12. For an interesting take on this episode, see Denys Turner, *Thomas Aquinas: A Portrait* (New Haven, CT: Yale University Press, 2013), 40–46.

On account of the sobriety of style that marks most of Aquinas's writings, it is helpful to remember that Aquinas (and Bonaventure too) was not the mid- or late-career professor, pontificating from a position of stability and institutional comfort; rather, he and Bonaventure were young university upstarts, writing their most important work in their thirties and forties.

In 1255, Paris began officially integrating Aristotle's philosophy into the liberal arts curriculum at the university. In the figure of Aquinas there converge two movements: one, a mode of learning, fortified over recent centuries, called *scholasticism*. In Aquinas's century this mode came to be expressed through the *quaestio*, reflected in Aquinas's crowning achievement, the *Summa Theologiae*. The *Summa* is comprised of thousands of questions. In the process of confronting the question, Aquinas marshals evidence from both sides before offering, through a combination of reason, judgment, and authority, an answer. The second movement that converges in the person and work of Aquinas is the integration of Aristotelean science into medieval Christian metaphysics. Aquinas leans heavily on Aristotle's understanding of science to explain just exactly how faith relates to reason or, in the formulation of his time, how theology is scientific. Many regard Aquinas's reflections on these matters as the crowning achievement, not just of his own work, but of the entire medieval church, which thereby was able to form a synthesis between faith and reason.

In order to get to the heart of Aquinas's reflections on these matters it will be helpful to focus on four key points or questions that he asks: (1) What kind of science is theology? (2) What is the kind of intellectual activity undertaken when one comes to believe in the gospel? (3) What distinguishes faith from reason as intellectual activity? (4) To what degree is reason, or philosophy, an activity independent from authority and divine intervention? Although the most obvious place to answer the first question would be the very beginning of the *Summa Theologiae*, when Aquinas takes up the question of whether theology is a science,[13] it is helpful for a fuller comprehension of his position to recall an important precursor to the *Summa*: his commen-

13. Aquinas, *Summa Theologiae*, I, q.1 a.2).

tary on Boethius's *de Trinitate*. Aquinas wrote this commentary shortly after he began teaching as a master in Paris, from 1256–59.[14]

The first three articles in part 1, question 2 of the *Super Boetium* shed light on how Aquinas thought about faith and reason during this stage of his career.[15] The first article asks, "Is it Permissible to Make Divine Realities an Object of Investigation?" After recalling a number of citations that lean toward fideism, Aquinas cites 1 Peter 3:15: "Always be prepared to make a defense to anyone who calls you to account (*rationem*) for the faith." In order to heed this precept, Aquinas says one needs to "inquire into what we hold on faith."[16] He outlines three ways that people can go wrong in the pursuit of deeper understanding of the faith: first, by presuming a comprehensive understanding of these matters; second, by putting reason prior to faith; and third, "by pursuing speculation into the divine beyond the measure of one's ability."[17] One argument seems to cause hesitation for Aquinas, and it comes from Gregory the Great's Easter homilies, where he says, "Faith has no merit where human reason supplies proof."[18] If one could know by human reason what faith claims to know, then there's no point in having faith. Aquinas makes a distinction: There are two kinds of human reasoning—demonstrative (*demonstrativa*) and persuasive (*persuasoria*). A good example of demonstrative reasoning would be geometry: If one understands the way the arguments work, one cannot deny the conclusions that are reached. Aquinas states that this kind of reasoning has no place in matters of faith, except for "disproving claims that faith is impossible."[19] Here

---

14. The title of the Latin original reads: *Super Boetium de Trinitate*. Bauerschmidt notes, "The commentary on Boethius might be seen as an attempt to think through the place of theology among the sciences—that is, a reflection on the relationship of faith and reason" (Bauerschmidt, *Thomas Aquinas*, 27).

15. Aquinas, *Super Boetium*, I, q.2, a.1–3; I have used the English translation of these questions from *Thomas Aquinas on Faith and Reason*, ed. Stephen Brown (Indianapolis: Hackett, 1999), 25–42. I have on occasion cross-checked the translation against the Latin and revised it. For the original I consulted http://www.logicmuseum.com/authors/aquinas/superboethiumq2.htm#pars1q2a1.

16. *Thomas Aquinas on Faith and Reason*, 26. The translation inserts "rationally" after "inquire," but the adverb is lacking in the Latin.

17. Aquinas, *Super Boetium*, I q.2, a.1; Brown, 27.

18. Aquinas, *Super Boetium*, I q.2, a.1, arg.5; Brown, 26.

19. Aquinas, *Super Boetium*, I. q.2, a.1, ad.5; Brown, 28.

Aquinas likely has in mind claims like "God does not exist," or "God is not simple." Demonstrative reason can only show that certain refutations have unstated presuppositions, and thus fail as logical arguments. Persuasive reasoning is another matter. This kind of reasoning makes a faith claim more plausible or believable. Since it is not demonstrative, assent is still voluntary, a matter of the will, rather than compulsive (*ad consensum*).

In the second article Aquinas asks, "Can there be a science of divine realities?"[20] This article is the true predecessor to the question that opens the *Summa Theologiae*: "Whether theology is a science?" After chronicling citations from different scriptural and patristic authorities, as well as Aristotle, Aquinas begins his exposition by noting a certain logic or order in science. He calls it the *ratio scientarum*, the "reason of science," better rendered as the "essence of science." The divine reality can be known from our natural creaturely perspective, but it can also be known "by God and the blessed."[21] Aquinas likely has in mind Paul's claim that we will know God "face to face" (1 Cor 13:12). From this twofold mode of knowing, Aquinas concludes that there are two kinds of theology (*duplex scientia divinis*). In the first mode we can know God through what later figures label "natural theology," that is, philosophical modes of enquiry like the cosmological and teleological argument. We also know God by faith, and come to know further things about God "by drawing conclusions from principles."[22] The key to this passage is understanding what Aquinas means by principles. Here we can recall Origen's classic text, *On First Principles*, in Latin *de Principiis*. The *principium* means the order or the basis; one example being Euclid's five postulates in geometry, which function as the foundation for any initiation into the study of geometry.

In his response to the fourth "objection," Aquinas explains how these principles work in relation to the reasoning or scientific activity that accompanies them. He writes, "The reasoning introduced in sciences precedes assent to the conclusions, but it follows assent to the

---

20. Aquinas, *Super Boetium*, I. q.2, a.2; Brown, 29.
21. Aquinas, *Super Boetium*, I. q.2, a.2; Brown, 31.
22. Aquinas, *Super Boetium*, I. q.2, a.2; Brown, 31.

principles because it flows from them."[23] One can think of the term "reasoning" (*ratio*) along the lines of the activity of playing a game like checkers or chess. In checkers there are rules, and the reasoning or "game playing" that leads one to be a good or a bad player succeed one's ability to think from within these rules, like moving diagonally and jumping over a piece if space permits. Playing chess involves a different and more elaborate set of rules. Likewise, playing chemistry involves a set of rules, quite different from the rules for playing history, or law. The common denominator in all of these activities is a rational capacity that understands the rules and then plays within them. The rules are the principles to which reason assents, and the conclusions result from playing the game well.

According to Aquinas, the articles of faith, by which he means the creedal claims to which all Christians assent, are "like principles, not conclusions."[24] In other words, reason only performs rearguard defense of the articles of faith, but it never demonstrates them. Yet the process of reasoning from these principles produces understanding that does not provide greater certainty—for faith provides its own certainty—though it does give rise to greater comprehension.[25] This process does not make theology less rational as a science, because, as Aristotle argues in the *Metaphysics*, first principles, like the principle of non-contradiction, cannot be proven, and yet these form the basis of the process of reasoning within a field or discipline.[26] Aquinas continues the argument in the next response when he gives the example of "subalternate" sciences, like engineering, that presuppose the science of math and physics.[27] Their derivative character makes subalternate sciences less pure, but it does not make them less scientific

23. Aquinas, *Super Boetium*, I. q.2, a.2, ad.4; Brown 32.

24. Aquinas, *Super Boetium*, I. q. 2, a.2, ad.4; Brown 32.

25. For this point, as well as an important articulation of how Aquinas relies on Aristotle's understanding of science that distinguishes between an *ordo inventionis* and an *ordo doctrinae*, see the essay by Bernard Lonergan, "Theology and Understanding," in *Collection: Papers by Bernard Lonergan, S.J.*, ed. F. E. Crowe (New York: Herder and Herder, 1967), 121–41, esp. 127–30.

26. Here Aquinas refers to book IV of the *Metaphysics* (1005b35–1011b22).

27. The classification of such sciences as "subalternate" likely came from Robert Grosseteste (c. 1175–1253), who wrote the first medieval commentary on Aristotle's *Posterior Analytics*. For this reference see Bauerschmidt, *Thomas Aquinas*, 53.

than the disciplines from which they are derived. Theology derives its principles, the articles of faith, from the apostolic witness of the divine truths revealed through Christ. In his next reply Aquinas notes how theology "does not make evident matters of faith, but by them it brings to light other things."[28] Here, returning to our example of checkers, the rules do not say that it behooves a player to protect the back row, but the reasoning process—playing the game to win—yields this among other lessons. All of these lessons are part of the "science" of checkers, or chess. If one imagined the game with no rules at all, then there would be no way to understand how to win. The rules, or principles, provide the framework for applying the reasoning process to it. So too with any science, including theology.

In the third article Aquinas asks whether one can use philosophy in theology, or reason in the science of faith. Aquinas distinguishes the sources of philosophy and theology: one comes from the "light of faith," and the other from "the light of natural reason."[29] Both of these activities depend on a light that comes from elsewhere (a point to which we will return). The source of this light is God, and since God is one, philosophy and theology—one derived from natural and the other from supernatural light—cannot contradict one another. Only a false-footed philosophy can contradict theology. Theology, meanwhile, can use philosophy or any other science to understand itself better. Despite a clear warning about the dangers of misapplying philosophy to theology, Aquinas considers all sciences, especially philosophy, as potential aids or handmaids to reach new insights in theology.

Around 1265 Aquinas began writing the first of his three-part *Summa Theologiae*, one of the most ground-breaking works in the history of theology. Though it took a few centuries, this work would eventually replace Lombard's *Sentences* as the standard text for theological education. Leo XIII's great nineteenth-century revival of Thomism recollected the special place that the *Summa* held at the Council of Trent: "In the midst of the Council of Trent, the assembled Fathers so willing it, the *Summa* of Thomas Aquinas lay open on the altar, with the Holy Scriptures and the decrees of the Supreme Pontiffs, that from

28. Aquinas, *Super Boetium*, I. q.2; a.2, ad.46; Brown 33.
29. Aquinas, *Super Boetium*, I. q.2; a.3; Brown 36.

it might be sought counsel and reasons and answers."[30] To his peers, it was not obvious that the future Angelic Doctor would scale such heights. In the 1260s, Aquinas was an early-career university professor and member of an upstart but growing religious order. He felt dissatisfied with available textbooks, including Lombard's *Sentences*, and sought to write one for beginners (*incipientes*), perhaps solely for the initiates in the Order of Preachers, or possibly for a wider audience.[31]

Aquinas opens with ten articles in his first question on the domain of theology. It will be helpful to focus on a couple of these articles to chart how he builds upon his understanding of theology as a science begun in the *Super Boetium*. In article 2 he asks, "Whether Sacred Doctrine is a Science?"[32] Here Aquinas maintains his distinction of two kinds of sciences. Of the sciences that proceed "by the natural light of the intellect," Aquinas lists geometry and arithmetic. Other sciences proceed "by the light of a superior science." Music, for instance, relies on the principles of arithmetic. Theology, or *sacra doctrina* "proceeds from the principles made known by the light of a higher science, namely, the science of God and the blessed."[33] Aquinas means that theology begins with revealed data—data whose truths can only be known by the light of faith—which for him are codified in the Nicene Creed.

Theology's status as a "sub-alternate science" may sound second-class. Aquinas tackles this question in article 5, when he asks whether theology is more reputable (*dignior*) than other sciences. In the second objection Aquinas references the claim that it is in the nature of a lower science to draw on a higher one. Since theology draws on other

---

30. Pope Leo XIII, *Aeterni Patris* (1879), cited from "Encyclical Letter of Pope Leo XIII," in St. Thomas Aquinas, *Summa Theologica*, trans. the Fathers of the English Dominican Province, vol. 1 (New York: Benziger Brothers, [1948] 1981), xvi. Bauerschmidt rightly calls this story a "pious fiction" (Bauerschmidt, *Thomas Aquinas*, 298).

31. The audience of the *Summa* and the subject of *incipientes* remains disputed. For a helpful discussion of audience see Anna Bonta Moreland, *Known by Nature: Thomas Aquinas on Natural Knowledge of God* (New York: Herder & Herder, 2010), 40–44.

32. Here and below I cite from *Thomas Aquinas on Faith and Reason*, 9–24, occasionally changing the translation based on the Latin taken from S. Thomae de Aquino, *Summa Theologiae. Primam Partem* (Ottawa, Impensis Studii Generalis O. Pr, 1941), 1–11.

33. Aquinas, *Summa Theologiae*, I, q.1, a.2; Brown, 12.

sciences, it is not higher, or more reputable, than them. This objection gets at the very heart of the "borrowing" that characterized scholastic theology, especially in the thirteenth century. Was theology just a set of faith claims, taken on authority, that only became "scientific" when it applied other, non-theological methods? And if this application was so necessary to earn for theology the designation of "science," would it not then be more in keeping with the nature of theology to retreat to the monasteries and become more sapiential, at the expense of being scholastic? In other words, what does Athens have to do with Jerusalem and the activities of a lived faith aimed toward leading practitioners to union with God?

Aquinas argued that theology could remain in the university despite receiving its first principles "immediately from God, by revelation."[34] The accent on "immediately" (*immediate*)—literally, not mediated—was lacking in the same discussion of *Super Boetium*, and indicates a greater urgency on the part of Aquinas to highlight the divine basis of theology. Yet the question resurfaces about whether theology has the same legitimacy as other sciences, especially when the truths gained in these sciences seem more certain. In the reply to question 1, article 5, he argues that this apparent certainty does not stem from the superiority of these sciences, but from the "weakness of the human intellect," a claim that does not come from Scripture or from a text of spiritual theology, but from book II of Aristotle's *Metaphysics*.[35] Here Aristotle, treating this question, writes: "Perhaps the cause of this difficulty [. . .] is in us and not in the facts."[36] Aquinas adds in the first objection that the lack of certainty we feel about theology may derive from "the weakness of our intellect" rather than from the field of study in question.[37] In the second objection, he picks up this point again to explain why theology can borrow so freely from the philosophical disciplines. The principles for theology come from revelation, so its reliance on philosophy is only extrinsic, rather than foundational. Aquinas continues, "That it thus uses them is not due

34. Aquinas, *Summa Theologiae*, I, q.1, a.5, ad.2; Brown, 15.

35. Aquinas, *Summa Theologiae*, I, q.1, a.5, ad.1; Brown, 15.

36. Cited from *Aristotle's Metaphysics*, Ia, 1 (993b), trans. Hippocrates G. Apostle (Grinell, IA: Peripatetic, 1966).

37. Aquinas, *Summa Theologiae*, I, q.1, a.5, ad.1; Brown, 15.

to its own defect or insufficiency, but to the defect of our intellect."[38] This response turns the tables on a mentality that marks the modern mindset, a mentality that tends to cast theology, or any humanistic mode of knowing, as less scientific, less rational, less rigorous than a natural scientific mode of knowing. To a person of this mentality, the truths from humanistic disciplines seem less certain. Citing Aristotle, the paragon of a natural scientist in the thirteenth century, Aquinas reminds his audience, which included many students adjusting to a university climate, that such inferences say more about us and the weakness of our intellects than they do about the nature of theology and other humanistic disciplines.

Article 8 continues the discussion about the rationality of faith by asking whether theology is argumentative, by which he means something disputable or falsifiable. Aquinas answers affirmatively by reminding his readers that theology, rather than "arguing in proof of its principles, argues from them to prove something else."[39] In this way theology mirrors other "inferior" sciences that do not prove their principles, but instead leave such matters to the "higher" sciences upon which they depend. But even metaphysics has trouble arguing with people who deny its principles. If there is no basis for agreement, then there is no basis for disagreement or for argument. Arguments about first principles cannot yield demonstrations, because first principles cannot be demonstrated or proven—in Aquinas, demonstration (*demonstrarare*) has more force than proof (*probare*). Arguments against theology's first principles cannot disprove the articles of faith, nor can arguments for these principles prove them. Far from concluding that arguing has no point, Aquinas insists on the argumentative nature of theology, both in terms of the conclusions it reaches and the disputes it carries out with non-believers and heretics (taken up in the *Summa Contra Gentiles*, treated below). But he wants to moderate expectations about the results to be gained from such arguments. Theology integrates the authority of revealed data with the history of conversation and disputation (the patristic lineage), as well as metaphysical and dialectical arguments, all of which help theo-

---

38. Aquinas, *Summa Theologiae*, I, q.1, a.5, ad.2; Brown, 15.
39. Aquinas, *Summa Theologiae*, I, q.1, a.8; Brown, 19.

logians come to conclusions and to reach a deeper understanding of revealed truth.

Before he had begun writing the *Summa Theologiae*, Aquinas composed, between 1258–60, another summa, the *Summa Contra Gentiles*. In this work he set out to "make known the truth that the Catholic faith professes, and to set aside the errors opposed to it."[40] The *Summa Contra Gentiles* differs in style and audience from his more familiar summa. Aquinas directs the *Summa Contra Gentiles* to a less obvious audience: unlike the *Summa Theologiae*, written for those needing an initiation into theology, this text's likely audience is Christians who might have needed to come into conversation with Muslims, although Thomas does not explicitly say so.[41] In this case the Angelic Doctor does not rely on the structure of a *quaestio*, and, at least until book IV, jettisons most scriptural and patristic authority. By doing so, it seems that Aquinas makes his argument based on "unaided human reason," leaving him susceptible to a number of charges, most importantly the separation of faith from reason that would belie his attempted synthesis.

This argument merits unpacking, as so much of the modern trajectory—outlined and traced in parts II and III of this book—departs from the distinction between unaided human reason, and aided faith. Later in book I, chapter 2, Aquinas remarks that Muslims and pagans, unlike heretics, do not accept the authority of the Christian Scriptures. When disagreeing with heretics, one can at least appeal to the Scriptures as a basis for solving the disagreement. In the case of non-believers, broadly speaking, one must find a common ground: "We must, therefore, have recourse to natural reason, to which all people are compelled to give their assent."[42] In addressing a non-Christian audience, the *Summa Contra Gentiles* appears to move theology beyond the Anselmian *faith seeking understanding*, and toward a space in which theology can be imag-

---

40. Aquinas, *On the Truth of the Catholic Faith. Summa Contra Gentiles. Book I: God*, trans. Anton Pegis (Garden City, NY: Doubleday 1955) I, ch. 2 (62). Henceforth *Summa Contra Gentiles*. Here and below I cite by book and chapter, with the page number from the Doubleday edition in parentheses. Below I stray occasionally from the Pegis translation, based on the Latin text available at http://www.corpusthomisticum.org/scg1001.html.

41. Bauerschmidt, *Thomas Aquinas*, 28.

42. Aquinas, *Summa Contra Gentiles, Book I*, ch. 2 (62).

ined prior to any specific faith commitment. By seeking common ground with non-believers, it would appear that "natural reason" exists in an autonomous sphere that, in the epigrammatic phrasing of John Milbank, describes a "modern philosophy" that paves the way to secularization, *not* a premodern philosophy that does not imagine reason without faith.[43] Could one fault Aquinas here for assuming that a "natural reason," bracketed from revealed truths and the wisdom that comes as a gift from the Holy Spirit, can serve as a common basis for discussion with non-believers? These questions raise the stakes in interpreting the opening chapters of the *Summa Contra Gentiles.*

In chapter 3 Aquinas distinguishes between two modes of knowing about God: revealed, or supernatural, and natural. The knowledge that God is triune, for instance, falls into the former category, while the knowledge that God exists falls into the latter category. From this distinction arises a temptation to conceive "natural reason" as autonomous and existing apart from the supernatural or from any divine assistance or grace. Yet an attentive reading of Aquinas allows for another interpretation. He writes of the latter category of truths that, "Such truths about God have been proved demonstratively by the philosophers, guided by the light of the natural reason (*lumen rationis naturalis*)."[44] The use of the metaphor of light connotes a decidedly non-autonomous model of human knowing. After all, if insight and knowledge derive from a light, on the basis of which certain realities can be seen, then natural reason seems like an activity in cooperation with divine light. Though Aquinas distinguishes this knowledge of God attained from this reasoning activity from the kind of knowledge gained through believing, one need not conclude that natural reason takes place in a realm totally sealed off from the supernatural. For one commentator, the distinction made clearly and unequivocally by Aquinas would eventually become a separation that Aquinas himself never would have accepted: "According to Thomist wisdom, then, there is in principle no theoretical necessity for reason and nature to

43. Milbank writes: "Modern theology on the whole accepts that philosophy has its own legitimacy, its own autonomy, apart from faith." See John Milbank, "The Theological Critique of Philosophy in Johann Georg Hamman and Friedrich Heinrich Jacobi," in *Radical Orthodoxy*, eds. Milbank, Pickstock, and Ward (London: Routledge, 1999), 21.

44. Aquinas, *Summa Contra Gentiles. Book I*, ch. 3 (63).

gain their rightful autonomy by turning the distinctions into separations. But as a matter of fact this is just what modernity has done."[45]

In these chapters of the *Summa Contra Gentiles* Aquinas develops and lends precision to the distinction between natural and supernatural that went largely ignored in the first millennium of Christian theology. He also distinguishes the theological truths known by human reason (books I–III), from those known by faith (book IV), writing, "We shall first seek to make known that truth which faith professes and reason investigates. [. . .] Then we shall proceed to make known that truth which surpasses reason."[46] The *Summa Theologiae* accepted the same classification, but the structure of the *Summa Theologiae* is not organized around it. In performing a dialogue with Muslims and non-believers, Aquinas carved out a space for reason to say quite a bit about God, independent of any faith claims. Despite Aquinas's repeated assertions that very few can attain even these natural truths about God, and that the preferred and straighter path is to accept them through faith, as they appear in the data of revelation, he still carries out an extended exercise in natural theology. This decision invites the question of how to understand the relationship between the quasi-autonomous spheres of reason and revelation in Aquinas. In his 1931/32 Gifford Lectures, the great medievalist Etienne Gilson caricatures the demarcation as follows:

> In Thomism alone [among medieval theological approaches] we have a system in which philosophic conclusions are deduced from purely rational premises. [. . .] Philosophy, doubtless, is subordinate to theology, but as philosophy, it depends on nothing but its own proper method; based on human reason, owing all of its truth to the self-evidence of its principles and the accuracy of its deductions, it reaches an accord with faith spontaneously and without having to deviate in any way from its own proper path.[47]

45. Frederick Lawrence, "Athens and Jerusalem: The Contemporary Problematic of Faith and Reason," *Gregorianum* 80 (1999): 228.

46. Aquinas, *Summa Contra Gentiles. Book I*, ch. 9 (78).

47. Etienne Gilson, *The Spirit of Medieval Philosophy*, trans. A. Downes (New York: Charles Scribner's Sons, 1940), 6.

Gilson's caricature, which his own scholarship sought to overcome, has doggedly persisted to the present, leading many to understand Thomism as one part philosophy and one part theology.[48]

In the tradition of "Hillbilly Thomism," a term coined playfully by Flannery O'Connor, Friedrich Bauerschmidt suggests that the Aquinas of both Summas is carrying out a consistent mission, fortifying the faith of believers through preaching.[49] The opening chapters of the *Summa Contra Gentiles* book II provide an important reminder about the nature of Aquinas's investigation. Book II, chapter 2 takes up the question of whether an investigation into creation is useful for instruction in the faith.[50] Aquinas responds affirmatively, noting this consideration (he calls it both a *consideratio* and a *meditatio*) enables a deeper appreciation of divine wisdom, power, and goodness.[51] In other words, study and reflection in the mode of natural philosophy can deepen a sense of reverence and piety for God. Book II, chapter 4 compares the mode of investigation employed by the philosopher to that of the theologian. Theology looks at the natural world differently. The "teaching of Christian faith" considers the natural world as *creation*, in other words, as it relates to the divine creator. The common denominator between the tree *qua* tree, and the tree *qua* creature is nonetheless "conveyed through different principles in each case."[52] The philosopher considers the natural cause of the tree, whereas the believer considers the first cause, God, when contemplating the tree. Christian teaching gives one the "highest wisdom," but "human philosophy serves this teaching as the first wisdom."[53] It is first wisdom in the sense that it awaits a completion, even though, on the basis of

48. For Gilson's place in scholarship concerning the Aquinas's philosophical project, see Bauerschmidt, *Thomas Aquinas*, 41–46.

49. O'Connor notes, "Everybody who has read *Wise Blood* thinks I'm a hillbilly nihilist, whereas I would like to create the impression [. . .] that I'm a hillbilly Thomist." See Flannery O'Connor, *The Habit of Being*, ed. Sally Fitzgerald (New York: Farrar, Straus and Giroux, 1979), 81. Bauerschmidt writes, "Those who wish to have an easy descriptor for this book can describe it as an essay in Hillbilly Thomism" (Bauerschmidt, *Thomas Aquinas*, xi).

50. Aquinas, *On the Truth of the Catholic Faith. Summa Contra Gentiles. Book II: Creation*, trans. James Anderson (Garden City, NY: Doubleday, 1956).

51. Aquinas, *Summa Contra Gentiles, Book II*, ch. 2 (30–31).

52. Aquinas, *Summa Contra Gentiles, Book II*, ch. 4 (35).

53. Aquinas, *Summa Contra Gentiles, Book II*, ch. 4 (35).

its own principles, it can claim to know the answer to a given question. Bauerschmidt astutely notes that in this section, "theology in a certain sense subsumes philosophy. [. . .] Furthermore, Thomas's discussion makes it clear that in the *Summa Contra Gentiles* he is following the order not of philosophy, but of theology."[54] Despite earlier appearances, the *Summa Contra Gentiles* does not bracket faith out of the organizational structure or methodological procedure. Instead, it applies a different, admittedly riskier form of faith seeking understanding, in which philosophy relates to theology as handmaid, not as independent contractor.

BONAVENTURE, THE SERAPHIC DOCTOR

Alongside Aquinas, Bonaventure (c.1217–74) is often credited for the great thirteenth-century synthesis between faith and reason. Analogous to the great cathedrals of the same century, this synthesis embodies the glory of the "High Middle Ages." Like his Dominican contemporary, Bonaventure was born in Italy, joined a recently founded order, and undertook his most important studies in Paris, where he would gain status as a master in 1257, which meant he could lecture on Lombard's *Sentences*. He later became master general of his order, the Franciscans, and eventually was made a cardinal. Bonaventure died in 1274, the same year as Aquinas.

Bonaventure's allegiance to the Franciscans has led to an unfortunate caricature of the "Seraphic Doctor." In this caricature, Aquinas, the Dominican, was the headier theologian, the truer scholastic, and the rightful heir of the Dominican tradition, with its emphasis on learning—"the bow is bent in study, and released in preaching," as the motto goes. By contrast, Bonaventure was the more mystical theologian, emblematized by his vision of the six-winged seraph, with which he opens his most popular and accessible work, *Journey of the Mind to God*. As the heir of Francis, Bonaventure's reputation has been shadowed, for better or for worse, by the Franciscan legacy. If one were to compare this text, his most available and notable text, to Aquinas's most recognized work, the *Summa Theologiae*, one might understand-

54. Bauerschmidt, *Thomas Aquinas*, 80.

ably conclude that Bonaventure, who placed Francis's vision of the six-winged seraph at the outset of *the Journey*, was the mystic and Aquinas, with his predictable and methodical *Summa*, was the scholastic.

A brief perusal of Bonaventure's work, however, reveals a theologian very much at home in the university climate in which he was trained. Like Aquinas, he wrote in a variety of genres, one of which was a *Sentences* commentary, and another of which was a *disputatio*, in which he took up the disputed questions of the day and answered them with a combination of authoritative citations—including copious references to Aristotle—mixing logic and subtle distinction. Bonaventure, beyond question, matched his Dominican contemporary as a scholastic. Even if one takes up a work like the *Breviloquium*, literally "brief treatise," one encounters a breathtaking complexity and synthesis of the theological tradition, as well as full command of different philosophical and logical categories.

The task at hand, however, does not so much involve contrasting Bonaventure to Aquinas as it does discovering the heart of Bonaventure's thought about the relationship of reason to faith. One glimpses this synthesis in a very short treatise by Bonaventure, *On the Reduction of the Arts to Theology (De Reductione Artium ad Theologiam)*.[55] In a work that may have been part of his inaugural lecture at Paris,[56] Bonaventure shows how all academic disciplines gain their ultimate meaning when read through a theological lens. *Reduction* comes from the Latin *reducere*, "to lead back."[57] Bonaventure opens by citing the letter of James: "Every good and perfect gift is from above, coming down

---

55. In what follows I cite from Bonaventure, *On the Reduction of the Arts to Theology*, trans. Zachary Hayes (St. Bonaventure, NY: Franciscan Institute, 1996). Henceforth cited as *On the Reduction*, with paragraph number. In certain instances, I have altered the translation to make it more literal.

56. Joshua Benson argues persuasively that this treatise, which had long been assumed to have come from a later period of Bonaventure's writing, in fact derives from his inaugural lecture. See Joshua Benson, "Identifying the Literary Genre of *De reductio artium ad theologiam*: Bonaventure's inaugural lecture at Paris," *Franciscan Studies* 67 (2009): 149–78.

57. Bonaventure writes, "Let us see, therefore, how the other illuminations of knowledge are to be led back (*reduci*) to the light of sacred Scripture" (Bonaventure, *On the Reduction*, 8). Bonaventure later writes, "It was most fitting that the eternal and invisible should become visible and assume flesh in order to lead us back (*reducederet*) to God" (Bonaventure, *On the Reduction*, 12).

from the Father of lights" (Js 1:17). Bonaventure mines the metaphor by connecting God with light to discuss how all of creation, under the purview of the various academic disciplines, reflects this light both in relation to the discipline that studies it, and in relation to the divine power that creates and sustains it: "This text speaks of the source of all illumination; but at the same time, it suggests that there are many lights which flow liberally from that fontal source of light."[58]

Bonaventure's "reduction" consists in arguing that there is no essence of chemistry, strictly speaking. What the chemist knows, the chemist knows through the illumination that comes from studying the reality at hand; in the case of chemistry, this means studying the changes at work in different bodies (organic, inorganic, physical). Yet to say, *chemistry is the study of change in bodies* is mistaken, for the true meaning of chemistry is only attained when one comprehends it as a "good gift" whose source is divine light. *Reduction* is the process of reducing or deriving the deeper theological meaning of each discipline. Put another way, all secular knowledge contains an intelligibility and a lack. To grasp this intelligibility involves some process of illumination, but to fail to see the lack is to fail to understand what the discipline truly is. Bonaventure explains, "And as all those lights had their origin in a single light [referring to the six days of creation, which begin with the divine declaration of light], so too all these branches of knowledge are ordered to the knowledge of sacred Scripture: they are contained in it, they are perfected by it, and they are ordered to the eternal illumination by means of it."[59]

Bonaventure structures his text by distinguishing four kinds of light: exterior, inferior, interior, and superior. The first corresponds to what Bonaventure, borrowing from Hugh's *Didascalicon*, calls the seven mechanical arts,[60] the second to the knowledge revealed by sense perception. Bonaventure follows Augustine's categories of natural light in elements, which correlates to the five senses. The third "is the light of philosophical knowledge," while the fourth light, "which provides illumination with respect to saving truth, is the light of sacred

---

58. Bonaventure, *On the Reduction*, 1.
59. Bonaventure, *On the Reduction*, 7.
60. Bonaventure, *On the Reduction*, 2.

Scripture."[61] In the subsequent chapters Bonaventure returns these disciplines to their theological source. For our purposes it will be helpful to recount the reduction of rational philosophy.

Bonaventure identifies *speech* as the principal concern of rational philosophy, most likely due to the Trinitarian form of speech that Augustine had outlined in his treatise on the Trinity.[62] Speech travels from the speaker to the hearer through the medium of sound waves. Before spoken, speech consists in an "inner word" that can be understood as the intelligibility contained within verbal speech. "Toddlers are playful" expresses a truth, but one can distinguish knowing the inner word from uttering it, just as one can distinguish between hearing the phrase and understanding the inner word corresponding to the vocalization. By connecting rational philosophy with speech, Bonaventure highlights the process of understanding, communicated from one intelligent being to another. Not being angels, humans learn through the outward expression of inner words. Even soundless gestures like a hug or a kiss express an inner word. When this happens, we give witness to the pattern through which God reveals Godself to us in the Incarnation. Bonaventure explains, "But that the Word might be known by human beings who are endowed with senses, the Word assumed the form of flesh."[63] What rational philosophy does, by conveying the intelligibility of truths from speaker to hearer, from author to reader, can be *reduced* to the incarnational pattern of all of created reality, for the world is a sacrament of God.

By taking up a few snippets of Bonaventure's dense argument in *On the Reduction*, the concluding remarks can be brought into relief. In the final paragraph Bonaventure notes, "It is likewise clear how wide the illuminative way may be, and how the divine reality itself lies hidden within everything which is perceived or known."[64] Yet Bonaventure was unwilling to grant these disciplines the same formal autonomy that Aquinas did. Like Hugh of St. Victor, whom Bonaventure singles out in his list of greatest theologians,[65] Bonaventure pro-

---

61. Bonaventure, *On the Reduction*, 4–5.
62. Bonaventure, *On the Reduction*, 15.
63. Bonaventure, *On the Reduction*, 16.
64. Bonaventure, *On the Reduction*, 26.
65. Bonaventure, *On the Reduction*, 5: "For Anselm excels in reasoning; Bernard, in preaching; Richard, in contemplation. But Hugh excels in all of these."

vided intellectual support for the connection between study and prayer as a way to combat the corrupting forces in university culture. This concern remained throughout his career, and informs how he articulated the relationship between faith and reason.

While affirming the conclusion from the previous paragraph, it is important to add a qualifier: Bonaventure's opposition to certain elements in the university climate was not restricted to the moral realm. His theological vision led him to chafe against conclusions drawn by the more radical Aristotelians mentioned at the outset of this chapter. This impression comes across most clearly in the *Itinerarium*. The point can be made more generally with reference to a number of scholars. One remarks that the *Itinerarium* as well as the unfinished *Hexaemeron* embody Bonaventure's "theophanic" understanding of the world.[66] By "theophanic" the interpreter means an understanding of the world in which creation itself manifests divine revelation. On a similar note, Rik Van Nieuwenhove adds, "Bonaventure's universe is, however, a deeply symbolic or sacramental one, in which creaturely things are the vestiges of the Trinitarian God. It is only with the eyes of faith that we can truly perceive this inner depth of creation."[67] Ernest Fortin highlights how transformative the discovery of Aristotle's physics was, especially in its encounter with a theophanic or sacramental understanding of the world. Fortin recalls that there is almost no concern for nature in the Bible, whereas the Greeks and Romans placed *natura* or *physis* at or near the center of so many of their treatises.[68] The medieval rediscovery of Aristotle meant a reconsideration of nature—less as a sacrament, and more as an entity best understood through observation aimed at uncovering laws, i.e., formulae inte-

---

66. Gregory LaNave, "Bonaventure's Theological Method," in *A Companion to Bonaventure*, eds. Jay Hammond, Wayne Hellmann, and Jared Goff (Leiden, The Netherlands: Brill, 2014), 81–120, at 98.

67. Van Nieuwenhove, *An Introduction to Medieval Theology*, 223.

68. Fortin writes, "There is no natural law teaching to be found anywhere in the New Testament," and goes onto explain that even Romans 2:14, so often used as a proof text for later natural law, is nothing like medieval and modern natural law. Fortin adds, "With the rediscovery of Aristotle's *Physics* during the early decades of the thirteenth century, the natural law was finally able to come into its own." See Ernest Fortin, *Classical Christianity and the Political Order*, ed. J. Brian Benestad (Lanham, MD: Rowman & Littlefield, 1996), 227, 229.

grally related to matter itself that disclosed natural essences. Edward Grant explains, "The conscious and systematic application of logic and reason to the natural world was the first major phase in the process that would eventually embrace modern science."[69] It would be mistaken to say that Bonaventure rejected Aristotle, but it is worth noting the qualification of another commentator: "Bonaventure reads Aristotle through the eyes of Augustine," and thus saw "his task as incorporating the Aristotelian insights into the intellectual heritage of Augustine and other authorities, most of whom are deeply formed by Neo-Platonism."[70]

Nowhere does this theological project manifest itself more plainly than in *The Journey of the Mind to God*, written in 1259, two years after Bonaventure became minister general of the Franciscans.[71] This classic in medieval mysticism begins with Bonaventure's recollection of Francis's vision of the seraph from the sixth chapter of Isaiah: "The figure of the six wings of the Seraph, therefore, brings to mind the six stages of illumination, which begin with creatures and lead up to God, into union with whom no one rightly enters save through the Crucified."[72] Bonaventure reads both Scripture and creation as books that lead their readers to God. Although many people associate *finding God in all things* with Saint Ignatius, the founder of the Jesuits, this phrase applies as aptly to Bonaventure's *Itinerarium* as to any other text in the Christian tradition. Bonaventure writes, "We may behold God in the mirror of the sensible, not only by considering creatures as vestiges of God, but also by seeing Him in them."[73] He leads the reader through six steps, concluding in the mind's union with God.

69. Grant, *God & Reason in the Middle Ages*, 150.

70. Christopher M. Cullen, "Bonaventure's Philosophical Method," in *A Companion to Bonaventure*, eds. Jay Hammond, Wayne Hellmann, and Jared Goff (Leiden, The Netherlands: Brill, 2014), 121–63, at 126.

71. For a helpful background to the text see Stephen Brown, "Introduction," in Bonaventure, *The Journey of the Mind to God*, trans. Philotheus Boehner, ed. Stephen Brown (Indianapolis: Hackett, 1993), ix–xxvi.

72. Bonaventure, *Itinerarium*, prologue, 3. Here and below I have relied on the above-mentioned *Journey of the Mind to God* in collaboration with *Saint Bonaventure's Itinerarium Mentis in Deum*, trans. Philotheus Boehner (St. Bonaventure, NY: The Franciscan Institute, 1998), which has the Latin and English facing one another. In what follows I will cite by chapter and number.

73. Bonaventure, *Itinerarium*, 2, 1.

As with *On the Reduction*, the *Itinerarium* is a short, tightly packed work of theology. Unlike the former text, the *Itinerarium* had a Franciscan, not a university audience in mind. For our purposes, it will be most helpful to examine the third chapter. Here the Seraphic Doctor borrows the psychological analogy from Augustine. Just as there are three consubstantial persons in one God, so does the soul contain memory, intellect, and will: "These three, the generating mind, the word, and love—exist in the soul as memory, intellect, and will, which are consubstantial, coequal, equally everlasting, and mutually inclusive."[74] By talking about the vestiges of the Trinity in creation, Bonaventure has something more in mind than the famous example of Saint Patrick explaining the Trinity by using a three-leafed clover. In good Augustinian fashion, Bonaventure affirms that our thinking and speaking reflect a triune structure. Yet Bonaventure goes further than Augustine: The disciplinary organization of medieval learning and the threefold division of philosophy also reveal this structure. He concludes: "And thus our mind, enlightened and suffused by so much brightness, unless it is blind, can be guided through itself to contemplate that eternal light."[75]

By ruminating on this sentence it is possible to unearth how radical this claim is. *Guided through itself.* In other words, the human being can—not just through contemplation of nature, or things outside of us, but through considering the interior life of the mind—be guided toward an understanding of the triune God. The architecture of our highest systematized modes of learning—what in Bonaventure's own time would have meant natural philosophy, ethics, and such, but in our own time might be genetic mapping, string theory, and computer coding—illuminates God. When one reflects on it honestly and truly, the apex of human reasoning power leads us to understand, in a deeper way than simple admiration of nature, the mind of the creator. There is of course the danger that we fail to do so, which the clause *unless it is blind* captures. Here one can recall T. S. Eliot's famous phrase, "We had the experience but missed the

---

74. Bonaventure, *Itinerarium*, 3, 5.
75. Bonaventure, *Itinerarium*, 3, 7.
76. T. S. Eliot, "Dry Salvages."

meaning."[76] Human sin, especially pride, can lead the knower into great confusion about the knowing process. In Bonaventure's model, reasoning is an activity on the way toward participation in God.[77] Some people study and reason without considering how undertaking these activities refracts divine light. Bonaventure calls such people the "unwise." They embody the inversion of Anselm's famous formula: "[T]hey do not believe with the aim toward understanding (*non credunt, ut intelligent*), and this fact leads to confusion.[78] Although Bonaventure distinguishes reason from faith, and thus arguments based on reason from arguments based on faith, his emphasis on a participatory model of human knowing rendered his aversion to isolate one from the other almost instinctive. To contemplate what reason can do prior to faith is, in a way, to fail to reason fully. What Bonaventure hints at, modern thinkers like Pascal and Blondel, both featured below, make explicit.

Between the 1250s and the 1270s, Bonaventure modified his reflections about the relationship between theology and philosophy. Like Aquinas, Bonaventure referred to Aristotle as "the Philosopher" in his commentary on Lombard's *Sentences*, and he cited Aristotle more frequently than any other non-Christian source.[79] When he was composing his *Collationes in Hexaemeron* (*Lectures on the Six Days of Creation*) in the spring of 1273, one year before his death, his opinion of secular learning became more critical. One commentator notes, "By the time of the composition of [the *Collationes*], Bonaventure is reacting against a conception of Aristotelian science that had developed on the Arts faculty and that sought, in some ways, to divorce philosophy from faith and from the ecclesial culture of the day."[80]

Read without context, the *Collationes* give off an anti-academic air, especially when they advocate retreat from the secular world. In

77. Bonaventure notes in his *Disputed Questions on the Trinity*, which dates from the mid-1250s, "There is innate to the mind a natural desire for, together with a knowledge and consciousness (*memoria*) of that reality in whose image it is made, and to which it naturally tends for its beatitude." See Bonaventure, *Disputed Questions on the Mystery of the Trinity*, trans. Zachary Hayes (St. Bonaventure: NY: The Franciscan Institute, 1979), 116 (q.1, art.1, conclusion).

78. Bonaventure, *Itinerarium*, 3, 7.

79. For this point see Cullen, "Bonaventure's Philosophical Method," 126n13.

80. Cullen, "Bonaventure's Philosophical Method," 127.

the First Collation Bonaventure complains about curious types who lack the proper spirit of obedience: "There are many men of this kind, empty of praise and devotion although filled with the splendors of knowledge. They build wasps' nests without honeycombs."[81] The problem is not just students, but professors as well: "For theologians have attacked the life of Christ as related to morals, and the teachers of the Arts have attacked the doctrine of Christ by their false statements."[82] Bonaventure continues by drawing a comparison to the Israelites who had been led out of Egypt. To seek secular knowledge so zealously is like rejecting the healthy manna from heaven for the junk food consumed in Egypt. The process of rational discernment, as Bonaventure explains, is not a good in itself: "For there is an argument of Christ and an argument of the devil. The argument of the devil leads to hell; it is a fallacy, a sophistic and destructive argument: the argument of Christ is constructive and restoring."[83] This kind of rhetoric, which draws such a contrast between the right and wrong way of thinking, almost seems as if it could be transplanted into the current-day religious blogosphere.

As hinted above, the context of the *Collationes* helps temper the initial impression given. Part of the context comes in properly identifying the genre. As Kevin Hughes has noted, the text should be read as *protreptic*: "Bonaventure's protreptic exhorts his Franciscan audience to pursue a life of Franciscan holiness even as they pursue their academic study in Paris, for it is only in the integration of holiness and insight that one may find the Wisdom of God."[84] When read

81. Bonaventure, *Collationes in Hexaemeron*, 1, 8. Here and below I work from Bonaventure, *Collations on the Six Days*, vol. 5 of *The Works of Bonaventure*, trans. José de Vinck (Paterson, NJ: St. Anthony Guild Press, 1970). I have also been aided by a new and greatly improved translation of the *Collationes* by Jay M. Hammond that was published in the *Works of Saint Bonaventure* series (Franciscan Institute, 2018). I thank my colleague for generously sharing his translations with me prior to its publication. For the Latin, I have consulted an online version of volume 5 of the *Opera Omnia* (Quaracchi edition) located at http://www.documentacatholicaomnia.eu/20_50_1221-1274-_Bonaventura_Bagnoregis,_Sanctus.html.

82. Bonaventure, *Collationes in Hexaemeron*, 1, 9. As Hammond relayed to me, the "teachers of the Arts" refers to the Latin Averroists at Paris.

83. Bonaventure, *Collationes in Hexaemeron*, 1, 26.

84. Kevin Hughes, "St. Bonaventure's *Collationes in Hexaëmeron*: Fractured Sermons and Protreptic Discourse," *Franciscan Studies* 63 (2005): 107–29, at 108.

in this manner, the *Collationes* and the *de Reductio*, despite being formally distinct, are entirely compatible.

Bonaventure reserves the sharpest rhetoric against secular learning for the Nineteenth Collation. In previous collations he recalls
how philosophy, even Aristotle, made erroneous judgments about
the natural world. Here, Bonaventure regards philosophy not so
much as a means of knowing natural truths, but as a handmaid to
knowing divine truths. Yet it exists several steps removed from the
source of these truths: Scripture. Between Scripture and philosophy,
or secular learning, lie "the writings of the saints" (the Church
Fathers) and "the opinions of the Masters" (the scholastic writings).[85]
These middle two sources of knowledge, along with philosophy, also
remain on an inferior level because they contain "no knowledge that
grants the remission of sins," for the aforementioned opinions "drew
from the original (patristic) authors, who in turn used Scripture as
their source."[86] The patristic authors, holy men like Augustine and
Athanasius, had the good sense to remind their readers to return to
the source, and to be conscious of the dangers that arose from ignoring Scripture. The various medieval summaries of the patristic legacy pose a "still greater danger," for "error is sometimes found in
them. Their authors believe they understand the originals, but they
do not understand them: they even contradict them."[87] Bonaventure
exhorts his Franciscan novices to learn from the sources and not to
trust commentaries blindly.

If the patristic writings do not suffice, and the great summas of
medieval theology can deceive, it is hardly a surprise that Bonaventure
warns his audience against philosophy. In the Nineteenth Collation,
he recalls the scriptural scene of Egypt and its spoils. He warns: "Let
the masters beware, then, not to commend or appreciate too highly
the sayings of the philosophers, lest the people take it as a pretext to
return to Egypt."[88] Bonaventure overlays this scriptural scene with the
wedding of Cana (John 2), where Jesus mixed water with wine. If the

---

85. Bonaventure, *Collationes in Hexaemeron*, 19, 6.
86. Bonaventure, *Collationes in Hexaemeron*, 19, 7.
87. Bonaventure, *Collationes in Hexaemeron*, 19, 11.
88. Bonaventure, *Collationes in Hexaemeron*, 19, 12.

masters of Paris dilute the wine too much, then instead of turning water into wine, they will turn wine into water.[89] Philosophy's role is as handmaiden to theology. The Franciscan brothers in Paris to whom Bonaventure preached these collations were trying to figure out how to integrate liberal arts studies and their religious calling. Bonaventure gave the following advice: "Anyone who wishes to obtain advantages from his studies should be holy and should work for a life that is reverent, pure, religious, and edifying."[90] A study of philosophy and a full exercise of reason that could not be integrated into a path toward holiness, or a journey to God, was fundamentally deficient. In this final, incomplete exhortation, Bonaventure expressed what some have called a "scholastic mystagogy."[91] In doing so, he offered an alternative vision for how faith related to reason than Aquinas, one that would also serve as the inspiration for important developments in later medieval theology.

Bonaventure and Aquinas had different theological visions, instincts, inclinations, and orientations. These differences are manifested in the way they sought to synthesize Aristotle into the Western theological tradition that they inherited. The reasons for their different approaches can be explained in part by the nascent religious orders they joined—Franciscan and Dominican—which helped to define their theological orientations. These theological giants also helped form their respective orders to such a degree that one can almost measure their impact alongside that of their founders, Dominic and Francis. As time went on, these orders inevitably lost touch with the questions that animated Bonaventure and Aquinas, and grew satisfied with knowing the answers and forgetting the questions underlying them. This narrowing had the effect of creating silos in which schools of faculty grew to see their Franciscan or Dominican counterparts as theological adversaries, and the agonistic world of medieval disputations only heightened divisions. These developments occurred to the detriment of both thinkers, who would have certainly found much

---

89. Bonaventure, *Collationes in Hexaemeron*, 19, 14. From this image Bonaventure pivots to commend how the earliest Christians burned books of philosophy. The Quaracchi edition cites Acts 19:19, where a great number of magic books were burned.

90. Bonaventure, *Collationes in Hexaemeron*, 19, 20.

91. See Hughes, "St. Bonaventure's *Collationes in Hexaëmeron*," 128–29.

more shared ground and agreement between their approaches than their spiritual progeny were capable of seeing.

DUNS SCOTUS AND THE
HAUNTED FRANCISCAN LEGACY

For at least one hundred years, historians of theology have celebrated the glorious thirteenth-century achievement of theological synthesis, most especially embodied in the Dominican system of Thomas Aquinas, and the Franciscan mystagogy of Bonaventure. As the story goes, this synthesis represented a great accomplishment, toward which medieval theology had been working at least since Abelard. For some, synthesis meant reconciling Platonism with the newly discovered Aristotle. For others, it meant synthesizing Aristotle with a Christian worldview. And still for others, it meant a more general synthesis of faith and reason. Whatever the synthesis, it showed strains already toward the end of the thirteenth century, and eventually unraveled. This rupture, so the story goes, explains in part why the Reformation happened, and also why modern intellectual movements seem to be at such odds with traditional theological claims. A few obvious questions arise from this narrative: first, why did the synthesis, if so glorious, not last longer? The two most commonly cited agents of destruction, Duns Scotus (c. 1266–1308) and William of Ockham (1288–1347), flourished just a few decades after Aquinas and Bonaventure. Put another way, why did Bonaventure and Thomas's contemporaries, given their proximity to these great masters, fail to appreciate the synthesis for what it was? Their bodies were practically still warm when Etienne Tempier, bishop of Paris, condemned 219 erroneous propositions in 1277, including many associated with Aquinas. The Archbishop of Canterbury issued a similar condemnation at the University of Oxford just a few days later.[92] These condemnations seem to indicate a lack of consensus about any perceived synthesis.

Such questions attend to the difficulty in understanding the relationship between the High Middle Ages and the Reformation-era the-

---

92. For the negative effect of these condemnations of the attempted synthesis between faith and reason, see Van Nieuwenhove, *An Introduction to Medieval Theology*, 225–28.

ology. Many have noted that Ockham and Scotus were Franciscans, and their thought, especially those aspects that seemed to undermine the earlier synthesis, derives from Bonaventure's theological vision. In short, the Franciscans were to blame. Van Nieuwenhove puts it only slightly less tersely: "Bonaventure's skepticism of Aristotelian philosophy (in its Averroist version) proved influential in the Condemnations of 1277, and those, in turn, would lead to a further separation of faith and reason, and philosophy and theology. It is out of this intellectual climate that the Modern period would emerge."[93]

The most pivotal theologian after Aquinas and Bonaventure was Scotus, whose theological work managed to attract more followers in the decades after his death than the work of either Aquinas or Bonaventure. Although born only four decades after Aquinas and Bonaventure, Scotus had to navigate a much different intellectual landscape marked by the aforementioned condemnations.[94] Scotus's academic career was fast-tracked and peripatetic. After his training in Oxford, he was sent to Paris in 1302, only to be exiled with many other Franciscans for political reasons. He returned the next year, but was appointed Regent Master of the Franciscans in 1305. In 1307 he was commissioned to teach in Cologne, where he died one year later.

Despite all of this motion, Scotus managed to write prolifically, most significantly in the genre of commentary on Lombard's *Sentences*. He wrote three such commentaries at different stages in his life, the most relevant for our purposes was the commentary known as the *Ordinatio*,[95] also referred to as the *Opus Oxoniense* ("Oxford Text") begun in 1300 but never completed. Mary Beth Ingram describes the

---

93. Van Nieuwenhove, *An Introduction to Medieval Theology*, 224. He later writes, "The growing separation of theology and spirituality should be partly attributed to the Franciscan skepticism of reason which finds its origins in Bonaventure's stance against the Aristotelian learning" (Van Nieuwenhove, *An Introduction to Medieval Theology*, 228). This claim, it should be noted, is at odds with what Richard Cross says. See note 99 below.

94. For the idea that the condemnations of 1277 marked a generational shift, see Gérard Sondag, "Réflexions sur la Vie de Jean Duns Scot et le Sense du Prologue de l'*Ordinatio*," in Jean Duns Scot, *Prologue de l'Ordinatio*, ed. and trans. Gérard Sondag (Paris: Presses Universitaires de France, 1999), 1–7, at 2.

95. Concerning the *Ordinatio*, noted scholar Philotheus Boehner writes that it is "the principle source for his doctrine." See Philotheus Boehner, *The History of the Franciscan School. Part III: Duns Scotus* (St. Bonaventure, NY: 1945), 8.

Ordinatio as "the sort of formal text that someone prepares for a final edition," meaning that it would be a revised version of a *Sentences* commentary that had been given publicly.[96] The *Ordinatio* thus presents a reliable overview of his theology.[97] The Preface, much like Aquinas's opening questions in the *Summa Theologiae*, serves as a helpful starting point to examine how Scotus relates faith and reason.

One can think of Lombard's *Sentences* as the most memorable jazz tune ever written. To become a master or professor of theology in a medieval university, one was required to comment on the *Sentences*. These commentaries often worked like jazz riffs, wherein the commentator could riff, that is, offer extensive commentary akin to a solo that remains bound to the melody of the tune but also expresses the musician's interpretation of it. Scotus's extensive and metaphysically complex riffs on the *Sentences* helped earn him the reputation as the "subtle doctor." Due primarily to the scholarship of the previous century's greatest medievalist, Etienne Gilson (1884–1978), many have read Scotus's subtle, Franciscan commentaries as a direct response to Aquinas.[98] Others have suggested the more direct object in Scotus's sights was the neo-Augustinianism represented by Henry of Ghent (c. 1217–93), who was the most influential master at Paris in the decades between the 1277 condemnations and Scotus's arrival in 1302.[99] Philotheus Boehner, however, concludes, "To see in [Scotus] only the critic of St. Thomas, or even of Henry of Ghent, is a complete misconception of the situation."[100] Like his Franciscan confrere, Bonaventure, Scotus took up the

---

96. Mary Beth Ingram, *Scotus for Dunces: An Introduction to the Subtle Doctor* (St. Bonaventure, NY: Franciscan Institute, 2003), 16.

97. Richard Cross describes the *Sentence* commentaries as "By far the most important set of works for understanding Scotus's theology." See Cross, *Duns Scotus* (Oxford: Oxford University Press, 1999), 6.

98. For Gilson's most extensive treatment, see the recently translated *John Duns Scotus: Introduction to his Fundamental Positions*, trans. James G. Colbert (London: T&T Clark, 2019), from the 1962 original. He notably concludes the text by contrasting Aquinas's analogical approach to Scotus's univocal approach (Gilson, *John Duns Scotus*, 491–523).

99. See, for instance, Gérard Sondag, "Réflexions sur la Vie de Jean Duns Scot et le Sense du Prologue de l'*Ordinatio*," 4–6.

100. Boehner, *The History of the Franciscan School. Part III*, 15. To this Richard Cross adds, "So the theological debate had moved on from Aquinas and Bonaventure, and very often we find Scotus engaging not with these earlier schoolmen but with his nearer contemporaries, thinkers from the 1280s and 1290s" (Cross, *Duns Scotus*, 5).

task of engaging in what one scholar calls "a critical reflection upon the legacy of Greek Aristotelian thought precisely in light of the *caveats* raised by the condemnations."[101] Nowhere does this come out more clearly than in the prologue to the *Ordinatio*, where Scotus takes up the controversy between philosophers and theologians.

Despite lacking the zeal of Aquinas to reconcile philosophy and theology, Scotus eagerly applied reason to matters of faith. In the realm of metaphysics, as Scotus lays it out, the truths obtained come by way of necessity; what one knows about God and being, one knows necessarily. The God of the Bible, however, is not that kind of God. Philosophy does not yield the truth about our ultimate end, to see God face to face. The reason for this shortcoming derives from God giving this truth about our ultimate end contingently.[102] Like any true gift, it is freely, and thus not necessarily given; it lies in the contingent, and thus not necessary realm of reality. Whether one would have been able to know this truth prior to the fall is beside the point for Scotus, and he is not so much concerned with what Aristotle failed to know. Revelation teaches us that God is free, and freely creates us, and freely chose to become incarnate in order to save us. Scotus occasionally sounds like a nominalist when he discourses on God's "absolute power to save anyone he likes"[103] when discussing the difference between what metaphysics and theology can know.

Nothing marks the paradoxical nature of Scotus's theological approach more perfectly than his argument that theology is a practi-

---

101. Ingram, *Scotus for Dunces*, 26. It should be mentioned that some, including Richard Cross, caution against making too much of "a Franciscan tradition of theology," because "Scotus disagrees with Bonaventure almost as much as he disagrees with the Dominican Aquinas" (Cross, *Duns Scotus*, 5).

102. Scotus, "Prologue" to the *Ordinatio*, #18 ("sed contingenter datur a Deo"). For this text, I have relied on the translation by Peter Simpson available at https://aristotelophile.com/current.htm. Simpson bases his translation on the critical edition *Ioannis Duns Scoti Opera Omnia*, vol. 1 (Vatican City: Typis Polyglottis Vaticanis, 1950). I have also consulted the dual-facing French-Latin translation (cited above as Jean Duns Scot, *Prologue de l'Ordinatio*, trans. Sondag) based on the same edition. Some, like Gilson, refer to the *Ordinatio* as the "Opus Oxoniense" and cite it according to question. Due to Scotus's penchant to go on long "jazz solos" I have opted to cite according to the standard paragraph number in both Simpson and Sondag. Henceforth it will be cited parenthetically as "Prologue, #X."

103. Scotus, "Prologue," #55.

cal, rather than a speculative science. In making this argument, Scotus offers an extremely complex, *speculative* justification. Unlike Aquinas and other scholastics so eager to demonstrate how theology was a science, Scotus walks right to the edge of denying the scientific character of theology due to the lack of necessity in it.[104] After recalling how Aristotle connects science with necessity and reminding his audience that theology concerns contingencies, Scotus admits that, "in an absolute sense, there is no science of what is contingent," before stating that theology concerns things seen, which means that theology can be science in a qualified way: "Therefore I say that theology is of necessity about what is possible."[105] Scotus calls the truths of revelation "practical necessities," and lists such norms as "God is to be loved." In one way, they are necessities; one must do these things in order to reach one's final end. But in another they are practical; Christianity is ultimately about a doing, not a knowing.

The doing at the heart of Christianity is charity,[106] a conclusion that reveals a fundamental fissure between the Aristotelian and Christian worldviews. As essentially related to free action, Christian religion would fit, in Aristotle's own classification, within the realm of a moral science. Aristotle defines happiness as "activity in conformity with virtue" and then identifies this activity with contemplation.[107] The one who lives a life of contemplation most closely approximates the gods, and therefore the most beloved and happiest of human beings. According to Scotus, Aristotle does not reason badly about the nature of moral science. Aristotle, however, does not have access to Scripture, which teaches that "the end of the law is love" (Rom 13:10).[108] For Christianity, therefore, the end of what Aristotle calls moral science is love, not contemplation, and love belongs to the will, not to the intellect.

Theology is still a science according to Scotus, but it is neither speculative nor subalternate. Scotus seeks to demarcate theology from metaphysics and does not concede Aquinas's argument in the first question of the *Summa Theologiae* that theology is a subalternate

104. Scotus, "Prologue," #210–11.
105. Scotus, "Prologue," #211, interpolation.
106. Scotus, "Prologue," #222.
107. Aristotle, *Nichomachean Ethics* X, 7; 1177a; 1178b.
108. Scotus, "Prologue," #222.

science. Theology, according to Scotus, is a practical science. This, on its face, seems difficult to square with the parts of theology dealing with, say, processions and emanations in the Trinity, or with understanding the hypostatic union. Scotus himself undertook some of the most sophisticated and seemingly impractical questions in all of medieval theology. He clarifies, "that knowledge is practical in which the determination of things to speculate on is no greater than pertains, on the part of knowledge of them, to practice or practical knowledge."[109] In other words, even the most speculative parts of theology exist only to fulfill the practical end, which is the salvation of our souls and the beatific vision of God.[110]

For Scotus, the intellect and the will—knowing and doing—perform an elaborate dance. According to the normally accepted scholastic schematic, they are distinct faculties of the soul, but Scotus brings out the various ways in which these faculties are related. Theology, he acknowledges, generates knowledge that is prior to will. Knowing the good precedes consciously doing the good. As Scotus puts it, "The intellect naturally understands the first object before the will wills it."[111] Yet the true purpose of humanity is not to understand, but to will, do, act, and love. Therefore, even the highest theological truths, like the Trinity, are practical truths.[112]

One already observes this shift of the center of the human soul toward willing in Augustine, who in books 7 and 8 in *Confessions* finds Platonism wanting; as he himself comes to experience, knowing the best way to live does not alone provide what is needed to alter the sinful life of one mired in bad habits. Remarking on this shift toward the will, Charles Taylor explains, "Where for Plato, our desire for the good is a function of how much we see it, for Augustine the will is not simply dependent on knowledge."[113] Faced with much different cir-

---

109. Scotus, "Prologue," #310.

110. Scotus, "Prologue," #312.

111. Scotus, "Prologue," #324.

112. Scotus, "Prologue," #322.

113. Charles Taylor, *The Sources of the Self: The Making of Modern Identity* (Cambridge, MA: Harvard University Press, 1989), 137. Taylor continues, "What is morally crucial about us is not just the universal nature or rational principle which we share with others, as with Plato and Aristotle, but now also this power of assent" (Taylor, *The Sources of Self*, 137).

cumstances, Scotus shifted the focus of human nature again toward the will, but this time by carefully repurposing Aristotelian arguments that had been used by earlier scholastics to the opposite effect.

Scotus also took up the problem of the divine will in the *Ordinatio*. Scotus never separates God's freedom from other divine properties like goodness. Divine freedom not only means that many of theology's truths reside in the realm of the contingent, but also that God is not subject to a higher law. This reality does not make God's actions arbitrary, as freedom and goodness coincide within one another. But in his assessment of his contemporaries, certain naturalizing tendencies among philosophers were infringing on theology's ability to preserve biblical truth.[114] In this environment, Scotus put his thumb on the scale of divine freedom by asserting that God is a free infinite being. This stance, according to Étienne Gilson, is "the principle of principles [. . .] and it decides everything" for Scotus.[115]

One finds both in Aquinas and in Scotus arguments and frameworks that seem to lead toward a backdrop in which theology and philosophy occupy realms that become easier to imagine as sharply divided from one another. Scotus's ordering of things, however, opened the door toward theologies that would accentuate divine freedom, even at the expense of other qualities or attributes.

One can observe some of these changes already in Ockham, the major theologian of import after Scotus. Ockham rejected the idea that one could call theology a science if one lacked immediate insight into the principles.[116] This judgment had the effect of further widening the distinction between faith and reason as two orders of knowing. The effects of this can be observed in comparing attitudes about whether humans can attain natural knowledge of God. Previous figures like Anselm and Aquinas affirmed this position. Ockham, however, rejects it: "God cannot be known in Himself" (*deus non potest cognosci in se*)

---

114. Both Cross (*Duns Scotus*, 11) and Gilson (*John Duns Scotus*, 521) argue that Scotus seemed particularly piqued by philosophical naturalism.

115. Gilson, *John Duns Scotus*, 507.

116. For Ockham on this question, see Jan Peter Beckmann, *Wilhelm von Ockham* (Originalausg: München, 1995), 142–49, and Alfred J. Freddoso, "Ockham on Faith and Reason," in *The Cambridge Companion to Ockham*, ed. Paul Vincent Spade (Cambridge: Cambridge University Press, 1999), 326–49.

by any kind of natural reasoning.[117] Such instances, when read in isolation, can obscure how much Ockham still shares in common with predecessors like Aquinas, but nonetheless they mark a shift. Likewise, in asserting, as Scotus did, that all of the commandments, save the first two, do not belong to natural law,[118] the impression was given that God's freedom might be an arbitrary freedom.

At this point it should be mentioned that social circumstances matter. Just as many theologians and scholars of religion turned to questions of religion and violence after 2001, so too did medieval theologians confront pressing issues. We would find it odd if somebody attempted to understand the theological attention in the last two decades by focusing on precursors in twentieth-century theology, without mentioning the 9/11 attacks, or the rise of global jihad, or increased awareness of global warming. Events like the Black Plague (mid-fourteenth century), European exploration and discovery, and increased urbanization, as well as practical and pastoral changes initiated by Church leadership, helped frame the questions and topics that theologians asked. The increasing turn toward emphasizing divine freedom coincided with the observation of incalculable human suffering during aforementioned plagues that ravaged Europe and coincided with Ockham's death in 1347. Although the subject of the next chapter marks a clear difference in perspective from high medieval theology, one cannot suppose that modern theology began with a clean slate.

---

117. William of Ockham, *Opera Theologica* II, 312. Cited from Beckmann, *Wilhelm von Ockham*, 144. Scotus thinks that God's existence can be proven through natural reason, but his attributes cannot (Van Nieuwenhove, *An Introduction to Medieval Theology*, 232).

118. Van Nieuwenhove, *An Introduction to Medieval Theology*, 239.

PART II

Modern Theology

Chapter 4

The Reformation

As underscored in the two previous chapters, Christianity embraced reason through integrating logic and dialectic into theological discourse. Initiated by Boethius, and continued by such figures as Anselm, Lombard, and Aquinas, scholastic theology became a widespread, if not universally accepted, mode of theology. Indeed, for authors like Robert Grant, in *God & Reason in the Middle Ages*, the growth of scholasticism offers strong evidence that theology wanted to be scientific and witnessed to Christianity's openness to reason and scientific understanding. Given this background, it comes as a surprise to learn that in the early modern period there arose a huge backlash against scholastic theology. One can find anti-scholastic polemics not just in Luther and other key Reformers, but also in such wide-ranging figures as Hobbes, Locke, Francis Bacon, Erasmus, and Thomas More.[1] In order to chart the trajectory of faith and reason in the modern period, it is imperative to begin with the reaction against scholastic theology.

THE RISE OF THE HUMANISTS

If one had to pick one movement to represent the shift from a medieval to a modern worldview, it would most likely be the humanism associated with the Renaissance. No figure did more to effect this shift than Petrarch (1304–74), the Italian poet. As one historian put it, "When Petrarch besought his countrymen to close their Aristotle and open their Cicero, he was most truly the Father of the Renaissance."[2] At one level, the whole notion of the Renaissance as a rebirth of affec-

---

1. Grant, "The Assault on the Middle Ages," in *God & Reason in the Middle Ages*, 283–355.

2. R. R. Bolger, *The Classical Heritage and Its Beneficiaries*, 264; cited in John O'Malley, *Four Cultures of the West* (Cambridge: Harvard University Press, 2004), 149.

tion for classical culture seems absurd. The previous thirteen centuries of Christian theology took a sustained and serious interest in preserving the pre-Christian legacy, both in the inclusion of the older Hebrew Scriptures in the Christian canon, and in the maintenance of Greek philosophy, especially Plato in the early centuries, and later—via Boethius and the subsequent medieval discoveries—Aristotle. The above quotation helps clarify just which sources were retrieved. Rather than focusing on logical and scientific treatises from the classical period, Petrarch initiated the turn to literature, especially the highly rhetorical, and thus more beautiful, writings from the classical period. This turn to literature, and the turn away from the intricate study of animals contained in many of Aristotle's treatises, involved a turn to the human, hence *humanism*.[3] One key offshoot of the Renaissance involved the search for reliable manuscripts. John O'Malley explains, "Petrarch's summons 'back to the sources' had helped launch humanists' search for good manuscripts from which to construct reliable versions of their texts, leading them ever deeper into the historical situations and literary forms that constituted them."[4] Of course this search would have dramatic consequences, but for the present purposes it is enough to note that it commenced the downfall of the scholastic hegemony over university life in Europe.

At this point one can summarize the critique leveled by humanists against scholasticism (and by consequence, scholastic theology). First, scholasticism relied too heavily on fine logical distinctions, and thus missed the forest for the trees. Second, its slavish devotion to Aristotle led to a kind of dogmatism. Third, it did not engage in the original languages or even show an interest in sources; thus, over the centuries both its text and its translations had been corrupted and were in need of correction. Fourth, it wrote in a bland, unattractive style, lacking in wit or beauty. These complaints were enough, in the minds of the humanists, not just to modify scholastic culture—after all, this is what theologians like Hugh of St. Victor and Bonaventure had already attempted—but to dismantle it completely.

---

3. For this point, see O'Malley, *Four Cultures of the West*, 151.
4. O'Malley, *Four Cultures of the West*, 159.

In their imitation of classical style, the humanists preferred rhetorical flourish over subtle distinctions, which the humanists dismissed as pointless logic-chopping. For humanists like Petrarch, the figure of Aristotle became emblematic of the problem, leading to savage portrayals.[5] Petrarch opined, "I snarl at the stupid Aristotelians, who day by day in every single word they speak do not cease to hammer into the heads of others Aristotle whom they know by name only."[6] Here the problem is not so much the master, Aristotle, but the pupils, who promote the cause in name only, and thus distort and corrupt the master's meaning. Petrarch's complaint would be applied to many pupils of many schools, most especially Thomists.

Petrarch's attacks became the standard for subsequent critiques. The fifteenth century expanded humanism's critique of scholasticism, exemplified in the thought of Lorenzo Valla (1407–57). Valla had discovered gaps between the Greek New Testament and the Vulgate translation, and his research revealed that a key early Christian text supporting Roman authority was in fact a forgery.[7] Like Petrarch, Valla savaged not so much Aristotle himself as Aristotelians: "They regard all other philosophers as non-philosophers and embrace Aristotle as the only wise man, indeed the wisest—not surprisingly, since he is the only writer they know. If one can call it 'knowing,' for they read him, not in his own language, but in a foreign, not to say corrupt, language. Most of his works are wrongly translated, and much that is well said in Greek is not well said in Latin."[8] In Valla's rendering, the Aristotelians care more about maintaining loyalty to Aristotle than the truth. In addition, after centuries in which Latin had been the dominant language of learning and culture, Valla's critique signals a tectonic shift in education. Passing through the necessary curriculum to become a "master of arts" in a university no longer counted as being learned, at

5. For this critique of scholasticism, see the chapter, "The Assault on the Middle Ages," in Grant, *God & Reason in the Middle Ages*, esp. 293–329.

6. Petrarch, "On His Own Ignorance and That of Many Others," cited from Grant, *God & Reason in the Middle Ages*, 295.

7. O'Malley, *Four Cultures of the West*, 159–60.

8. See Erika Rummel, *The Humanist-Scholastic Debate in the Renaissance & Reformation* (Cambridge: Harvard University Press, 1995), 160. Taken from Grant, *God & Reason in the Middle Ages*, 296.

least in humanist eyes. The new model was the *vir trilinguis*, the "tri-lingual person" who knew Latin, Greek, and Hebrew, and could refer to the original source material to ensure proper reception.

Nobody in the sixteenth century carried the humanist torch higher than Desiderius Erasmus (c. 1466–1536), the Dutch-born scholar best known for editing a critical edition of the Greek New Testament in 1516. Despite middling family resources, Erasmus received a fine education, learning Greek in high school (as a result of new humanistic reforms), and later studying theology at Louvain. Valla's efforts inspired him to create a critical edition of the New Testament, and he acquired the best possible knowledge of the relevant ancient languages to do so.[9] Unlike Petrarch and even Valla, Erasmus's humanism arose from a deeply theological framework.[10] Theological questions mattered to him, borne out not only in his work on the New Testament, but also in his patristic scholarship, especially on Jerome, and in his disputes over free will with Luther. It is no great stretch to compare Erasmus to twentieth-century Catholic *ressourcement* theologians like Henri de Lubac and Hans Urs von Balthasar. Like these later theologians, Erasmus sought to enrich theology by bypassing decadent scholasticism and replacing it with earlier, and from his standpoint more authentic theological forms. Unfortunately, too much of Catholic history remembers and blames Erasmus for "laying the egg that Luther hatched."[11]

Erasmus penned his most infamous jeremiad not only against scholasticism, but against the sixteenth-century church more

9. This point appears in much of the literature. Michael Legaspi writes, "Valla is often credited with stimulating Erasmus's interest in biblical philology. After encountering Valla's critical notes on the Vulgate New Testament, Erasmus eagerly produced a new edition of them in 1505. In subsequent years, he devoted himself to a study of the Greek text, and in 1516 his *Novum Testamentum* appeared" (Michael Legaspi, *The Death of Scripture and the Rise of Biblical Studies* [Oxford: Oxford University Press, 2010], 12–13).

10. While conceding how much his 1505 discovery of Valla's critical work inspired his own efforts, Erasmus added that Valla "was more a rhetorician than a theologian" (Erasmus, *The Praise of Folly*, trans. Clarence H. Miller [New Haven, CT: Yale, 1979], 171).

11. This metaphor has been in circulation since Erasmus's time. See Daniel Preus, "Luther and Erasmus: Scholastic Humanism and the Reformation," *Concordia Theological Quarterly* 46, no. 2 (1982): 219. Erasmus disagreed, answering that Luther hatched a different bird entirely. For an example of the Catholic bent against Erasmus, see Joseph Sauer, "Desiderius Erasmus," in *The Catholic Encyclopedia*, vol. 5 (New York: Robert Appleton Company, 1909), 510–14.

broadly. It began as an encomium to amuse Thomas More, written as Erasmus set out for London to visit his close friend in the summer of 1509.[12] *The Praise of Folly* cast the elites of Europe in a most unflattering light by showing the hypocrisy among the political, ecclesiastical, and academic classes. Despite the uproar that it caused, Erasmus authorized several revised editions in subsequent decades.[13]

The Praise of Folly continues the humanist line of critique that began with Petrarch. Erasmus lambasts almost every kind of university man before turning to the theologians: "As for the theologians, perhaps it would be better to pass them over in silence [. . .] for they might rise up en masse and march in ranks against me with six hundred conclusions and force me to recant."[14] In this section, Erasmus's encomium to folly attends to the gap between theological questions and pastoral concerns: "There are numberless *petty quibbles* even more fine-spun than these, concerning notions, relations, instants, formalities, quiddities, ecceities."[15] Erasmus contrasts scholastic theology with the theology of lived experience that permeates the Apostolic fathers. In his judgment, scholastic distinctions, borne from logic and dialectic, and formed in a culture of rational debate, did not matter: "For who could perceive these things unless he had spent thirty-six whole years studying the physics and metaphysics of Aristotle and the Scotists? So too, the apostles preach grace very forcefully, but nowhere do they distinguish between *gratis data* and *gratificans*. They exhort us to good works, without distinguishing *opus operans* from *opus operatum*."[16] Erasmus lamented a decadent scholastic theology that divorced faith from life. The relationship that the Church Fathers had discerned between faith and reason always bound itself to living, practical concerns. Erasmus explains: "Chrysostom, Basil, and Jerome certainly did confute pagan philosophers and Jews [. . .] but they did it

---

12. My familiarity with the background of the text comes from the superb introductory "Note on the Text," by Clarence Miller in, Desiderius Erasmus, *The Praise of Folly*, ix–xxxiv.

13. Miller, "Note on the Text," xxxiv.

14. Erasmus, *The Praise of Folly*, 87.

15. Erasmus, *The Praise of Folly*, 89.

16. Erasmus, *The Praise of Folly*, 92–93.

by the lives they led and the miracles they performed rather than by manufacturing syllogisms."[17]

In Erasmus's account, the millennium-long effort to seek greater understanding within the horizon of faith did not result in continual improvement and progress, but rather in a kind of decline. This narrative of decline has become a defining feature for so much of modern theology. In both *The Praise of Folly* and his letter to Martin Dorp, Erasmus makes the qualification that his critique only extends to bad theologians (admittedly, thick on the ground), not to the few noble theologians, or to the discipline itself, which he reveres. Still, Erasmus makes the case for a devolution or decline, and thereby contrasts the living springs of the Bible and patristic theology with torpid, late medieval theology:

> They distort and reshape Holy Scripture however they like, while they demand that their conclusions should be [...] more binding than the papal decretals [...] while they deliver their oracular pronouncements [...] so that not even baptism, not the gospel, not Paul or Peter, not even St. Jerome or St. Augustine, in fact not even Thomas [Aquinas], himself *Aristotelicimmus* [most Aristotelian], can make someone a Christian unless he has the vote of these theologians.[18]

The Praise of Folly, chock full of such statements, caused great rancor and eventually landed on a list of forbidden books compiled by the Sorbonne faculty of theology in 1543.[19]

In 1514, Erasmus's confidant and friend, Martin Dorp, wrote to complain that *The Praise of Folly* was too severe in its critique, and that Erasmus failed to display the spirit of charity at the heart of the gospel he had accused the medieval church of corrupting. Erasmus's long response appeared in subsequent editions of *The Praise of Folly*.[20] According to one commentator, *The Praise of Folly* and the letter to Dorp, when read in conjunction, constitute the most concise articulation of the humanist critique of university education, especially in theology.[21]

17. Erasmus, *The Praise of Folly*, 94.
18. Erasmus, *The Praise of Folly*, 95–96.
19. Miller, "Note on the Text," xiii.
20. "Erasmus's Letter to Martin Dorp (1514)," in Erasmus, *The Praise of Folly*, 139–74.
21. Miller, "Note on the Text," xi.

As the following analysis of his letter to Dorp will show, Erasmus's critique was not directed at the integration of faith and secular learning, but instead at the wrong kind of secular learning. Too many theologians thought that acquainting themselves with Aristotelian logic and dialectic excused them from the task of philology, the study of classical languages. Erasmus brought this point home: "These are the people who ridicule Greek, Hebrew, and even Latin literature, and though they are more stupid than any sow and do not have even ordinary common sense, they think they have reached the very pinnacle of wisdom."[22] Scholastic Latin as it had developed in the medieval period was often stripped down for clarity's sake to the most rudimentary form of expression; its prose came to resemble that of modern manual for a kitchen appliance. Erasmus had fallen in love with the beauty of classical Latin, still preserved in patristic theologians like Jerome and Augustine, whom he repeatedly extols. In a university climate so focused on parsing fine distinctions, the humanistic style of patristic theology had been lost. Erasmus speaks directly to this: "As for modern theology, I pass over the base monstrosities of its barbarous and factitious language. I pass over its complete lack of literary culture, its ignorance of languages."[23] Erasmus offered an alternative mode of educated theology, one steeped in languages and literary form.

In order for the humanists to triumph over the decadent scholastics of his day, Erasmus needed to fell the strongest tree of the latter camp. This tree was Aristotle. Erasmus offers the starkest possible contrast between Aristotle and Christian theology: "But [theology] is so contaminated with Aristotle [. . .] that I hardly see how it can preserve the true savor of Christ, who is pure and uncontaminated." And a few sentences later: "What connection is there, I ask you, between Christ and Aristotle? or between sophistical quibbles and the mysteries of eternal wisdom?"[24] Erasmus later reminds Dorp that, whatever problems he had with Aristotle, the scholastics of Erasmus's day were not even drinking from that source. Aristotle and sixteenth-century Aristotelianism were not the same thing. Recalling an old papal decree that allocated

22. "Erasmus's Letter to Martin Dorp," 151.
23. "Erasmus's Letter to Martin Dorp," 155.
24. "Erasmus's Letter to Martin Dorp," 155.

funds for language study, Erasmus laments the lack of interest in learning them, and the perils that result from it: "But even in the study of Aristotle the same thing happens as in their handling of Holy Scripture. Everywhere they encounter their Nemesis, who takes revenge on their contempt for language: with Aristotle, as with all the others, they wander in a fog, they dream, they bump into things blindly."[25] In short, there was no way, in Erasmus's mind, for theologians to practice "faith seeking understanding" within the confines of institutions devoted to narrow conceptions of scholastic training; for "understanding" in the fullest sense would be foreclosed without the capacity to engage texts in their original languages. With regard to Aristotle, Erasmus criticized scholastic theologians for failing to read him in the Greek. In the case of the New Testament, the Vulgate translation suffered a number of flaws: mistakes had been made in copying Jerome's Vulgate, which crept into common printed versions; Jerome himself made mistakes in his translation, due to working from a corrupted version of the Greek New Testament. Nobody interested in questions of truth, concluded Erasmus, could afford to neglect these realities. The time had come to replace outmoded forms of education that failed to equip students with the necessary tools—language skills. To this end, Erasmus exhorted Dorp himself to study Greek, and warned of his not doing so: "If you think you can get a true knowledge of theology without skill in languages, especially in that language in which almost all of Holy Scripture has come down to us, you are completely off track."[26]

Before moving on to Erasmus's contemporary and subsequent opponent, Martin Luther, it bears remembering how Erasmus's critique came from a place of considerable familiarity. He himself had studied theology, and throughout both *The Praise of Folly* and the letter to Dorp, Erasmus reminds his reader that he does not oppose theology, just as he does not oppose monarchy: What he opposes is bad theology and bad theologians, and he insists that the good and wise theologians in his own time would agree with him. Nevertheless, Erasmus, more than almost anyone before Luther, fueled subsequent efforts to jettison entire centuries of theology. He gave the impression

25. "Erasmus's Letter to Martin Dorp," 155.
26. "Erasmus's Letter to Martin Dorp," 163.

that these eras could be forgotten with no great loss. Although the decadent scholastic theology of Erasmus's day had forgotten much from the first centuries of theology—each era of theology exercises its own form of forgetting and retrieval—this forgetting resulted more from accident than design. Maintaining the corpus of early Christian theology was a nearly impossible task for a medieval center of learning on account of the political, geographical, and technological factors that made the preservation of texts so challenging. The humanistic assault on scholasticism, and with it the Middle Ages, inaugurated a new era in Christian intellectual history by setting up a "narrative of decline." In many ways this imaginative construct of decline made the possibility of Protestant reformation possible.

MARTIN LUTHER

Over five hundred years after Martin Luther (1483–1545) nailed his Ninety-Five Theses to a door in Wittenberg, his legacy remains as contested as ever. Luther's theology represents the most radical rearticulation of the relationship between faith and reason in the history of Christian thought, one that recalls Tertullian's skepticism from the third century, and paves the way for modern fideism, the notion that "faith alone" suffices for theology. In John O'Malley's taxonomy, Luther belongs more to the prophetic than the humanist culture, but he nonetheless benefitted immeasurably from the humanist educational reforms, especially the study of Greek and Hebrew.[27] Luther undertook this study to become a professor of Scripture for his religious order, the Augustinians. The story of Luther's intensive engagement with the Psalms and the Pauline epistles in the second decade of the sixteenth century, and the discovery of salvation "by faith alone, by grace alone" has been well-documented. The study at hand begins with another set of Luther's theses from 1517, the "Disputation Against Scholastic Theology."[28]

27. O'Malley, *Four Cultures of the West*, 9–10.
28. Luther, "Disputation against Scholastic Theology," in *Early Theological Works*, trans. James Atkinson (Louisville: Westminster John Knox, 1962), 251–73. For the original Latin, see Luther, *Werke, kritische Gesamtausgabe*, vol. 1 (Weimar: Herman Böhlau, 1883), 221–28. From this edition I have slightly revised Atkinson's translations.

By the time of the composition of these theses, Luther had come to understand the gospel of grace as the central Christian message: On our own, we are hopeless sinners; through the gift of grace, we can be saved. This grace precedes any movement in us, and it is unmerited by any prior action. Luther had studied scholastic theology in depth, and had even lectured on Lombard's *Sentences*, a rite of passage for anyone planning to make a university career in theology. Luther became convinced that the attempt to fuse Aristotle's ethical teaching with Christianity had clouded the judgment of scholastic theology. It is perhaps illustrative to list a few of his theses to capture Luther's mood:

> 41. The whole Aristotelian ethic is grace's worst enemy (against the scholastic theologians).
> 42. It is a wrong thing to hold that the teaching of Aristotle on happiness is not repugnant to catholic doctrine (against the moral philosophers).
> 43. It is wrong to say that one cannot become a theologian without Aristotle (against the common viewpoint).
> 44. The truth is that one cannot become a theologian unless one becomes so without Aristotle.
> 50. In short, the whole of Aristotle is to theology as darkness is to light (against the scholastic theologians).[29]

None of the major medieval theologians, even if critical of Aristotle, ever expressed such a blatant aversion. *Aristotle* in these theses both indicates the historical figure of Aristotle as received in the Latin West, and also serves a synecdoche for all of secular learning. Here we can note both the continuity between Luther's and the humanist critique of scholasticism, and also ask about the nature of Luther's aversion: How did Luther come to understand the task of the theologian in such a way that made it diametrically opposed to the theology he had studied in Erfurt, which could claim a multi-century lineage?

One place to start is in Luther's understanding of the task and nature of theology. He lays this out programmatically, if elliptically, in his 1518 Heidelberg Disputation: "21. The theologian of glory calls

29. Luther, "Disputation against Scholastic Theology," 269–70.

the bad good and the good bad. The theologian of the cross says what a thing is. [...] 24. Nevertheless, this wisdom [that beholds the invisible things of God] is not bad nor is the law to be fled. But without a theology of the cross one misuses the best things in the worst way."[30] These comments come in the context of his critique of works righteousness, outlined in the "Disputation" and given flesh in his 1519 sermon, "Two Kinds of Righteousness."[31] For Luther, a theology of glory, like a religious attitude based in works righteousness, calls the bad good. In the life of a believer, it means taking a good action, like serving in a soup kitchen, as a mark of one's own righteousness. Like the Pharisee who thanks God that he is not like other men (Luke 18:11), the one who tries to become righteous through his own work calls the bad good. Spiritual writers since Luke the Evangelist have pointed out different forms of hypocrisy in an effort to help keep the Christian consciousness wedded to the elusive virtue of humility. At one level Luther simply magnified that tradition. As he explains, "Men of this kind wish to be like God, sufficient in themselves, pleasing themselves, glorifying in themselves, under obligation to no one."[32] Luther's unique contribution, however, came in his application of this insight to the realm of university theology, where he equated scholastic theological constructs to a form of works righteousness. Instead of beginning with the human incapacity, on account of original sin, to know God, theologies of glory sought to conform a notion of God with human expectations and demands. Luther scholar Robert Kolb states, "These scholastic theologians sought to fashion—with biblical citations, to be sure—a God worthy of the name, according to the standards of emperors and kings, whose glory and power defined how glory and power were supposed to look."[33] In short, a theology of glory looks at God from a human perspective.

30. Luther, "Theses for Heidelberg Disputation," in *Selections from His Writings*, ed. John Dillenberger (New York: Anchor Books, 1962), 503. For the Latin see Luther, *Werke*, vol. 1, 353–74.
31. Luther, "Two Kinds of Righteousness," in Dillenberger, *Selections from His Writings*, 86–96.
32. Luther, "Two Kinds of Righteousness," 90.
33. Robert Kolb, "Luther on the Theology of the Cross," *Lutheran Quarterly* 16 (2002): 443–66, at 446.

Against this tendency, a theology of the cross humbles itself in obedience unto death on a cross (Phil 2:8). Whatever righteousness we have comes to us first as Christ's alien righteousness (*justitia aliena*). Luther cites Psalm 31:1—"in thy righteousness deliver me"— and adds: "It does not say 'in my' but 'in thy righteousness,' that is, in the righteousness of Christ my God which becomes ours through faith and by the grace and mercy of God."[34] Integrating this perspective, a perspective that Luther thought the gospels, and especially Paul's epistles, made plain, meant undergoing an epistemological asceticism. Instead of thinking about working at a soup kitchen as an action that makes one good, one learns to understand the action as a product of God's creation of a new heart in oneself. Alien righteousness precedes my own, proper righteousness: "The second kind of righteousness is our proper righteousness, not because we alone work it, but because we work with that first and alien righteousness."[35] In the reception of Luther's theology, there has often resulted a caricature of faith as an all-at-once, one-off commitment. This caricature distorts Luther, who writes of a constant struggle to overcome bad religious psychology: "But the carnal nature of man violently rebels, for it greatly delights in punishment, in boasting of its own righteousness, and in its neighbor's shame and embarrassment at his unrighteousness. Therefore it pleads its own case, and it rejoices that this is better than its neighbor's. [. . .] This perversity is wholly evil, contrary to love, which does not seek its own good, but that of another."[36] The abiding religious danger is to think like the Pharisee in Luke 18. To transpose this language into Catholic or Orthodox Christianity, one could examine the lives and writings of the saints. No saint ever says that she is a good person. In becoming Christ-like, one becomes ever more attuned to one's sinfulness, so that one's prayer becomes the prayer of the publican: "God, be merciful to me a sinner" (Luke 18:13).

Luther thought this matter of religious epistemology could be transposed into the theological realm. Scholastic theology, as interpreted by Luther, did not reflect the humility of the believer who under-

---

34. Luther, "Two Kinds of Righteousness," 88.
35. Luther, "Two Kinds of Righteousness," 88.
36. Luther, "Two Kinds of Righteousness," 93.

stands that his righteousness comes from another. Kolb points out this problem: "Luther found in medieval theological systems an emphasis on the glory of human performance, of works that can capture God's favor by sheer human effort, plus some help from divine grace."[37] Coming to regard oneself as saved "by grace, through faith" (Eph 2:8) includes an existential reorientation. Everything looks different in the life of the believer, whose status as saved does not derive from any personal initiative. In Luther's judgment, scholastic theology refracted none of the humility and existential urgency that the gospel requires. Since it did not view other realities through a cruciform lens, it "misuses the best things in the worst way," including human reason.[38]

Luther's polemical barbs have attained a legendary status.[39] Medieval university culture, and even the development of medieval Latin, was geared toward verbal combat. Just as many Protestants wince at Luther's verbal torrents, so too do some Catholics blush at the bluntness of the anathemas in the Council of Trent and elsewhere. Perhaps Luther's strongest condemnation of reason comes in a late 1546 sermon: "Reason, the devil's bride, the pretty harlot [. . .] is the greatest whore that the devil has."[40] Such statements, alongside other remarks from Luther about the consequences of original sin, have led many to conclude that Luther's post-lapsarian anthropology—the human being is "curved in on itself" (*incurvatus in se*)[41]—forces him, and the entire Lutheran tradition, into a position that puts reason and faith, philosophy and true theology (*theologia crucis*) into permanent con-

---

37. Kolb, "Luther on the Theology of the Cross," 447.

38. Luther, "Heidelberg Thesis," 24.

39. See, for instance, the insult generator: http://ergofabulous.org/luther/.

40. Luther, "Predigten des Jahres 1546," in *Weimar Ausgabe*, vol. 51, 126. See also, *The Devil's Whore: Reason and Philosophy in the Lutheran Tradition*, ed. Jennifer Hockenberry Dragseth (Minneapolis: Fortress Press, 2011), especially the article by Denis Janz, "Whore or Handmaid," 47–52.

41. The literature on Luther generally associates Luther's citation of this term with his 1516 "Lectures on Romans." For an accessible translation, see Martin Luther, *Lecture on Romans*, ed. and trans. Wilhelm Pauck (Louisville: Westminster John Knox, [1961] 2006). In Luther's comments on Romans 5:4 he writes, "Due to original sin, our nature is so curved in upon itself at its deepest levels that it not only bends the best gifts of God toward itself in order to enjoy them [. . .] but it does not even know that, in this wicked, twisted, crooked way, it seeks everything, including God, only for itself" (Luther, *Lectures on Romans*, 159; see also 112).

flict.[42] Although such conclusions have a textual basis, they hardly do justice to the complexity of Luther's thought.

In their attempts to give a more balanced account of Luther's attitude about faith and reason, leading scholars Denis Janz and Oswald Bayer both point to Luther's 1536 "Disputation Concerning Man," which assesses human reason more positively.[43] The fourth thesis reads, "And it is certainly true that reason is the most important and the highest in rank among all things and, in comparison with other things of this life, the best and something divine."[44] At first glance, such a statement seems irreconcilable with statements about reason being a harlot. And lest one think that Luther is referring only to reason before the fall of humanity, he adds in the ninth thesis: "Nor did God after the fall of Adam take away this majesty of reason, but rather confirmed it."[45] Still, Luther does argue that the fall alters the use of reason. Following Augustine, Luther insists that original sin imputes guilt to each human being.[46] Every natural endowment after the fall belongs in some way to the power of Satan. From this Luther concludes in thesis twenty-six: "Therefore, those who say that natural things have remained untainted after the fall philosophize impiously in opposition to theology."[47] For Luther, it was imperative to remind

---

42. Bayer cites two converging forces for this misapprehension: Karl Barth and Martin Heidegger, with Bultmann serving as a bridge between them. Citing Heinrich Bornkamm, he notes, "Recent theological movements, especially dialectical theology, have made a sharp in-principle distinction between biblical-reformational and philosophical thought and have tried to think of Luther's opposition to the Catholic tradition in precisely this way" (Bayer, "Philosophical Modes of Thought of Luther's Theology as an Object of Inquiry," in *The Devil's Whore*, 203n14; Bornkamm, *Luther im Spiegel der deutschen Geistesgeschichte*, 2nd ed. [Göttingen: Vandenhoeck & Ruprecht, 1970], 154). Bayer continues, "Dialectical theology, of a Bultmannian character, was strengthened here by the thesis, as put forward by Heidegger, that it is necessary to draw a sharp boundary between theology and philosophy" (Bayer, "Philosophical Modes of Thought of Luther's Theology as an Object of Inquiry").

43. Janz, "Whore or Handmaid," and Bayer, "Philosophical Modes of Thought of Luther's Theology as an Object of Inquiry," in *The Devil's Whore*, 13–21. For the text in English, see *Luther's Works*, vol. 34, ed. Lewis Spitz (Philadelphia: Muhlenberg, 1960), 137–44. For the Latin see Luther, *Werke*, vol. 39, no. 1, 174–80.

44. Luther, "The Disputation Concerning Man," 137.

45. Luther, "The Disputation Concerning Man," 137.

46. Here Luther also had in mind Paul, especially Romans 5:18a: "One man's trespass led to condemnation for all men."

47. Luther, "The Disputation Concerning Man," 139.

his audience that reason, like any natural good, was vulnerable to abuse, especially about the most important thing: our sinful state before God.

As his theology developed, Luther came to place greater emphasis on the proper order between faith and reason than focusing on affirming the inherent incompatibility between the two. Though he never says it, one can reasonably conclude that he spoke so strongly against reason, and more precisely, against the use of Aristotle by scholastic theology, in an effort to swing the pendulum toward greater reliance on faith. He was not concerned that Christian civilization would discard learning, or academic culture, as a result of his diatribes. Instead, he worried that scholastic theology would obscure faith's distinctive mode of knowing. Even if reason can discover some of God's attributes—Luther writes, "That is as far as the natural light of reason sheds its rays—it regards God as kind, gracious, merciful, and benevolent. And that is indeed a bright light"[48]—reason cannot supplant faith as a way of knowing God. Coming to understand oneself as a forgiven sinner involves something like an "undergoing," quite different from the grasping that accompanies acquisitive reason.[49] To presuppose that a human faculty like reason can know anything of God's saving message is to make a categorical mistake. As Denis Janz summarizes: "Reason is a marvelous gift of God, but it has its limitations. What is disastrous, according to Luther, is when reason oversteps its bounds and attempts to be the supreme judge in matters of faith."[50]

PHILIPP MELANCHTHON

As fate had it, an incredibly talented humanist, Philipp Melanchthon (1497–1560), began teaching Greek in Wittenberg just one year after Luther posted his Ninety-Five Theses. Melanchthon quickly joined

48. Luther, *Works*, vol. 19, 54. Cited in Janz, "Whore or Handmaid?," 48–49.

49. Curiously, it is a Catholic who draws this distinction most effectively to my mind. See James Alison, *Undergoing God: Dispatches from the Scene of a Break-In* (New York: Continuum, 2006). Alison explains, "The very word 'to undergo' is an oddity, an active verb with a passive meaning. [. . .] Thomas Aquinas, borrowing from Dionysius the Areopagite, held that doing theology implies a certain *pati divina*—an undergoing of 'divine things'" (Alison, *Undergoing God*, 2–3).

50. Janz, "Whore or Handmaid?," 49.

Luther's cause, and became just as formative for the Lutheran tradition as Luther himself. Within a year of arriving at Wittenberg, Melanchthon turned his attention to theology, taking a bachelor's degree in divinity in 1519, and lecturing on the Pauline epistles in 1520. In 1521 he wrote the first edition of his *Loci communes rerum theologicarum*, or "Fundamental Theological Themes," which sought to replace Lombard's *Sentences* with a theological introduction centered more directly on the Scriptures. According to a humanist method developed by Erasmus, by noting the topics, or *loci communes* of a given text, one could better extract its content. Melanchthon "took from *Romans* the central themes of sin, law, and grace as his organizing principles" for the *Loci* in 1521, although he expanded the topics in subsequent editions.[51] This publication, as well as the esteem in which Luther held Melanchthon, propelled his meteoric rise: "In place of the outlawed Luther, Melanchthon became the most important theological spokesman of the Protestants at imperial diets and religious colloquies, beginning in Speyer in 1529."[52] Melanchthon later played a leading role in composing the 1530 *Augsburg Confession*, a text regarded as constitutional for Lutheran identity. He also helped organize both the German secondary education system (the *Gymnasium*), and the Protestant university system, thereby earning the nickname *praeceptor Germaniae*, or "teacher of Germany."

Melanchthon's relationship to philosophy evolved during his lifetime. His early writings on Paul parroted the humanistic critique seen above. The early Melanchthon, for instance, laments, "All philosophy is darkness and untruth."[53] Yet by the end of the 1520s, Melanchthon, perhaps in response to more radical, enthusiastic reform movements, turned to Aristotle, and later Plato, with greater regularity.[54] As one

51. Heinz Scheible, "Philipp Melanchthon," in *The Oxford Encyclopedia of the Reformation*, vol. 3, ed. Hans Hillerbrand (Oxford: Oxford University Press, 1996), 41–45, at 42.

52. Heinz Scheible, "Philipp Melanchthon," 43.

53. Cited from Wilhelm Pauck, "Editor's Introduction" to the *Loci Communes* in *Melanchthon and Bucer*, ed. Wilhelm Pauck (Philadelphia: Westminster, 1969), 3–17.

54. Sachiko Kusukawa writes, "He began to feel keenly the threat of evangelical radicals who advocated the right to disobey civil governments. [...] All these people [the Thuringian Anabaptists] seemed to claim some special access to the Holy Spirit or sacred knowledge, imposed arbitrary human interpretations on the Bible, and drew out radical

commentator summarizes: "Melanchthon wrote philosophical works, he studied and critiqued the work of philosophers past, and he praised philosophy. Melanchthon did what philosophers have always done."[55] This activity has led to the persistent complaint that Melanchthon violated the fundamental principle of Lutheran thought by diluting the gospel with philosophy. No less an authority than Jaroslav Pelikan wrote, "Melanchthonianism, Orthodoxy, Rationalism, and Hegelianism all sought a comprehensive rational system. To that extent they all constitute a misrepresentation of Luther."[56] Such an accusation assumes an essentially anti- or a-rational quality to Protestantism, or at least its Lutheran branch.

In subsequent centuries Lutheran theology followed two divergent tracks that would define its legacy regarding the question of faith and reason. One track, inspired by the later Melanchthon, developed its own tradition of scholasticism through such figures as Johann Gerhard (1582–1637) and George Calixt (1586–1656). Another track produced the Pietists, who gained steam in the eighteenth century, and are treated in chapter 5. The latter track recalled Luther's accent on feeling, sentiment, and personal encounter as an antidote to Lutheran scholastic categories.[57] In view of this complexity, such interpreters as Jaroslav Pelikan not only fail to do justice to Melanchthon, but also to Luther himself. Indeed, as Oswald Bayer notes, Luther's "engagement with philosophy is not something secondary but constitutive" for his theological project; even further, this engagement took place in an (admittedly qualified) Aristotelian mode.[58]

---

messages of action which would have resulted in resisting or overturning the existing political order. Melanchthon saw poor education and confusion of philosophy and theology as the root of the problem." See Sachiko Kusukawa, "Introduction" in Philip Melanchthon, *Orations on Philosophy and Education*, ed. Sachiko Kusukawa (Cambridge: Cambridge University Press, 1999), xvii.

55. Charles Peterson, "Philipp Melanchthon: The First Lutheran Philosopher," in *The Devil's Whore*, 69–75, at 69.

56. Jaroslav Pelikan, *From Luther to Kierkegaard: A Study in the History of Theology* (Saint Louis: Concordia, 1950), 115; cited in Peterson, "Philipp Melanchthon," 74.

57. For this split in the context of Melanchthon's legacy see Ralph Keen, "Philipp Melanchthon," in *The Encyclopedia of Protestantism*, vol. 3, ed. Hans Hillebrand (New York: Routledge, 2004), 1194.

58. Bayer, "Philosophical Modes of Thought," 15–16. Bayer leans heavily on what he calls the "groundbreaking research" on the relationship between Luther and Aristotle by

Scholars generally regard Melanchthon's *Loci Communes* as the first work of Protestant systematic theology. Although the work presents some textual problems—Melanchthon constantly revised and even corrected it, and did not always authorize or approve the German translations—it gained almost immediate popularity upon publication, and has remained a foundational text in the history of Protestant theology.[59] It takes up Luther's insistence that we know the relevant Christian truths *sola scriptura*, through Scripture alone. Luther's own theological corpus reflects this methodological conviction. Much of his theology is occasional and polemical. His most important writings take the form of homilies, commentaries, and expositions. One can draw a parallel, in terms of theological genre, between Luther and patristic theology; no Luther text offers something like an alternative to Lombard's *Sentences* in the way that the *Loci Communes* does.

Not unlike the *De Reductione*, Melanchthon is concerned that students had drifted too far away from the biblical text, and similar to Bonaventure, he offers a humble contribution to help keep the student focused on Scripture. He writes, "I am setting forth in only a few words the elements on which the main points of Christian doctrine are based. I do this not to call students away from the Scriptures to obscure and complicated arguments but, rather, to summon them to the Scriptures if I can."[60] Melanchthon then laments that so many commentaries replace the unfiltered word of Scripture with muddled philosophical jargon. He does not merely disparage the efforts of later, second-rate scholastics, but instead directs his aim at Lombard, John Damascene, and even Origen of Alexandria. By flagging both Eastern and Western, both pre-scholastic and scholastic theology, he seems to posit a deviation in the tradition as having occurred much earlier than

---

Theodor Dieter: *Der junge Luther und Aristoteles: Eine historisch-systematische Untersuchung zum Verhältnis von Theologie und Philosophie* (Berlin: Walter de Gruyter, 2001). See Bayer, "Philosophical Modes of Thought," 21 and passim.

59. For a brief account of the varying editions, see Clyde Manschreck, "Preface" to *Melanchthon on Christian Doctrine: Loci Communes 1555*, trans. Manschreck (Oxford: Oxford University Press, 1965), vi–xxiv; and Pauck, "Editor's Introduction," in *Melanchthon and Bucer*, 14–17. Between the 1521 and 1555 edition, one is dealing with almost two entirely different books.

60. Melanchthon, *Loci Communes* in *Melanchthon and Luther*, 19. Below I cite from this, the 1521 version, unless otherwise noted.

previous critics had asserted. One could even say that such a sweeping dismissal is used to justify *sola scriptura* as a method. Melanchthon, rhetorically at least, sidesteps the theological tradition entirely. In light of the attention he gave to the Pauline corpus in 1520, it is no surprise that he identifies three "fundamentals" in the scriptural message: sin, law, and grace.[61] He imagines this knowledge as a bulwark against scholastic theology:

> This, then, is Christian knowledge: to know what the law demands, where you may seek power for doing the law and grace to cover sin. [. . .] Do the Scholastics teach those things? In his letter to the Romans when he was writing a compendium of Christian doctrine, did Paul philosophize about the mysteries of the Trinity, the mode of incarnation, or active and passive creation? No! But what does he discuss? He takes up the law, sin, grace, fundamentals on which the knowledge of Christ exclusively rests.[62]

Theologians do not need to systematize or impose order on the scriptural narrative because Scripture has already done so via the "compendium of Christian doctrine" otherwise known as *Romans*. As for Luther, so too for Melanchthon does *Romans* function as a short summa of the Christian faith. Therefore, scholastic efforts to bring understanding to Christian revealed data, that is, Scripture, are otiose and unnecessary at best, since so many of these efforts deviate from the biblical message.

One gets a sense of how Melanchthon reads the Christian theological tradition when revisiting his section from the *Loci* on original sin. Rather than identifying a continuity between Augustine and the medieval tradition on original sin, Melanchthon finds a fissure, referring to "the new Pelagians of our times" who underestimate the effects of sin and thus fail to understand grace correctly.[63] Instead of regarding the development of theology, including the attempt to integrate the rediscovered Aristotle into Christian faith claims, as part of a long

---

61. Melanchthon, *Loci Communes*, 21.
62. Melanchthon, *Loci Communes*, 22.
63. Melanchthon, *Loci Communes*, 33. Melanchthon borrows wholesale Luther's law-gospel categorization of Scripture (Melanchthon, *Loci Communes*, 70–71).

but worthwhile effort at faith seeking understanding, Melanchthon dismisses it entirely: "I am not concerned to make this agree with the philosophy of Aristotle. For what do I care what that wrangler thought?"[64] Scholastic theologians, or "Sophists" as Melanchthon calls them, have distorted the biblical message, and the surest way to restore that message is by going to the source, not by endlessly drawing distinctions about the meanings of words, logic-chopping to the point of incomprehension, and devoting oneself to a particular school, be it Thomism, Ockhamism, Scotism, or something else. He dismisses it all with one fell swoop: "You now know how we must evaluate the Scholastic view of faith: the Sophists teach nothing but lying, vanity, and hypocrisy."[65]

At this point it may be instructive to name out loud a conclusion that many readers have already reached about the inevitable split between faith and reason essential to any Protestant approach: Melanchthon's orientation to the theological tradition seems to echo the dark anthropology upon which Luther based so many of his theological convictions. Luther's account, which arose from his acute concerns about the selling of indulgences, led to a post-lapsarian anthropology in which the entire human being was vitiated by sin. Working from this perspective, Luther and those taking their cue from him looked skeptically at any possible synthesis between faith and reason. Where the medievals had sought a synthesis, the Reformers resigned themselves to an unbridgeable chasm. Comments by Luther or Melanchthon that seem to unsettle this conclusion only underscore the point, for when one jettisons reason, one does not concern oneself with bald-faced contradiction.

Despite the urge to draw this conclusion, it is important to caution against it and to reach a sound and historically accurate modification. Although the connection between post-lapsarian anthropology and skepticism about reconciling faith with reason seems causative, too much evidence stands in the way. First, both Luther and Melanchthon praised human reason and employed different forms of philosophy:

64. Melanchthon, *Loci Communes*, 50.
65. Melanchthon, *Loci Communes*, 91.

Even the Lutheran mantra *sola scriptura* does not require one to disregard reason.[66] They did so in full awareness of their earlier comments, and understood the later appreciation of reason as at most a coherent development of their earlier position. Second, they valued and promoted humanistic education, and applied it to theology. Their attacks against scholasticism should be read in continuity with Erasmus's criticism of the same. Erasmus's critique was based on *how* the scholastics applied reason and logic to theology, and not *that* they applied it. Luther and Melanchthon supplanted the scholastic approach, rooted in logic and dialectic, with the humanistic approach concerned with reading the most authentic versions of texts in the original languages. Doing so, they thought, involved a new and different *fides quarens intellectum*, not a *fides contra intellectum*. Along these lines, they applied a specific hermeneutic to Scripture. The law-gospel hermeneutic so central to Lutheran theology applied the use of reason to the problem of interpretation. Luther and Melanchthon did not spend much energy explaining this point, and one could reasonably conclude that they wanted to obscure it. Nevertheless, the imperative to read Scripture through the genres of law and gospel does not appear in the Bible. Third, Luther and Melanchthon both excoriated the "enthusiasts" (*Schwärmer*), a term that included such radical reformers as the Zwickau prophets. At the extreme edge, this branch of the Reformation claimed direct access to the Holy Spirit, and thus could bypass any custom or educational training. Both Luther and Melanchthon advocated for a well-trained clergy and an educated laity. Still, if Erasmus laid the egg that Luther hatched, then could one not claim that Luther did the same with the Radical Reformation?

TWO OFFSHOOTS OF THE REFORMATION

Perhaps it is apt to say that Luther hatched two eggs, pietism and Protestant scholasticism, both of which could claim to be his legitimate offspring. Both movements helped shape how future theologians and

---

66. See Ward Holder, "Revelation and Scripture," in *T&T Clark Companion to Reformation Theology*, ed. David Whitford (London: Bloomsbury, 2012): "*Sola scriptura* did not mean Scripture alone in the sense of Protestants refusing to use reason or the Church's tradition" (32).

ordinary Christians thought about how faith relates to reason. Although justice cannot be done to the multiplicity of the various off-shoots inspired by Luther in the years and decades after his split from Rome, a brief outline of the logic behind such movements can be offered.[67] When Luther met resistance to his interpretation of salvation by faith alone, Catholic opponents like Johannes Eck quickly turned the debate from the question about salvation to the matter of authority: Did Luther claim that his own interpretation subverted that of the theological schools, his local bishop, the pope, and Church tradition, including Church councils? In response Luther claimed that he did not need biblical teaching mediated to him through church authority, be it understood as the history of interpretation (the Church fathers and scholastics), or magisterial authority (bishops, theology faculties, or popes). In the five hundred years since Luther split from Rome, it is worth noting that the abiding differences that keep mainline Protestant churches separated from the Catholic Church have much less to do with indulgences and salvation by faith alone, and much more to do with matters of authority.[68] By questioning the validity of ecclesial authority, Luther allowed for his contemporaries to reimagine various ecclesial-political structures.

Luther's critique of authority arose in the context of the humanistic educational revolution and the Catholic Church's response to it. When Erasmus edited the New Testament and promoted educational structures that would emphasize the original languages, the Magisterium, while not anathematizing Erasmus, did not welcome this gesture with open arms. Even several decades later, at the Council of Trent, the session on Scripture did not mention the original Greek and Hebrew, and basically canonized the Vulgate Latin trans-

---

67. Already the name, "Radical Reformation," poses just as many problems as "The Reformation." It hints that groups with Catholic, Lutheran, or Calvinist allegiances could not be radical. It also coopts the word "radical," from the Latin *radix* (root), by presuming that this version of Christianity went back to, and reduplicated, the roots of the earliest or primitive Christianity. For a comprehensive overview of the movement, see George Huntston Williams, *The Radical Reformation*, 3rd ed. (Kirksville, MO: Truman State University Press, 2000).

68. For an extended treatment of this argument, see Grant Kaplan, "Revisiting Johannes Eck: The Leipzig Debate as the Beginning of the Reformation," *Logos: A Journal of Catholic Thought and Culture* 24, no. 2 (2021): 73–97.

lation.[69] Luther's rejection of ecclesial authority did not necessitate a total disavowal of authority; his training in the university system and his appointment as professor gave him qualifications that made additional institutional mediation unnecessary. Not all of his contemporaries picked up on this distinction.

Since the conversion of Constantine in 309, European Christianity found itself interwoven with political structures and powers, and the Church eventually acclimated itself mostly, if not entirely, to a state of compromise. Against this backdrop, Luther's attacks on the institutional church felt like an earthquake. As any student of medieval Europe knows, the tectonic plates beneath the surface shifted with regularity, but on the surface the terrain seemed stable. Luther's actions created dozens of aftershocks, some easily anticipated and others unforeseen. If ecclesiastical authority was such a sham, what was the basis of political authority, especially since the highest political actor, the Holy Roman Emperor, derived this authority from the Roman pontiff?[70] And if Luther had challenged the highest theological authorities about matters of justification, what prevented anybody else from challenging Luther on the same scriptural basis about his teaching on infant baptism or the real presence of the Eucharist?

Scholars generally date the "Radical Reformation" to late 1521, when a group from Zwickau, less than 100 miles south of Wittenberg, traveled north to Luther's university town and advocated for deeper and more fundamental changes, like communion under both species and the eradication of graven images.[71] Upon returning from Wartburg, Luther condemned the short-lived uprising and recommended

---

69. Council of Trent, Session 1; The text of the session can be found in Latin-English edition, *Enchiridion Symbolorum: A Compendium of Creeds, Definitions, and Declarations of the Catholic Church*, 43rd ed., ed. Peter Hünermann (San Francisco: Ignatius Press, 2012). The text will be abbreviated below as Denzinger, with the traditionally referenced pagination: Denzinger, 1501–8.

70. For a recent and riveting account of the Holy Roman Empire, see Peter Wilson, *Heart of Europe: A History of the Holy Roman Empire* (Cambridge: The Belknap Press of Harvard University Press, 2016).

71. These paragraphs lean heavily on the following two articles: C. Scott Dixon, "The Radicals," in *The Oxford Handbook of the Protestant Reformations*, ed. Ulinka Rublank (Oxford: Oxford University Press, 2017), 189–213; Geoffrey Dipple, "Radical Theology," in *T&T Clark Companion to Reformation Theology*, 291–314.

slower, more gradual reform. In addition, he demanded the exile of one of the uprising's leaders, Andreas Karlstadt. This hardly ended the problem, as various figures took what they understood as Luther's cue and preached a purportedly purer gospel, even if it meant challenging authority at their own peril. In the case of Thomas Müntzer, Luther's cue led to inciting the German Peasants' Rebellion, a popular uprising in protest against injustices perpetuated by ruling powers. Luther infamously railed against this uprising in a pamphlet whose title says everything: "Against the Murderous, Thieving Horde of Peasants."[72] From a personal standpoint, Luther owed his life to Friedrich of Saxony, the prince who protected him. He dismissed reformers like Karlstadt and Müntzer as *Schwärmer* (enthusiasts).[73]

When Luther wrote about the "Babylonian Captivity" of the Catholic Church, he assailed what one might call the "sacramental system." Subjects in this system avoided eternal damnation through ecclesial mediation, beginning with baptism, extending through penance and the Eucharist, and ending with last rites, without which one's salvation was in peril. The radicals took complaints against such mediation even further than Luther by questioning infant baptism and by dissolving entirely the need for clergy. One scholar writes, "Like Karlstadt and Müntzer, the early Anabaptists took the interpretation of scripture, and with it religious authority, out of the hands of the learned divines and placed it in the hands of the spirit-filled lay person—the requirements for the true interpreter of scripture were possession of the Spirit and an outward life that bore witness to one's inner spiritual renewal."[74] How could Luther savage Roman ceremonialism while defending the baptism of children not yet old enough to understand the experience? The radicals emphasized direct experience, often resulting from an inpouring of the Holy Spirit. This theological vision, when carried all the way through, meant the eradication of the professional class of Christians, and the need to build and sustain educational institutions for such a purpose.

72. In *Luther's Works*, vol. 46, 49–55.
73. For a summary of Luther's position against the *Schwärmer*, see Amy Nelson Burnett, "Luther and the Schwärmer" in *The Oxford Handbook of Martin Luther's Theology*, eds. Robert Kolb, Irene Dingel, and Ľubomír Batka (Oxford: Oxford University Press, 2014), 511–24.
74. Dipple, "Radical Theology," 303.

Both Luther and Melanchthon saw these movements as a grave threat. And as several scholars have noted, the movements caused Melanchthon in particular to rethink how faith and reason related. Early in his career he had used a Pauline phrase to critique scholasticism: "See to it that no one makes a prey of you by philosophy and empty deceit" (Col 2:8). By 1827, Melanchthon had revised his interpretation of this passage, writing: "Paul did not say 'philosophy is bad,' but he said 'See to it that no one makes prey of you by philosophy.'"[75] The problem is not philosophy itself, but the abuse of philosophy, a qualification that makes all the difference. Concerned with protecting the left-flank of the reform efforts against the radicals, Melanchthon's appropriation of philosophy continued through the rest of his life. As one commentator notes, "Melanchthon's confidence in the positive value of philosophy never wavered after 1527."[76] This stance, as noted above, led to what might have seemed in 1520 like an impossible development within the Lutheran tradition: its own version of scholasticism.

Theology in the Middle Ages had been a university discipline and it bore this stamp. Luther pointed out the problem of theological expertise divorced from a transforming conversion experience. Theology became just another way of holding the gospel captive. Within such a framework, it became difficult to reimagine how one could both create a system that gave the different doctrines a coherent structure, and apply the tools of secular learning, including philosophy, to theological problems.

Melanchthon attempted to deal with this tension by distinguishing between knowledge and true knowledge, or "between theology as a theoretic knowledge based on the intuitive recognition of the truth of its principle, and theology as an *acoustic* knowledge mediated by the word which is concretely heard as the voice of God."[77] This audial metaphor came from Luther's emphasis on Paul's axiom: *fides ex auditu*—"faith comes from hearing" (Romans 10:17). Following

75. Melanchthon, *Corpus Reformatorum Philippi Melanthonis*, XII, 695. My knowledge of this passage comes from Sachiko Kusukawa, *The Transformation of Natural Philosophy: The Case of Melanchthon* (Cambridge: Cambridge University Press, 1995), 66.

76. Kusukawa, *The Transformation of Natural Philosophy*, 68–69.

77. Robert Scharlemann, "Theology in Church and University: The Post-Reformation Development," *Church History* 33, no. 1 (1964): 23–33, at 23.

Luther, Melanchthon recognized the vast gap between affirming a truth "out there" and a truth "for me" (*pro me, pro nobis*). An influential Lutheran theologian in the subsequent century, Johann Gerhard, attempted to bridge the revival in Aristotle (in part inspired by Melanchthon) with Lutheran existential theology in the preface to his *Loci Theologici*. The ideal theology student "is not only instructed in the divine mysteries through an illumination of the mind so that, in a saving way, his intellectual knowledge also becomes the object of his heart's affection and the guide of his life."[78] Although Scharlemann insists on a sharp distinction between medieval and post-Reformation forms of scholasticism, the preceding quotation echoes the medieval distinction, brought out especially by Aquinas and Bonaventure, between knowledge and wisdom.

In both Catholic and Protestant realms, novel scholastic constructions, even if modeled closely on older ones, reflected the changes of many centuries. Lutheran scholastics in particular attempted new ways to show the rationality of faith. The aforementioned article by Robert Scharlemann discloses the emergence of a more territorial understanding of faith and reason. Instead of conceiving faith and reason as two distinct modes of thought, both illumined, albeit in different degrees, by divine grace, Lutheran scholasticism forged a peaceful relationship between faith and reason by according them distinct realms:

> In seventeenth-century scholasticism the whole ontological realm, the realm of the knowable, was divided into two parts. One part was knowable by *ratio*; this coincided with finite being. The other part was knowable by faith; this extended to infinite being. [. . .]
> This division of the ontological realm provides the key for relating theology and other areas of knowledge.[79]

In thus partitioning the different realms of knowledge, early modern scholastics sought to preserve the authenticity of theological and scientific truths. This model would persist, with some modifications and

---

78. Cited in Scharlemann, "Theology in Church and University," 25.
79. Scharlemann, "Theology in Church and University," 27. In the same article Scharlemann offers a genealogy connecting this distinction of realms to Kant's later distinction between the knowable sensible realm, and the unknowable supersensible realm.

too few exceptions, for several centuries. Unlike such medieval reform efforts as Bonaventure's *Reductio*, Gerhard's *Loci* did not attempt anything as radical as proposing a unifying vision of knowledge based on the principle of the Incarnation, which Bonaventure had done.

CALVIN'S REFORMATION

Besides Luther, no figure impacted the direction of the Protestant Reformation more than John Calvin (1509–64), the French-born reformer whose ideas inspired reform efforts throughout the continent and the rest of the Christian world. Calvin's most famous work, *The Institutes of Christian Religion*,[80] first appeared in 1536, and was revised and reissued several times. Alongside Melanchthon's *Loci*, the *Institutes* constitutes the most impactful work of Protestant systematic theology, and is still read today in theological surveys.[81] A brief analysis of certain key passages reveals how Calvin understood the relationship between faith and reason, and how these insights shaped so much of the modern theological trajectory.

Running parallel to the relationship between faith and reason is that of nature and grace. Both relationships manifest the difficulty in attempting to balance human and divine causation. Especially during the sixteenth century, key theologians of the reform wing like Luther and Calvin emphasized the effects of the Fall in order to prioritize the

---

80. It is a mis-translation to add a definite article between "of" and "Christian." Like most early modern thinkers, Calvin did not think of Christianity as one of many religions. To render it: *Institutes of Christian Piety* better conveys what he intends the text to do. To this point Brian Gerrish writes, "From Desiderius Erasmus and Martin Bucer [Calvin] learned that genuine theology, unlike the 'sophistry' of the late medieval schoolmen, is eminently practical: its aim is piety." Later in the same paragraph Gerrish calls the *Institutes* a "*pietatis summa*" (summary of piety). See Brian Gerrish, "The Place of Calvin in Christian Theology," in *The Cambridge Companion to Calvin*, ed. Donald McKim (Cambridge: Cambridge University Press, 2004), 289–304, at 300.

81. Carl Trueman writes that Calvin's own preface to the *Institutes* "perhaps legitimates the use of the term 'systematic theology' to describe what he is writing—but only with the important proviso that we realise this is systematic theology as pursued within a trajectory stemming from the twelfth century and not be understood by the crude imposition of later models of systematic theology onto the sixteenth century." See Carl Trueman, "Calvin and Calvinism," in *The Cambridge Companion to John Calvin*, 225–44, at 232. In the same volume John Hesselink echoes this claim: "It is not a dogmatics or systematic theology in the modern sense" (John Hesselink, "Calvin's Theology," in *The Cambridge Companion to John Calvin*, 74–92, at 76).

need for grace, and, in the case of Calvin, to glorify God's gracious agency. Calvin filters his account of how faith relates to reason through his reading of the fall and its effects. According to Calvin, the fall distorted all of our rational faculties, especially the will and the intellect. He writes, "We are so vitiated and perverted in every part of our nature that by this great corruption we stand justly condemned and convicted before God."[82] Although similar sounding versions of this understanding of the fall had been expressed previously, Calvin argues that it too frequently faded from consciousness, and thus led to grave errors. Augustine used similar language to describe the effects of the fall, whereas Aquinas distinguished between nature and certain "goods of nature" when he talked about the effects of the fall. Nature remained intact, but certain goods were lost. Discussing these matters, Calvin was dismissive of medieval qualifications like Aquinas's: "For our nature is not only destitute and empty of good, but so fertile and fruitful of every evil that it cannot be idle."[83] Such strong language about the effects of the fall has led many to conclude of Calvin and the Reformed[84] tradition that it downgrades human rational capacity and thus replaces the faith-seeking-understanding of Anselm and the medievals with something like "knowledge by faith alone."[85]

As with the Lutheran narrative of pure fideism recounted and rejected above, this picture of the Reformed account of how faith relates to reason is overly tidy, and thus cannot account for evidence to the contrary. Even more than the Lutherans, the Reformed branch of Protestantism developed a robust scholasticism and supported the development and promotion of the intellectual life through institutions like

82. Calvin, *Institutes of the Christian Religion*, ed. John McNeill, trans. Ford Lewis Battles (Philadelphia: Westminster, 1960), II, 1, 8 (251 in McNeill); henceforth *Institutes* with book, chapter and number, and McNeill pagination in parenthesis.

83. Calvin, *Institutes*, II, 1, 8 (252).

84. Here and below I use the capitalized "Reformed" to refer to the churches and theological tradition owing and professing genealogy to Calvin, for whom the term "Calvinist" would have been abhorrent.

85. At times, Reformed scholars themselves have understood Calvin in this way. See, for instance, Dewey Hoitenga, *Faith and Reason from Plato to Plantinga: An Introduction to Reformed Epistemology* (Albany: SUNY Press, 1991), 170: "It has to be said that the Augustinian dynamic of faith seeking understanding is absent [in Calvin]." Hoitenga, *Faith and Reason*, 174: "Calvin does not, however, incorporate into his position or into his thinking the Augustinian formula, faith seeks understanding."

universities and publishing houses.[86] The tradition of Reformed scholasticism can call itself a legitimate heir to Calvin.[87] Additionally, Calvin's *Institutes* betray something of "faith seeking understanding" insofar as it represents a logically ordered and coherent attempt to explain the revealed data of Scripture and to express proper Christian piety. In his theology, Calvin did not denigrate reason per se, but rather distinguished three kinds of reason—natural, vicious and redeemed—two of which could be compatible with faith.[88] Rather than identify Calvin and the Reformed legacy as creating an unbridgeable chasm between faith and reason, what follows shows how Calvin underwent an imaginative shift, whereby he came to conceive faith and reason as covering distinct territories of knowing. This shift, while innocent of the accusations of fideism, still managed to play a major role in developing the modern division between faith and reason.

Calvin's focus on the effects of the fall and the infinite capacity for human self-deception should not obscure his affirmation of natural theology, which he states quite clearly: "There is within the human mind, and indeed by natural instinct, an awareness of divinity (*sensum divinitatis*)."[89] Human reason, even after the fall, has the capacity to perceive the existence of God, and indeed still possesses something like the natural desire to know. Calvin continues: "For we see implanted in human nature some sort of desire to search out the truth to which man would not at all aspire if he had not already savored it. Human understanding then possesses some power of perception, since it is by nature captivated by love of truth."[90] Like Luther, Calvin employed heightened rhetoric about the effects of the fall, and like

86. For a helpful guide to Reformed scholasticism, see Willem Van Asselt, *Introduction to Reformed Scholasticism* (Grand Rapids, MI: Reformation Heritage Books, 2011).

87. As Ward Holder notes, Francis Turretin, one of the most influential Reformed scholastics, "could allow for no possible difference between the truths of right reason and faith, and found this in the tradition stemming from Calvin" (Holder, "Calvin's Heritage," in *Cambridge Companion to Calvin*, 245–73, at 257).

88. See John Calvin, "The Clear Explanation of Sound Doctrine concerning the True Partaking of the Flesh and Blood of Christ in the Holy Supper," in *Calvin: Theological Treatises*, trans. Reid (Philadelphia: Westminster, 1954). My awareness of this classification comes from Barry Waugh, "Reason within the Limits of Revelation Alone: John Calvin's Understanding of Human Reason," *Westminster Theological Journal* 72 (2010): 1–21, at 5.

89. Calvin, *Institutes*, I, 3, 8 (43).

90. See Calvin, *Institutes*, II, 2, 12 (252).

Luther, he also acknowledged some place for natural theology and for the human capacity to know God. Yet due to the fall, according to Calvin, our natural faculties have become misaligned, which explains how so many different kinds of people and cultures have come to such wildly inaccurate understandings of God.

Calvin famously opens the *Institutes* with something like a vicious cycle. He begins with the Delphic oracle, *know thyself*, and adds that one cannot really know oneself without knowing God: "It is certain that man never achieves a clear knowledge of himself unless he has first looked upon God's face, and then descends from contemplating him to scrutinize himself."[91] This cosmic separation resulting from the fall means that humans lose both knowledge of God and knowledge of themselves. Even worse, a misrecognition follows, in which our human pride exaggerates our virtues and underestimates our vices. Consider a few examples. First, contemplate how often a friend has relayed in confidence, "I am a good person," regardless what has been done. The very duty of being a friend means affirming the goodness of that person. So in the future, if somebody calls that goodness into doubt, the friend can say, "But all my friends tell me I'm a good person." Second, recall how we relay the events that led to the break-up of a friendship or a relationship. We tend to tell the story in such a way that almost all the guilt lies with the other person, and almost none lies with us. The inability to find fault in ourselves marks the excess of pride, the sin that overcame Adam and Eve in the garden. Calvin puts it succinctly: "For, because all of us are inclined by nature to hypocrisy, a kind of empty image of righteousness in place of righteousness itself abundantly satisfies us."[92] Without knowing God as creator and, more importantly, redeemer, we cannot come to recognize ourselves as sinners.

Calvin prioritizes God's glory in his theological vision. Much like Luther, he spurns any theological thinking that would credit or justify humans at the expense of God. If pride is the arch-sin, then Pelagianism—achieving one's own justification—is the arch-heresy. The proper

91. Calvin, *Institutes*, I, 1, 2 (37).
92. Calvin, *Institutes*, I, 1, 2 (37–38).

Christian religious attitude, or piety, demands giving God God's due: "For until men recognize that they owe everything to God, that they are nourished by his fatherly care, that he is the Author of their every good, that they should seek nothing beyond him—they will never yield him willing service."[93] Elsewhere he writes, "The awareness of [our condition after Adam's fall], when all our boasting and self-assurance are laid low, should truly humble us and overwhelm us with shame."[94] The Reformed tradition's attitude about the consequences of the fall has been crystallized into the phrase *total depravity*, often associated with the doctrinal synod at Dordt, in the Netherlands in 1618. Though Calvin himself never articulated the phrase "total depravity" as a doctrine or a confessional claim, it is not hard to conceive how the Reformed tradition connected this phrase with Calvin's theology. The *Institutes* declare: "We are so vitiated and perverted in every part of our nature that by this great corruption we stand justly condemned and convicted before God, to whom nothing is acceptable but righteousness, innocence, and purity."[95] Calvin rejects scholastic frameworks that distinguish the components of human nature corrupted from the fall. Total depravity means that every part of the human being was affected, as Calvin interprets the Apostle: "Paul removes all doubt when he teaches that corruption subsists not in one part only, but that none of the soul remains pure or untouched by that mortal disease."[96] It does not mean corruption beyond the point of recognition, as though the human faculties were no better than a dog's, but instead that the corruption extends into all parts of those faculties: One cannot say that the will is damaged, but the reasoning faculties remain the same.

One could render Calvin's thinking through the metaphor of performance. Before the fall, one could perform a duty like being an effective policeman. After the fall, one can still write tickets, drive a police car, work a speed gun, operate one's equipment, but the different functions do not come together to police effectively: A choleric temper

---

93. Calvin, *Institutes*, I, 2, 1 (41).
94. Calvin, *Institutes*, II, 1, 1 (242).
95. Calvin, *Institutes*, II, 1, 8 (251).
96. Calvin, *Institutes*, II, 1, 9 (253).

generates unpleasant interactions and poor judgments with citizens; the projecting of one's own sins and fears onto certain segments of the community leads to a heightened prejudice; lapses in memory and concentration portend an inability to solve cases; and general loss in company morale instigates abuse of alcohol or drugs. In short, the corruption after the fall involves a combination of factors through which performance lags.

In this way it is possible to comprehend how human reason functions after the fall. It is not eliminated, but it is, in the words of one commentator, "vicious."[97] Reason will not perform up to capacity unless it undergoes the redemption afforded through God's grace purchased on the cross. Reason, emotions, and desires do not integrate as intended by the creator. Instead, they are like ships passing in the night. Calvin considered medieval theology to be overly optimistic about human reasoning, and far too uncritical in appropriating philosophy. He describes the problem with philosophy as follows:

> Certainly I do not deny that one can read competent and apt statements about God here and there in the philosophers, but these always show a certain giddy imagination. As was stated above [Book I, 3, 1], the Lord indeed gave them a slight taste of his divinity that they might not hide their impiety under a cloak of ignorance. [. . .] But they saw things in such a way that their seeing did not direct them to the truth, much less enable them to attain it![98]

Absent the recovery of the knowledge of God whereby pride would wane and humility would wax, fallen human reason cannot perform the kind of tasks it wants to accomplish.

In his commentary on the *Acts of the Apostles*, Calvin offers a lengthy discourse on philosophy when discussing Paul's speech in Athens (Acts 17). Interpreting philosophy through the lens of pride, Calvin casts first-century Athens as a site of human folly rather than as a seat of human wisdom. According to Luke's account, Paul encountered Epicurean and Stoic philosophers, who brought him to the Are-

---

97. Waugh, "Calvin's Understanding of Human Reason," 8–12.
98. Calvin, *Institutes*, II, 2, 18 (277).

opagus (Acts 17:17–19). Calvin comments: "But just as we know what sort of religion springs from the human understanding, and that human wisdom is nothing else but a factory of all the errors, so let us realize that the Athenians, being intoxicated by their own pride, wandered from the truth more shamefully than the rest."[99] If you cannot be truly wise without coming to realize the urgent need for God, then any anthropocentric pursuit will not just fall short, it will enhance the error.[100] Referencing Paul's phrase in 1 Corinthians—*the world did not know God through wisdom* (1:21)—Calvin declares, "No one can be fit to learn the first principles of the Gospel, except the man who has first renounced that wisdom."[101] Such statements seem hostile to philosophy and to granting human reason a role in religious pursuit. It is best to read these passages through the lens of Calvin's understanding of pride, and especially how pride inhibits reason's capacity to fulfill the Delphic oracle.

In his speech at the Areopagus, Paul cites a Greek poet who declared, "For we are [God's] offspring" (Acts 17:28). Paul's usage of Greek poetry, paired with the metaphor of plundering the Egyptians, had traditionally served as the textual warrant for applying extra-Christian philosophy to theology. Calvin explicitly rejects this analogy, as it had been applied in the schools: "The method of the Papists is far different. For they are so dependent on the testimonies of men that they place them over against the oracles of God. [. . .] Yes, and what is more, they have not been afraid to give so much authority to Aristotle that, compared with him, the apostles and prophets were silent in the schools." In *Acts*, Paul confronts the errors of pagan thinking, and contrasts the gospel with worldly wisdom. In Calvin's interpretation of pre-Reformation Christianity, theologians made the gospel subservient to worldly wisdom, thereby distorting, not applying, the biblical model for relating faith to reason. Calvin litters the *Institutes* with attacks on "the Schoolmen," and most frequently Peter Lombard, for

---

99. Calvin, *The Acts of the Apostles 14–28*, trans. John Fraser (Grand Rapids, MI: Eerdmans, 1965), 104.

100. As one commentator puts it, "The greater the learning of these lovers-of-wisdom the greater is their foolishness" (Waugh, "Calvin's Understanding of Human Reason," 8).

101. Calvin, *The Acts of the Apostles 14–28*, 107.

distorting the faith. Writing almost half a century after Erasmus's *Praise of Folly* and forty years after Luther's 1517 attacks on scholasticism, Calvin integrated what had by his time become a familiar anti-scholastic trope into his systematic theology of piety.

In contrasting the understanding gained through faith with that of reason, Calvin tends to emphasize certain affective qualities of the former. One of the longest chapters in the *Institutes* is the chapter on faith.[102] In the middle of this chapter, Calvin discusses the nature of this understanding: "For as faith is not content with a doubtful and changeable opinion, so it is not content with an obscure and confused conception; but requires full and fixed certainty, such as men are wont to have from things experienced and proved."[103] This certainty serves as the effect of the grace that yields faith. Calvin highlights the passages in the Pauline epistles that talk about the assurance and confidence that come from accepting Christ. Whatever uncertainty or doubt believers experience, says Calvin, comes not from the complexity of the life of faith, but from their own persistent unbelief. While discussing doubt, Calvin asks and answers the obvious question: "But if in the believing mind certainty is mixed with doubt, do we not always come back to this, that faith does not rest in a certain and clear knowledge, but only in an obscure and confused knowledge of the divine will toward us? Not at all."[104] For Calvin, faith implies an assurance, and therefore occupies a higher status than truths gained through alternative means: "Faith is much higher than human understanding. And it will not be enough for the mind to be illumined by the Spirit of God unless the heart is also strengthened and supported by his power. In this matter the Schoolmen go completely astray, who in considering faith identify it with a bare and simple assent arising out of knowledge, and leave out confidence and assurance of heart."[105] Calvin's concern with the subjective/affective standard for knowledge also extends to his commentary on *Acts*, where he contrasts the uncertainty of the Athenians with the confidence of Christians: "Moreover whoever worships God with-

---

102. Calvin, *Institutes*, III, 2, 1–43 (542–92).
103. Calvin, *Institutes*, III, 2, 15 (41).
104. Calvin, *Institutes*, III, 2, 18 (564).
105. Calvin, *Institutes*, III, 2, 33 (581).

out any certitude is merely worshipping his own fabrications in the place of God. [. . .] Therefore, we see how wretched is the lot of those who do not possess the certain light of the truth, because they are always restless in themselves, and labour in vain in the sight of God."[106] If faith provides the certainty, then it is not immediately obvious what would be gained by seeking additional understanding, which had been an important goal for medieval theology.[107]

Historians of ideas usually associate the quest for certainty with Descartes, who would lay out these ideas in his *Meditations* a full half century after Calvin's *Institutes*. Yet in reading Calvin and the other Reformers treated in this chapter, they sound more modern than their medieval predecessors. This sense comes from a renewed emphasis on interiority and the subjective difference between faith and other modes of knowing. In a previously cited article, Robert Scharlemann located in Luther and other Reformation figures the seeds of Kant's subsequent division between faith and reason.[108] The point here is not to find the cause or the roots of later secular philosophy in the Reformers, especially Calvin. Up to now this essay has intentionally avoided overly determined readings of intellectual history. As detailed above, some theological currents in post-Reformation theology tended toward developing a new scholasticism. Other developments, like pietism, tended to give even more attention to the subjective side of belief. The sixteenth-century reformers treated above—Erasmus, Luther, Melanchthon, and Calvin—helped make that possible. But before turning to that development, a cursory glance at important movements in sixteenth-century Catholicism will help round out the current chapter and prepare for what is to come.

---

106. Calvin, *The Acts of the Apostles 14–28*, 110.

107. Dewey Hoitenga writes, "When Calvin defines *faith* as knowledge, he is not really introducing a brand new kind of knowledge into the world but emphasizing the certainty of the content of Christian belief, certainty which is based on the authority of God who speaks in Scripture" (Hoitenga, *Faith and Reason from Plato to Plantinga*, 149).

108. Scharlemann, "Theology in Church and University" 32: "The post-Reformation development of the distinction in theology [. . .] also provided the basic impulse for Kantian critical philosophy (which elaborates the conviction that the intuitive reason cannot transcend finite reality)."

CATHOLIC REFORMERS: IGNATIUS OF LOYOLA

One can mention at this point some important historical movements, especially from the Catholic side, that impacted the development of theology. First, the missionary movements that accompanied the great age of exploration, which made Catholicism truly
global. Second, the growth in natural sciences and the influence of
the humanists, which radically destabilized university life. Third, the
Council of Trent (1545–63), whose calls for reform took at least a
century to implement. Fourth, a boom in religious orders—including the rise of several important orders for women.[109] These orders
provided intellectual leadership, renewed lived Catholicism, and
created new institutions while reviving existing ones. Most prominent among these orders was the Society of Jesus, founded by Ignatius of Loyola (1491–1556). A brief engagement with Ignatius will
allow us to move onto the proper beginnings of modernity, but first
a few words about labels.

These Catholic reform efforts are often grouped under the head-
ing "The Counter Reformation," but this label itself poses problems.[110]
It indicates that Catholic reform efforts during the century operated
in a reactive mode to Protestant initiatives, which additionally implies
that reform efforts were absent before 1517. Yet Ignatius' biography
calls this narrative into question. In comparison with a later Spanish
Catholic reformer, Teresa of Ávila (1515–82), who invokes the dangers
of Protestantism in the opening of *The Life of Perfection* (c. 1565),
Ignatius almost never mentions the looming threat of Protestantism.
Indeed, one could read the *Spiritual Exercises* and his *Autobiography*
and have no idea that European Christianity was in turmoil. When
the Spanish Dominicans in Salamanca confronted Ignatius about his
street preaching in 1527, the only dangerous thinker mentioned was

---

109. The two most important were the Ursulines and the Discalced Carmelites,
founded by Teresa of Avila. The Ursulines placed a great value on education, eventually
opening the oldest girls' school in the United States, and giving the Louisiana-territory its
first female pharmacist.

110. For a helpful essay on jettisoning "Counter Reformation" and replacing it with
"Early Modern Catholicism," see John O'Malley, *Trent and all That: Renaming Catholicism
in the Early Modern Era* (Cambridge: Harvard University Press, 2000).

Erasmus, not Luther or Melanchthon.[111] From Salamanca Ignatius walked to Paris, where he lived for eight years and studied for a time in the same college as John Calvin, although there is no record of the two meeting.

First in Spain, and then in Paris, Ignatius had been honing a method of prayer that would form the basis of what became known as "Ignatian spirituality." He convinced some of his dorm mates, including future Jesuit saints Francis Xavier and Peter Favre, to perform these exercises. Ignatius eventually decided to form the "Society of Jesus," which received papal approval in 1540. At the heart of the Society lay the Exercises. These exercises cultivated an intensely interior form of Christianity, in which one could have direct access to God through prayer. This method corresponded more to the modern consciousness and social horizon, in which people began to experience privacy, and socio-economic changes made private reading more of a reality. By means of reading the Bible and of private, meditative prayer, one could encounter God directly. This raised suspicion in the eyes of those accustomed to thinking about divine encounter in a more traditional, sacramental manner. During his run-in with the Spanish Inquisition in Salamanca, there is no record of Ignatius wanting to leave the Catholic Church, but his hallmark spiritual achievement seems to overlap in certain ways with what was associated with a more Protestant, individualized practice. Seen another way, Ignatius' spiritual method undercut the heart of the Protestant critique: Catholicism insists that the Church mediate, in a particularly public and impersonal manner, one's relationship to Christ.

The "Second Prelude" in the First Exercise of the First Week of the *Exercises* gives the following imperative: "to ask God our Lord for what I want and desire,"[112] which happens by contemplating different gospel episodes from the life of Christ. In the process of doing these exercises, the retreatant should not only shed many tears, but also experience

---

111. Ignatius, "The Autobiography," in *Ignatius of Loyola: The Spiritual Exercises and Selected Works*, ed. George Ganss (New York: Paulist, 1991), 96: "The friar insisted, 'Well, now that there are so many errors of Erasmus and of so many others who have deceived the world, you do not wish to explain what you say.'"

112. Ignatius, "The Spiritual Exercises," in *Ignatius of Loyola: The Spiritual Exercises and Selected Works*, 136.

consolation and desolation appropriate to the particular exercise, such as contemplating how one's sins put Christ on the cross, or how God dwells in all things. Alongside these Exercises, Ignatius presumed that the retreatant would make confession and attend mass, but the program of prayer is intensely personal, and the idea was that the authentic Christian message would be received one person at a time.

Despite developing a method of prayer tied so closely to the affections, and creating a group of followers known for their missionary zeal, Ignatius became a legendary founder of institutions, especially educational institutions. One chronicler notes, "Between 1547 and 1556 [Ignatius] opened thirty-three colleges and approved six more."[113] Over the next two centuries these numbers multiplied exponentially, with the Jesuits having founded over six hundred new colleges by the early eighteenth century.[114] Despite his own conversion being more affective than intellectual, Ignatius did not conceive of the life of the mind in opposition to the movements of the heart.

Like their Protestant counterparts, early modern Catholics had to confront a number of perceived tensions, including those between: (1) a personal encounter with the Lord and a need to understand the truths of faith intellectually; (2) scholastic and humanistic models of education; (3) the secular success of educational institutions and their religious and missionary roots. One finds all of these tensions at work in *The Constitutions of the Society of Jesus*, written shortly before Ignatius died.

The fourth chapter of *The Constitutions* tackles education and gives a framework to ensure that Jesuit colleges and universities, spreading from Europe, to India, to the Americas, would form their students with a similar, if not identical, ethos. Four points are worth mentioning. First, *The Constitutions* integrate the educational task with the saving of souls. At several points the text mentions that the end of study is helping souls.[115] Young members of the Society would

---

113. "Introduction," in *Ignatius of Loyola: The Spiritual Exercises and Selected Works*, 278.

114. "General Introduction," in *Ignatius of Loyola: The Spiritual Exercises and Selected Works*, 49.

115. *The Constitutions of the Society of Jesus and their Complementary Norms*, ed. John Padberg (Saint Louis: The Institute of Jesuit Sources, 1996), 307, 351.

need a sound education to work effectively in the Lord's vineyard. Second, the experience undergone in the *Exercises* would spread to these institutions. Scholastics—young Jesuits in training—would learn to use this method of prayer as a "spiritual weapon." The text expounds: "Their explanation of the Exercises should be such that it not only satisfies people but also moves them to a desire to take advantage of the Exercises."[116] Although *The Constitutions* distinguish between the life of prayer and of study, they do not separate them. Third, *The Constitutions* mandate the study of Aristotle. They recommend both Aquinas and Peter Lombard's *Sentences* as texts for the theological curriculum: "In theology there should be lectures on the Old and New Testaments and on the scholastic doctrine of St. Thomas. [. . .] The Master of the Sentences will also be lectured on."[117] Though a new order with a dynamic new form of spirituality, the Jesuits did not want to abandon or ignore the medieval theological legacy. This extended to the use of Aristotle as well: "In logic, natural and moral philosophy, and metaphysics, the doctrine of Aristotle should be followed, as also in the other liberal arts."[118] Whatever blows the humanists delivered to Aristotelian scholasticism, they were not fatal, as evidenced by the continued use of Aristotle by this fast-growing educational program. Fourth, despite continued allegiance to scholasticism, the Jesuits appreciated and appropriated the humanists' critique and contribution. *The Constitutions* confirm the value of learning languages besides Latin, especially in order to read the Bible in the original. They also criticize scholasticism for its dry formality: "Similarly, [scholastics] will exercise themselves in preaching and delivering lectures in a manner suited to the edification of the people, which is different from the scholastic manner."[119] As *The Constitutions* imagined it, scholasticism and humanism need not be mutually exclusive in Jesuit schools.

This brief nod to the Jesuit impact on early modern Christianity, especially in regard to the challenges faced by Catholic educational

---

116. *The Constitutions of the Society of Jesus*, 408, 409.
117. *The Constitutions of the Society of Jesus*, 464–66.
118. *The Constitutions of the Society of Jesus*, 470.
119. *The Constitutions of the Society of Jesus*, 402; see *The Constitutions of the Society of Jesus*, 367, 447 for the need for Greek and Hebrew.

institutions, hardly does justice to the Catholic thought of the period, or even to the Jesuit thought. Indeed, perhaps the two greatest early modern Catholic theologians, Francisco Suarez and Robert Bellarmine, were both Jesuits, and both developed sophisticated articulations of the rationality of faith. Instead, it merely gestures to the reality that both Catholics and Protestants were dealing with the tension between a growing realization that Christianity had to be authentically appropriated through an encounter with Christ, and yet it also had to provide intelligent answers to the questions of the day. The next chapter traces this out, both by following the tension, especially within the Lutheran trajectory, between the head and the heart, and also by chronicling the challenges presented by modern scientific discovery and philosophy.

Chapter 5

Early Modernity and the Separation of Faith from Reason

This chapter visits a handful of events, movements, and figures emblematic of and causative to what became an increasingly reified—at least in the minds of many leading theologians—gulf between faith and various secular modes of knowing, in particular natural science and philosophy. Amidst exploration, colonization, "wars of religion,"[1] and the birth of modern science, the Western churches required a theology nimble enough to respond to various events of the day and to the reshaping of the sociology of knowledge. The diversity of theological approaches voiced during these centuries is astounding, yet no period of theology is more under-explored than this one. The aim is not to remedy that situation, but instead to examine a few of the episodes that shaped how theology imagined the relationship between faith and reason in this period.

SITUATING GALILEO

When Nicolaus Copernicus (1473–1543) published a book that argued for heliocentrism, it hardly caused a stir. Indeed, although the Council of Trent met from 1545–63, and found time to comment on a number of pressing issues, it did not utter a word against Copernicus. This changed with Galileo (1564–1643), whose condemnation stands as a black mark against the Catholic Church. The figure of Galileo, whispering his conviction of heliocentrism in a theocratic Italian court, represents in the minds of many modern people their image of

---

1. See William Cavanaugh, *The Myth of Religious Violence* (Oxford: Oxford University Press, 2009), 123–80.

an intrinsic conflict between faith and science, dogma and free enquiry, medieval justice and modern values. As numerous scholars have shown, however, the Galileo trial was largely an anomaly in the history of Catholicism. In the early modern period, it was far more common for religious institutions, especially the Catholic Church, to embrace with zeal the latest scientific discoveries, which by and large confirmed their worldview. Nowhere was this more apparent than in the case of Isaac Newton, whose system of mechanics seemed to confirm an unmoved mover.[2] The antagonism between religion and science became a more definite marker in the nineteenth and twentieth centuries, and it would be anachronistic to read that battle back into the seventeenth century.[3] With regard to the popular rendering of the conflict between Galileo and the magisterial authorities, prefiguring later ecclesial opposition to Darwin, Freud, and others, one respected commentator notes, "This reading of Galileo's conflict with the Catholic Church is wrong. Not *entirely* wrong, of course, since cosmological issues were obviously involved in the opposition to Galileo on the part of the Roman Curia, but substantially wrong nonetheless."[4]

Early modernity was not the first occasion for conflict between science and religion. Already in the third and fourth centuries, such authors as Origen and Augustine recognized certain incompatibilities between some scientific theories and biblical accounts of the natural world. These two theologians cautioned against reading Scripture literally with the aim of discerning highly technical theories about cosmological or biological truths. In *De Genesi Ad Litteram* (*On the Literal Meaning of Genesis*), Augustine writes,

> It is also frequently asked what our belief must be about the form and shape of heaven according to Sacred Scripture. Many scholars

---

2. For a groundbreaking study of theological responses to Newton, see Michael J. Buckley, *At the Origins of Modern Atheism* (New Haven, CT: Yale University Press, 1987). See also Michael J. Buckley, *Denying and Disclosing God: The Ambiguous Progress of Modern Atheism* (New Haven, CT: Yale University Press, 2004).

3. For this point see Peter Harrison, *The Territories of Science and Religion* (Chicago: University of Chicago Press, 2015).

4. Ernan McMullin, "Galileo on Science and Scripture," in *The Cambridge Companion to Galileo*, ed. Peter Machamer (Cambridge: Cambridge University Press, 1998), 271–347, at 272.

engage in lengthy discussions on these matters, but the sacred writers with their deeper wisdom have omitted them. Such subjects are of no profit for those who seek beatitude, and, what is worse, they take up very precious time that ought to be given to what is spiritually beneficial.[5]

Augustine not only considered such activities a waste of time and a distraction from the proper pastoral duties, but he also declared that they could undermine a believer's faith:

But the credibility of Scripture is at stake, and as I have indicated more than once, there is danger that a man uninstructed in divine revelation, discovering something in Scripture or hearing it from something that seems to be at variance with the knowledge he has acquired, may resolutely withhold his assent in other matters where Scripture presents useful admonitions, narratives or declarations. Hence, I must say briefly that in the matter of the shape of heaven the sacred writers knew the truth, but that the Spirit of God, who spoke through them, did not wish to teach men these facts that would be of no avail for their salvation.[6]

Augustine asserts that the Bible avoids cosmological truths because they do not relate directly to matters of salvation, the real topic of the Bible. And if somebody wants the Bible to tell us about evolution, or to provide the date on which the universe came into existence, she faces disappointment, for the Bible exists to instruct us in our salvation, not in matters unrelated to our salvation. Somewhere in the Galileo controversy, however, Augustine's warning was lost.

At certain milestones of the nearly two-decade long debate— roughly 1613 to 1633, the year Galileo was condemned—Galileo sought to retrieve these earlier arguments. When first challenged that

---

5. Augustine, *De Genesi Ad Litteram*, book II, chapter 9; cited from *The Literal Meaning of Genesis*, trans. John Hammond Taylor, vol. 1 (New York: Paulist, 1982), 58–59. It may be helpful to remember that when Augustine practices a "literal" reading of Scripture, it means only a scrupulous attention to the words on the page, not a commitment to interpret in the literal sense of a modern-day fundamentalist. For more on this point, see David Bentley Hart, "Ad Litteram," in *A Splendid Wickedness and Other Essays* (Grand Rapids, MI: Eerdmans, 2016), 274–77.

6. Augustine, *The Literal Meaning of Genesis*, vol. 1, 59.

his books *The Starry Messenger* (1610) and *Sunspot Letters* (1613) contradicted the biblical viewpoint, Galileo wrote a letter to Princess Christina of Tuscany, his former pupil.[7] In contemplating how to defend his support of Copernicus, Galileo asked a priest friend to supply him with some theological ammunition that would quiet challengers. His friend obliged him in 1615, and Galileo used this ammunition in his *Letter to the Grand Duchess of Tuscany*.[8] In this text Galileo defends himself against his theological detractors, especially against the claim that his findings "go against the Bible." It is worth noting how theologically Galileo argued against his attackers: "It is most pious to say and most prudent to take for granted that Holy Scripture can never lie, as long as its true meaning has been grasped; but I do not think one can deny that this is frequently recondite and very different from what appears to be the literal meaning of the words."[9] Here Galileo sounds more like an early Christian theologian than a New Atheist. Just as it would be wrong to say that God is a large creature because Scripture talks about God's hands, so too it would be wrong to interpret passages about the sun standing still to mean that the Bible teaches geocentrism. Echoing Augustine, Galileo declares that the Bible was written for salvific, not scientific purposes. Therefore, one should not turn to it, and against reason and experience, to establish geological or biological positions, "which are very remote from popular understanding and not at all pertinent to the primary purpose of the Holy Writ, that is, to the worship of God and the salvation of souls."[10] Scripture does not seek to answer questions under the domain of natural science. Therefore, natural scientists should be able to use their God-given reason in order to pursue these questions: "So it seems that a natural phenomenon which is placed before our eyes by sensory experience or proved by necessary demonstrations should not be called into question, let alone condemned, on account of scriptural passages whose words appear to have

---

7. For a reliable guide to these events, see Maurice Finocchiaro, "Introduction," in *The Galileo Affair: A Documentary History*, ed. Maurice Finocchiaro (Berkeley: University of California, 1989), 1–43.

8. For an accessible version, see Galileo, "Galileo's Letter to the Grand Duchess Christina," in *The Galileo Affair*, 87–118.

9. "Galileo's Letter to the Grand Duchess Christina," 92.

10. "Galileo's Letter to the Grand Duchess Christina," 93.

a different meaning." As long as theology's (and cosmology's) area of concern is properly marked, there is no need for a turf war. Scripture and natural science can be complementary, but only if natural scientists are free to pursue answers to questions by means of the tools proper to natural science, for which the correct, non-literalist biblical hermeneutic is required.

Galileo thought he could win the argument on terms that theologians would accept. He cited a letter from Augustine on just this point:

> For if reason be found contradicting the authority of Divine Scriptures, it only deceives by a semblance of truth, however acute it be, for its deductions cannot in that case be true. On the other hand, if, against the most manifest and reliable testimony of reason, anything be set up claiming to have the authority of the Holy Scriptures, he who does this does it through a misapprehension of what he has read, and is setting up against the truth not the real meaning of Scripture, which he has failed to discover, but an opinion of his own; he alleges not what he has found in the Scriptures, but what he has found in himself as their interpreter.[11]

Quite justly, Galileo takes this to mean that, if heliocentrism proves itself to fall under the category of "reliable testimony of reason," then theologians might just have it wrong. Theologians, as well as practitioners of other disciplines, have methods for attaining their truths, and these methods might be right- or wrong-headed; alchemy, for instance, may turn out to be an illegitimate discipline. But whatever truths theologians arrive at truthfully cannot, logically speaking, contradict any other discipline. Galileo writes, "Two truths cannot contradict one another."[12] Galileo's theological opponents thought they had stumbled across a contradiction, but this only arose from their inadequate and narrow principles for interpreting Scripture.

Galileo's claim that truths cannot contradict had already been affirmed at the Fifth Lateran Council in 1513: "truth cannot contra-

---

11. Augustine, *Letter 143*, in *NPNF*, vol. 1, 492, cited in "Galileo's Letter to the Grand Duchess Christina," 96.

12. "Galileo's Letter to the Grand Duchess Christina," 96.

dict truth."[13] Galileo thought his critics were overstepping their bounds. At least in his argument to the Grand Duchess, Galileo respected religious authority to proclaim on matters related to religion. He affirms the magisterial authority of theology, but he says it has its limits: "I cannot deny having some qualms, which I consequently wish could be removed; for in disputes about natural phenomena they seem to claim the right to force others by means of the authority of Scripture to follow the opinion they think is most in accordance with its statements." Galileo continues, "They say that theology is the queen of all the sciences and hence must not in any way lower herself to accommodate the principles of other less dignified disciplines subordinate to her; rather, these others must submit to her as to a supreme empress."[14] To this level Galileo would not stoop, and on this point it is easy to sympathize with Galileo. As the controversy would develop, Galileo was not without error, especially regarding the demonstrative value of sunspots and tidal movements for heliocentrism.[15] But Galileo's admirable attempt to forge a workable truce between theology and the natural sciences has too often been overlooked.

If the case of Galileo does not support an argument for the incompatibility of science and religion, then what function does it have for our current purposes? It would seem that the previous citation provides a clue. The Galileo affair symbolizes, and also portends, a shifting architectonic of knowledge in early modern Christianity. The humanist critique of scholasticism, described in detail in the previous chapter, captured two different approaches to theology. Medieval universities from the outset made a place for natural philosophy, but they could not imagine the advances that these disciplines would make when scientists began applying mathematics to empirical observation. Aristotle, no less than Darwin, was a tireless observer of nature, and the medieval period, with Aristotle serving as the model scientist, oversaw an explosion of new inventions that transformed society. Yet nobody could have predicted how technological advances like the telescope

13. Denzinger, 1441.
14. "Galileo's Letter to the Grand Duchess Christina," 99.
15. For this point see Buckley, *Denying and Disclosing God*, 3–10.

would fundamentally alter the capacity of reason and observation to fuel an unprecedented knowledge explosion.

In my one and only dinner with a billionaire, he asked a question to his theologian dinner guests: what counts as progress in theology? The question was sincere, and the billionaire in question studied and values the humanities. Like law, the advances in theology are less easily marked. Biology can find the cure to different diseases, and physics can construct experiments that lead to new technologies and inventions. Yet theology advances often through reading and reinterpreting sacred texts, or applying ethical theories like the just war theory to new situations. It is not a discipline that regards discovery as the goal. Almost no discipline before the sixteenth century thought the point of science was to make discoveries. Instead, it was to understand the principles of the discipline, and their connection to other disciplines. Yet by the time of Galileo and Kepler, natural sciences were making discoveries, and many of these discoveries challenged or even seemed to undermine settled truths about the world. This caused many disciplines to lose their footing, and it also set the trajectory for replacing the medieval university with the modern one.

FROM HANDMAIDEN TO RIVAL: PHILOSOPHY'S EARLY MODERN SEPARATION

If the natural sciences seemed to emerge out of nowhere as a rival to theology, philosophy's rebellion against theology was easier to predict. Throughout the history of Christian theology distinctions have been made between faith and reason, secular and sacred. Gradually these distinctions came to seem like divisions. Modern philosophy forged its identity in large part by distinguishing its method and first principles from those of theology. Though the figure most closely associated with this separation is René Descartes (1596–1650), Baruch Spinoza (1632–77) also came to a similar conclusion about philosophy's relation to theology through means quite distinct from Descartes's. It will be helpful to review these two figures to locate the origins of certain modern modes of thinking that have become permanent features of the modern landscape. When these modes of thinking become habitual, it is almost impossible for faith and reason *not* to end in conflict.

Descartes

Already in the medieval period, leading lights distinguished clearly between proceeding from revealed truths and proceeding from truths known through reason. As shown above, no less a figure than Aquinas made a distinction between what could be known by reason and what could be known by revelation. Yet on the heels of major scientific breakthroughs, especially those of Galileo, seventeenth-century thinkers began to formulate an even sharper distinction that would become a separation of reason from faith. In part, this happened because reason came to be understood as autonomous, carrying out its activities in a natural arena sealed off from the supernatural.

Reaching maturity just when the Thirty Years' War (1618–48) was getting underway, and a few years after the shocking regicide of Henry IV in 1611, Descartes's abstract philosophical concerns did not arise in a vacuum. The theological failure to peacefully resolve sixteenth-century disputes, or at least to bracket these disputes for the sake of political tranquility, led to a loss of prestige for the queen of sciences. Remarking on this setting, the noted historian of philosophy Stephen Toulmin connects the political unrest to the purportedly abstract and a-political project of Descartes: "Living in a time of high theological passion, the only other thing thinking people could do was to look for a new way of establishing their central truths and ideas: one that was independent of, and neutral between, particular religious loyalties."[16] After his 1637 *Discourse on Method*, Descartes penned the *Meditations on First Philosophy* in 1641. These two short texts mark the modern turn that would value universality over particularity, certainty over skepticism, and theory over practice. They would also initiate the separation of philosophy from theology, a step that Descartes justifies even though it is not at all

16. Stephen Toulmin, *Cosmopolis: The Hidden Agenda of Modernity* (Chicago: The University of Chicago Press, 1990), 70. On the same page Toulmin continues: "As matters stood, there was no alternative to circumventing the theological dogmatists, by arguing in their own idiom—the idiom of *certainty*."

"The 17th-century philosophers' 'Quest for Certainty' was no mere proposal to construct abstract and timeless intellectual schemas, dreamed up as objects of pure, detached intellectual study. Instead it was a timely response to a specific historical challenge—the political, social, and theological chaos embodied in the Thirty Years' War" (Toulmin, *Cosmopolis*, 70).

obvious he would favor shutting out theology from the secular academy, as happened in the West in subsequent centuries.

In an attempt to correct a misunderstanding conveyed in his *Discourse on Method*, Descartes opens the *Meditations* with a letter to the faculty of theology at Paris.[17] Here he argues that the existence of God and the human soul "ought to be demonstrated with the aid of philosophy rather than theology."[18] Descartes points out that doubters and unbelievers cannot be convinced on the authority of the Bible that God exists, for the authority of the Bible depends on belief in its divine authorship. Descartes wants the freedom to do this, and gives a seemingly straightforward reasoning for his request: Theologians themselves "affirm that one can prove the existence of God by natural reason,"[19] a point affirmed in chapters 2 and 3 (though one can ask whether Descartes meant the same thing by *ratio naturalis* that an Anselm or an Aquinas might have meant). The novelty of the project does not have to do with subject or conclusion—here he rightly regards himself as echoing past theological arguments affirming the existence of the soul through natural reason. The novelty, however, lies with the method. Descartes explains why he applied a new method to philosophy: "I was strongly urged to do this by some people who knew that I had developed a method for solving all sorts of problems in the sciences."[20] Only this method would produce a true *demonstration*, the highest form of proof in scholastic thought. Descartes writes, "I now make bold to propose these as most certain and evident demonstrations [. . .] that even surpass those of geometry in certitude and obviousness."[21] Descartes suffers from what some in the humanities call *science-envy*. He wants other fields to generate the same results as science, and to bring this about he applies a universal method to areas of study that traditionally used other methods.

17. Here and below I cite from the English edition, René Descartes, *Discourse on Method and Meditations on First Philosophy*, 3rd ed., trans. Donald Cress (Indianapolis: Hackett, 1993). For the Latin I have consulted an online edition: http://www.thelatinlibrary.com/des.html.

18. Descartes, *Meditations*, 47.

19. Descartes, *Meditations*, 47.

20. Descartes, *Meditations*, 48.

21. Descartes, *Meditations*, 48–49.

Descartes implements his method in six "meditations" or reflections on God and the soul. These meditations recall the project of Anselm by asking the reader to walk through a series of thought exercises that delimit normal modes of enquiry. For Anselm, this meant thinking about God absent any revealed data. For Descartes these exercises serve to try on methodological doubt, including doubt of the senses. Contrary to some critics who want to make Descartes the willing precursor to all skepticism and atheism, the *Meditations* make Descartes no more a skeptic than the *Proslogion* makes Anselm a denier of the Bible. On the contrary, one can fairly ask whether Descartes's *Meditations* could have been written for spiritual edification.[22]

The *Meditations* lay out what Descartes intended to do: "begin again from the original foundations" so as to replace false opinions with truths that could be "firm and lasting," which means withholding assent from anything unless it can be known as "certain and indubitable."[23] The first idol to fall in Descartes's meditation exercise are the senses. We observe a sun sink below the ocean and we believe it to be moving. But it stands still. We look at an object on a desk and it appears static. But it moves, both as part of a constantly rotating earth, and on the atomic level, where electrons race around a proton. The contrast between observation and scientific reality means that the senses deceive. The second idol is the presumption of God's goodness. In the first "Meditation" Descartes supposes that God, rather than being good, is a *genius malignus*, an "evil genius" who aims to deceive creatures. Descartes eventually affirms God's existence and God's goodness, but does not presuppose these attributes during the meditative exercise of radical doubt.

If we put ourselves in an ocean of radical doubt, what is the nearest island of certainty we can find? In walking his readers through these mental exercises, Descartes invites his readers to perform a number of exercises: Thinking of a ball of wax in order to strip away

22. Pierre Hadot takes this line of argument in *Philosophy as a Way of Life*, trans. Michael Chase (Malden, MA: Blackwell, 1995), 271: "It was no accident that Descartes entitled one of his works *Meditations*. They are indeed meditations—*meditatio* in the sense of exercise—and [. . .] Descartes recommends that they be practiced over a certain period of time."

23. Descartes, *Meditations*, 59.

all imagined properties; conceiving of oneself as a thinking subject (*cogito ergo sum*). Through these exercises one learns that the intellect, rather than the senses or the imagination, offers the most reliable path to understanding: "[Objects] are not perceived through their being touched or seen, but only through their being understood."[24] This same method results in the discovery, in the Third Meditation, that God necessarily exists as first cause. Through these exercises the human mind is able to generate certainty that satisfies personal doubts. These exercises also convince unbelievers of the basic questions about God and the soul.

It is easy to exaggerate the differences between Descartes and his medieval precursors if one does not keep in mind other differences between the seventeenth century and the thirteenth, or the eleventh. Descartes was a peripatetic intellectual, but also detached from any religious order or clerical vow. The shift from a feudal economy to a more modern economy allowed for a growing percentage of the population to work outside ecclesial settings. In the wake of the dispute between humanists and scholastics, it also meant that aspiring intellectuals could follow diverse paths to find an education. Anselm wrote for monks, and Bonaventure wrote for friars confronting a "secular" space of learning still entirely controlled by the Church. Descartes wrote for an entirely different audience. As intellectuals began to inhabit physical and imagined space not formally encompassed by churches—and here the new, post-Reformation plurality of ecclesial authority in Western Europe surely hampered the task of presenting a united front—they began to conceive of reason detached from participation in the mind of God. This detachment is hard to trace, but Descartes, whether he intended or not, and whether he thought this way or not—paved the way for modern, "autonomous" reason. Bringing faith and reason back into union would become either a central goal or a fool's errand for theologians that followed. Before turning to them, it will be helpful to chart how the most important philosopher in the second half of the seventeenth century navigated these waters.

---

24. Descartes, *Meditations*, 69.

Spinoza

If Descartes was only marginally connected to mainstream European institutions of learning, Spinoza was as far away from them as possible. Born into a family of Jewish *conversos* from Spain that had fled to Amsterdam—*Spinoza* is just the Germanized version of *Espinosa*—Spinoza began entertaining doubts at an early age about Jewish metaphysics and the status of the biblical books. At the age of twenty-four, Spinoza was excommunicated from the Amsterdam synagogue, never to return. Neither Jewish nor Christian, Spinoza can rightly be called the first secular European. He continued his "underground" education and eventually located to The Hague, where he ground lenses and philosophized in his free time. His greatest philosophical work was his *Ethics*, which challenged Cartesian dualism by replacing it with a monism. Yet for our purposes we will focus on his 1670 *Theological-Political Treatise*, one of the first and best-known repudiations of revealed religion and the Bible. In the words of one commentator, "No one else during the century 1650–1750 remotely rivalled Spinoza's notoriety as the chief challenger of the fundamentals of revealed religion, received ideas, tradition, morality, and [. . .] divinely constituted political authority."[25]

The *Theological-Political Treatise* challenged the fundamentals of revealed religion to devastating effect. In chapter 7, Spinoza employs a two-pronged attack, not so much on the Bible, but on traditional approaches to interpreting the Bible. This attack is central in his move to separate faith from reason. The first prong is Spinoza's insistence that the interpretation of Scripture follow the rules for interpreting nature. Spinoza writes, "the method of interpreting Scripture is no different from the method of interpreting Nature. [. . .] For the method of interpreting Nature consists essentially in composing a detailed study of Nature from which, as being the source of our assured data, we can deduce the definitions of the things of Nature."[26] Spinoza here

---

25. For a recovery of Spinoza's centrality to the true, "radical" Enlightenment, see Jonathan Israel, *Radical Enlightenment: Philosophy and the Making of Modernity 1650–1750* (Oxford: Oxford University Press, 2001), cited here at 159.

26. Spinoza, *Theological-Political Treatise*, trans. Samuel Shirley (Indianapolis: Hackett, [1991] 1998), 89.

does not propose a proto-rationalist method that would dissolve the miracles in Scripture. His approach is more akin to structuralism. Scripture has its own language-world, and only from inside this world can its intelligibility be apprehended. Just as nature can only be known by looking at nature, as opposed to, say, imposing an outside theory on it, so too Scripture is only known from internal investigation. Within it, miracles, signs, and historical narratives have their own intelligibility. Spinoza concludes, "Therefore knowledge [. . .] of almost all the contents of Scripture must be sought from Scripture alone, just as knowledge of Nature must be sought from Nature itself."[27]

The second prong relates to the first, and is almost indistinguishable from it, but concerns the role of confessional identity and interpretation. Spinoza's critique sets its sights on post-Reformation controversy. Take a question like the real presence of the Eucharist. Once the dust settled in the first generations after Luther, the Western churches articulated a variety of doctrinal positions on beliefs like Eucharistic presence. Theologians representing the different churches took on the task of demonstrating how the biblical texts supported their church's position on topics ranging from church polity to Trinitarian theology. Instead of moving from Scripture to confession, the churches moved from creed and confession to Scripture. One can practically feel the effect of religious strife in Spinoza's diagnosis:

> Now if men were really sincere in what they profess with regard to Holy Scripture, they would conduct themselves quite differently, they would not be racked by so much quarrelling and such bitter feuding, and they would not be gripped by this blind and passionate desire to interpret Scripture and to introduce innovations in religion. On the contrary, they would never venture to accept as Scriptural doctrine what was not most clearly taught by Scripture itself.[28]

In Spinoza's rendering, churches do not teach people how to read the Bible correctly. Instead, they contort the Bible so that it corresponds to their preconceived notions: "To make Scripture appear more won-

---

27. Spinoza, *Theological-Political Treatise*, 90. It should be added that Spinoza modifies his method when he shifts from the historical to the prophetic writings.

28. Spinoza, *Theological-Political Treatise*, 88.

derful and awe-inspiring, they endeavor to explicate it in such a way that it seems diametrically opposed both to reason and to Nature."[29] Spinoza's argument results in clear interpretive norms: One should replace confessional forms of scriptural reading with a free-thinking style in accord with reason.

The Spinoza of the *Theological-Political Treatise* is anything but a rationalist, as he does not demand that Scripture conform to the canons of modern rationality, or that miracles and prophecy be distilled into the terms amenable to the modern mind. He merely wants to look at the Bible by removing the hermeneutical lens of ecclesial identity, and, as chapters 13 and 14 demonstrate, this means understanding it for what it is. The Bible is not a text of philosophy or of scientific knowledge. Spinoza explains, "Nothing whatsoever of a purely philosophic nature is to be found in Scripture's teaching." And later in the same paragraph: "Scripture's aim was not to impart scientific knowledge."[30] This conclusion coincides with what Galileo had retrieved from Augustine. Spinoza declares that the word of God can be distilled to the two-fold love commandment, thus the Bible has more to do with obedience than with rational comprehension. Concepts like Trinitarian procession and sacramental efficacy do not appear in the Bible, and it is only through the effort of scholastic, confessional apologists that people come to debate the Bible's stance on such matters. Spinoza reduces Scripture to its essentials: "The message of the Gospel is one of simple faith; that is, belief in God and reverence for God, or—which is the same thing—obedience to God."[31] Faith is less a *fides quae*—content or doctrines to be held—than *fides qua*—the faith that leads one to trust in God. Spinoza writes, "Faith must be defined as the holding of certain beliefs about God such that, without these beliefs, there cannot be obedience to God."[32] The Bible aims to impress this faith and the living out of this faith through acts of mercy and pursuit of justice.

In these chapters Spinoza returns to Tertullian's age-old question: *what has Jerusalem to do with Athens*? Although his book ostensibly

---

29. Spinoza, *Theological-Political Treatise*, 88–89.
30. Spinoza, *Theological-Political Treatise*, 158.
31. Spinoza, *Theological-Political Treatise*, 164.
32. Spinoza, *Theological-Political Treatise*, 165.

covers biblical interpretation and the political consequences of revealed religion, it also turns to discuss faith and reason. Here Spinoza is worth quoting at length:

> Between faith and theology on the one side and philosophy on the other there is no relation and no affinity, a point which must now be apparent to everyone who knows the aims and bases of these two faculties, which are as far apart as can be. The aim of philosophy is, quite simply, truth, while the aim of faith, as we have abundantly shown, is nothing other than obedience and piety. Again, philosophy rests on the basis of universally valid axioms, and must be constructed by studying Nature alone, whereas faith is based on history and language, and must be derived only from Scripture and revelation [. . .] So faith allows to every man the utmost freedom to philosophize.[33]

To Tertullian's question Spinoza answers, *very little*. Faith may seek understanding, but not with the help of philosophy, which demands an autonomy at odds with the very principle of faith. According to Spinoza, any theology that demands that the Bible reproduce the same truths as those of science or philosophy leads to bad theology. Likewise, any philosophy forced to conform to the biblical worldview inevitably cripples itself: "He who seeks to make Scripture conform with philosophy is sure to ascribe to the prophets many ideas which they never dreamed of. [. . .] On the other hand, he who makes reason and philosophy ancillary to theology has to accept as divinely inspired utterances the prejudices of a common people of long ago."[34] Philosophical theology is an oxymoron: Theology has to do with the will, and philosophy with the intellect.

Spinoza extends the arguments of Galileo and the position of Descartes into the latter half of the seventeenth century. In addition, he substitutes Galileo's non-overlapping magisterium of theology and science with a non-overlapping magisterium of theology and

---

33. Spinoza, *Theological-Political Treatise*, 169.
34. Spinoza, *Theological-Political Treatise*, 170. Later in chapter 15 he makes an even pithier formulation: "Neither must Scripture be made to conform to reason, nor reason with Scripture" (Spinoza, *Theological-Political Treatise*, 174).

philosophy. Implicit here is that reason is its own master. While the bulk of Christian institutions would fight this claim, some movements seemed quite happy to accept it, and instead of comingling faith and reason, sought a more authentic faith unaffected by reason's refinement.

PIETISM

This book's preface recalled the famous passage by Tertullian that ended with the exhortation "I believe because it is absurd." One could argue that Tertullian's extreme claims—associated with the idea of fideism, or knowledge by faith alone—are an outlier, both because they do not accurately represent Tertullian's thoughts on the matter, and because the subsequent direction of theology and Christian institutions diverged from Tertullian's recommendation. Yet one could also contend that Tertullian's claims represent a magnetic pole in the history of theology, around which has gathered a family of arguments against an overly rationalistic interpretation of faith. Like Tertullian, Martin Luther made many extreme rhetorical statements that seemed to advocate fideism as the best course for Christian theology. More importantly, he offered a more proximate and more authoritative example of this position for those concerned to preserve their faith in a rapidly changing intellectual climate. The previous chapter presented a balanced account of Luther's theology while tracing two strands derivative of Luther's theology: scholasticism and a theology more rooted in feeling. The latter strand, which emerged in the second half of the seventeenth century, is taken up in this section.

Doctrinal orthodoxy and scholasticism represented the dominant modes of theological engagement across the largest Christian bodies during this period. Surveying the Lutheran scene, one commentator notes, "By the middle of the seventeenth century [. . .] we find very little criticism of the scholastics for their philosophy."[35] This would change in the coming decades, as the Pietists found the scholastic and orthodox responses to problems of the day woefully insufficient. In

---

35. Pelikan, *From Luther to Kierkegaard*, 55; Pelikan depends on Emil Weber, *Die philosophische Scholastik des deutschen Protestantismus im Zeitalter der Orthodoxie* (Leipzig, 1907).

their reaction, the Pietists help set the trajectory for future centuries by rejecting much of the institutional consensus and coming up with a radical alternative to the synthesis of faith and reason.

While the most direct inspiration for pietism came from Johann Arndt (1555–1621), a Lutheran spiritual writer, the movement properly began with the publication of Philipp Jakob Spener's *Pia desideria* ("Pious Desires") in 1675.[36] The title of this book provided the label for this new movement, pietism, which flourished in the late seventeenth and early eighteenth century. Pietism downplayed confessional identity and instead emphasized individual conversion. Many pietists remained within older church structures while others founded sectarian movements, some of which had mystical leanings. Perhaps the most influential Pietist was Count Zinzendorf (1700–60), an aristocrat who gave asylum on his German estate to the Moravians, a long-persecuted Christian community. They called their new community Herrnhut, and in 1727 Herrnhut was home to a religious awakening. They soon exported this religious enthusiasm to other parts of Europe, and even to North America. One prominent visitor to Herrnhut was John Wesley, the founder of Methodism. His contribution helped make pietism a global Christian movement.

Although Pietists did not share a common language, creed, or doctrinal orientation, it is entirely justified to group these figures together and to emphasize the role this movement played in the historical panorama of perceptions of how faith and reason relate. One can categorize them according to their positions on three matters: (1) their emphasis on personal conversion as affective; (2) their suspicion toward institutional Christianity, conjoined with antipathy toward scholasticism and confessional polemics; (3) their tendency to contrast reason, often perceived as cold and abstract, to personal experience and encounter. These features led Pietists to judge faith as largely divorced from reason.

Pietism emphasized interior conversion as the *sine qua non* for authentic discipleship. Though almost all of the famous Pietists came

---

36. For a helpful overview of pietism see Peter Erb, "Introduction," to *Pietists: Selected Writings*, ed. Peter Erb (New York: Paulist, 1983), 1–27; see also Douglas Shantz, "Pietism," in *Oxford History of Modern German Theology*, eds. Grant Kaplan and Kevin Vander Schel, vol. 1, *1781–1848* (Oxford: Oxford University Press, forthcoming).

from Christian households, they portrayed their earlier faith as dry and listless. This was not without merit, as one historian, not entirely sympathetic to the movement, admits that pietism "represented a legitimate protest against the excesses of the Orthodox [sic] period," during which time "Christian faith had been equated with intellectual assent to a body of revealed truth for so long that the Christian way of life received far less than its share of attention."[37] The Pietists did not just raise this complaint to Catholics, but to their own churches and communities.

Three leading Pietists exemplify this interior turn: Wesley, Francke, and Zinzendorf. In his journals, John Wesley recalled meeting a prominent Moravian and balking at the question of his knowing Jesus personally. This encounter unsettled Wesley, for although he was a committed Christian, he had not yet experienced this deeply personal event. The moment for Wesley occurred when reading Luther on Romans in 1737: "About a quarter before nine, while he was describing the change which God works in the heart through faith in Christ, I felt my heart strangely warmed. I felt I did trust in Christ, Christ alone, for salvation; and an assurance was given me that He had taken away my sins, even mine, and saved me from the law of sin and death."[38] Accepting Christ in Wesley's orbit has a similar arc to the experience of falling in love, and he portrays it as an experience outside the realm of the intellect. Such declarations were typical. The truth of the Christian revelation needed to be verified on a personal level.

Like Wesley, but a half century earlier, August Hermann Francke recalls the problem of having studied theology for seven years with the aim of being a pastor, but not really knowing God. Eventually Francke, at the age of twenty-three, underwent a crisis of skepticism and borderline atheism. The solution was not found in more and better theology, but instead in prayer, whereupon God heard the cries of Francke and answered his prayers: "My doubt vanished as quickly as one turns one's hand. I was assured in my heart of the grace of God in Christ Jesus and I knew God not only as God but as my Father. All

---

37. Pelikan, *From Luther to Kierkegaard*, 80.
38. John Wesley, *The Heart of John Wesley's Journal*, ed. Percy Livingston Parker (Peabody, MA: Hendrickson, 2008), 66. Cited in Erb, "Introduction," 23.

sadness and unrest of my heart was taken away at once, and I was immediately overwhelmed as with a stream of joy. [. . .] I arose a completely different person from the one who had knelt down."[39] Francke later describes this as his "true conversion."[40]

Such conversion accounts accentuate the affective over the intellectual. One finds a similar emphasis on the affective in a text like Augustine's *Confessions*. Augustine, however, intermixes these affective moments with a recollection of his intellectual struggles concerning matters like the problem of evil. The Pietists, on the other hand, give the impression that a focus on the intellectual component of faith can impede God's entrance into our hearts. This one-sidedness comes across in Count Zinzendorf's public lectures from 1746. The Count laments the efforts of those "who think that if they have [non-Christians] memorize the catechism or get a book of sermons into their heads or, at the most, present all sorts of well-reasoned demonstrations concerning the divine being and attributes, thus funneling the truths and knowledge into their heads, that this is the sovereign means to their conversion."[41] Zinzendorf laments the misguided nature of this method, and compares it to going "against wind and current with full sails."[42] Like Wesley and Francke, Zinzendorf requires that conversion work at the affective level, for at this level God transmits an understanding deeper than words and concepts.

The Pietist foregrounding of an intimate, personal experience places the most essential Christian experience beyond the Catholic sacramental framework and Protestant confessional identity. If one experienced the "strange warming" described by Wesley, then one knew Christ personally. This shared experience transcends confessional identity, dogmatic dispute, and such institutional forms as baptism or confirmation. The Pietist suspicion toward institutional Christianity, scholasticism, and confessional polemics, was intertwined with their conversion narratives. Notwithstanding the influence of humanism in university life, these institutions in the latter half of the sev-

---

39. Francke, "Autobiography," in *Pietists: Selected Writings*, 105.
40. *Pietists: Selected Writings*, 106.
41. Zinzendorf, "Nine Public Lectures," in *Pietists: Selected Writings*, 305.
42. Zinzendorf, "Nine Public Lectures," in *Pietists: Selected Writings*, 305.

enteenth century were still dominated by scholasticism and disputation. In Spener's treatise on theological studies from 1680, he contrasts university theology with a more authentic theology. Too many students, complains Spener, "consider [theology] only a human discipline which like the other liberal arts has its foundation in human reason and is intended to sharpen and intensify reason."[43] No amount of reasoning can generate the kind of experiences that marked the authentic Christian life. One learns about Christianity without necessarily encountering it. Such a situation is lamentable, Spener explains: "Most of those people who seek and find education in the universities discover nothing other than a certain literal knowledge of spiritual things and an empty learning bereft of all divine power."[44] Universities and formal theological studies seemed at best neutrally ordered toward the real experience of God that signifies authentic Christianity.

Spener's concerns were not limited to the university's emphasis on head over heart. They extended to the kind of theology often undertaken. Catholic, Reformed, and Lutheran faculties of theology focused on polemics and apologetics. This focus required taking one's confessional dogmatic commitments and showing how the ecclesial bodies that rejected these commitments were out of step with Scripture, church tradition—admittedly a more salient concern for Catholics than Protestants—and rational understanding or logic. Increasingly, even Protestant theological faculties relied on philosophy, including logic, to buttress theological claims.[45] Spener considered it counterproductive to focus on such matters when so many students and perhaps even professors had not encountered Christ in a personal way that led to interior rebirth. Peter Erb summarizes Spener's main line of argument: "Rather than maintain polemical attack, Christians should endeavor to come to agreement through dedicated prayer, examples of moral well-being, and heartfelt love. Antagonistic scholastic disputation must be ended."[46] If medieval Christianity imagined philosophy as a handmaiden to theology, the

---

43. Spener, "On Hindrances to University Studies," in *Pietists: Selected Writings*, 66.
44. Spener, "On Hindrances to University Studies," in *Pietists: Selected Writings*, 67.
45. Pelikan, *From Luther to Kierkegaard*, ch. 3, esp. 59–60.
46. Erb, "Introduction," in *Pietists: Selected Writings*, 5–6.

queen science, then the Pietists saw philosophy as a kept woman, best hidden from view.

Gottfried Arnold (1666–1714) carried this skepticism further than Spener and most mainstream Pietists. He abandoned a university position to become a pastor, and would come to represent the more radical branch of Pietism. Arnold's treatises make it seem as though academic theology actively impedes knowledge of God. He writes, "Furthermore, because doctrine concerning God in himself is for the most part hidden to reason and too high for it, the truly learned of God cast aside the simplistic misuse of the carnal scholastic theologians and understood under the name of theology generally the secret wisdom of God revealed to the faithful alone."[47] If, in general, the Catholic Church emphasized the ecclesial mediation of God's grace, then Protestants reacted by highlighting the direct encounter of the individual with God, which in the Catholic view occurs in and through the sacraments, but which for Protestants came to be symbolized by Luther's insistence that he could know what one needed to be saved *sola scriptura*, by Scripture alone. Friedrich Schleiermacher, a leading Protestant theologian with Pietist roots, would later articulate the difference: "[Protestantism] makes the individual's relation to the Church dependent on his relation to Christ, while [Catholicism] contrariwise makes the individual's relation to Christ dependent on his relation to the Church."[48] It is easy to see how pietism further diminished the need for mediation. Why go to school if you can have the Holy Spirit instruct you? Arnold continues, "The Pope, emperors, and universities can make us doctors of the fine arts. But be certain no one will make you a doctor or a teacher of the Scriptures except the Holy Spirit."[49] Further, no human can replace the interior illumination that comes from the Holy Spirit. The purpose of theology is to grant one the possibility of a deeper understanding of the mysteries of faith, but Pietists like Arnold imagine this understanding as of another order than experience, and thus they only value theology that

---

47. Arnold, "History and Description of Mystical Theology or of the Mystical Doctrine of God," in *Pietists: Selected Writings*, 229.

48. Friedrich Schleiermacher, *Glaubenslehre*, §24. Cited from *The Christian Faith*, eds. H. R. Mackintosh and J. S. Stewart (Edinburgh: T&T Clark, 1989), 103.

49. Arnold, "History and Description," in *Pietists: Selected Writings*, 231.

refrains from analysis. Institutions themselves are at best neutral, and the kinds of skills that they gave to students in the seventeenth century—logic to help make distinctions, metaphysics to understand the nature of God and God's relationship to the world, polemics to aid in articulating the distinctions and differences needed to grasp confessional claims—largely prevented the students from having an experiential encounter with the risen Lord. Having framed the issues in this manner, the Pietists created a movement that downplayed the mediation of Christian institutions in an overwhelmingly Christian culture.

In their critique of institutions and their interpretive authority, many of the Pietist texts cited above also discuss reason and make claims about reason's relationship to faith. To summarize their response, it will be helpful to begin with their conceptualization of how the Holy Spirit grants inner illumination. In a challenge both to scholastics and to humanists, Spener's "Spiritual Priesthood" asks the question: "Whence do simple pious Christians receive the understanding of the Scriptures?"[50] First it should be noted that, although this question derives from Luther's claim that the knowledge necessary for salvation is gained from Scripture alone, the question above is not, strictly speaking, Luther's question. Luther translated the Bible into German with the hopes that ordinary Germans could have their faith sustained and strengthened by reading the Scriptures. He did not imagine a "free-for-all" in which every person decided for herself what Scripture meant. Luther's chief concern was that Roman Catholicism had allowed tradition to usurp the primacy of Scripture: A more authentic Christianity could be recovered by going back to the Bible, where the meaning was plain. But as every student of the Reformation knows, Protestant churches, despite claims to have found a more reliable means of clarity through *sola scriptura*, came to different conclusions about matters like communion, baptism, and predestination. Still, many theologians continued to insist on the plain meaning of Scripture. Spener, for instance, maintains that the Old Testament "was given to instruct the simple" and that "the New Testament is still more clear."[51] Therefore, although learning Greek and Hebrew could not

50. Spener, "Spiritual Priesthood," in *Pietists: Selected Writings*, 56.
51. Spener, "Spiritual Priesthood," in *Pietists: Selected Writings*, 55.

hurt the pursuit, Spener argues that simple pious Christians can understand the Bible "From the enlightenment of the Holy Spirit. [. . .] By [the Holy Spirit's] anointing and illumination they, therefore, understand all in the Scriptures that they need for their salvation and growth in the inner man."[52] Understanding the Gospels does not even need to be mediated through preaching. And if the Holy Spirit gives this inner illumination, what is to stop the same Spirit from communicating the necessary truths directly, thus making it possible to bypass the Bible as well?

Even if the majority of Pietists refrained from such a withering critique of reason, their emphasis on inner illumination and direct experience put reason in the crosshairs. In the same text, Spener warns against those who "follow the judgment of their *reason* and let it count for more than the words of the Holy Spirit." The Pietists conceived of reason as cold, analytic calculation, and it therefore comes as no surprise that they contrast it so sharply with affective experience. In his autobiography Francke recalls the aridity of his old life spent in seminary: "I had read the Scripture through and through again, indeed I was not lacking in the other practical books but since all this was grasped by me only in my reason and in my thought and since the Word of God was not changed in my case into light [. . .], I had to make a beginning anew to become a Christian."[53] Reasoning occupies a different part of the mind, Francke thought, than the part where the Holy Spirit touched and illumined the believer. In Francke, these parts eventually play off against each other. On the brink of his conversion, he was reading the Bible in Greek, when Paul talks about the gospel message being contained "in earthen vessels" (2 Cor 4:7). At that moment the words "entered into my heart a little and I thought that it was really not strange that this should thus happen—it seemed thus that a hidden consolation sank into my heart but my atheistic mind immediately brought forth corrupted reason as its instrument to tear the power of the godly word once again out of my heart."[54] Reason is not merely unnecessary for conversion, it actively impedes it, in Francke's account.

52. Spener, "Spiritual Priesthood," in *Pietists: Selected Writings*, 56.
53. Francke, "Autobiography," in *Pietists: Selected Writings*, 100–1.
54. Francke, "Autobiography," in *Pietists: Selected Writings*, 104.

Francke was not the only Pietist to harbor such an opinion. Spener also wrote about the danger of too much reason and philosophy. Gottfried Arnold favorably invoked the "pre-Hellenized" theology of the first centuries of Christianity, during which time "the clergy and their book-learning and worldly ways which they learned from the heathens, along with their merely reasoned wisdom, had not been mixed in nor troubled the clear water."[55] Francke wanted to return Christianity to a time before philosophy had corrupted theology, before Athens had anything to do with Jerusalem. In his advice to students, Count Zinzendorf shows a frank indifference for reason, declaring, "Religion can be grasped without the conclusions of reason," and that it can "be grasped through experience alone without any concepts."[56] For Zinzendorf, logic and dialectic give the illusion that one can get at reality by avoiding direct experience. He counsels just the opposite, and thus demands that reason, "which weakens experience," yield: "Religion cannot be grasped by reason as long as it opposes experience."[57] These examples substantiate the accusation that Pietism paved the way for future anti-intellectualism.[58]

It is possible now to draw a few conclusions about faith and reason in the seventeenth and eighteenth centuries. The reigning presuppositions about faith and reason, whether discussing a key modern philosopher like Descartes or a Pietist like Francke, seem to conceive of the two as more at odds than in the premodern period. Faith and reason, according to figures from totally different thought traditions, had little or nothing to do with one another. They no longer represented different steps or degrees of assent to God. Faith increasingly connoted the non-rational part of the mind, whereas reason became aligned with autonomous human capacities taking place in a natural realm that God may have created, but from which he was removed.

---

55. Arnold, "History and Description," in *Pietists: Selected Writings*, 232.

56. Count Zinzendorf, "Thoughts for the Learned and yet Good-Willed Students of Truth," in *Pietists: Selected Writings*, 291.

57. Zinzendorf, "Thoughts for the Learned," in *Pietists: Selected Writings*, 292.

58. Erb states, "Pietism's concern with the priesthood of all believers tended in popularist [sic] democratic circles to merge with anti-intellectualism and support only the most simplistic theological positions" ("Introduction," 25).

Like the Protestant world, the Catholic world was largely scholastic, but it too saw growing spiritual movements represented through religious orders as well as newer, modern forms of piety. These modern movements raised similar concerns about the inability of mainstream institutions to foster interior renewal. By the mid-seventeenth century, the Jesuits, upstarts just one century earlier, became Catholicism's most powerful order. They took a leading role in missions, and also dominated many of the leading faculties in theology.[59] They also became embroiled in a controversy over grace that began as scholarly and obscure, but ended up engulfing the Catholic Church, especially in France, in a nearly intractable controversy. Opposed to the Jesuits were the "Jansenists," named after a Belgian bishop, Cornelius Jansen, who had composed a three-volume work in Latin called *Augustinus*. Jansen focused on Augustine's controversy with the Pelagians about nature and grace, and his work was only published after his death in 1638. The controversy spread like wildfire, from the academic halls of Louvain to the streets of Paris. On a seemingly unrelated note, a sickly mathematical genius had undergone a profound conversion experience at the Jansenist abbey of Port-Royal. This genius, however, entered the controversy in 1656 by writing a series of anonymous letters against the Jesuits. His name was Blaise Pascal.

BLAISE PASCAL

Pascal (1623–62) made enough of an impact in mathematics to have a computer language named after him. He also left two writings—one anonymous, and one published posthumously—that have shaped the Christian intellectual tradition: *The Provincial Letters* and the *Pensées*. These writings came after Pascal's religious conversion mediated by the Jansenists of Port-Royal: At this abbey, his sister, Jacqueline Pascal, took her vows in 1652, against her brother's wishes. It is hard to imagine somebody who had written breakthrough texts in conic geometry in his twenties later being regarded as a true master of prose, but it was just so with Pascal, whose *Provincial Letters* have earned the des-

---

59. For a brief overview of this period, see John O'Malley, *The Jesuits: A History from Ignatius to the Present* (Lanham, MD: Rowman & Littlefield, 2014), 28–82.

ignation as the first manifestation of modern French prose. In them he excoriates the Jesuits for their scurrilous attacks on Antoine Arnauld, by then the leading figure of the Jansenist movement.[60] Pascal objected to the entire Jesuit mode of operating, which obfuscated more than enlightened. He especially highlighted the problem of casuistry, which gave license to transgress moral laws by ignoring the moral principle and instead focusing on the particulars of the case. For Pascal, reason could lead religion astray if it became reduced to instrumentality.

The *Pensées* (in English we might render them "musings" or, more literally, "thoughts") constitute a decisive breakthrough in understanding the relationship between faith and reason. After Pascal died, they were discovered as files of topically arranged papers around the theme of a Christian apologetic. Two interpretations, almost diametrically opposed, have animated discussions of Pascal. The first sees Pascal as a fideist. This derives from his frequent appeal to the heart: "The heart has reasons of which reason knows nothing."[61] So Nietzsche, for instance, regards Pascal as epitomizing Christianity's abandonment of the intellect. He calls the faith of Pascal "a gruesome manner of continual suicide of reason" and refers to a "sacrifice of the intellect à la Pascal."[62] Others, however, judge Pascal as having prioritized reason excessively on the basis of his famous "wager." In this section, Pascal formulates the argument for God in terms of a wager and suggests that, if one cannot know of God's existence with certainty, and heaven and hell are real options, it makes more sense to believe in God than to reject God.[63] Both interpretations, as demonstrated below, fundamentally misread Pascal.

---

60. It is notable that Arnaud's sister, Angelique, was the abbess at Port-Royal who persuaded Jacqueline Pascal to take her vows despite the lack of a dowry. Both women were theologians in their own right, and both influenced their famous brothers, whose conversions were subsequent to theirs.

61. Blaise Pascal, *Pensées*, trans. A. J. Krailsheimer (New York: Penguin, [1966] 1995), #423 (#277). The Krailsheimer edition orders the aphorisms differently from the older Brunschvicg edition. The parenthetical following Krailsheimer nods to this discrepancy. I have occasionally altered Krailsheimer against the following French edition: Pascal, *Les pensées de Pascal*, ed. Francis Kaplan (Paris: Editions du Cerf, 1982).

62. Friedrich Nietzsche, *Beyond Good and Evil/On the Genealogy of Morals*, trans. Adrian Del Caro (Stanford, CA: Stanford University Press, 2014), #46, 229.

63. See, for instance, the collection, *Gambling on God: Essays on Pascal's Wager*, ed. Jeff Jordan (Lanham, MD: Rowman & Littlefield, 1994).

It is helpful to keep in mind that Pascal wrote just one generation after Descartes, who placed certainty at the center of his project. Pascal counters the skeptics who doubt that faith and revelation suffice without some "natural intuition (*sentiment*):" "Now this natural intuition affords no convincing proof that they are true. There is no point of certitude, apart from faith, as to whether the human being was created by a good God, an evil demon, or just by chance, and so it is a matter of doubt, depending on our origin, whether these innate principles are true, false, or uncertain."[64] The reference to an evil demon makes it obvious that Pascal has Descartes in mind. Pascal does not divorce faith from reason, or even insist on faith's superiority. He merely points out that reason provides no greater route to certainty than faith. This becomes explicit in an aphorism that opens the subsection titled "Reason." Pascal declares, "We know the truth not only through our reason but also through our heart. It is through the latter that we know first principles, and reason, which has nothing to do with it, tries in vain to refuse them."[65] Pascal's heart (*coeur*) cannot be equated with the seat of emotions. The heart, in Pascal's understanding, is the basis for our knowledge of first principles.[66] Without first principles vouchsafed by the heart, we could not even undertake Descartes's meditations, which rely on prior assent or trust that, for instance, we are awake rather than asleep. These first principles or capacities belong to a realm anterior to rationality, and are as solid as any principles that reason builds upon. Pascal's point is not fideism, then, but a proper acknowledgment that neither active reason nor faith suffice on their own to achieve the knowledge they desire: "It is just as pointless and absurd for reason to demand proof of first principles from the heart before agreeing to accept them as it would be absurd for the heart to demand an intuition of all the propositions demonstrated by reason before agreeing to accept them."[67]

---

64. Pascal, *Pensées*, #131 (#434).

65. Pascal, *Pensées*, #110 (#282).

66. Balthasar makes this point. See Hans Urs von Balthasar, *The Glory of the Lord: A Theological Aesthetics*, eds. John Riches and Joseph Fessio, SJ, trans. Andrew Louth et al., vol. 3 (San Francisco: Ignatius Press, 1986), 184: "*Le coeur* [. . .] can be understood only in light of the Augustinian *cor*, and not at all as pointing to a theology of feeling; *coeur* is *sensorium* for the whole."

67. Pascal, *Pensées*, #110 (#282).

Reason does not need to be vanquished—Pascal does not go as far as the most extreme Pietists—but it does need to be humbled, as Pascal concludes in the aphorism under question.

Given his Jansenist lineage, and Jansenism's almost Calvinistic suspicions about reason's capacity after the fall, it is no surprise that Pascal regards reason as needing help. Reason does not lead us away from God, or corrupt our faith, but it requires other faculties in order to reach correct judgments. Pascal writes,

> One must know when it is right to doubt, to affirm, to submit. Anyone who does otherwise does not understand the force of reason. Some men run counter to these three principles, either affirming that everything can be proved, because they know nothing about proof, or doubting everything, because they do not know when to submit, or always submitting, because they do not know how to judge.[68]

Here Pascal sounds like a premodern author, less beholden to the modern contrast between autonomous reason and authority-reliant faith, and more focused on reason as *ratio*, in the sense of understanding proportion.[69] Reason at its pinnacle limits, rather than increases, its territory: "Reason's last step is the recognition that there are an infinite number of things which are beyond it. It is merely feeble if it does not go as far as to realize that."[70] The final purpose of reason is to understand its own limits.

This critique of reason brings Pascal's balancing act between faith and reason into relief. His effort does not, however, aim at a division of labor between faith and reason, each aware and respectful of the other's bailiwick, but otherwise having nothing to do with one another. Faith and reason need each other, otherwise they cannot be faithful or rational. Pascal exclaims, "Two excesses: to exclude reason, to admit nothing but reason," and elsewhere: "If we submit everything to reason

---

68. Pascal, *Pensées*, #170 (#268).
69. On Pascal as premodern, see Thomas Hibbs, "Habits of the Heart: Pascal and the Ethics of Thought," *International Philosophical Quarterly* 45, no. 2 (June 2005): 203–20. This article pushes back effectively against the fideistic reading of Pascal.
70. Pascal, *Pensées*, #188 (#267).

our religion will be left with nothing mysterious or supernatural. If
we offend the principles of reason our religion will be absurd and rid-
iculous."[71] Pascal also critiques a distorted piety closed off from reason:
"Piety differs from superstition. To carry piety to the point of superstition is to destroy it."[72] Pascal felt that the Cartesian turn had left reason too disconnected from lived reality. To escape into a different,
superstitious fantasy would be equally mistaken.

Pascal's attempt at mediation gives the proper perspective on his
more excessive statements about the heart: "The heart has its reasons
of which reason knows nothing."[73] This aphorism is best understood
against the backdrop of aphorism #110, summarized as follows: The
heart gives us our first principles. Reason can only work from these,
not generate them. In the next aphorism Pascal continues, "It is the
heart which perceives God and not the reason. That is what faith is:
God perceived by the heart, not by the reason."[74] God is not so much
something that we see, but an orienting reality that lets us see everything else as it should be. If reason gave us first principles, in Pascal's
sense, then reason could perceive God. But it is the heart, which gives
us a *sense*[75] of the whole, that does this. Even the famous and seemingly un-Pascalian "wager," when read to the end, confirms this view.
After insisting that one must wager, and that the smart wager is on
believing, Pascal reaches an odd conclusion: "If you are unable to
believe, it is because of your passions, since reason impels you to
believe and yet you cannot do so. Concentrate then not on convincing
yourself by multiplying proofs of God's existence but by diminishing
your passions."[76] Pascal offers a practical solution to a theoretical problem. Reason unaware of its limits often fools the unbeliever into thinking that she is making a rational decision, when in fact the passions
provide a greater barrier than reason realizes. Pascal's advice is not

71. Pascal, *Pensées*, #183 (#272); #173 (#273).
72. Pascal, *Pensées*, #181 (#255).
73. Pascal, *Pensées*, #423 (#277).
74. Pascal, *Pensées*, #424 (#278).
75. In Jane Austen's understanding of the term, in which sense and sensibility are
contrasted, and, in the novel (*Sense and Sensibility*), both are shown as insufficient as a
universal principle upon which to guide one's life.
76. Pascal, *Pensées*, #418 (#233).

unlike Father Zossima's in Dostoevsky's great novel, *The Brothers Karamazov*. In consultation with a woman who finds the idea of God incredible, Zossima does not provide arguments. Instead, he advises her to love somebody concretely and unreservedly: *This way has been tried. This way is certain*. Pascal's "wager" does not make a case for God based on rational calculation. Instead, it uses this calculation to demonstrate how the passions can present a greater barrier to accepting Jesus than the faculty of reason.

CONCLUSION

Both the Pietists and Pascal exemplify how early-modern Christianity attempted to confront an increasing chasm between faith and reason. At the beginning of the chapter, three seminal figures—Galileo, Descartes, and Spinoza—were examined in order to understand how leading thinkers both reacted to and created new intellectual paradigms that seem closer to a contemporary or modern way of seeing things than to their medieval predecessors. Such factors as geographic exploration, shifts in political economy, and the creation of the modern nation state, while themselves not concerned with the project of *fides quarens intellectum* or with its destruction, offered scant support for the idea of a "Christendom" that would unite political and ecclesial life and that would create an intellectual "imaginary" conducive to such a project. These circumstantial factors only multiplied in the coming centuries, and thus created even greater challenges for any politico-ecclesial synthesis in the nineteenth century. Nevertheless, it is in this century where Christian intellectuals gave greater attention than any of the previous centuries to the relationship of faith to reason. It is to this challenge and to the leading responses to it that the next chapter turns.

Chapter 6

The Nineteenth Century

No century presented as many problems to the church and to Christian belief as the nineteenth century. By comparison, the challenges facing the seventeenth century were child's play: In the nineteenth century, theologians had to confront Darwinian theory, Marxism, the ramifications of the French Revolution, the Industrial Revolution and its impact on lived faith, modern warfare, the birth of modern biblical criticism, modern historiography, especially the kind that challenged traditional histories of Christianity, the invention of archaeology, comparative religion, colonial backlash, the moral crisis of slavery, nationalism, positivism, scientism, and psychoanalysis. It is no wonder that Pius IX, the longest reigning pope in history, began to imagine the church as a besieged fortress, and concluded the 1864 "Syllabus of Errors" by decrying the assumption that the pope "should reconcile and adapt himself to progress, liberalism and modern culture."[1]

Rather than addressing how Christian theology reimagined the relationship between faith and reason in light of all of the issues mentioned above, this chapter instead turns its focus on Germany—with important detours in Oxford and Copenhagen—as a site of fervid intellectual output that would provide the fuel for much of the twentieth- and twenty-first-century theological discourse. It begins by summarizing the Enlightenment critique of Christianity as expostulated by perhaps its most representative figure, Immanuel Kant (1724–1804). The chapter then treats four emblematic figures: Johannes Kuhn (1806–87), John Henry Newman (1801–90), Soren Kierkegaard (1813–55), and Ferdinand Christian Baur (1792–1860), each of whom represented the best of their traditions while responding to the crises of their day in ways that both recalled earlier theological conversations, and shaped subsequent conversations. They held in common the desire to be in

1. Denzinger, 2980.

conversation with movements and developments of a distinctly modern faith that took for granted many of the assumptions of modernity that overturned the world of medieval scholasticism. Although their responses covered a range of outcomes between fideism and rationalism, they all confronted the modern dilemma directly.

ENLIGHTENED CRITIQUE: IMMANUEL KANT

A movement as vast and far-ranging as the Enlightenment problematizes any attempt at definition. Both secular devotees and religious opponents have attributed an anti-Christian, anti-religious animus in the Enlightenment. It is easy to see why: The predilection for modern scientific thinking was often wedded to Enlightenment thinkers' skepticism about claims based on authority. This modern mode of thinking frequently grew out of or led to a political liberalism rooted in contract theory (as opposed to a variation of divine right sovereignty), and a concept of liberty that exalted the individual's freedom of conscience regarding both thought and worship. From the perspective of established churches, these ideas could appear to present an intellectual-political program aimed at uprooting Christian Europe and replacing it with something new.[2] Yet for at least a century, historians of the Enlightenment have noted that the Enlightenment and religious traditions often worked in harmony, and sometimes produced intriguing offspring.[3] Despite some understandable interpretations to the contrary, it would be a mistake to conceive the historical movement known as "The Enlightenment" as advancing a never-ending battle with religion in general, and historical Christianity in particular. Even if one accepts this rejoinder, however, it still remains that leading Enlightenment thinkers inherited certain assumptions about faith and reason revisited in the previous chapter. These assumptions led many thinkers occupying a newly created secular sphere to presuppose a

2. For a classic articulation of this understanding of Enlightenment see Peter Gay, *The Enlightenment: An Interpretation*, vol. 1, *The Rise of Modern Paganism* (New York: W. W. Norton, 1966).

3. For an excellent overview, see David Sorkin, *The Religious Enlightenment: Protestants, Jews, and Catholics from London to Vienna* (Princeton: Princeton University Press, 2008).

hostility between these two terms, and this presupposition often undergirded much religious speculation as well.[4]

This chapter engages Germany's most well-known *Aufklärer*— Immanuel Kant—in light of such tendencies. Kant's philosophy has come to embody the most permanent feature of modernity's strained relationship with Christianity, yet the man himself regarded his work as reconciling, rather than pulling apart, faith and reason. In this regard he continues the legacy of earlier German philosophers like Gottfried Leibniz (1646–1716) and Christian Wolff (1679–1754), both moderates who attempted to unite Christian faith with modern science and philosophy. Yet upon closer inspection, Kant imported certain assumptions about reason that made conflict with faith inevitable. Kant's impact on theology comes through his desire to carry out this project of reconciliation via his new critical philosophy, mostly known through terms like "Idealism," "the turn to the subject," and "the Copernican revolution" in human understanding. Despite Kant's desire to bring harmony between theology and philosophy, his plan for peace, like the Versailles Treaty that subsequently served as a poison pill for Germany, left theology permanently crippled.

This new, critical philosophy led Kant, in his three *Critiques*, to conclude that God could only be known through practical, not theoretical reason. In his overview of modern German religious thought, Heinrich Heine explains how Kant eventually opened the door to God after seemingly closing it in the *Critique of Pure Reason*: "Kant distinguishes [in the first two *Critiques*] between theoretical reason and practical reason, and by means of the latter, as with a magician's wand, he revivifies deism, which theoretical reason had killed."[5] What Heine meant is that Kant allowed a place for God in his system, but it was through ethics, not metaphysics. This, of course, represented a drastic departure from the mainstream tradition, from Augustine through Aquinas, which affirmed the capacity to know God by means of theoretical reason.

---

4. For an introduction and fine analysis into the growing tension in eighteenth-century France, see Jonathan Israel's chapter, "Faith and Reason: Bayle versus the *Rationaux*," in *Enlightenment Contested: Philosophy, Modernity, and the Emancipation of Man 1670–1752* (Oxford: Oxford University Press, 2006), 63–93.

5. Heinrich Heine, *Religion and Philosophy in Germany*, trans. John Snodgrass (Boston: Beacon, 1959), 119.

The best way to understand Kant's critical philosophy is through what has been called "science envy." Like Descartes, Kant wanted philosophy to rest on sure and certain ground and to produce truths that could not be discounted as opinions. Through his encounter with Hume's empiricist epistemology of doubt, Kant came to realize that the pre-critical philosophy, to use Kant's terminology, rested on a kind of dogmatism.[6] In order to ensure that philosophy was properly scientific, it would need to produce universal and necessary truths. Kant makes this point clearly and loudly in the preface to the second edition of his *Critique of Pure Reason* (1787), the book that launched a philosophical revolution. In his preface Kant recalls the source of this science envy: not science's empiricism, or its capacity to generate data, but its ability to produce necessary truths through pure, *a priori* reason. Mathematics embodied the ideal science: "The secure course of a science was entered on and prescribed for all times and to an infinite extent."[7] In recalling the discovery of the isosceles triangle, Kant notes that it was not a matter of reading off the qualities from a triangle in nature, "but rather that he had to produce the [triangle] from what he himself thought into the object and presented (through construction) according to *a priori* concepts, and that in order to know something securely *a priori* he had to ascribe to the thing nothing except what followed necessarily from what he himself had put into it in accordance with its concept."[8] For Kant, what made the scientific revolution *scientific* did not involve more or better observation; mere observation never produces necessity. In reflecting on the breakthroughs of Galileo and others, Kant explains: "In order to be taught by nature, reason must approach nature with its principles in one hand, according to which alone the agreement among appearances can count as laws, and, in the other hand, the experiments thought out in accordance with these principles—yet in order to be

---

6. Kant writes, "I freely admit, it was the recollection of David Hume that first, many years ago, interrupted my dogmatic slumber." See *Prolegomena to Any Future Metaphysics*, "Introduction." Cited and translated from *Kants gesammelte Schriften (Akademie Ausgabe)*, ed. Königlich Preussischen Akademie der Wissenschaften (Berlin: de Gruyter, 1902), 4:260.

7. Kant, *Critique of Pure Reason*, B xi. Here and below I employ the standard A and B pagination. I have used the following translation and edition: *Critique of Pure Reason*, trans. and ed. Paul Guyer and Allen Wood (Cambridge: Cambridge University Press, 1998).

8. Kant, *Critique of Pure Reason*, B xii.

instructed by nature not like a pupil [. . .] but like an appointed judge who compels witnesses to answer the questions he puts to them."[9] To give a more recent example, the scientists who discovered the double-helix genetic structure did not do so by inventing a better microscope to observe a double-helix. They came to realize that something like a double-helix structure must exist in order to make sense of their data. They imagined this structure before conducting experiments that allowed them to affirm the knowledge made possible by a rational faculty that discerned the necessity of the double-helix. Likewise, Darwin did not see survival of the fittest in nature, he instead posited something like this law, and then was able to perceive how the data of genetic mutation corresponded to the theory. Kant concludes: "This is how natural science was first brought to the secure course of a science after groping about for so many centuries."[10]

Compared to the natural sciences, metaphysics had been groping in the dark, unable to make any progress while mired in intractable dispute. Kant summarizes: "Hence there is no doubt that up to now the procedure of metaphysics has been a mere groping, and what is the worst, a groping among mere concepts."[11] Kant's *Critique of Pure Reason* constitutes a dizzying and virtuoso application of this basic insight into the questions of the existence of the soul and of God, the traditional objects of metaphysical concern. In addition, it tackles how the human mind knows and understands objects through what Kant calls "sense intuition." His explanation of how the mind works unleashed a revolution comparable to Copernicus's cosmological revolution to heliocentrism. Yet what is the upshot of this revolution for theology? The main consequence of Kant's mode of procedure seems obvious: If theology aims to be a science—in other words, if it aims to legitimize its existence in the university—then it too must demonstrate how the results of its enquiry are universal and necessary.[12] Kant

9. Kant, *Critique of Pure Reason*, B xiii.
10. Kant, *Critique of Pure Reason*, B xiv.
11. Kant, *Critique of Pure Reason*, B xv.
12. For a helpful account of German Protestant theology's attempt to legitimize itself in the newly organized universities of the nineteenth-century, and the role played by Kant, see Zachary Purvis, *Theology and the University in Nineteenth-Century Germany* (Oxford: Oxford University Press, 2016).

himself thought through these consequences in his important late work, *Religion within the Limits of Mere Reason* (1794).

Kant did not think the exercise of theoretical reason, whose parameters he established in the *Critique of Pure Reason*, could safely and sufficiently demonstrate the existence of God. In his subsequent *Critique of Practical Reason* (1788), he introduced God as a postulate of practical reason, that is, as something that must exist in order for the realm of human freedom and morality to achieve intelligibility. His affirmation of God, despite qualifying how one can come to know God through reason, meant that Kant's attitude toward religion was not purely destructive. He did not set out to demonstrate the absurdity of Christian belief. This being so, it might be reasonable to ask: What made Kant so different from an Anselm, or indeed from the long project of lending understanding to belief, *fides quarens intellectum*? A distillation of the third part of *Religion within the Limits* provides an answer.

Mainline Buddhism teaches four noble truths about the nature of reality and proposes an eightfold path to attain enlightenment or nirvana. These truths are timeless and universal. Like Buddhism, Christianity proposes timeless and universal truths, both in its basic moral theology—do good and avoid evil—and in its creed, which speaks of God's oneness, and of one Lord, "eternally begotten of the Father," and so on. Besides affirming these timeless truths, Christians believe in historical, contingent truths, not just about the Incarnation of the Son, but also about the person who crucified him, and the number of days between crucifixion and resurrection. In short, Christianity, as a revealed religion, is also an historical religion. Christianity has put its faith in the validity of these historical truths to the point of making them eternally meaningful: The birth and death of Jesus of Nazareth give permanent intelligibility to human identity and destiny. Yet by attempting to bring religion within reason's scope of judgment, with the aim of making theology like natural science, Kant turns historical events into intractable barriers to scientific legitimacy as he defines it.

With Western monotheistic religions in mind, Kant sets before himself the task of reconciling the contingent events that mark these religions with the need for a universal faith open to all. Kant explains,

"Pure religious faith alone can found a universal church; for only such rational faith can be believed in and shared by everyone, whereas an historical faith, grounded solely on facts, can extend its influence no further than tidings of it can reach."[13] Kant admits religions often originate with either a charismatic leader or a witness to a theophany. Sound use of reason, however, compels us to move beyond this beginning stage. Likewise with morals. One might base one's morals on the historical theophany of the Ten Commandments; God gave Moses the tablets, and being moral for ancient Israelites meant obeying those Commandments, or what Kant calls "divine statutory laws." Yet basing one's moral code on contingent commands, Kant argues, is neither rational nor even moral, because they cannot be universally applied. He continues, "And even admitting divine statutory laws [. . .], pure moral legislation, through which the will of God is primordially engraved in our hearts, is not only the ineluctable condition of all true religion whatsoever but is also that which really constitutes such religion; statutory religion can merely comprise the means to its furtherance and spread."[14] Loving one's neighbor as oneself (Lev 19:18) appeared to the Jewish people first as a divine command in their Torah. It was part of keeping their covenant with God. Yet it was *their* covenant with *their* God, and thus not applicable to other peoples who did not worship Yahweh. The Commandments have the capacity to become universal moral laws, and the Jewish people served as a vehicle for this process. The only way to have a universal standard is to have a moral law, and the only way this can be transmitted is through reason, which does not rely on belief in an event on Mount Sinai to be valid and applicable. Stated another way, the morality of "Thou shalt not steal" cannot depend on the historical veracity of the Sinai encounter. Practical reason, not historical confirmation, determines the validity of this law.

How should particular laws become universal? One might imagine achieving universality through missionary work: spreading the news of the resurrection, or faithfully proclaiming Gabriel's revelation to

---

13. Kant, *Religion within the Limits of Reason Alone*, trans. Theodore Greene and Hoyt Hudson (New York: Harper & Row, 1960), 94.
14. Kant, *Religion*, 95.

Muhammed. Yet this universality would not really be universal in the Kantian sense, for it would lack necessity. Kant explains, "The token of the true church is its universality; the sign of this, in turn, is its necessity."[15] Recall the task of making natural science scientific. One has to find the pattern that makes something necessarily so. For Kant, this pattern was the moral law as rendered through practical reason. Missionary work inevitably fails to bring universality because it spreads merely particular, contingent statutes based on claims of divine revelation at particular points in history. Although there can be several kinds of faith, there can be only one true religion.[16] Kant explains:

> The so-called religious wars which have so often shaken the world and bespattered it with blood, have never been anything but wrangles over ecclesiastical faith. [. . .] When, as usually happens, a church proclaims itself to be the one church universal (even though it is based upon faith in a special revelation, which, *being historical, can never be required of everyone*), he who refuses to acknowledge its (particular) ecclesiastical faith is called by it an unbeliever and is hated wholeheartedly.[17]

Later Kant makes this point even more clearly: "A church dispenses with the most important mark of truth, namely, a rightful claim to universality, when it bases itself upon a revealed faith. For a revealed faith, being historical [. . .] can never be universally communicated so as to produce conviction."[18] Unlike efforts to bring order or intelligibility to historical events or data, Kant's project eliminates any need for historical events, and he takes this position based on his understanding of the way reason relates to truth. For Kant, only reason, by its own light and operating at full capacity, can find the patterns and the universal laws in phenomena. In the natural sciences, this means imagining the law of gravity or of thermodynamics, and subsequently ordering the data. In religion, it means finding the universal principle. Consequently, historical data can never be the *sources* of the universal principle, they can

---

15. Kant, *Religion*, 105.
16. Kant, *Religion*, 98.
17. Kant, *Religion*, 99, italics mine.
18. Kant, *Religion*, 100.

only be an example of this principle. Just as in the natural sciences, reason is not pupil to the data of religion, but instead teacher. Speaking of the Scriptures, Kant writes: "[T]he historical element, which contributes nothing to the purpose of making humans better, is something which is in itself quite indifferent, and we can do with it what we like."[19] Playing off James 2:17, Kant reminds the reader that (historical) faith without works is dead: "[I]t contains nothing, and leads to nothing, which could have any moral value for us."[20] Later in the same section, Kant talks of the historical element as a vehicle, implying that it can be dispensed of when one attains pure religious faith.[21]

Kant's attempt at reconciling faith and reason presented certain challenges for Christianity. These challenges were less antagonistic than those presented by a Voltaire or a Diderot, which made the question of how best to respond less obvious. In the Kantian system, reason does not refine faith so much as eliminate it, at least in the sense of faith being based in an experience or an encounter. The truths that really matter are universal and necessary, and therefore timeless, so history cannot, by definition, reveal. Kant's repositioning of religion, now under the judgment of reason in a new and particular way, further cornered a theology already in retreat after Hume's devastating blow to natural theology dealt in his *Dialogues Concerning Natural Religion*. Would theology accept a reduction to philosophical ethics, which would translate into a message of: *Jesus wants you to be a good person*, or *God wants you to follow the categorical imperative*? Nineteenth-century theologians had a daunting task before them.

JOHANNES KUHN AND THE CATHOLIC TÜBINGEN SCHOOL

Roman Catholics hardly found themselves in agreement about how to respond to the challenges of the Enlightenment as exemplified in the critical philosophy of Immanuel Kant. Some Catholics were in conservative states like Portugal and Spain, where revolutionary ideas

19. Kant, *Religion*, 102.
20. Kant, *Religion*, 102.
21. Kant, *Religion*, 106.

felt distant. Others lived as small minorities in England, the United States, and elsewhere, and inhabited a social context largely outside mainstream intellectual life. In France, the revolution and subsequent reign of terror left Catholics more likely to defend monarchy.[22] The German context contained a little of both. Some German Catholics were relatively undisturbed by growing political and intellectual challenges. Others had to confront a new reality of being confessional minorities in kingdoms without a Catholic ruler, an inevitable outgrowth of greatly reducing the number of kingdoms in the former Holy Roman Empire. Such was the case in Swabia, a southwestern region close to Switzerland and France. It contained many Catholic towns and cities formerly in tiny duchies now consolidated into larger states. Instead of having their own seminary and university, in a comfortably Catholic climate, Catholics (as well as Protestants) in these areas found their educational institutions dissolved or relocated into larger, "state" universities. In Swabia the Catholic seminary in sleepy Ellwangen was relocated, in 1817, to Tübingen, a university town with no Catholic churches and only one or two score of Catholic citizens. Tübingen was a stone's throw from Rottenburg, the seat of the local bishop, but another world away in confessional terms.[23]

From the outset, the Catholic theological faculty in Tübingen, which would come to be known as the "Catholic Tübingen School," felt compelled to become conversant with the trends that their Protestant counterparts were dealing with. This meant engaging not only Kant, but the other German Idealists like Fichte, Schelling, and Hegel, along with such leading German Romantics as Friedrich Schlegel, Friedrich Schleiermacher, and Novalis. The Catholic faculty started a

22. For an overview of Catholic responses and contributions to the Enlightenment, see Ulrich Lehner, *The Catholic Enlightenment: The Forgotten History of a Global Movement* (Oxford: Oxford University Press, 2016). Lehner's book is especially helpful in emphasizing the global nature of the Catholic Enlightenment, highlighting forgotten thinkers in places like India and the Americas. He also demonstrates how the French Revolution, on account of its violence against clergy and seizure of Church property, decisively turned Catholics away from Enlightenment thinking.

23. On the founding of the Catholic Tübingen School, see Grant Kaplan, "The Catholic Tübingen School in its First Generation," in *Oxford History of Modern German Theology*, eds. Grant Kaplan and Vander Schel, vol. 1, *1781–1848* (Oxford: Oxford University Press, forthcoming).

journal, the *Theologische Quartalschrift*, in 1819, which is the oldest surviving journal of Catholic theology in the world. The "founder" of the school, Johann Sebastian Drey, produced an influential book on restructuring seminary education, the *Brief Introduction to the Study of Theology*. His most promising student, Johann Adam Möhler, returned to Tübingen as a faculty member in 1823, and wrote what many consider to be the first truly modern ecclesiology, *Unity in the Church* (1825), which combined certain Romantic motifs into a Catholic understanding of the Church. But it was not until the 1830s that the Tübingen School took up the question of faith and reason in a systematic way, and by so doing, confronted the challenge presented by the Enlightenment.

Johannes Kuhn, a student of both Möhler and Drey, rejoined the faculty in 1838, the same year that Möhler died. Kuhn sensed keenly that the magisterial winds were changing in the 1830s, when he began his academic career. Under Pope Gregory XVI's papacy (1831–46), the Vatican began to intervene more aggressively in theological matters, specifically around questions of faith and reason. Within a few years of Gregory's papacy, the Vatican issued statements against the work of Louis Bautain, a Strasbourg theologian, for being too fideistic, and against the system of Georg Hermes, an influential theologian in Bonn, for being too rationalistic.[24] These condemnations were the first concrete evidence that, on an institutional level, the Catholic Church saw the problem of relating faith to reason as a danger to the very fabric of Catholic faith and life. Before the nineteenth century, Rome rarely intervened in theological matters concerning an individual theologian; it would certainly intervene in ecclesial-political matters, but it left theological disputes to be handled on the local level, most often through the judgment of a theological faculty or local ordinary. This practice changed in the nineteenth century, accounted for both by increased speed of communication and concern to re-establish papal authority after the military and political threats at the beginning of the century, including the captivity of Pope Pius VII.

24. For a trajectory of Catholicism dealing with the growing tension between faith and reason that begins with these figures, see Aidan Nichols, *From Hermes to Benedict XVI: Faith and Reason in Modern Catholic Thought* (Herefordshire: Gracewing, 2009).

In 1835 the Vatican issued a brief, *Dum acerbissimas*, which condemned the writings of Georg Hermes (1775–1831), who had formed a leading school of theology in Bonn. Hermes's writings fell under condemnation because they claimed "that reason is the chief norm and only medium whereby people can acquire knowledge of supernatural truths."[25] According to the Vatican's judgment, Hermes privileged reason at the expense of faith. Ecclesiastical authorities also concerned themselves with the other end of the pole: fideism. After being removed from his professorship in Strasbourg in 1834, Bautain was required to sign a set of "Theses on Faith and Reason against Fideism," including one that stated "Reason can prove with certitude the existence of God."[26] Although this process began in Strasbourg, it continued in Rome, and precipitated the 1846 encyclical *Qui pluribus*, which treated "The Errors of Rationalism" and "The Correct Attitude of Human Reason toward the Faith."[27] Given the challenge posed by the German philosophical tradition from Kant to Hegel, Tübingen Catholics took keen interest in the movements against Hermes and Bautain, especially in light of their own attempts, both prior and ongoing, to establish the scientific legitimacy of Catholic theology.

In his writings Kuhn used the same framework as the authorities in Rome and Strasbourg, but supplemented it with profound subtlety of mind and fluency with the most recent trends in Kantian and post-Kantian philosophy.[28] Kuhn's concerns about faith and reason predated any of the condemnations. Already in 1832, at the young age of twenty-six, he defined his speculative theological project as follows: "It has as its ultimate goal to bring about the aforementioned recon-

---

25. Denzinger, 2738. For Hermes's place in modern Catholic discussions of faith and reason, see Nichols, *From Hermes to Benedict XVI*, 25–47.

26. Denzinger, 2751–56.

27. Denzinger, 2775–86. It should also be noted that the leading theologian in Rome and teacher of future Pope Pius IX, Giovanni Perrone, engaged and critiqued the thought of both Hermes and Bautain. For a careful treatment of Perrone on faith and reason, especially concerning Bautain and Hermes, see Charles M. Shea, "Faith, Reason, and Ecclesiastical Authority in Giovanni Perrone's *Praelectiones Theologicae*," *Gregorianum* 94, no. 1 (2014): 159–77.

28. For an English translation of Kuhn's contribution, see *Faithfully Seeking Understanding: Selected Writings of Johannes Evangelist von Kuhn*, ed. and trans. Grant Kaplan (Washington: The Catholic University of America Press, 2009), 45–83.

ciliation of Christianity with reason."[29] As Kuhn saw things, too many Catholics found themselves rattled by the Kantian and later Hegelian challenge. On one hand, thinkers like Hermes capitulated to modern notions of reason, as if that were the only way to understand reason. On the other hand, Bautain and others had disavowed reason to such a degree that, from Kuhn's perspective, they had ceded the ground of rationality to a modern philosophy that itself failed to be wholly rational. Kuhn's project was to articulate how theology could remain an academic discipline, within the university, while not being coopted by or reduced to philosophy.

Kuhn's aim at synthesis had precedent; his theology of faith and reason not only echoes, but explicitly recalls many of the conversations that animated previous chapters. A master of both Greek and Latin, deeply learned in patristic, scholastic, and modern theology, Kuhn not only provided his own response to the contemporary crisis about faith and reason, but also referred to and retrieved, often in great detail, the previous efforts of such luminaries as Clement of Alexandria, Augustine, and Aquinas. Kuhn addressed the contemporary problematic of faith and reason, but did so in full awareness of, and in conversation with, a rich theological tradition.

Kuhn's theology held together two seemingly contradictory principles, which helps explain some of the confusion about his writings.[30] The first principle concerns the compatibility of faith and reason. From his 1832 essay to his 1860 treatise on philosophy and theology, Kuhn consistently upheld their compatibility. He frequently cited the famous declaration from the Fifth Lateran Council in 1513: "And since truth

---

29. Kuhn, "Ueber den Begriff und das Wesen der speculativen Theologie oder christlichen Philosophie," *Theologische Quartalschrift* 14 (1832): 253–304, at 260.

30. In his later dispute with the neoscholastic Jakob Clemens, Kuhn expressed exasperation at doubts about the soundness of his approach to questions of faith and reason. He writes, "I am completely justified in saying that no theologian of the modern period holds more steadfastly and strictly than I do to the orientation expressed in the encyclical [*Qui pluribus*] concerning the principle of theological understanding: *fides quarens intellletum*" (Johannes Kuhn, *Philosophie und Theologie: eine Streitschrift* (Tübingen: Laupp-'schen, 1860), 24–25. For the most thorough treatment of Kuhn's disagreement with neoscholastics, see Karl Joseph Mattes, *Die Kontroverse zwischen Johannes v. Kuhn und Constantin v. Schäzler über das Verhältnis von Natur und Gnade* (Freiburg, Switzerland: Universitätsverlag Freiburg, 1968).

cannot contradict truth in any way, we define every statement contrary to the truth of the illumined faith to be entirely false."[31] Since truths cannot contradict, the faith cannot be irrational or contradictory with reason, which can, at minimum, reveal falsity. The second principle declares that faith and reason belong to two different orders, which cannot be collapsed into one. Kuhn does not mean the exercise of natural faith, which we carry out when we find our parents trustworthy. Instead, Kuhn means saving faith—a virtue infused by God (Romans 5:5). This faith is graced, and as such, can never strictly be owed to anyone, or confined to a natural order of causality. Maintaining the compatibility between these two claims became Kuhn's lifelong project.

In his 1839 essay, Kuhn uses Aquinas to explain the rationality of faith. Reason does not prove faith, but it lends intelligibility to the articles of faith. Glossing the first question of the *Summa Theologiae*, Kuhn writes, "Theology employs rational insight under the presupposition of the faith, and of its truth and certainty, in order to articulate the essential aspects of this faith into the necessity of the concept and the intelligibility of science."[32] Beginning with revealed truths, that is, the articles of faith, theology uses reason to understand them. Doing so reveals their intelligibility by showing the connection of one truth to another, or by finding analogies between truths of faith and common human experiences. The understanding that builds on faith represents a real advance over a faith uninformed by reason. Kuhn declares: "It is better to understand what one believes than to believe without understanding."[33] Reason has a place in theology, and Catholics need not reject wholesale the Kantian project.

Kuhn faults Hermes, however, for eradicating the distinction between the two orders of truth. In his *Introduction to Catholic-Christian Theology*, Hermes had sought to put faith on a safe footing by providing

31. Denzinger, 1441; The First Vatican Council would cite this passage in *Dei Filius* (Denzinger, 3017). A digested version of Kuhn's article is translated as "The False Choice between Faith and Rational Understanding," 45–69 in Kaplan, *Faithfully Seeking Understanding*, at 46.

32. Kuhn, "The False Choice between Faith and Rational Understanding," 60.

33. Kuhn, "The False Choice between Faith and Rational Understanding," 69. Here it is notable that Kuhn softens the sharper edges of Hegelianism, which declares religion the realm of representation, to be subsumed into the purified understanding of the concept, which only philosophy can produce.

for it a philosophical foundation prior to faith. He had written: "There is no secure criterion for truth except necessity."[34] Theology done in this mode assumes the validity of the Kantian paradigm, in which theological truths need to match the formal qualities that Kant had desired for metaphysics, which metaphysics borrowed from the natural sciences. Kuhn upbraids this approach for replacing the tradition of Augustine and Anselm with *intelligo ut credam*: "I understand so that I may believe."[35] Hermes erred, according to Kuhn, because he bound truth to necessity; the truest truths must proceed necessarily from a priori principles, as is the case in the pure sciences. Hermes writes: "For we know two methods to decide with certainty on matters of truth and reality: the necessary custody of theoretical reason and the necessary acceptance of obligatory reason."[36] For Kuhn, this understanding of reason capitulates to Kantianism, with deleterious consequences for faith.

Recall from the previous chapter Pascal's quip: The purpose of reason is to show the limits of reason. A properly functioning reason understands that certain elements of reality lie beyond its grasp. In his *Catholic Dogmatics*, Kuhn spells out this principle:

> Philosophizing reason, the more that it is truly self-conscious, will grant less room for the illusion that it has the final say about the truth and the knowledge of the truth. The same reason will carefully guard against ascribing to its results the qualities of exclusivity and completion. Just the opposite will take place: philosophizing reason will consider the realm of truth infinite and not to be exhausted by philosophy.[37]

To be truly rational, philosophy needs to cede final judgment over the elements of reality that lie outside its grasp. Not all of reality falls under the category of necessity, therefore not all of reality need clear the bar

---

34. Hermes, *Einleitung in die christkatholische Theologie. Erster Theil: Philosophische Einleitung* (Münster: Coppenrath, 1819), xi.

35. Kuhn, "The False Choice between Faith and Rational Understanding," 46. Kuhn's conclusive critique of Hermes is located in "Ueber Glauben und Wissen," 444–45.

36. Hermes, *Einleitung*, 258; cited in Kuhn, "Ueber Glauben und Wissen," 459.

37. Kuhn, "The Precedence of Faith over Reason," 70–83 in Kaplan, *Faithfully Seeking Understanding*, at 77–78. For an argument that Aquinas ascribes to a similar understanding, see the chapter, "Intellect," in Denys Turner, *Faith, Reason and the Existence of God* (Cambridge: Cambridge University Press, 2004), 75–88.

of rationality set by Kant for philosophy. This condition applies to theology, which includes both supernatural truths and historical realities that elude Kant's standard of universality. Kant equated this standard with truth, an unprovable assertion whose weaknesses become evident through further scrutiny.

Picking up a thread that runs through Aquinas and Pascal, Kuhn provides an alternative to the instinctive gesture to conceive Enlightenment critiques like Kant's as usurping faith's territory through an expansion of reason. Kuhn takes a less obvious course by criticizing a false understanding of reason. Like John the Baptist's words about himself in relation to Christ, reason's truest aim is not to draw attention to its mission as if it were comprehensive, but instead to point toward something else, in which it has already begun to participate. So too, reason at full capacity reveals its own limits. Only a reason fully engaged with reality could come to this conclusion.

At this juncture, the relation between faith and reason comes closest to mapping onto another familiar relation: nature and grace. Kuhn intuits a parallel between Augustine's critique of Pelagianism and his own critique of rationality. Just as Augustine had outlined the problem of a theology that supposed that humans do not need divine assistance in order to achieve salvation through Christ, so too there was an intellectual, or epistemological Pelagianism at work in certain forms of modern philosophy, and in theologians that depended too much on them. Kuhn did not mince words: "To put the matter succinctly: one cannot philosophize one's way into Christianity."[38] But this mistaken attempt becomes the inevitable path if one begins with doubt, as Descartes did in his famous *Meditations*. For Kuhn, if one begins with nothing, one can never get anywhere: "The self-proclaimed speculative philosophy of Hegel begins with nothing, and then emulates the process of the becoming of things."[39] Such a method could never confirm the revealed truths of Christianity: "From nothing only nothing can result."[40] Theologians who follow modern phi-

---

38. Kuhn, "The Precedence of Faith over Reason," 80.

39. Kuhn, "The False Choice between Faith and Rational Understanding," 54.

40. Kuhn, "The False Choice between Faith and Rational Understanding," 54; Kuhn intentionally recalls Lucretius's famous dictum from *De Rerum Natura: ex nihilo nihil fit.*

losophy too closely create a system rooted in this intellectual analogue to Pelagianism. This pattern results in the naïve belief that if one reasons well enough, one can move, one step at a time, into Christianity. Such a presupposition ignores the distinction between the natural and supernatural orders.

Reason alone does not contain the capacity to explain how reason relates to faith. To bridge this gap Kuhn applies the distinction between rational and supernatural faith. Rational faith might be the act of assenting to the claim that New Zealand is an island without ever circumnavigating it. This kind of faith differs in kind from the faith that compelled the disciples to abandon their fishing nets and to place all of their trust in Jesus. Kuhn concedes that rational faith requires no particular grace. But supernatural faith certainly does, and therefore requires a commensurate religious epistemology.

The inability to distinguish between rational and supernatural faith explains how both Hermes and Bautain erred so badly. Kuhn's treatment of Bautain recalls how the Strasbourg theologian appealed to the canons from the Synod of Orange in 529, which declared that the beginning of faith was not due to our effort, but to the grace of God, and that, consequent to humanity's fall, we were not free to believe in God without divine grace.[41] Hermes seemed to deny this canon, but Bautain, himself an ex-Kantian, sought to affirm it so wholeheartedly that he rejected both reason's capacity to attain natural knowledge of God, and the existence of a natural faith to which fallen human beings still have access. For all their differences, Bautain and Hermes shared the urge to dissolve the difference between the natural and supernatural faith, albeit for different epistemological ends.

In nineteenth-century Germany, theology needed to legitimize itself as a university discipline; it could not seal itself off in a supernatural realm. The Kantian paradigm excludes from the university not only theology, at least as traditionally practiced, but also *history*. The German playwright and theological provocateur, Gotthold Lessing (1729–81), made a quip in the 1770s that attained prophetic status: "Accidental truths of history can never become the proof of necessary truths of rea-

---

41. Kuhn, "Ueber Glauben und Wissen," 473. For the reference to the Council of Orange, see Denzinger, 375.

son."[42] By this Lessing meant that historical truths, by their very historicity, can never realize the qualities of necessity and universality that the natural or pure sciences attain. The Tübingen Catholics had digested enough Lessing to grasp the danger in following Kant's reduction of Christianity to a religion of mere ethical precepts. Kuhn explains, "Philosophy cannot accept anything authenticated by an authority other than that of the thinking mind. Philosophy cannot accept experiences that lay claim to something beyond those made under normal circumstances."[43] By philosophy Kuhn does not mean the handmaid model of philosophy as conceived in medieval theology. Instead he means modern autonomous philosophy that aimed to be judge not just of supernatural truths, but also of quotidian historical truths outside its grasp. These truths concern a part of reality not contained by philosophy, and thus outside its boundaries of judgment. Necessity fails both on a logical level, because it cannot account for historical truths, and also on a Christian metaphysical level, in that, if the saving truths are equated with necessary conclusions, then grace becomes superfluous for the attainment of these truths. Kuhn adds, "Just as the content of rational ideas is totally independent from experiential knowledge, even more so is revelation [. . .] independent from this rational understanding."[44] Reason cannot deduce its way to revealed teachings that exceed its capacity to prove, although it can have a grasp of those teachings that shows their reasonability and illuminates their intelligibility.

The place of reason in theology, which Kuhn affirms, does not mean that theology and philosophy can be melded into one discipline. Kuhn lamented this tendency, which he associated with Hegelians and neo-scholastics. As early as his long 1841 article,[45] and more concisely

42. Gotthold Ephraim Lessing, "On the Proof of Spirit and of Power," in *Lessing's Theological Writings*, ed. and trans. Henry Chadwick (Cambridge: Cambridge University Press, 1956), 53.

43. Kuhn, "The Precedence of Faith over Reason," 80.

44. Kuhn, *Einleitung in die katholische Dogmatik*, 127–28.

45. Kuhn, "Princip und Methode der speculativen Theologie," *Theologische Quartalschrift* 23 (1841): 1–80. Kuhn wrote this essay in response to criticism of his 1839 article on faith and reason, for which he had been accused of "making the Church Fathers into Hegelians." For an account of this exchange, see Grant Kaplan, *Answering the Enlightenment: The Recovery of Historical Revelation in Nineteenth Century Germany* (New York: Crossroad/Herder, 2006), 119–22.

in the 1859 introduction to the *Catholic Dogmatics*, Kuhn insists that philosophy and theology each have their own principles of knowledge. Theologians like Philip Marheineke affirmed Hegel's claim that philosophical and theological truths were materially identical, and only formally distinct. This claim went beyond any notion of a unity between truths articulated at the Fifth Lateran Council. In Hegelianism, the task was to translate unmediated understanding or mere representation into a higher, mediated idea or concept. Like the Kantian project, Hegel's flattened the supernatural quality of faith by subordinating it into "absolute knowledge," which is identical to Hegel's understanding of what philosophy should be.[46] By distinguishing between rational and supernatural faith, Kuhn's religious epistemology prevented the subsumption of theological truths into philosophy.

Kuhn insisted that theological truths drew from a different source than those of philosophy, thereby echoing Aquinas's explanation in the first question of the *Summa Theologiae*: "Theology's cognitional principle is not reason, but the authority of the prophets and apostles, and later, the teaching Church."[47] From this it did not follow that theology should either buffer itself, or allow itself to be buffered, from the scientific standards of modern university life. Kuhn criticized tendencies in Schleiermacher that led to such a buffering: "[Theologians like Schleiermacher] have declared that religious belief occupies a position inaccessible to philosophy, and they have taken refuge in the realm of feeling."[48] The same conviction led Kuhn to oppose efforts that would create a Catholic university in Germany, for fear that such a university would buffer theology from scientific rigor.[49] At times his delicate balancing act seemed to please nobody. Kuhn desperately wanted to promote a theological method and religious epistemology that would make it possible to preserve a modern symbiosis between faith and reason, lest theology lurch into the abyss of rationalism or the illusion of fideism.

---

46. See Kuhn, "Princip und Methode," esp. 6–9.

47. Kuhn, "The Precedence of Faith over Reason," 74.

48. For the dispute with Schleiermacher, see "Religion as Feeling or Illusion?" 246–54 in Kaplan, *Faithfully Seeking Understanding*, 247. In the footnote Kuhn cites from Schleiermacher, *On Christian Faith*, #16.

49. See Kuhn's address from 1863: "The Place of Theology in a University: A Response," in Kaplan, *Faithfully Seeking Understanding*, 277–86.

Kuhn offered perhaps the most thoughtful and insightful response by a Catholic theologian on the continent. Yet over the course of his career, the tides had turned against non-scholastic theologians in Germany. Though he had fashioned himself a defender of the faith, taking on not only Protestant liberalism, but Catholic semi-rationalism, Kuhn fell afoul of ecclesial leadership due to his opposition to the newly imagined Catholic university. This fallout led to a decade-long dispute over nature and grace that lasted all the way up to the onset of the First Vatican Council, in 1869–70. Neither Kuhn nor any of the leading German theologians went to Rome as advisors during the Council, and therefore his theology of faith and reason did not have the impact it could have had during the session that produced *Dei Filius*, and his vision was largely eclipsed with the resurgence of Thomism as articulated in *Aeterni Patris* (1879) a few years later.

JOHN HENRY NEWMAN

John Henry Newman (1801–90) preferred to understand himself as a controversialist rather than a theologian,[50] and there is no reason why he should not be taken at his word. Unlike Kuhn, Newman never wrote a book of Christology or Trinitarian theology, a life of Jesus or a treatise on grace. He also never grappled seriously with the German philosophical tradition; there existed no comparable philosophical movement in the England of his day, although the specter of John Locke's cognitional theory hovered over England. Despite these differences, Newman managed to home in on certain matters in almost the exact same way as Kuhn, but added to this a retrieval of Aristotle's notion of *phronesis*, or practical wisdom, as a way to justify the rationality of the assent of faith.

Like Kuhn, Newman realized that the working definitions of faith and reason would be the die that cast the perceived compatibility between the two terms. Newman reflected on these matters through-

---

50. In his correspondence, Newman stated words to this effect on numerous occasions. For one instance, see his February 1869 letter to Maria Giberne, "Really and truly I am not a theologian" (*LD* 24:212). For another, see Newman's February 1866 letter to William Ward: "I am a controversialist and not a theologian," cited from *The Quotable Newman*, ed. Dave Armstrong, vol. 2 (Self-published, 2013), 264–65.

out his life, both in private correspondence and published work. During his Anglican period, Newman, a well-known public intellectual, had given a series of sermons at Oxford that came to be known as the *University Sermons*.[51] Those that deal most specifically and helpfully with faith and reason—numbered X through XIII—were given between 1839 and 1840. Newman gave a much lengthier reflection on faith and reason in perhaps his greatest work, *An Essay in Aid of a Grammar of Assent*, which belongs to Newman's Catholic period.[52] He worked on it over two decades. Of this period of gestation Newman wrote to a friend:

> For twenty years I have begun and left off an inquiry again and again, which yesterday I finished [. . .] I began it in my Oxford University Sermons [. . .] but though my fundamental ideas were ever the same, I could not carry them out. Now at last I have done all that I can do according to my measure.[53]

If *The Grammar of Assent* was difficult for Newman to write, it has been even more difficult for his audience to read.[54] As Newman's admission makes clear, it extends and deepens the arguments from the earlier *Sermons*. By reading them together, one can arrive at a coherent picture of Newman's account of how faith relates to reason.

In Newman's reflections on how he thought people actually reason, he was unable to find any theory, save Aristotle's, that mapped onto the reality of human thinking, both in terms of the manner that humans reason, and how they come to believe and to feel certain in their belief. An account of Newman's explanation starts with his examination of reason itself. Newman calls for an expanded scope of human reason that does not constrict it to formal logic, and includes

51. John Henry Cardinal Newman, *Fifteen Sermons Preached before the University of Oxford*, 3rd ed. (Notre Dame, IN: University of Notre Dame Press, [1872] 1997).

52. John Henry Cardinal Newman, *An Essay in Aid of a Grammar of Assent* (Notre Dame, IN: University of Notre Dame Press, [1870] 1979).

53. Newman to Richard Hutton, on February 13, 1870; cited in Nicholas Lash, "Introduction," in Newman, *A Grammar of Assent*, 1.

54. Frederick Aquino declares, "The *Grammar* qualifies as the most difficult text to read within the entire corpus of Newman's writings." See Frederick Aquino, *Communities of Informed Judgment: Newman's Illative Sense and Accounts of Rationality* (Washington: The Catholic University of America Press, 2003), 48.

faith as a species of reason. Besides expanding the definition of reason, Newman also personalizes reason: Newman insists that the personal nature of reasoning means that one cannot predetermine how humans should reason through a methodological scaffolding. The other central element to Newman's account concerns the illative sense, a term coined to account for the highly personal assent made in concrete matters. Newman employs this phrase to explain how people—both believers and non-believers—reach a conviction about something that has not been conclusively proven. Newman argues that such "leaps of faith" are entirely reasonable, and we do them with great regularity in everyday matters. To round out an account of Newman, I will look at Newman's understanding of how faith is best safeguarded. This examination will lead to the conclusion that Newman's deep antipathy to rationalism recovers, rather than abandons, the proper use of reason, in a fashion similar to Kuhn's understanding.

With good reason, scholars have noted Newman's attempt to broaden the understanding of reason beyond the parameters set by modern rationalism.[55] Andreas Koritensky notes that Newman was eager to explain the shortcomings of a mentor at Oxford, Richard Whately, who had written a textbook called *Elements of Logic*.[56] One finds traces of this concern in Newman's "Twelfth University Sermon," where he states: "Faith, considered as an exercise of reason, has this characteristic—that it proceeds far more on antecedent grounds than on evidence."[57] Newman then compiles a wide range of activities that

---

55. For a sampling, see Maurice Nédoncelle, "Le Drame de la Foi et de la Raison dans les Sermons Universitaires de J. H. Newman," *Études* 247 (1945): 66–83; Lash, "Introduction," in *A Grammar of Assent*, esp. 8–10; and Andreas Koritensky, "The Early John Henry Newman on Faith and Reason," *Newman Studies Journal* 14, no. 1 (2017): 46–68. Nédoncelle writes, "L'un des mérites incontestables des Sermons universitaires aura été d'élargir la notion d'intelligence, trop étroitement définie par le rationalism classique" (Nédoncelle, "Le Drame de la Foi et de la Raison," 75).

56. Koritensky, "The Early John Henry Newman on Faith and Reason," 50–51. Koritensky writes, "Whately's decisive mistake, for Newman, however, consists in underestimating the phenomenological richness of this psychology insofar as he limits reasoning to the rules of syllogisms," (Koritensky, "The Early John Henry Newman on Faith and Reason," 51). For a more intensive examination of Newman's relationship to Whately, see Gillian Evans, "'An Organon More Delicate, Versatile and Elastic': John Henry Newman and Whately's *Logic*," *The Downside Review* 97 (1979): 175–91.

57. Newman, *University Sermons*, 222.

fall under the purview of reason: "By the exercise of Reason, indeed, is properly meant any process or act of the mind, by which, from knowing one thing it advances on to know another."[58] Some theologians, working with a territorial understanding of how faith and reason relate, might have welcomed a restricted terrain for reason, leaving more room for faith to operate, yet Newman saw a restricted notion of reason as a danger to thought in general and to theology in particular.

Although he opposed Locke on many fronts, Newman may have inherited this aspect of his argument from Locke. In his famous work on cognition, *An Essay Concerning Human Understanding*, Locke maintained that, while few people know how to construct a syllogism, it does not follow that people reason poorly: "And therefore we may take notice, that there are many men that reason exceeding clear and rightly, who know not how to make a syllogism."[59] People managed to reason well before Aristotle published his logic, and they continue to reason well knowing nothing of it. Locke continues, "[God] has given them a mind that can reason, without being instructed in methods of syllogizing: the understanding is not taught to reason by these rules; it has a native faculty to perceive the coherence or incoherence of its ideas."[60]

Though he eschewed Lockean empiricism and his theory of innate ideas, Newman picked up this thread from Locke to counter Whately's claim that only those who considered themselves intellectuals, or who had logic, reasoned well. In "Sermon XI" he remarked, "In truth, nothing is more common among men of a reasoning turn than to consider that no one reasons well but themselves."[61] What Newman goes on to

58. Newman, *University Sermons*, 223.
59. John Locke, *An Essay Concerning Human Understanding*, ed. Alexander Fraser, vol. 2 (New York: Dover, 1959), 389 (book IV, 17). Whereas Mark McIntosh highlights the contrast between Locke and Newman, Koritensky notes their similarity, at least in this regard. McIntosh correctly outlines how the Lockean legacy made reason the arbiter of faith, but Locke nonetheless was an ally to Newman against Whately. See Mark McIntosh, "God as First Truth, the Will's Good and Faith's Cause: The Theology of Faith and Newman's *University Sermons*," *International Journal of Systematic Theology* 15 (2013): 416–36, esp. 418, 427–29. Koritensky remarks, "Locke's model of reason allows Newman to fill the gaps in the conception of spontaneous moral and religious judgment, as well as to divide it into various operations" (Koritensky, "The Early John Henry Newman on Faith and Reason," 59).
60. Locke, *An Essay Concerning Human Understanding*, 391 (IV, 17).
61. Newman, *University Sermons*, 209.

say about how people process differences of opinion on political and other questions could apply to our own day, as seen in those who assume their political opponents are "blind followers," or "brainwashed" by certain media. In this account, everyone who disagrees—whether a communist or a capitalist, a conservative or a liberal—reasons badly. Of course, many people reason poorly, and some have been brainwashed. But Newman concerns himself with those who trace all difference in judgment to the power of reason, or lack thereof. And in Newman's time this criticism had been directed with greater frequency toward people of faith. Newman had little patience for these kinds of thinkers, whom he described as: "men of exact or acute but shallow minds, who consider all men wrong but themselves [. . .], who regard the pursuit of truth only as a syllogistic logic."[62] Newman reached this judgment not simply on the authority of Locke; he also rooted it in observation: "For the experience of life contains abundant evidence that in practical matters, when their minds are really roused, men commonly are not bad reasoners."[63] Recall the American TV series, "The Wire," which gives an intimate portrayal of the drug trade in urban Baltimore. In the first season, one character laments that his younger siblings cannot solve basic math problems assigned in school. They give the wrong answer until their older brother puts the question into a word problem with examples from the drug trade. They immediately know the right answer. When queried, they respond that, whereas nothing is at stake in school failure, their wellbeing could be threatened by an accounting error in the exchange of drugs for cash. Even if they could not articulate the principles employed in reaching the right number, they still reason correctly. Newman captures this dynamic when he writes of the mass of human beings: "They may

62. Newman, *University Sermons*, 210–11. In his autobiography Newman famously described Anglicanism as a "paper religion," but, more notable for the argument at hand, he complained about a "paper logic." Newman writes of the role of logic in his conversion: "I had a great dislike of paper logic. For myself, it was not logic that carried me on; as well might one say that the quicksilver in the barometer changes the weather. It is the concrete being that reasons; pass a number of years, and I find my mind in a new place; how ? [sic] the whole man moves; paper logic is but the record of it." See John Henry Cardinal Newman, *Apologia Pro Vita Sua*, ed. William Oddie (London: Dent, 1993), 218.

63. Newman, *University Sermons*, 211.

argue badly, but they reason well; that is, their professed grounds are no sufficient measure of their real ones."[64]

If this can be true of farmers and masons, it can also be true of people of faith. In documentaries like "Religulous," such cultured despisers as Bill Maher have tried to capture how people of faith reason poorly. The same failure would be easily demonstrable of almost any group in almost any sphere of knowledge. Even trained logicians and philosophers give absurd and silly justifications for how they choose to spend their money or pick their spouses. For Newman, the answer to religious skepticism resides not in airtight proofs or "evidences" of the reasonableness of Christianity. He suggests giving reason space to breathe before considering whether religious reasoning is of a similar kind as the sound reasoning that takes place among less learned people engaged in practical matters.

Besides expanding the scope of reason, Newman seeks to clarify how certitude corresponds to sound reasoning, given the seemingly superior disposition of doubt. Newman wrote during a time when natural sciences demonstrated a growing capacity for certitude, while humanities' disciplines engendered greater skepticism. It was the nineteenth century that witnessed the linguistic preference both for the word "scientist" to designate the natural sciences, and the "scientific method" as a term that divided liberal arts from natural sciences through the assumption that only one method, induction, could be scientific.[65] Newman did not think that this model would work for faith and theology; if it did, then one single argument would suffice for all believers. Anyone who teaches or catechizes knows this not to be so. Newman describes how the mind comes to know things beyond the realm of immediacy: "It makes progress not unlike a clamberer on a steep cliff, who, by quick eye, prompt hand, and firm foot, ascends how he knows not himself, by personal endowments and by practice, rather than by rule, leaving no track behind him, and unable to teach another."[66] We reach judgments about whether somebody is trustwor-

---

64. Newman, *University Sermons*, 212.
65. For this point, see Peter Harrison, *The Territories of Science and Religion* (Chicago: University of Chicago Press, 2015), esp. 164–70.
66. Newman, *University Sermons*, 257.

thy, or whether we can find a location without asking for help, if an email is spam, or if a job candidate will write well enough to get tenure, not in all cases by predetermined rule, but by a more varied route. Newman compares this process to mountain climbing, and calls it both "unsafe," and "precarious": "And such mainly is the way in which all men, gifted or not gifted, commonly reason,—not by rule, but by an inward faculty."[67]

Between the *Sermons* of 1839/1840, and *A Grammar of Assent* published nearly three decades later, Newman would give more precise terminology to describe this process, especially through his term "illative sense." In the case of concrete reasoning, both the early and the late Newman agreed:

> In no class of concrete reasonings, whether in experimental science, historical research, or theology, is there any ultimate test of truth and error in our inferences besides the trustworthiness of the Illative Sense that gives them its sanction; just as there is no sufficient test of poetical excellence, heroic action, or gentleman-like conduct, other than the particular mental sense, be it genius, taste, sense of propriety, or the moral sense, to which those subject-matters are severally committed.[68]

Before spelling out what Newman means by the illative sense, it will be helpful to explore what Newman understands to be the personal element of reasoning, and his consequent critique of rationalism.

In Martin Luther's theology and its reaction against the medieval sacramental system, there emerged the following truism: Just as nobody else can do your dying for you, so nobody can do your believing for you. Whatever social pressures there were to attend mass, go on pilgrimage, give confession, and the like, Luther insisted that your parents, or your community, could not ultimately do your believing for you. It is in part this insistence that makes so many assess Luther as a modern thinker, geared toward individual exercise of conscience. Newman makes a similar claim and also occupies a place as a defender of conscience. Popular religious authors like Samuel Clarke (1675–

67. Newman, *University Sermons*, 257.
68. Newman, *A Grammar of Assent*, 281.

1829) and William Paley (1743–1805), both Anglican clergymen, persuaded their learned countrymen for most of the eighteenth century with arguments about the "evidences" that bespoke of a divinely and benevolently ordered universe. For Clarke and Paley, a sober, objective view of the evidences would lead any rational person to belief.[69] David Hume would greatly disrupt many of these arguments in the *Dialogues Concerning Natural Religion*, perhaps the greatest treatise ever written against natural religion. Newman felt uneasy about the lessons some theologians had derived from natural theology, even if they had proven initially effective.[70] In his final chapter of *A Grammar of Assent*—"Inference and Assent in the matter of Religion"—Newman takes up this topic: "In religious inquiry each of us can speak only for himself, and for himself he has a right to speak. His own experiences are enough for himself, but he cannot speak for others: he cannot lay down the law; he can only bring his own experiences to the common stock of psychological facts."[71] In light of this reality, Newman calls for humility, not agnosticism.

Each year dozens of aspiring conservative biblical scholars enter seminary and encounter historical-critical interpretation in their theological training. For a few, this exposure leads to radical doubt, and they leave their seminaries and churches, finding homes in more liberal establishments, or in something other than Christianity. One cannot easily explain how the digestion of these experiences affects some so strongly, and others not at all. In Newman's example, each person must take up the evidences on their own—the wonders of creation, the luminosity of being, the gift of children, the witness of holy people, the scope of church history—in order to determine what these evidences yield. Newman addresses the matter of diverse evidences in a memorable passage:

> But, however that may be, he brings together his reasons, and relies
> on them, because they are his own, and this is his primary evidence;

69. For a summary of the "Evidential School," see Aquino, *Communities of Informed Judgment*, 16n6.

70. For Newman's direct engagement with Paley, see *A Grammar of Assent*, 329–31, and *University Sermons*, 195–97.

71. Newman, *A Grammar of Assent*, 300.

and he has a second ground of evidence, in the testimony of those who agree with him. But his best evidence is the former, which is derived from his own thoughts [. . .] and therefore his true sobriety and modesty consists, not in claiming for his conclusion an acceptance or a scientific approval which is not to be found anywhere, but in stating what are personally his own grounds for his belief.[72]

If for Luther, nobody else can do your believing for you, then for Newman, nobody else does your reasoning for you. The evidence for either belief or unbelief is never something we *have*; instead it is something we *weigh*, and we will not all weigh it in the same manner. In the Gospels, it is the devil, not Jesus, who suggested a circus performance over Jerusalem to leave no doubt in people's minds as to Jesus's supernatural mission (Luke 4:9–10; Matt 4:5–7). For Newman, people fail to believe in the gospel because of sin, not insufficient judgment.[73] Through the mysterious intermingling of grace with nature, some come to believe truly in their hearts, and others do not. Arguments may constitute a late, or important step, but prior moral and religious formation prepares the heart for this step.[74]

Newman's insistence on the concrete particularity of the reasoning process and his aversion to strictly logical method—couched so delicately in his subtle Victorian prose—have led many to attribute Newman's contributions to the genius of his mind, and to be less anxious about influence. But Newman's understanding of how faith and reason relate, especially as articulated in his notion of the "illative sense," shows his debt to Aristotle.[75] Although this debt is on display in *A*

72. Newman, *A Grammar of Assent*, 301.
73. Newman writes, "Further, they perhaps would say, that to insist much on matters which are for the most part so useless for any practical purpose, draws men away from the true view of Christianity, and leads them to think that Faith is mainly the result of argument, that religious Truth is a legitimate matter of disputation, and that they who reject it rather err in judgment than commit sin" (Newman, *University Sermons*, 198).
74. In this same paragraph, Newman cites Matthew 5:8: "The pure in heart shall see God" (Newman, *University Sermons*, 198).
75. For a short but helpful examination of Newman's relationship to Aristotle, see Joshua Hochschild, "The Re-Imagined Aristotelianism of John Henry Newman," *Modern Age* 45, no. 4 (2003): 333–42. Hochschild surmises: "Aristotle is clearly the master even of what is taken to be most original in *A Grammar of Assent*, Newman's notion of 'the Illative Sense'" (Hochschild, "The Re-Imagined Aristotelianism of John Henry Newman,"

Grammar of Assent, where Newman writes, "As to the intellectual position from which I have contemplated the subject, Aristotle has been my master,"[76] scholars have also traced Aristotle's influence on Newman to earlier writings, including the *University Sermons*.[77] In chapter 9 of *A Grammar of Assent*, which Newman subtitled "The Illative Sense," he gives an account of how humans move from experience or data to certitude, which he identifies as a mental state.[78] Since one person can be certain she is in love after a week, and another might take years, it is nonsense to talk as though certitude existed on an objective level, like a merited conclusion. When Newman says certitude is a mental state, he means that it exists nowhere else but in particular minds, about particular matters. The statement "it is raining" also exists in the mind, but it corresponds to a perceived reality in the world. The statement "I am certain it is raining" exists more properly and exclusively in the mind. How does one come to this certitude?

Newman asks this question because the Christian tradition talks about conviction and certitude as fruits of belief. Certain skeptics asked whether certitude did not require an unjustified leap, and recommended in its place caution. Newman was responding to Christians who proposed something akin to the "epistemological Pelagianism" that Kuhn associated with Georg Hermes. Newman wanted to occupy a space between these positions; convictions about matters not strictly provable were neither earned, on the one hand, nor unreasonable, on the other. A passage from *A Grammar of Assent* captures Newman's position:

---

336); he later concludes, "Newman communicates Aristotelian ideas, not hardened and familiar in the technical terminology of scholastic manuals, but renovated and re-imagined in the vigorous language of his personal style. Newman's learned Aristotelianism is a re-imagined Aristotelianism," (Hochschild, "The Re-Imagined Aristotelianism of John Henry Newman," 341).

76. Newman, *A Grammar of Assent*, 334.

77. Besides Hochschild, who traces it to the *Idea of a University*, begun in 1852, see Koritensky, "The Early John Henry Newman on Faith and Reason." Koritensky writes, "The practical philosophy of Aristotle with its epistemological implications became Newman's guideline to outline his ideas [in the *University Sermons*]. Upon this foundation, Newman developed an epistemology of faith" (Koritensky, "The Early John Henry Newman on Faith and Reason." 48).

78. Newman, *A Grammar of Assent*, 271.

Not that I deny that demonstration is possible. Truth certainly, as such, rests upon grounds intrinsically and objectively and abstractedly demonstrative, but it does not follow from this that the arguments producible in its favour are unanswerable and irresistible. [...] The fact of revelation is in itself demonstrably true, but it is not therefore true irresistibly; else, how comes it to be resisted? There is a vast distance between what it is in itself, and what it is to us.[79]

If certitude is not earned, on what grounds can it be justified? How is it distinguished from prejudice or superstition? In both *A Grammar of Assent* and the *University Sermons*, Newman points to a number of moral and intellectual habits described by Aristotle that help answer this question and complement Newman's point about the personal nature of reasoning.[80]

In the *Nicomachean Ethics*, Aristotle claims that questions of moral goodness cannot be answered by means of *theoria*, and instead find resolution in the activity of *phronesis*, or judgment. Newman explains: "[*Phronesis*] is the directing, controlling and determining principle in such matters, personal and social."[81] This faculty of judgment provides the answers for how to act well and justly: "Judgment then in all concrete matter is the architectonic faculty; and what may be called the Illative Sense, or right judgment in ratiocination, is one branch of it."[82] Rules cannot predetermine how the illative sense will operate in particular cases: "For the answers in fullness and accuracy to these and similar questions, the philosopher refers us to no code of laws, to no moral treatise, because no science of life, applicable to the case of an individual, has been or can be written." Even so, Newman does not advocate moral relativism. His point is that the application of general rules to particular cases is done by individuals through the activity of *phronesis*: "An ethical system may supply laws, general rules,

79. Newman, *A Grammar of Assent*, 318–19.

80. For this point see McIntosh, "God as First Truth," 421: "The certitude of authentic faith *can* be distinguished from mere doggedness or prejudice or superstition precisely by the moral and epistemic character that really guides the life of a believing person, by his or her genuine humility, authentic love of what is good, and persistent and reverent desire to know and serve the truth."

81. Newman, *A Grammar of Assent*, 277.

82. Newman, *A Grammar of Assent*, 269.

[. . .] but who is to apply them to a particular case? whither can we go, except to the living intellect, our own, or another's?"[83] For this reason Aristotle focuses his treatment of ethics on character formation.

Aquinas notably transposed Aristotle's association of virtue and habit into an analogical understanding of how acquired and supernatural virtues relate in the Christian life.[84] Newman draws upon the same Aristotelian association of virtue with habit to explain how a believer reaches certitude about matters of faith. Certitude comes to the believer through antecedent judgment and inference, and when believers apply these moral and intellectual habits to their life of faith, their certitude about Christian mysteries is entirely, though analogically, compatible with the operation of reason. Newman opines, "Though truth is ever one and the same, and the assent of certitude is immutable, still the reasonings which carry us on to truth and certitude are many and distinct, and vary with the inquirer."[85] Newman correlates this crowning act of judgment with the illative sense, and in practical matters *it*, not any other science, is the test of truth or error. One does not judge, strictly speaking, whether New Zealand, lying off the western coast of Australia, is a real place, unless of course one has been there; one judges whether or not the people making this claim are trustworthy. Just as it is rational to trust scientific authorities, so too is it rational to trust generally reliable religious authorities. Newman conveys these points, with a hint of wistfulness, as though he wishes there were a more certain path to faith. Given the limits of human cognition, he offers his best and only account of how humans come to believe in God.[86]

This certitude, however, cannot be conceived as a subsequent step; there is something of a leap in it. Jaime Ferreira highlights how certi-

---

83. Newman, *A Grammar of Assent*, 277.
84. See especially Aquinas, *Summa Theologiae*, Part Two.
85. Newman, *A Grammar of Assent*, 278.
86. In emphasizing the shaky ground upon which Newman puts assent to Christian faith, some have understandably identified Newman as a fideist or an irrationalist. Nicholas Lash notes these accusations: "It is therefore not surprising that, from the Modernist crisis to our own day, Newman has frequently been charged with 'irrationalism,' 'fideism,' and cognate vices" (Lash, "Introduction," 8). For the most notable instance of this, see Frank Turner, *John Henry Newman: The Challenge to Evangelical Religion* (New Haven, CT: Yale University Press, 2002). For a refutation of Turner on this point, see Hochschild, "The Re-Imagined Aristotelianism of John Henry Newman," at 338.

tude functions for Newman: "Newman thus makes certitude [. . .] a 'threshold' concept, a concept which is not applicable at all until it is simply and totally applicable. [. . .] A threshold concept refers to a state or condition which is not expressed gradually or by degrees."[87] Ferreira then refers to Newman's own example of water coming to a boil: It's either boiling or it's not.[88] Water is never half-boiling, and a person is never partially certain. Newman uses another metaphor—the contrast between an iron rod and a cable: "An iron rod represents mathematical or strict demonstration; a cable represents moral demonstration, which is an assemblage of probabilities. [. . .] A man who said 'I cannot trust a cable, I must have an iron bar,' would in certain given cases, be irrational and unreasonable."[89] Or to put it conversely, a person who trusts in a cable is neither irrational nor unreasonable. Certitude is accompanied by a sense of relaxation, analogous to no longer worrying whether a mentor or friend really likes you.[90] As Newman notes, certitude does not admit of degree; one is either certain or not.[91]

If faith gives rise to an analogical certitude as proportionate to the truths of faith, how does one safeguard oneself against the fanaticism and enthusiasm that serve as misleading simulacra of authentic faith? Newman addresses this question in "Sermon XII," where he writes: "such a view [about faith] may be made an excuse for all manner of prejudice and bigotry, and leads directly to credulity and superstition."[92] One might expect Newman, an Oxford man to the bone, to recommend some form of continuing education or application of reason as a way to steady faith. Newman describes this position in the same section of the sermon: "Give them, then, education; open their

87. Jaime Ferreira, "Leaps and Circles: Kierkegaard and Newman on Faith and Reason," *Religious Studies* 30, no. 4 (1994): 385.

88. Ferreira, "Leaps and Circles," 386; see Newman, *Letters and Diaries*, vol. 27, 161–62 (27 November, 1874).

89. Newman, *Letters and Diaries*, vol. 21, 146; cited in Lash, "Introduction," 16.

90. Nobody makes this point to greater effect than James Alison in *Jesus the Forgiving Victim* (Glenview, IL: Doers, 2013), 187–231.

91. For Newman on certainty, see *A Grammar of Assent*, chapter 7, 173–208. For this specific quotation, see Newman, *Theological Papers of John Henry Newman on Faith and Certainty* (Oxford: Clarendon, 1976), 124: "Certitude does not admit of more or less—but is a state of mind, definite and complete, admitting only of being and non-being." I owe this reference to Ferreira, "Leaps and Circles," 385.

92. Newman, *University Sermons*, 232.

minds; enlighten them; enable them to reflect, compare, investigate, and infer; draw their attention to the Evidences of Christianity."[93] Newman, however, rejects the idea that reason should serve as faith's safeguard. For if reason does not produce faith, it cannot, strictly speaking, maintain it. Newman explains:

> The safeguard of Faith is a right state of heart. This it is that gives it birth; it also disciplines it. [. . .] It is holiness, or dutifulness, or the new creation, or the spiritual mind, however we word it, which is the quickening and illuminating principle of true faith, giving it eyes, hands, and feet. It is Love which forms it out of the rude chaos into an image of Christ.[94]

Newman then appends the scholastic formula *fides formata caritate* ("faith formed by charity") to his argument. The heart, not the mind, prevents the believer from becoming a fanatic. In light of almost two hundred years' worth of additional data since Newman's 1839 appeal, he seems to have it right. Fanaticism can fell the best skeptic, or atheist, or scientist, or believer of any stripe, for anyone can fail to love. Recalling the last century's many gulags and torture chambers, the one common denominator between both secular and religious fanatics seems to be a want of charity.

FERDINAND CHRISTIAN BAUR

German Protestantism produced a dizzying array of movements, schools, trends, and reconfigurations of theology. So much of this reconfiguration took place in connection with seismic shifts in conceptions of sciences and in the structure of universities. As the understanding of science changed, so too did the corresponding sense about whether theology could be scientific. To capture what was at stake in this debate, the rest of this chapter will examine one Protestant theologian who embraced the modern paradigm—Friedrich Christian Baur (1792–1860)—before turning to another who rejected it, the great Danish thinker, Søren Kierkegaard (1813–55).

93. Newman, *University Sermons*, 233.
94. Newman, *University Sermons*, 234.

Born in a small village near the birthplace of Johannes Kuhn, Baur was the son of a Lutheran pastor. He followed in his father's footsteps, studying theology in Tübingen where he would return as a professor in 1828. Eventually he came to be regarded as the guiding light of the "Tübingen School" approach to New Testament studies and church history.[95] Baur grappled with all of the major currents that impacted theology during his time. As a student, he was immersed in the Tübingen "supernaturalism" associated with Gottlob Storr, which arose in reaction to an Enlightenment rationalism that sought to strip Christianity of anything supernatural. Baur broke from strict supernaturalism through his encounter with Friedrich Schleiermacher, whose *The Christian Faith*, first issued in 1821, called into question the necessity of the resurrection for Christianity. Baur also learned a great deal from Friedrich Schelling, whose post-Kantian "Absolute Idealism" took both history and Christianity more seriously than did Kant. Yet the figure who seemed to function as the moon in the bountiful tides of Baur's writings was Hegel. Recent scholars have noted that Baur did not discover Hegel until the 1830s, when Baur was already a professor and author of many books. Still, Baur's mature thought bore the stamp of this Hegelian influence from 1835 until his death in 1860. And this stamp entailed a conviction about the precise manner in which Christianity could be rational and scientific, the implication being that Christianity needed to catch up if it wanted to be taken seriously by an intellectual elite becoming more cultured and more inclined to despise Christianity.

The aforementioned influences—Schleiermacher, Schelling, and Hegel—shaped the trajectory of thought on how faith related to reason in light of the assumptions of the modern world. Yet in none of these thinkers do the struggles of the age and the drive for theology to be scientifically viable come to the forefront as they do in Baur. Unlike Kierkegaard, who looked with so much skepticism at the age, Baur saw an age ripe with possibility, able to overcome the tension between naturalism and supernaturalism, and saw himself as equipped to use the tools of modern historical research to understand aright the

---

95. For a classic but flawed account of the school, see Horton Harris, *The Tübingen School* (Oxford: Clarendon, 1975).

essence of Christianity, which had been obscured by past dogmatism and bad historiography.

Though Protestantism, especially the Lutheran variety, contained elements that led to fideism, Baur regarded Protestant Christianity as the only viable context in which faith and reason could be shown as compatible. Notwithstanding the synthesis of faith and reason achieved by medieval Catholicism, Baur considered the Catholic system misbegotten and ill-equipped for the age. Only Protestant Christianity, based on the inviolable rights of the individual to pursue the truth, could protect this pursuit from the suffocating clutches of authority. Baur did not identify Protestantism's essence with Luther's *sola scriptura* or *sola fide*; instead, he located it in a freedom that Luther foretold in so many ways: "Protestantism in its innermost nature is the principle of autonomy, of liberation and withdrawal from everything in which the self-conscious spirit does not recognize its own nature."[96] This position, which owed as much to the Enlightenment as it did to the sixteenth century, highlighted the role of the theologian working in the university. In Baur's account, academics like himself were not merely pursuing arcane interests; they were manifesting the spirit of Protestantism by inquiring into the rationality of their faith. Those Protestants who retreated into the dogmatism of their confession defied the deepest truth of their own tradition, and were formally Catholic, regardless of their material loyalty to the Augsburg Confession, the Westminster Catechism, or the Synod of Dort.

Baur came to understand supernaturalism as a barrier to a coherent, rational understanding of Christianity. His eventual abandonment of supernaturalism represented a decisive break from the Tübingen of his student days. Beginning with Spinoza, whose rationalism was

---

96. Ferdinand Christian Baur, *Church and Theology in the Nineteenth Century*, ed. Peter Hodgson, trans. Robert Brown and Peter Hodgson (Eugene, OR: Cascade Books, 2018), 37. Although these lectures were from the latter part of Baur's career, his concern for Catholicism's lack of intellectual freedom manifested itself already in the 1830s. In an 1835 letter to a leading Protestant organization, Baur defines being Protestant as "pursuing true enquiry," and opposition to such enquiry conceals a "Catholic principle of authority," which is also "the principle of lazy reason [*das Princip der faulen Vernunft*]." See "Ferdinand Christian Baur an den Evangelischesn Verein in Tübingen," in Ferdinand Christian Baur, *Die frühen Briefe (1814–1835)*, ed. Carl Hester (Sigmaringen: Jan Thorbecke, 1993), 129–44, at 134.

combined with political radicalism, and continuing through the high Enlightenment of Immanuel Kant, rationalism posed a challenge that Baur took seriously: If the universe functioned according to, in Spinoza's words, "fixed and immutable laws," then biblical events should conform to these laws.[97] David Hume largely agreed with Spinoza when he defined "miracle" as a violation of the (fixed and immutable) laws of nature.[98] Christian history needed to be filtered through rational exegesis in order to maintain rational religion. In reaction to this novel way of understanding the relationship of reason to the data of Christian faith, the supernaturalists defended biblical miracles. Based on a biblical understanding of divine intervention, the supernaturalists conceived a God who not only created the laws of nature, but intervened selectively in history.[99]

Educated in a supernaturalist hotbed, Baur's initial sympathies lay with that position. Baur's encounter with Schleiermacher's *The Christian Faith* in 1821 led him to reject the terms set by both sides. For Baur it made no sense to believe in a God who both created the laws of nature and interrupted them at will. Baur's nature was not a closed system, and his God was more the God "in whom we live and move and have our being" (Acts 17:28), than the clockmaker God associated with deism. But as a historical theologian committed to the reigning standards of the discipline of history, Baur saw the task at hand as one of understanding the causal connection between events, so as to render Christianity intelligibly. For if historical events were not intelligibly connected, Baur thought, then one could only construct an arbitrary relationship between contemporary Christianity and its founding. Miracles, viewed by Baur as supernatural interruptions with no connection to historical events, made it impossible for Christianity to cohere as a historical reality.

97. See Spinoza, *Theological-Political Treatise*, chapter 6, "Of Miracles."

98. See David Hume, *An Enquiry Concerning Human Understanding*, ed. Eric Steinberg (Indianapolis: Hackett, 1977). In chapter 10, "Of Miracles," Hume writes, "A miracle is a violation of the laws of nature" (Hume, *An Enquiry Concerning Human Understanding*, 76).

99. For the supernaturalists, and Baur's relationship to them, see Stefan Alkier, "Belief in Miracles as the Gateway to Atheism: Theological-Historical Remarks about Ferdinand Christian Baur's Critique of Miracles," in *Ferdinand Christian Baur and the History of Early Christianity*, eds. Martin Bauspiess, Christof Landmesser, and David Lincicum (Oxford: Oxford University Press, 2017), 261–86.

One can draw a parallel from evolutionary biology to illustrate Baur's concern.[100] Imagine nature progressing along for millions of years, according to laws of evolutionary biology. Then, at the end of the Jurassic period, God beams down a new species like a sea otter, which has no discernible biological connection to the creatures preceding it. From the standpoint of evolutionary biology, this new species would be biologically unintelligible. Thus it was with biblical supernaturalism, as Baur explains: "He who regards [the virgin birth] as simply and absolutely a miracle, steps at once outside of all historical connection. A miracle is an absolute beginning, and since as such it must needs qualify all that follows, the whole series of phenomena which fall within the range of Christianity must bear the same miraculous character."[101] Miracles understood as supernatural entities made it impossible to connect events historically, and made the hope of serious study of the past unfeasible. Given his embrace of this reasoning, it becomes clear why Baur considered the supernaturalist option a dead end for the scientific study of theology.

As Baur saw it, historical theology performed two tasks essential for the project of making faith intelligible. First, it used philosophy to inform how to connect events in order to render them intelligible. Second it employed scientific resources, which in this instance meant a critical, rather than dogmatic approach to the sources of Christian history. It did so because the stuff of history on its own did not form itself into a rational whole. Regarding the first point, Baur declared already in 1824, in the preface to *Symbolik und Mythologie*: "I do not at all fear succumbing to the well-known accusation of co-mingling philosophy and history. Without philosophy, history remains for me forever dead and dumb."[102] This is perhaps the most cited line from all of Baur's works. For Baur, it meant that one requires a leading idea in order to connect the facts, and on this point he was following the

---

100. This point is made in a review by Grant Kaplan of *Ferdinand Christian Baur and the History of Early Christianity*, in *International Journal of Systematic Theology* 20:3 (2018): 443–47.

101. Ferdinand Baur, *The Church History of the First Three Centuries*, ed. and trans. Allan Menzies, 2 vols. (London: Williams & Norgate, 1878), I, 1.

102. Ferdinand Baur, *Symbolik und Mythologie, oder die Naturreligion des Alterthums. Erster oder Allgemeiner Theil* (Stuttgart: J. B. Metzler, 1824), xi.

thought of Schelling and Schleiermacher: One could not understand religious history, for instance, without some guiding principle, in this case a comparative study of symbol and myth, hence the title of Baur's book. Recalling his infamous statement opens the door to correct a common stereotype of Baur. According to this stereotype, Baur imposed Hegelian philosophy onto church history, wherein a dyad of thesis and antithesis rounded into a synthesis: In the New Testament, Pauline antinomianism, opposed by James's emphasis on works, resulted in the Petrine synthesis. Later scholars complained that Baur's account of church history, to avoid being judged deaf and dumb by Baur, was forced to conform to this triad, sometimes at the expense of the historical record. If making theology "scientific" involved such ideological cant, then to many it seemed justified to reject Baur's project.

A closer look at Baur reveals the fragility of this stereotype. The first and most obvious point is that Baur had not yet even read Hegel when he famously defended the place of philosophy in history.[103] Other philosophies of history, especially Schelling's, had gained influence before Hegel, and Baur had fallen under their influence. The infamous triadic interpretation itself was not even true to Hegel.[104] Further, even after Baur discovered Hegel—a discovery that made Hegel perhaps Baur's most abiding intellectual partner—the incorporation was never uncritical and in some instances Baur stretched Hegel to the point of misrepresenting him.[105] Baur was his own man, with his own historical program that meant interpreting Christian history not as a random collection of events or facts around a place or

103. For this point, see, among others, Peter Hodgson, *The Formation of Historical Theology: A Study of Ferdinand Christian Baur* (Harper & Row, 1966), 15; Baur, *Church and Theology in the Nineteenth Century*, 316–17n1; Johannes Zachhuber, "The Absoluteness of Christianity and the Relativity of all History," and Martin Wendte, "Ferdinand Christian Baur: A Historically Informed Idealist of a Distinctive Kind," in *Ferdinand Christian Baur and the History of Early Christianity*, 287–304 (at 291) and 67–79. Wendte cites the famous judgment of Emanuel Hirsch: "Hirsch's evaluation has lost nothing of its relevance: 'Whoever accuses him [Baur] of an a priori historical construction has never read him seriously.'" For Hirsch, see *Geschichte der neuern evangelischen Theologie*, 3rd ed. (Gütersloh: G Mohn, 1964), 521.

104. See Gustav Mueller, "The Hegel Legend of Thesis-Antithesis-Synthesis," *Journal of the History of Ideas* 19, no. 3 (1958): 411–14.

105. Zachhuber, "The Absoluteness of Christianity," 301–3.

person, but instead according to certain ideas, like reconciliation, or incarnation, that explained where history was going.

For Baur, Christianity was irreducibly historical; he did not follow the Kantian reduction of Christianity to ethical norms. Peter Hodgson writes about "a basic continuity" that animated Baur's work: "This continuity was provided by a conviction about the irreducibly historical nature of the Christian Church, its Gospel and its faith."[106] But from its origins, Christianity sought to transform these historical events into more permanent categories and concepts. Jesus of Nazareth walked from one town to another, preached the Kingdom of God, and was crucified by Pontius Pilate. Yet already in the earliest record the evangelists go beyond these events: Even Mark has the centurion declare, "Surely this man was the Son of God" (15:39). Likewise, John's Gospel begins with the famous prologue, which describes the Word becoming flesh (John 1:14). Baur cites this example in a letter, where he also states that the content of faith is not merely empirical, but is also the object of spiritual intuition (*geistige Anschauung*).[107] The emerging critical history, which doubted the authenticity of certain aspects of the gospels, including events, authorship, and objectivity, was in line with, rather than a contradiction of, the basic tendency already present in the earliest writings, to employ universal concepts in order to understand this history, and to extract ideas and concepts from it. If the New Testament is the basis for understanding Christian origins, then a believing Christian should want it to be accurate, and faith itself should be open to revision from a critical, scientific-historical investigation.[108] A faith that seeks understanding, transposed from Anselm's eleventh-century abbey to Baur's nineteenth-century Germany, means subjecting the Christian narration of history to historical criticism.

The greatest threat to this principle, for Baur, was the Catholic principle of authority, to which Protestants clung as well, albeit in a different form. When Baur considered the possibility, and even the actuality, of churches limiting historical research, he judged it a failure

106. Hodgson, *The Formation of Historical Theology*, 22.
107. Baur, *Die frühen Briefe*, 137.
108. Baur, *Die frühen Briefe*, 133.

to bring rational reflection to faith. For Protestants this means nothing less than the failure of Protestantism to realize its essential quality.[109] Baur did not march in lockstep with Hegel's effort to elevate religious representation to the absolute knowing of the concept, which only philosophy could accomplish, but he did glean from Hegel the inspiration to transform faith into a more refined form of understanding that replaced religious representations or symbols with philosophical concepts. In doing so, he also displayed the hopeful optimism of the nineteenth century, in this case an optimism in the scientific legitimacy and objectivity of historical enquiry that still animates much of academic theology.

SØREN KIERKEGAARD

More than almost any modern figure, Kierkegaard reacted against Enlightenment systems of reasoning and against the secularizing academic trends that many came to see as undermining Christianity. Kierkegaard's emphasis on subjectivity, his aversion to system, and his irony have contributed to his reputation as a precursor both to the existentialism associated with the twentieth century, and to postmodern theory, especially the deconstruction of the self. Despite being relatively uninfluential in his own lifetime, Kierkegaard has become a canonical author, read alongside Friedrich Nietzsche, Fyodor Dostoevsky, and Jean-Paul Sartre in the existentialist catalogue.[110] Kierkegaard's writings echo many of the themes already seen in earlier figures, especially Luther and Pascal, but he put their ideas and themes in his own key, and responded to issues postdating what animated the sixteenth and seventeenth century. In order to chronicle how Kierkegaard developed his peculiar understanding of faith and reason, it will be helpful to review his Lutheran background and influence, in the context of his biography, before examining his reaction to Hegelian

---

109. Baur, *Die frühen Briefe*, 134.

110. For this point, see Steve Wilkens and Alan Padgett, *Christianity & Western Thought*, vol. 2, *Faith & Reason in the 19th Century* (Downers Grove, IL: InterVarsity, 2000), at 156: "At his death [Kierkegaard] was almost completely unknown outside the Scandinavian countries, and there was little evidence he would become the father of one of the most potent philosophical schools of the twentieth century: existentialism."

philosophy, and his understanding of faith in the context of subjectivity and passion.

The arc of Kierkegaard's life is known to many who have not even
read his works. Like a figure in a movie by the great Swedish filmmaker,
Ingmar Bergman,[111] Kierkegaard could not disentangle his relationship
with his father from his relationship with God, both of whom he perceived as loving him with a severe, harsh love. The father, Michael
Kierkegaard, rose from poverty to wealth and prestige in Copenhagen.
Søren attended the university in Copenhagen, and as a young man
began his tortured relationship with an even younger Regine Olsen,
who, next to Dante's Beatrice or Abelard's Heloise, is perhaps the most
famous love interest of a major Christian figure. Kierkegaard broke off
his engagement to Olsen on the grounds that he did not think himself
fit for marriage despite being, among philosophers, the one who had
written most frequently and deeply about love and passion. Around
the same time, Kierkegaard completed his theology degree and began
his career as an author, producing voluminous books and shorter writings, some under various pseudonyms (including Johannes Climacus,
Johannes de Silentio, Constantin Constantius, Anti-Climacus, and
Hilarius Bookbinder) in addition to his own name. Kierkegaard
afforded his lifestyle through the inheritance from his father, and wrote
frenetically right up to his early death, having never married, and having achieved great notoriety but little recognition.

In Kierkegaard's Denmark, Lutheranism was the official church of
the Danish state, which meant that almost all non-Jewish citizens were
baptized and incorporated into the Lutheran Church. The head of the
Danish Lutheran Church for most of Kierkegaard's life, Jacob Mynster,
was a friend and former pastor to Michael Kierkegaard. His replace-
ment, a Hegelian theologian named H. L. Martensen, took over in 1854,
one year before Kierkegaard's death. Kierkegaard lamented how being
Christian had become a matter of course in Denmark, and the restraint
he had shown out of respect for his father's friend, Mynster, now gave
way to a torrent of criticism, perhaps amplified because Martensen represented the worst kind of Hegelian theologian in Kierkegaard's eyes.

111. See in particular "Fanny and Alexander" (1982).

Both Luther and Kierkegaard detested an ecclesiastical system that removed the responsibility of believing from the individual—nobody else can do your believing for you! Though Kierkegaard was familiar with Luther from his student days in the 1830s, he did not read him intensively until 1846, at which point he was able to discern the parallel between Luther's *pro nobis* theology and his own emphasis on subjectivity and inwardness.[112] According to Luther, we know God not as a God *in se*, but instead as a God we encounter personally.[113] Therefore one's faith must begin with a personal encounter. In the Denmark of Kierkegaard's time, the church did your believing for you. Your parents baptized you and took you to church, and next to nothing was required to remain in it; at no point did one make a personal decision for Christ. In a series of letters and self-published pamphlets later collected and translated as *Attack Upon Christendom*, Kierkegaard sets out his complaints:

> When one sees what it is to be a Christian in Denmark, how could it occur to anyone that this is what Jesus Christ talks about: cross and agony and suffering, crucifying the flesh, suffering for the doctrine, being salt, being sacrificed, etc.? No, in Protestantism, especially in Denmark, Christianity marches to a different melody, to the tune of "Merrily we roll along, roll along, roll along"—Christianity is enjoyment of life, tranquillized, as neither the Jew nor the pagan was, by the assurance that the thing about eternity is settled.[114]

If being Christian conforms wholly to the norms of bourgeois respectability, or to basic citizenship, then how can a Christian believer be salt or leaven to the world? Kierkegaard complains that church leadership,

112. For this point, see David Gouwens, "Søren Kierkegaard: Between Skepticism and Faith's Happy Passion," in *The Devil's Whore*, 115–21, at 117. It remains unclear whether Kierkegaard was able to disentangle Luther from Lutheran theology. For this point see Rebecca Skaggs, "The Role of Reason in Faith in St. Thomas Aquinas and Kierkegaard," *Heythrop Journal* 58 (2017): 612–25, at 622n6.

113. In "Freedom of a Christian," Luther writes: "Rather ought Christ be preached to the end that faith in him may be established that he may not only be Christ, but be Christ *for you and me*, and that what is said of him and is denoted in his name may be effectual *in us*." See *Martin Luther: Selections from his Writings*, ed. John Dillenberger (New York: Doubleday, 1962), 66; emphasis mine.

114. Søren Kierkegaard, *Kierkegaard's Attack Upon "Christendom" 1854–55*, trans. Walter Lowrie (Princeton: Princeton University Press, 1944), 34–35.

attached to the honor and prestige to which it has become accustomed, cannot both live in that comfort and preach the gospel honestly: "For if things were to remain as they were, if only a few poor, persecuted, hated men were Christians, where was the silk and velvet to come from, and honor and prestige, and worldly enjoyment[?]"[115] Such church leaders cannot preach the gospel with probity, or compellingly lead their flock to conform their lives to the New Testament ideal. They are, in Kierkegaard's judgment, indistinguishable from the world.

In his pamphlets, Kierkegaard repeatedly attacks the practice, still in place in many Western European countries, of having the state pay the salaries of church officials. In this arrangement, the accommodation of Christianity to the ethos of the state seems preordained. Kierkegaard also scrutinizes infant baptism, especially in the case of more or less secular Danes with no strong religious opinion who still baptize their children in the Lutheran Church: "And this they dare to present to God under the name of Christian baptism. Baptism—it was with this sacred ceremony the Saviour of the world was consecrated for His life's work, and after Him the disciples, men who [...] promised to be willing to live as sacrificed men in this world of falsehood and evil."[116] Instead of baptism signifying a turning away from the world, it had become an embrace of the world. And in this system, the individual never chose to become a Christian. The choice is made for them, and thus the likelihood that they will be salt or leaven is minimal.

This ecclesial situation had direct bearing on Kierkegaard's stinging critique of reason. Kierkegaard notoriously emphasized the need for a "leap of faith." Reason only gets one so far and can even prevent one from attaining faith. Kierkegaard, according to this account, prescribes a "leap" into the super- or even ir-rational, making him the modern inheritor of the tradition of fideism that moves from Paul, through Tertullian and Luther, up to Kierkegaard and his postmodern offspring. Yet this portrayal faces problems when one tries to pin down Kierkegaard's irrational fideism. While Kierkegaard does talk a great deal about leaps, he never uses the Danish equivalent for "leap of

115. Kierkegaard, *Attack Upon Christendom*, 35.
116. Kierkegaard, *Attack Upon Christendom*, 205.

faith."[117] Despite this persistent caricature of Kierkegaard the irrationalist, scholars since at least the 1980s have conceded that Kierkegaard
does not forsake reason in favor of a crude fideism.[118] To understand
how Kierkegaard related faith to reason, it will be helpful to begin with
an examination of how he conceived this leap.

In his *Concluding Unscientific Postscript*, which continued an
argument from his *Philosophical Fragments*, Kierkegaard writes, "Lessing has said that contingent historical truths can never become a demonstration of eternal truths of reason, also that the transition whereby
one will build an eternal truth on historical reports is a leap. I shall
now scrutinize these two assertions in some detail and correlate them
with the issue of *Fragments*: Can an eternal happiness be built on historical knowledge."[119] Kierkegaard inherited the notion of the leap
from Gotthold Lessing, who borrowed it from Aristotle; it was not
Kierkegaard's invention.[120] Regardless, Kierkegaard made it his own.
Lessing was a leading figure of the German Enlightenment, and a
thorn in the side of eighteenth-century Lutheran orthodoxy. He col-
luded with the children of Hermann Samuel Reimarus to posthumously publish their father's *Fragments*, a groundbreaking work of
New Testament criticism.[121] In addition, Lessing highlighted contradictions in many of the arguments offered by leading theologians.
Kierkegaard took Lessing's central question—*how can one move seam-*

117. For this point, see Jamie Ferreira, "Faith and the Kierkegaardian Leap," in *The
Cambridge Companion to Kierkegaard*, eds. Alastair Hannay and Gordon Marino (Cambridge: Cambridge University Press, 1998), 207–34, at 207.

118. Rebecca Skaggs writes, "Until recently, Kierkegaard was considered by some
scholars [. . .] to be a fideist but scholars such as Louis Pojman and Steven Evans [. . .] have
managed to change this perception," in Skaggs, "The Role of Reason in Faith in St. Thomas
Aquinas and Kierkegaard," 623n11.

119. Søren Kierkegaard, *Concluding Unscientific Postscript to Philosophical Fragments*,
eds. and trans. Howard Hong and Edna Hong, vol. 1 (Princeton, NJ: Princeton University
Press, 1992), 93. For Lessing's analogy of a ditch and the need for a leap, see his 1777
rejoinder, "On the Proof of the Spirit and of Power," in Gotthold Lessing, *Philosophical and
Theological Writings*, ed. and trans. H. B. Nisbet (Cambridge: Cambridge University Press,
2005), at 85, 87. For a critique of Lessing, see Kaplan, *Answering the Enlightenment*, 7–22.

120. Lessing writes, "But to make the leap from this historical truth into a quite different class of truths [. . .] if this is not a 'transition to another category,' I do not know
what Aristotle meant by that phrase." ("On the Proof of the Spirit and of Power," 87); See
Aristotle, *Posterior Analytics* I, 6–7.

121. Hermann Reimarus, *Fragments*, trans. Ralph Fraser (Cambridge: SCM-Canterbury, 1970).

lessly from a historical event to an eternal truth?—and flipped it on its head: Instead of using the ditch to show the irrationality of Christianity (as most assumed that Lessing was doing), Kierkegaard commandeered Lessing's argument to demonstrate the necessity of faith.

Perhaps unique among religions, Christianity places not a text or an idea, but a person—Jesus of Nazareth—at the center of its faith. Yet the act of belief involves much more than the simple affirmation of historical events, even miraculous ones. Focusing on the same short treatise of Lessing, Kierkegaard explains: "Lessing opposes what I would call quantifying oneself into a qualitative decision; he contests the direct *transition* from historical reliability to a decision on an eternal happiness."[122] Kierkegaard rejects this transition as an intellectual ruse. People accept the veracity of any number of historical events, from an important court case to an episode in military history. But Christianity does not simply demand, as the creed says, that one accept that Jesus Christ was crucified under Pontius Pilate, or rose again on the third day. Kierkegaard continues:

> Lessing is willing to believe that an Alexander who subjugated all of Asia did live once [. . .] "but who, on the basis of this belief, would risk anything of great, permanent worth?" [. . .]
> It is the transition, the direct transition from historical reliability to an eternal decision, that Lessing continually contests.[123]

Believing in the truth of Christianity is not the same as believing that Caesar crossed the Rubicon; unlike the latter claim, believing in Christianity means placing all of one's trust in God while turning away from one's prior, sinful self. The convert's life now spins on a different axis. This kind of belief, or conversion, reorients one's entire world, and invites one into a truth that changes the light in which one understands everything else. It is less like bringing a logical point to conclusion, and more like falling in love with a person.[124] Kierkegaard

---

122. Kierkegaard, *Concluding Unscientific Postscript*, 95–96, emphasis mine.

123. Kierkegaard, *Concluding Unscientific Postscript*, 96; Lessing, "On the Proof of the Spirit and of Power," 87.

124. In his discussion of Kierkegaard, Merold Westphal notes how faith in this sense makes no sense outside of a relational context, in which God is not an object, but a

delights in the irony that Lessing, an Enlightenment playwright and critic of traditional Christianity, understood this point better than the leading figures in establishment Christianity, whose perspective in Lessing's Germany was echoed by the religious elite in Kierkegaard's Denmark half a century later.

To become a Christian meant taking a leap, and one cannot tiptoe oneself into a leap. Lessing's "ditch" was not just a ditch, it was "ghastly and wide." Kierkegaard concludes: "To have been very close to doing something already has its comic aspect, but to have been very close to making the leap is nothing whatever, precisely because the leap is the category of decision."[125] Kierkegaard observed the Copenhagen of his day and found very few people grappling with or in a state of frenzy about the decision before them. But nineteenth-century Denmark, at least in this respect, was not much different from sixteenth-century Wittenberg, or twelfth-century Paris, or any place where a Christian civilization has become culturally dominant. On this point neither Kierkegaard, nor Denmark, held much originality. Kierkegaard objected not so much to the general malaise in the population, but to the religious and intellectual establishment that propped up a system in which belief followed logically from respectable thinking. And Kierkegaard saw the Hegelian invasion in Denmark, incarnated in bishop Martensen, as representing this perspective.[126] No one can do your believing for you.

In his discussion of Lessing, Kierkegaard seized the metaphor of the leap to relate the reality at hand. One step at a time works for a paved footpath. But if one wants to traverse a brook of several feet, it will not do. One must get a running start and jump. It would be both foolish and unreasonable to think one could cross the flowing brook the way one walks on a path. Earlier in his *Postscript*, Kierkegaard highlights the role of the individual. His "Johannes Climacus" is not a

---

person. See Merold Westphal, "Kierkegaard on Faith, Reason, and Passion," *Faith and Philosophy* 28, no. 1 (2011): 82–92, esp. 84.

125. Kierkegaard, *Concluding Unscientific Postscript*, 99.

126. As he notes in his journals, "Hegel has never done justice to the category of the transition." See Kierkegaard, *Journals and Papers*, eds. Howard Hong and Edna Hong, vol. 1 (Bloomington, IN: Indiana University Press, 1967), 210; cited in Ferreira, "Faith and the Kierkegaardian Leap," 211.

believer, yet he understands how much Christianity concerns the individual: "Although an outsider, I have at least understood this much, that the only unforgivable high treason against Christianity is the single individual's taking his relation to it for granted."[127] The transformation of one's life into a participation in the life of the Holy Trinity does not happen to everybody; it happens to an individual, qua individual, based on the way that she lives her life and responds to God's call.

Kierkegaard's suspicion toward reason, or understanding (*forstand*, in Danish) stems from the association of understanding with universality, and thus against individuality. Like Luther, Kierkegaard showed little concern about making statements that one could interpret as rendering faith and reason inimical. In various writings, Kierkegaard describes belief as a paradox, and Christianity as an absurdity;[128] famously, in *Fear and Trembling*, he dwelt on the absurdity that Abraham faced when the God who had promised him descendants that outnumbered the stars, also commanded him to kill his only son.[129] In his steadfastness to preserve the individual from dissolving into the universal, he makes statements that would explain the association of his thought with fideism. One finds such claims near the end of the *Postscript*: "[The Christian] believes Christianity against the understanding and here uses the understanding—in order to see to it that he believes against the understanding."[130] Such statements are scattered throughout Kierkegaard's corpus, and while an attentive reading of Kierkegaard demonstrates that they do not condemn him to a fideist opposition between faith and reason, there are grounds to suppose a severe tension, and thus to read Kierkegaard as representing

127. Kierkegaard, *Concluding Unscientific Postscript*, 16.
128. Kierkegaard, *Concluding Unscientific Postscript*, 540: "The mark of Christianity is the paradox, the absolute paradox." See also, Kierkegaard, *Concluding Unscientific Postscript*, 558, where Kierkegaard talks about the qualitative distinction between what one understands, and what one does not understand: "If he stakes his whole life on this absurd, then his movement is by virtue of the absurd, and he is essentially deceived if the absurd he has chosen turns out not to be the absurd. If this absurd is Christianity, then he is a believing Christian. But if he understands that it is not the absurd, then he is *eo ipso* no longer a believing Christian, until once again he wipes out the understanding as an illusion and a misunderstanding and relates himself to the Christian absurd."
129. See Søren Kierkegaard, *Fear and Trembling/Repetition*, ed. and trans. Howard and Edna Hong (Princeton: Princeton University Press, 1983), 5–123.
130. Kierkegaard, *Concluding Unscientific Postscript*, 568.

an extreme within the Christian intellectual tradition regarding the question of how faith relates to reason.

CONCLUSION

This chapter, which concludes part II, takes four leading figures in Western Christianity, all of whom deal with problems foretold in the two preceding chapters. These problems, however dimly foretold in earlier centuries, rose to the fore in the nineteenth. All four of the thinkers featured above sought ways to create a synthesis between faith and reason in the face of the problems facing modernity. This was necessary because, for the first time, one could no longer assume that leading intellectuals in Western communities presupposed the validity of Christianity. The prospect of uniting faith and reason seemed increasingly unlikely, and correspondingly grew in importance. This urgency would only gain momentum in subsequent generations.

PART III

The Twentieth Century
and Beyond

Chapter 7

Neo-Thomist Revival, Maurice Blondel, and Karl Barth

The final panel of this historical triptych reckons with the several key trends in twentieth-century theology, all of which impact the relationship between faith and reason. As with part II, it remains a Western account while focusing on key figures rather than institutions or fields.

Beginning with the official authorization of neo-scholasticism and neo-Thomism that dominated Catholic theology for the first half of the century, this chapter examines two influential texts—*Dei Filius* and *Aeterni Patris*—with a view to showing the ways in which these documents perpetuate a distinctive understanding of how faith and reason relate. It then engages the work of Maurice Blondel, a bridge figure, both historically and intellectually, between Pascal and Newman, on the one hand, and the many leading Catholic theologians treated in chapter 8. It concludes by pivoting to Karl Barth and the movement of dialectical theology and demonstrates how this movement reacted against a theological mentality embodied in the previous chapter by F. C. Baur. In Barth one finds a noteworthy response to certain rationalistic trends, which makes him the greatest twentieth-century heir to Tertullian, Luther, and Kierkegaard.

Both dialectical theology and neo-Thomism would shape much of the theological discourse in their respective schools and confessions with regard to how faith relates to reason. On the Catholic side, one observes a response to neo-Thomism in the *ressourcement* movement by tracing the thought of Maurice Blondel through Henri de Lubac and others. Similarly, one finds in transcendental Thomists like Joseph Maréchal and Karl Rahner a new form of Thomism that employed modern methods to allow faith to seek understanding. The development of Protestant theology shows the gradual acceptance, despite

Barth, of modern biblical criticism, as well as the turn toward more philosophical modes, in thinkers like Wolfhart Pannenberg and even Eberhard Jüngel, a student of Barth. Sometimes through Barth, and sometimes despite Barth, Protestantism also turned toward postmodern theory, embodied in the postliberal theology of George Lindbeck and the Radical Orthodoxy of John Milbank.

Due to rapid technological advances that affected almost all areas of life, the twentieth century saw the world become both wealthier and smaller. Besides "world wars," the twentieth century also realized, for perhaps the first time in human history, a "global economy" and a "world hunger." To this one could add a global church, one that not only stretched across continents, but also acted in concert with the needs and trends from communities around the globe. Although many communities in Africa, Asia, and North America encountered the gospel for the first time through missionary work, they also made the faith given to them their own, just as the Mediterranean and later European communities had done when the gospel spread from Galilee. This dynamic has always informed Christianity, but it became more deliberate and explicit in the twentieth century due to the aforementioned changes, which gave different Christian communities much greater awareness of the God worshipped by their sister churches across the globe.

THE CATHOLIC ARC:
VATICAN RETRENCHMENT AND NEO-THOMISM

From the perspective of how faith relates to reason, one can begin the long twentieth century of Catholic theology with the First Vatican Council in 1869–70. In the Council's dogmatic constitution, *Dei Filius*, the Catholic Church declared that God is known through both faith and reason. This document, along with Pope Leo's *Aeterni Patris* in 1879, set the course for twentieth-century accounts of faith and reason. Rather than follow the model of Newman or Kuhn, who put premodern sensitivities into a modern mode of expression, *Dei Filius* and *Aeterni Patris* sought to restore wholesale the premodern formulae and arguments. The authors of these documents, however, did not see the magisterial texts as eliminating reason from faith; rather, they thought that a retrieval of medieval scholasticism would offer the best chance for a renewed synthesis.

Dei Filius's fourth chapter contains the most important framework for relating faith to reason. The chapter opens by affirming the scholastic category of the *duplex ordo* ("twofold order") of knowledge, wherein natural reason reveals natural truths, and faith orients itself to divine mysteries.[1] There are truths that can be known by reason, and others that require revelation. For the human mind to know these truths, it must be "illumined by faith"; that is, it needs the grace of God. Here the text insists on the overlap between these two orders, between what some consider to be an unbridgeable gulf. The document also affirms a certain dissimilarity based on the objects of knowledge. One knows a supernatural object differently than a natural object, despite the similarity resulting from the fact that the *same* mind knows both objects. "Divine mysteries," by their very nature, "exceed the created intellect" and "remain covered by the veil of faith."[2] After distinguishing between these two orders, *Dei Filius* insists that there can never be a "true discrepancy (*dissensio vera*) between faith and reason" since all truth is rooted in the same God.[3] Although discrepancies between revealed and natural truths emerge, these can and must be reconcilable, either because the former have not been properly understood, or the latter have been acquired through a faulty use of reason. Ideally, faith and reason each protect the other from misunderstanding and error.

The next section of *Dei Filius* affirms the Church's long support of the arts and sciences and encourages the benefits that come from such disciplines. The document ends on an optimistic note by citing Vincent of Lerins: "Therefore let there be growth and abundant progress in understanding, knowledge, and wisdom, in each and all, in individuals and in the whole Church, at all times and in the progress of ages."[4] This hopeful conclusion belies the dark clouds that seem to form around the claims to authority made in the text.

In the previous chapter, F. C. Baur expressed concern that Catholicism did not allow for freedom of inquiry, and thus could not be compatible with reason. Although *Dei Filius* upholds the compatibility

---

1. Denzinger, 3015.
2. Denzinger, 3016.
3. Denzinger, 3017.
4. Denzinger, 3020. Vincent of Lerins, *Commonitorium*, 23.

between faith and reason, it also grants to the Magisterium the power to judge what constitutes a failure of reason in regard to faith and morals. Besides safeguarding the deposit of faith, the Church "has also from God the right and the duty to proscribe what is falsely called knowledge."[5] Although the council Fathers may not have intended it, such a statement might lend the impression that the Church serves as final arbiter over not just faith, but science. *Dei Filius* goes on to describe a scenario in which scientific claims contradict the claims of faith. In this scenario, the faithful "are bound to account them as errors."[6]

There are instances in the history of science in which a certain truth seemed undeniable, and when this is so, the truths of faith, while not identical to it, become difficult to untangle from this scientific truth. Geocentrism, as chapter 5 recalls, is a prominent example. *Dei Filius* raises the question about how its principles sustain scientific freedom. Suppose, for instance, that the field of anthropology came to the consensus that human origins came about through polygenism and not the monogenism that the Church declared in *Humani Generis* (1950).[7] According to *Dei Filius*, the Catholic anthropologist would have to reject this consensus. On the one hand, the sacred constitution argues that no conflict can truly arise. On the other, it seems to require assent not only to the contents of the deposit of faith, but also to judgments about whether and which truths of science conform with this deposit. These circumstances lend the impression that the Catholic Church's understanding of authority eclipses its confirmation of the place of reason in the life of faith.

The spirit that emerged from the Council gave the impression that the Church had come to imagine herself as a besieged fortress, carefully guarding the deposit of truth from pernicious modern tendencies that manifested themselves in revolution, anti-clericalism, post-Christian secularism, and moral degeneracy. The Catholic Church was not the only religious body to raise these concerns. Many conservative movements arose within Protestant and Orthodox churches in

---

5. Denzinger, 3018.
6. Denzinger, 3018.
7. See especially Denzinger, 3896–97, for the Church's position in *Humani Generis* on monogenism.

response to secularizing tendencies. These responses corresponded to the growing perception of conflict between faith and reason, sometimes eliciting reactions that encompassed biblicism, the emphasis on personal encounter, the preference for mysticism over rational deduction, and a form of ecclesiolatry.

Within the Catholic Church, such reactions became symbolized in the long papacy of Pius IX (1846–78), who suffered the loss of the papal states and the unification of the Italian nation, a development that weakened papal temporal power.[8] Nowhere was this mentality better crystallized than in the eightieth and final error in Pius's 1864 "Syllabus of Errors": "The Roman pontiff can and should reconcile and adapt himself to progress, liberalism, and the modern culture."[9] Although the same pontiff oversaw and affirmed the teachings on faith and reason recited above, many took the later years of Pius's papacy as an indication that the world's largest Christian Church would unqualifiedly oppose modernity.

Although some might consider the long history of an institution like the Catholic Church disadvantageous in reckoning with modernity, many Catholics regarded the Church's history as advantageous because it permits present-day believers to look to the past for answers. By the end of the decade that occasioned *Dei Filius*, the magisterium turned to the great medieval synthesis of the thirteenth century and, in particular, to the work of Thomas Aquinas. Within a year of succeeding Pius IX, Leo XIII institutionalized the return to Thomas, known as "neo-Thomism," through the 1879 encyclical *Aeterni Patris*.[10] This program deemed efforts to integrate modern thought forms and philosophy into orthodox Catholic theology to be misguided. As an antidote, it recommended not just scholastic thought and method, but more specifically Thomism. Only the latter could

---

8. For a recent and not entirely sympathetic account of Pius IX's attempt to reconcile the papacy with the modern age, see Thomas Albert Howard, *The Pope and the Professor: Pius IV, Ignaz von Döllinger, and the Quandary of the Modern Age* (Oxford: Oxford University Press, 2017), esp. 16–56.

9. Denzinger, 2980.

10. For an overview of the rise of scholasticism during the nineteenth century, see Gerald McCool, *Nineteenth-Century Scholasticism: The Search for a Unitary Method* (New York: Fordham University Press, 1977).

reliably confront modernity and maintain theological orthodoxy while avoiding heresy and error.[11] Nobody laid out the stakes more clearly or more effectively than Joseph Kleutgen in his magisterial texts, *Die Philosophie der Vorzeit* (1860–63) and *Die Theologie der Vorzeit* (1853–70).[12] McCool writes, "Kleutgen took over as prefect of studies at the Gregorian University and Leo [XIII] made it clear that he desired to see the philosophy and theology of the Angelic doctor given a more prominent place in the instruction at the Gregorian."[13] Leo XIII also enlisted Kleutgen and other neo-Thomists to draft and prepare *Aeterni Patris*, the encyclical that shaped the Catholic Church's response to modernity.[14]

Aeterni Patris begins with an ominous diagnosis.[15] In contrast to what Kleutgen had referred to as the "earlier era" or "pre-modernity" (*Vorzeit*), the current period is characterized by "bitter strife." Upon examination of the current state of affairs:

> [one] must come to the conclusion that a fruitful cause of the evils which now afflict, as well as those which threaten us lies in this: that false conclusions concerning divine and human things, which originated in the schools of philosophy, have now crept into all the orders of the State, and have been accepted by the common consent of the masses.[16]

11. For this point see McCool, "The Scholastic Reaction," in *Nineteenth-Century Scholasticism*, 129–44; and Grant Kaplan, "Roman Catholic Perspectives: The Nineteenth Century," in *Oxford Handbook of the Reception of Christian Theology*, eds. Sarah Coakley and Richard Cross (Oxford: Oxford University Press, forthcoming).

12. Joseph Kleutgen, *Die Theologie der Vorzeit*, 5 vols. (Münster: Theissing'schen, 1853–70). For an overview, see McCool, "Kleutgen's Theological Synthesis," in *Nineteenth-Century Scholasticism*, 188–215. The former text has recently appeared in English as Joseph Kleutgen, *Pre-Modern Philosophy Defended*, trans. William Marshner (South Bend, IN: St. Augustine's, 2019). For an assessment, see Justin Coyle's review in *Pro Ecclesia* 29, no. 4 (2020): 498–503.

13. McCool, *Nineteenth-Century Scholasticism*, 228.

14. McCool states definitively: "The relation of speculative theology to philosophy and apologetics described in the encyclical is the relationship proposed by Kleutgen in his *Die Theologie der Vorzeit*" (McCool, *Nineteenth-Century Scholasticism*, 232).

15. For summaries of *Aeterni Patris* see McCool, *Nineteenth-Century Scholasticism*, 226–36, and Nichols, *From Hermes to Benedict XVI*, 7–23.

16. Leo XIII, Encyclical Letter *Aeterni Patris* (August 1879), 2. For an online translation of the text, see http://w2.vatican.va/content/leo-xiii/en/encyclicals/documents/hf_l-xiii_enc_04081879_aeterni-patris.html.

If one begins on the wrong philosophical foot, then one's ethics, politics, and religion suffer. The social order itself depends on the soundness of its underlying philosophical principles. Leo's encyclical affirms the role of divine revelation in correcting error, but then, in classic "both-and" fashion, affirms that the "natural helps" supplied to human beings, chief among which is philosophy, can work with divine wisdom "to restore humanity to its primeval dignity."[17] Although philosophy has caused the problem, it can contribute to the solution.

Aeterni Patris reaffirms the First Vatican Council's teachings that natural reason can know the existence of God and therefore the Church encourages its proper use. Philosophy, a manifestation of natural reason, can serve both as a propaedeutic to theology and as a necessary tool to mold "sacred theology" into scientific form.[18] But the encyclical distinguishes sharply between kinds of philosophies, and how proper philosophy understands its role. In contrast to those philosophies that reject systems built upon divine authority, "those who unite obedience to the Catholic faith to the study of philosophy are philosophizing in the best possible way."[19] *Aeterni Patris* insists that philosophy must know her place as "handmaid and servant."[20] Similar to *Dei Filius*, *Aeterni Patris* concludes that, just as natural science and revealed faith are compatible, so too are philosophy and theology. But when contradictions appear to emerge between revealed truths and philosophical wisdom, philosophy has most likely succumbed to error.

Besides making normative claims about how philosophy should relate to theology, Leo XIII's encyclical also narrates the history of this relationship, a first for a magisterial document. Indeed, in many ways, not least among them length, *Aeterni Patris* is the first modern encyclical. It recalls how the earliest Christian theologians used the "spoils of the Egyptians," that is, pagan philosophy, to defend and explain revealed doctrines before the Scholastics took up the task of "diligently collecting, and sifting, and storing [them] up, as it were, in one place."[21]

---

17. Leo XIII, *Aeterni Patris*, 2.
18. Leo XIII, *Aeterni Patris*, 6.
19. Leo XIII, *Aeterni Patris*, 9.
20. Leo XIII, *Aeterni Patris*, 8.
21. Leo XIII, *Aeterni Patris*, 14.

Nobody did this synthesizing better than Bonaventure and Aquinas: "With surpassing genius, by unwearied diligence, and at the cost of long labors and vigils [. . .] they arranged these fertile crops in the very best way [. . .] and handed it on to their successors."[22] With this line, it appeared that *Aeterni Patris* called for a multi-pronged approach to combat modern error by retrieving both Franciscan and Dominican riches. Within just a few paragraphs, however, the encyclical disabuses readers of this assumption.

After lavishing such praise on Bonaventure in section 14, *Aeterni Patris* never mentions him again. Subsequent paragraphs center on Aquinas, who, in the judgment of *Aeterni Patris*, "towers above all other scholastic theologians," and on the basis of his achievement he is "deservedly reckoned a singular safeguard and glory of the Catholic Church."[23] Aquinas receives such praise because he started from the correct principles, which not only forestalled subsequent errors but made possible the right understanding of the relation between faith and reason, making him uniquely equipped to guide subsequent theology: "With his own hand he vanquished all errors of ancient times and still he supplies an armory of weapons which brings us certain victory in the conflict with falsehoods ever springing up in the course of years."[24] Leo continues, "Carefully distinguishing reason from faith, as is right, and yet joining them together in a harmony of friendship, Aquinas guarded and watched the rights and dignity of each."[25] Aquinas permitted both faith and reason to flourish in their own way. Modernity has abandoned the Angelic Doctor's thought and replaced it with an abundance of contradictory approaches. By doing so, it has sown confusion and doubt, causing the dissolution of Aquinas's synthesis of faith and reason.

Leo does not simply lament this loss, but also calls for a corrective. Aquinas's achievement possesses an ongoing validity, and students, especially those faithful to the Church, would benefit by learning from

---

22. Leo XIII, *Aeterni Patris*, 14. Leo XIII cites Pope Sixtus V's 1588 Bull, *Triumphantis Hierusalem*, which named Bonaventure a doctor of the Church.

23. Leo XIII, *Aeterni Patris*, 17.

24. Leo XIII, *Aeterni Patris*, 17.

25. Leo XIII, *Aeterni Patris*, 18.

it: "There is nothing which we have longer wished for and desired than that you should give largely and abundantly to youths engaged in study the pure streams of wisdom which flow from the Angelic Doctor."[26] This teaching, along with a general grounding in patristic and scholastic philosophy, opens students to a sound worldview built on the firm foundation of faith and "faith's perfect harmony with reason."[27] Modern thought had gone astray because it had forgotten the wisdom of Aquinas, and therefore a return to him could result in transforming those muddy mental waters into pristine streams.

Aeterni Patris witnessed to a revival already underway, while giving that revival an official sanction that allowed it to grow and flourish. Two points can be made about that neo-Thomist revival as relates to faith and reason. First, it became institutionalized as a set of philosophical claims. By reasoning correctly about the universe and constructing a proper (i.e., Aristotelian) philosophical foundation, one would be less prone to fall into error. This was the hope of the Vatican's Congregation for Studies when, in 1914, it issued a list of twenty-four theses on Thomistic philosophy, which instantiated Aristotelian *philosophy* more than Aquinas's *theology*.[28] Bad philosophy continued to be regarded as the root of much error. Aquinas himself was lauded not primarily as a theologian, but as a philosopher, whose theology simply followed through on the principles vouchsafed by the philosophy.[29]

At this point it is helpful to distinguish between the text of *Aeterni Patris* and its implementation. Through textbooks and seminary instruction, the implementation often fell short of the task that would prove so transformative for later figures like Bernard Lonergan: to reach up to the mind of Aquinas (for a discussion of Lonergan's appro-

---

26. Leo XIII, *Aeterni Patris*, 26.

27. Leo XIII, *Aeterni Patris*, 27.

28. Denzinger, 3601–24; see also the editorial preface to this text in the 43rd edition of *Enchiridion Symbolorum*, ed. Hünermann.

29. For this point, see Erich Przywara, "Die Problematik der Neuscholastik," *Kant Studien* 33 (1928): 73–98, at 75–81. The 1917 *Code of Canon Law* likewise recommends Aquinas for philosophy, followed by theology (Canons 589, 1366). My reprint translation of Aquinas's *Summa Theologiae*, originally issued in 1920 and reissued in 1948, includes both *Aeterni Patris* and the canons from the 1917 *Code* in its preface (ix–xviii).

priation, see chapter 8). The somewhat caricatured version of Aquinas frequently presented in seminary education monopolized the conversation in Catholic theology for roughly fifty years before historical studies of Aquinas—made possible in part by *Aeterni Patris*'s stated demands for more accurate textual recovery of Aquinas's texts—began to uncover a different Thomas than the one exalted by doctrinaire neo-Thomists.[30] Eventually the Catholic Church would end up attempting new syntheses of faith and reason that incorporated modern modes of thought, but these attempts were retarded by a magisterium leery of the modern project *writ large*.

BLONDEL'S BREAKTHROUGH

Despite the writings of theologians like Kuhn and Newman paving the way forward for post-Enlightenment Catholic theology, by the end of the nineteenth century there was still little room for a non-Thomist, non-scholastic mode of Catholic theology to maneuver. Besides reinforcing a commitment to Thomism, mainstream institutional Catholicism railed against what it had termed "Modernism." The Modernist controversy came to a head during the papacy of Pius X. In 1907, the Vatican issued a syllabus—*Lamentabili sane exitu*—and the anti-Modernist encyclical *Pascendi Dominici Gregis*. In 1910, the Vatican demanded that priests and theologians pledge the "Oath Against Modernism." The Magisterium had acute concerns that the faithful would misconstrue the relationship between faith and history, and, as a corollary, adopt an evolutionary understanding of doctrine that prioritized historical context over truth and thus called into question the stability of Christian truth. Due to the Anti-Modernist campaign, "Modernism" appeared to have a coherence that it did not in fact have; it was never an organized movement, although its best-known representatives did share some qualities in common. As a result of the amorphous nature of Modernism, those on the hunt for Modernists were able to look both backward, to figures like Newman and members of the Tübingen

---

30. For a litany of citations that underscore this claim, see Grant Kaplan, "Roman Catholic Perspectives: The Nineteenth Century."

School, and forward to the *nouvelle théologie*, to find precursors and students of Modernism.

Between earlier efforts and the subsequent disputes about Modernism and the realignment of Catholic theology after *Aeterni Patris* stands Maurice Blondel (1861–1949).[31] Born to a prosperous family in Dijon, France, Blondel turned toward philosophical questions and set out to make a career in a French university. To write the thesis required for his graduate degree, Blondel studied for several years in isolation, eventually emerging to defend his thesis at the Sorbonne in 1893. The text that resulted from this period, *L'Action*, has been compared to Hegel's *Phenomenology of Spirit*, and it made comparable demands on readers. Blondel wanted to do for (Catholic) France what philosophers like Kant, Fichte, and Hegel had done for (Protestant) Germany. Blondel wrote to a friend: "I have tried to do [in *L'Action*] for the Catholic form of thought what Germany has long since done for and continues to do for the Protestant form."[32] After a delay he was appointed professor of philosophy at Aix, in the Provence region, where he remained for the rest of his life.

At the turn of the century Catholic theology was at a standstill, with neo-scholastics on one side and those desirous for history to play a more determinative role on the other. More decisively than any other thinker at the time, Blondel charted another course, not between those two options, but of an entirely different kind. By doing so he set the terms for subsequent conversations that would dominate the next hundred years of Catholic theology, including but not limited to: the debate in the 1930s concerning the possibility of a Christian philosophy, the mid-century argument over nature and grace, the discussion about the nature of tradition, and of course the relation between faith and reason.[33] This history prompted one commentator to discuss "the

31. This paragraph relies on Alexander Dru's "Introduction: Historical and Biographical," in Maurice Blondel, *The Letter on Apologetics* and *History and Dogma*, trans. Dru and Illtyd Trethowan (Grand Rapids, MI: Eerdmans 1964), 13–79.

32. Maurice Blondel, *Lettres Philosophiques de Maurice Blondel* (Aubier, 1961), 34; cited in Dru, "Introduction," 47.

33. For Blondel's role in the Catholic philosophy debate, see Gregory Sadler, *Reason Fulfilled by Revelation: The 1930s Christian Philosophy Debates in France* (Washington, DC: The Catholic University of America Press, 2011).

pervasive yet 'quietly unobtrusive' influence Blondel has had over modern Catholicism."[34] What interests us in Blondel is the application of certain themes in *L'Action* to questions of Christian apologetics and to the controversies surrounding Modernism, especially the work of Alfred Loisy, the most influential French Modernist. He developed these ideas in two texts, *The Letter on Apologetics* (1896) and *History and Dogma* (1903), which refract and make theologically explicit— or at least less nebulous, as Blondel is a famously difficult thinker— what *L'Action* had only intimated. To get a sense of Blondel's vision, the rest of this section will focus on: (1) Blondel's dissatisfaction with both scholasticism and historicism; (2) his articulation of the limits of "secular reason," which primarily means philosophy, but applies also to science; (3) his phenomenology of gift, and how the supernatural meets humanity on the plane of human experience; (4) his new, modern synthesis of faith and reason that would inspire almost every subsequent generation of Catholic theology.

Blondel's complaints about scholasticism can be read, at this point in the book, like a musical theme in a long fugue. They echo theologians ranging from St. Bonaventure to Luther, from Pascal to Newman. Blondel, however, faced a new challenge: a virtual identification of Catholic theology with not just scholasticism, but its late-nineteenth-century form: neo-Thomism. Blondel's thought, however, revealed that there was more than one way to think as a Catholic. To do so meant a frontal attack on the neo-Thomism of his day, which Blondel found wanting. He writes: "Once a man has entered this [Thomist] system, he is himself assured, and from the center of the fortress he can defend himself against all assaults. [. . .] But first he must effect his own entrance."[35] Aquinas reached an understanding of the relationship between faith and reason by using the leading philosophy and science of his day (Aristotelianism) to extend the insights of Christian faith and dogma. However well this worked in the thirteenth century, it could not have the same effect in Blondel's era. Blondel explains:

34. Robert Koerpel, *Maurice Blondel: Transforming Catholic Tradition* (Notre Dame, IN: University of Notre Dame Press, 2019). Koerpel cites Phyllis Kaminski, "Seeking Transcendence in the Modern World," in *Catholicism Contending with Modernity*, ed. Darrell Jodock (Cambridge: Cambridge University Press, 2000), 115.

35. Blondel, *The Letter on Apologetics*, 146.

And since the Thomist starts from principles which, for the most part, are disputed in our time; since he does not offer the means of restoring them by his method; since he presupposes a host of assertions which are just those which are nowadays called into question [. . .] one must not tend to treat this triumphant exposition as the last word. [. . .] We must not exhaust ourselves refurbishing old arguments and presenting an *object* for acceptance while the *subject* is not disposed to listen.[36]

Blondel's description overlaps with Newman's complaints outlined in the previous chapter. Unlike Newman, his engagement with modern philosophy, especially Kantian Idealism, went much deeper. Certain aspects of the "turn to the subject" made Thomist metaphysics and epistemology implausible to large swaths of intellectuals. Hence Blondel's reference to the entrance of the Thomist system, and to its first principles. Thomism did not need replacing, but it would not have the desired apologetic effect if it could not at least gesture toward certain modern assumptions.

In the course of his critique, Blondel takes aim at the appeal to miracles that had become a mainstay in Christian apologetics. Though appeals to miracles were not intrinsic to scholasticism, they were part of an effort to show the invincibility of faith. Blondel takes up these arguments in the opening sections of his *Letter on Apologetics*: "The proofs are valid only for those who are thoroughly prepared to accept and to understand them; that is why miracles which enlighten some also blind others." Later in the same paragraph he adds, "Miracles are truly miraculous only for those who are already prepared to recognize the divine action in the most usual events."[37] Blondel does not attack miracles themselves, nor those who believe in them for being naïve or practicing bad faith. Instead he puts them in proper perspective by accenting the role of prior disposition. Miracle apologists—those who make an apology for Christianity based on the credibility of miracles—wanted arguments to overwhelm skeptics. Blondel points out the hermeneutical presupposi-

---

36. Blondel, *The Letter on Apologetics*, 146.
37. Blondel, *The Letter on Apologetics*, 135.

tion, either for acceptance or rejection. If one is predisposed toward the mysteries of faith, then this predisposition is a grace, infused in us by God, and as a consequence, miracles seem perfectly reasonable. But this is not the case for everyone. To acknowledge this point would be to admit a subjective quality to these arguments, a quality that Blondel was eager to introduce, but his opponents feared would cause the whole system to collapse.

Blondel also recognized that history itself, not just the confirmation of miracles, was becoming a site for navigating how faith related to reason. As a secular science, history could either confirm or deny the historical claims upon which Christian faith rests. History purported to be, from the perspective of historians, a neutral arbiter in the battles between faith traditions that relied on historical testimony. Yet Blondel chafed at how historians confused the data of history with data analyzed in a lab. He noted: "To some people the answer appears simple. All they ask of the facts is that they should serve as signs to the senses and as common-sense proofs. Once the signs have been supplied, an elementary argument deduces from them the divine character of the whole to which these signifying facts belong."[38] Yet a sign is not the same thing as a brute fact; signs convey meanings, and meanings are more than data. Though Christianity is unintelligible without historical facts—for example, that Jesus really preached in Galilee and rose from the dead after his crucifixion—one cannot simply proceed from apprehension of fact to an assent to faith. To suppose so is to eradicate the subject, the individual believer. Blondel writes,

> While it is true that historical facts are the foundations of the Catholic faith, they do not of themselves engender it, nor do they suffice to justify it entirely; and reciprocally, the Catholic faith and the authority of the Church which it implies guarantee the facts [. . .] that convinces the believer [. . .] but on other grounds than those which the historian is able to verify.[39]

In between facts and faith stands the believer. It is the believer who makes an assent, trusts that what the authority is saying is true, and

38. Blondel, *History and Dogma*, 226.
39. Blondel, *History and Dogma*, 223.

takes the meaning of a given event and makes it a measure for under-standing her present situation.[40]

Like the decadent scholasticism he derided, historicism and extrinsicism—both of which fall under Blondel's withering gaze—fail to take the subject into proper account. But whereas extrinsicism sought to link doctrinal claims to historical facts, as if no interpreta-tion were required, historicism attempted to put all claims of reality upon the sure edifice of historical fact. In either case, the role of the subject in deciding which historical data count, how they are related, or what kind of value judgments should frame the historian's data col-lection, remains undetermined. Blondel describes the problem as fol-lows: "Only the matter of a testimony and the chain of facts linked together by a natural determinism can be the raw material of history."[41] He has in mind a conception of history that clings too closely to the natural sciences, as if this "chain of facts" did not need a human sub-ject to make the required connection: "A sort of dialectical evolution-ism is deduced from this scientific determinism which claims to have penetrated the spiritual secret of the living chain of souls because it has verified the external joints of the links which are no more than its corpse."[42] The facts do not arrange themselves or form a chain of inter-related events on their own. History, in other words, cannot be Arnold Toynbee's *one damn thing after another*. Realities like the Roman Empire do not subsist on the same plane of existence as a bridge, or a tribe of people. They are constructs of the human mind, passed down through social and collective memory, referring not, strictly speaking, to an object taking up space in time, but instead an idea brought to life in history. Historical facts in themselves cannot, however, replace the human process, undertaken by thinking subjects, to make mean-ing. History as conceived by historicists is unable to deliver the goods that certain kind of apologists want it to deliver, nor can it refute Christian dogmatic or metaphysical claims through the discovery of a new hidden gospel, or the refutation of a pious legend.

---

40. Blondel's contributions on this question are both put in context and deepened, to some degree, in the magisterial work by Roger Aubert, *Le Problème de L'Acte de Foi. Troisième Édition* (Louvain: E. Warny, 1958), esp. 62–71, 277–94.

41. Blondel, *History and Dogma*, 240.

42. Blondel, *History and Dogma*, 240.

The same goes for philosophy, despite the protestations of those who wished that France could turn back the clock to the *ancien régime*. There is no reviving of a golden era, when theology was the queen of the sciences and philosophy was its handmaiden. Philosophy's role is both greater and lesser than it had been; greater in the sense that it is free to carry out its own investigations, unencumbered with the role of handmaiden, but lesser in the sense that it is also unable to prove the supernatural realities through merely natural means. Blondel expounds:

> Is there, strictly speaking, a philosophical apologetics? Yes and no—no if this means that philosophy lends its services [. . .] or that its conclusions can be homogenous or continuous with those of theology or subordinate to them. [. . .] Yes if it means that [. . .] it and only it is capable of clearing away the fundamental objections, of determining the nature of the supernatural and of throwing clear light on the requirements and insufficiencies of our nature.[43]

In Blondel's judgment, Christian philosophy cannot function as theology *sub rosa*, dressing itself up as a secular activity, but secretly importing Christian assumptions and presuppositions that render faith credible. Neo-scholasticism, however, had sought that. In its account, philosophy had grown too big for its britches after Kant, and should return to its role as handmaiden to theology. By contrast, Blondel was convinced that philosophy should be allowed, with full theological permission, to perform the tasks inherent to the discipline. As a secular discipline it could only shed light on the concavity of secular reason, meaning the inherent limitations of reason, but in doing so it could accomplish a new, humbler apologetic task.

Twentieth-century Catholic discussions of how faith and reason relate inevitably touch upon the debate about grace, and the proper order between the natural and the supernatural. As his "disciple" Henri de Lubac would later clarify, neo-scholastics seemed not merely content to distinguish between nature and supernatural desire; they

---

43. Blondel, *The Letter on Apologetics*, 165.

also tended to separate these desires into two separate realms.[44] Neo-scholastics argued that since God could not give us natural desires if they could not be naturally fulfilled, there must be a natural beatitude, toward which human beings naturally strive, a beatitude that falls well short of the supernatural beatitude Christ promises his followers.

Blondel challenged this logic head-on. Secular reason, or philosophy, when pushed to its logical limit comes to a paradox: we are made for an end that we cannot achieve on our own. This understanding begins to take shape when reason takes up the difference between itself and faith. Blondel states, "Since, by hypothesis, faith is a gratuitous gift, no apologetic, however demonstrative we may suppose it to be, can communicate it or produce it."[45] The movement from a natural desire for God, pursued through natural lines of enquiry, does not proceed seamlessly toward a desire for something like union with Christ and faith in the triune God. The gap between them is more like a chasm, or what Blondel calls "the supernatural insufficiency of human nature."[46]

This insufficiency, however, is not bad news:

> If Christianity claims to satisfy man's natural needs, it also claims to arouse and fulfil new ones, far beyond anything which we could hope for or suspect, and that the need for the gift, the request for the gift is, like the gift itself, already a grace.[47]

One cannot cheat one's way into supernatural faith by supposing that rigorous logic leads to acceptance of God as first cause, and then gradually opens one to the mysteries. The insufficiency of this kind of epistemological Pelagianism has been covered in the last chapter. An unbelieving philosophy can also discover the same concavity of reason, which does not lead in step-wise fashion to faith, because the faith that follows is not a next step. This higher fulfilment is, in Blondel's formulation, "beyond the reach of our premises."[48]

44. For a superb account of this conversation, see Randall Rosenberg, *The Givenness of Desire: Concrete Subjectivity and the Natural Desire to See God* (Toronto: University of Toronto Press, 2017), 13–62.

45. Blondel, *The Letter on Apologetics*, 134.

46. Blondel, *The Letter on Apologetics*, 141.

47. Blondel, *The Letter on Apologetics*, 143.

48. Blondel, *The Letter on Apologetics*, 143.

To have a desire for something fundamentally not achievable would seem to portend endless disappointment and frustration. And indeed, philosophy both secular and sacred sought ways to avoid such a fate. Blondel demands, however, that his readers entertain a metaphysics of gift, for one has no other option: "Even if (to suppose the impossible) we were to recover by some effort of human genius the whole letter and content of revealed teaching, we should have nothing, absolutely nothing, of the Christian spirit, because it does not come from us."[49] What does it mean to say that if humans produced, say, the entire contents of the New Testament, they would have "absolutely nothing"? For Blondel, it has to do with the nature of the truth in question, from which its content cannot be separated. In this scenario, one would not have the teachings of the New Testament, because one cannot attain them; one must instead receive them. As anyone who has been caught up in the unpleasant dynamic of family gift giving knows, a gift is not a gift if it is owed or taken. Blondel continues: "To have this not as given and received but as found issuing from ourselves is not to have it at all."[50]

Blondel's method unsettled almost all parties invested in the relationship between faith and reason—neo-scholastic, modernist, secular, historicist and scientist. Blondel hit upon an aporia in secular philosophy. He concludes the *Letter on Apologetics* by noting, "Philosophy cannot demonstrate or produce the supernatural, for it cannot even provide or contain the reality of natural action."[51] He does not write this with the aim of placing the mysteries of faith into it, like a roof on top of a house. He simply shows that the gap revealed through good secular reasoning would be filled by these mysteries if they were the kind of reality that secular thought could realize.[52] Likewise, history cannot turn the leap of faith into a step. Blondel's philosophy of action required that one enter into the life of faith in order for it to be intelligible. The believer has access not only to dead texts, but to "another history formed of living relics."[53] One can think of Blondel

---

49. Blondel, *The Letter on Apologetics*, 153.
50. Blondel, *The Letter on Apologetics*, 153.
51. Blondel, *The Letter on Apologetics*, 198.
52. For this point, see Nichols, *From Hermes to Benedict XVI*, 176.
53. Blondel, *History and Dogma*, 248.

as a corrector of misbegotten shortcuts. Whether in historical or philosophical apologetics, these shortcuts would harm faith in the long run, for they violated the nature and proper scope of reason. After highlighting these problematic approaches, he notes at the end of *History and Dogma*, "One cannot fail to see that an attitude which proposes to reason [i.e. "think"] a faith without reason is as unjust to reason as it is dangerous to faith."[54]

KARL BARTH AND DIALECTICAL THEOLOGY

At the dawn of the twentieth century, the split in Western Christianity had become so entrenched that Protestant and Catholic theology proceeded as if independent of one another. Different confessional (and post-confessional) identities allowed for the illusion of quasi-autonomous theological traditions forgetful of their own past. Yet if the previous six chapters have attested to anything, it is the benefit of looking to previous generations in order to ameliorate a habitual forgetting of prior achievements.

Perhaps no figure in the twentieth century served more as a bridge between confessions than Karl Barth (1886–1968), the German, Reformed theologian and leading figure of dialectical theology. Barth not only shaped the theological conversation among Protestants on both sides of the Atlantic, but he also corresponded with and influenced such leading Catholic figures as Hans Urs von Balthasar, Erich Przywara, and Hans Küng.[55] Barth reacted to the dominant mode of academic theology that took its cue from Baur. By doing so he shaped twentieth-century developments in both Protestant and Catholic theology while playing a pivotal role in plotting the trajectory of twentieth-century theology's attempt to relate faith and reason.

Like so many of his generation, Barth was profoundly affected by the "Great War," and the sense of shock and despair it provoked. Four years of trench warfare, in which almost all of Europe and even non-

---

54. Blondel, *History and Dogma*, 259.
55. For an overview of Barth's influence, see Benjamin Dahlke, *Karl Barth, Catholic Renewal* (London: Bloomsbury, 2012).

European countries became engulfed for no justifiable reason, caused tens of millions of casualties. During these years the Western front remained relatively stable, having moved no more than a couple of miles, thus underscoring how futile the war had become. Twenty million deaths for nothing. To Barth's horror, the previous generation of theologians were more likely to support than oppose the war, and this group tended to conflate the aims of the German nation with the Christian church. Barth recalled with dismay "what [Franz] Overbeck called 'Bismarck-religion,' or the confusion of Christianity and German nationalism."[56] Barth later mused: "Ninety-three German intellectuals issued a terrible manifesto, identifying themselves before all the world with the war policy of Kaiser Wilhelm II. [. . .] And to my dismay, among the signatories I discovered the names of all of my German teachers," including towering figures like Adolf von Harnack and Wilhelm Herrmann.[57]

What had made such a blunder possible? How could those purporting to follow the gospel have endorsed not just any war, but this war? For Barth, too many theologians had been swept up by the spirit of the times, characterized by an optimism and a naïve belief in progress. For over a century, theology, especially German Protestant theology, had sought to "engage the culture" through some form of correlation between the gospel and the human experience of the divine, embodied most clearly in the project of Friedrich Schleiermacher to translate the God-human encounter into a "feeling of absolute dependence."[58] One commentator summarizes, "As a result [of the war, Barth] broke with the theology in which he had been trained."[59] Protestantism had drifted away from its sixteenth-century roots, informed by a biblical pessimism that cautioned against hubris by appealing to the reality of human fallenness, and a correspondingly realistic attitude about the human proclivity to evil. Instead of using Schleiermacher, Kant, or Hegel to clear space for theology to operate—which

56. Livingston and Fiorenza, *Modern Christian Thought*, 2nd ed., vol. 2, *The Twentieth Century* (Minneapolis: Fortress Press, 2006), 64.
57. Karl Barth, "Nachwort," in *Schleiermacher-Auswahl*, ed. Heinz Bolli (Hamburg: Siebenstern Taschenbuch, 1988), 290–312, at 294; cited from Livingston and Fiorenza, *Modern Christian Thought*, vol. 2, 62.
58. Schleiermacher, *The Christian Faith*, §4.

would have amounted in his own eyes to a failure to reckon with human fallenness—Barth sought a new beginning. Together with his friend Edward Thurneysen, Barth recalled,

> We tried to learn our theological ABCs all over again, beginning by reading and interpreting the writings of the Old and New Testaments, more thoroughly than before. And lo and behold, they began to speak to us—but not as we thought we must hear them in the school of what was then "modern theology." [. . .] I began to apply myself to Romans [. . . and] to read it as though I had never read it before.[60]

Barth's theology continued the legacy represented in earlier chapters by Kierkegaard, the Pietists, and Martin Luther. Yet he forged his own style, developed in conversation with other young Turks beginning academic careers.[61]

Barth's relearning of the ABCs led to his commentary on *Romans* in 1918, which he revised a few years later to incorporate his subsequent engagement with Nietzsche and Dostoevsky.[62] His second edition of *The Epistle to the Romans* (1921) ignited the movement that came to be known as dialectical theology. Barth described its impact as accidental, as if someone were climbing a church tower in darkness, and while fumbling for a handrail, this person "got hold of the bell rope instead. To his horror, he had then to listen to what the great bell had sounded over him and not over him alone."[63]

---

59. Daniel W. Hardy, "Karl Barth," in *The Modern Theologians*, 3rd ed., ed. David Ford (Malden, MA: Blackwell, 2005), 21–42, at 22. Barth's critique of Schleiermacher is sharpest in his *Letter to the Romans*: "The Gospel of Christ is a shattering disturbance, an assault which brings everything into question. For this reason, nothing is so meaningless as the attempt to construct a religion out of the Gospel, and to set it as one human possibility in the midst of others. Since Schleiermacher, this attempt has been undertaken more consciously than ever before in Protestant theology—and it is the betrayal of Christ" (Barth, *The Letter to the Romans*, 225).

60. Barth, "Nachwort," 294; cited from Livingston and Fiorenza, *Modern Christian Thought*, vol. 2, 64.

61. For an overview, see the previously cited Fiorenza and Livingston, "The Dialectical Theology: Karl Barth, Emil Brunner, and Friedrich Gogarten," in *Modern Christian Thought*, vol. 2, 62–95.

62. The best account of the differences between these two editions is Barth's own. See Barth, "The Preface to the Second Edition," in Karl Barth, *The Epistle to the Romans*, trans. Edwyn Hoskyns (Oxford: Oxford University Press, 1933), 2–15.

63. Cited from Livingston and Fiorenza, *Modern Christian Thought*, vol. 2, 65.

The early Barth traced an account of how humans know God that upended several presuppositions and permitted a new, dialectical account of how reason and faith relate. Barth explains this dialectic in his preface: "What, then, do I mean when I say that a perception of the 'inner dialectic of the matter' [. . .] is a necessary and prime requirement for their understanding and interpretation?" Barth unfolds his dialectic with a nod to Kierkegaard: "If I have a system, it is limited to a recognition of what Kierkegaard called the 'infinite qualitative distinction' between time and eternity."[64] Dialectic for Barth meant, in the words of one commentator, that "the only basis for Christian faith was in the contrast between the Holy God and sinful humanity, Creator and creature, revelation and religion, gospel and church, sacred history and profane history."[65] This dialectic was not the logical dialectic of Hegel, but instead the paradoxical dialectic of Kierkegaard.

Rather than bridging a gap between humans and God, divine revelation made transparent the distance between the two. Barth offers the image of revelation as a crater left by a meteor, whose impact is known only through concavity.[66] God reveals God's self as interruption or negation, not as confirmation of human presupposition. Commenting on Romans 1:16–17, Barth accents the paradoxical nature of the righteousness promised to humanity through Christ:

What men on this side [of the] resurrection name "God" is most characteristically not God. Their "God" does not redeem his creation, but allows free course to the unrighteousness of men; does not declare himself to be God, but is the complete affirmation of the course of the world and of men as it is. [. . .] But in Christ God speaks as He is, and punishes the "No-God" of all these falsehoods. He affirms Himself by denying us as we are and the world as it is. [. . .] He acknowledges Himself to be our God by creating and maintaining the distance by which we are separated from him.[67]

64. Barth, *The Letter to the Romans*, 10.
65. Hardy, "Karl Barth," 25.
66. Barth, *The Letter to the Romans*, 36.
67. Barth, *The Letter to the Romans*, 40–41.

Barth rejects an ideology of uninterrupted progress, idealistic about the power of human imagination and ingenuity to rid the world of its problems. This bland optimism led to a naiveté about the evils of war, resulting in death totals hitherto unseen in human history. Through a similarly misplaced confidence, humans boast of the compatibility between their desires and God's, between their time and God's, between their efforts at justice and Christ's promise of the kingdom to come. Only by speaking a "No" to sinful humanity does the biblical God reveal the falsity of human constructs and create the possibility for humanity to come to grips with the distance separating us from God.

Not surprisingly, this dialectical approach had repercussions for how faith relates to reason. Barth not only retrieves the theme of faith as trust, but also harnesses, from Kierkegaard as well as Luther, the full force of faith as a superior mode of knowing. In the chapter "The Law" in *Letter to the Romans*, Barth writes, "Faith is the faithfulness of God, ever secreted in and beyond all human ideas and affirmations about Him, and beyond every positive religious achievement."[68] Barth's account of faith prioritizes God's movement toward us. For Barth, one cannot inherit faith, or have it passed down; each believer must make her own leap. Faith is not a sober judgment from a properly educated modern person, but rather a "leap into the void," that any who would be disciple of Christ must take, regardless of his station.[69]

Barth transforms Luther's *sola fide* from a soteriology into an epistemology.[70] One does not only receive salvation "by faith alone"; one also knows God "by faith alone"—"God can be apprehended only through Himself and His faithfulness. He is intelligible only by faith."[71] In order to underscore his dialectic, Barth even cites Tertullian's *credo quia absurdum* alongside Luther's claim that faith "grips reason by the throat and

---

68. Barth, *The Letter to the Romans*, 98.

69. Barth, *The Letter to the Romans*, 99.

70. Barth has precedent in the German Protestant tradition. As John Milbank notes of Johann Georg Hamann and Friedrich Heinrich Jacobi, two contemporaries of Kant: "There is absolutely no doubt as to the Lutheran character of both of these thinkers: what they articulate is a kind of theory of 'knowledge by faith alone' to complement the notion of 'justification by faith alone.'" See John Milbank, "Knowledge: The Theological Critique of Philosophy in Hamann and Jacobi," in *Radical Orthodoxy*, eds. Mark Milbank, Catherine Pickstock, and Graham Ward (London: Routledge, 1999), 21–37, at 23.

71. Barth, *The Letter to the Romans*, 112.

strangles the beast."[72] Echoing the Pauline aim to know nothing but Christ crucified (1 Cor 2:2), Barth adds, "This is the only aspect of the truth visible to us: only in the Cross of Christ can we comprehend the truth and meaning of His resurrection. We can only believe in what is new, and, moreover, our capacity reaches no further than believing *that* we do believe."[73] The order of knowing that is faith radically transcends more terrestrial modes of knowing, and Barth feels no compulsion to downplay or mitigate this reality in the second edition of the *Römerbrief*.

Although Barth made his initial splash with his commentary on *Romans*, his lasting contribution was the thirteen-volume *Church Dogmatics*, a stunning achievement that spanned four decades and ran over nine thousand pages. In the midst of that work, Barth made his most important public action, drafting the Barmen Declaration, the 1934 document of the "Confessing Church" which took a clear, theological stance against Nazism. Barth's theological and moral leadership gained him a wide following and brought him into numerous conversations. Near the end of his life, he was invited to observe sessions at the Second Vatican Council. He also appeared on the cover of *Time* magazine in 1962.

While dialectical features remained in Barth's theology, deeper engagement with the theological tradition led to him softening some of the harder edges in his earlier theology.[74] Yet Barth maintained certain theological and epistemological presuppositions that led to a rupture among the dialectical theologians.[75] Most relevant for our purposes is Barth's engagement with Anselm, forged through multiple seminars from 1926–30, which resulted in his 1931 book, *Fides*

---

72. Barth, *The Letter to the Romans*, 112, 144.

73. The English translation capitalizes the first "believe" in the second quotation. In the German it is left in lowercase, whereas "that" is italicized. See Karl Barth, *Der Römerbrief 1922* (Zurich: Theologischer Verlag, 1989), 137.

74. In the 1958 preface to the second edition, Barth writes, "Only a comparatively few commentators, for example Hans Urs von Balthasar, have realized that my interest in Anselm was never a side issue for me or [. . .] realized how much it has influenced me or been absorbed into my own line of thinking. Most of them have completely failed to see that in this book on Anselm I am working with a vital key, if not the key, to an understanding of that whole process of thought that has impressed me more and more in my *Church Dogmatics* as the only one proper to theology" (Barth, *Anselm*, 11).

75. For Barth's break with Gogarten and Brunner, see the subsection, "The Breakdown of the Dialectical Theology," in Livingston and Fiorenza, "The Dialectical Theology," 75–76.

Quarens Intellectum.[76] As mentioned in chapter 2, Anselm proposed a radical manner of re-thinking theology by almost entirely jettisoning scriptural arguments in establishing the existence of God. At first glance he seems an odd dialogue partner for Barth.

In his commentary on Anselm, Barth recalls Anselm's prioritization of faith over reason and brings it to bear on his own project. For Barth, Anselm's *credo ut intelligam*—I believe so that I can understand—constitutes neither an "intellectual storming of the gates of heaven," nor a sacrifice of the intellect.[77] Faith is the presupposition for the intelligibility and rationality of the exercise that Anselm performs. Barth offers memorable imagery:

> A science of faith, which denied or even questioned the Faith would *ipso facto* cease to be either "faithful" or "scientific." Its denials would *a priori* be no better than bats and owls squabbling with eagles about the reality of the beams of the midday sun.[78]

Theology is about making intelligible something one already believes. The rational method proposed by Anselm does not threaten Barth, or the Protestant theology he represented, because faith, an act of the will, precedes understanding and functions as a fundament.

To put into relief the importance of Barth's commentary on Anselm, it is helpful to recall a much earlier episode in the history of theology. In his fight with the Pelagians, Augustine frequently returned to 1 John 4: *God loved us first.* God moves toward us prior to any action on our part. The same principle underlies Anselm's most basic insight. Anselm's *intellegere*, Barth insists, "would be of no avail if God did not 'show' himself, if the encounter with him were not in fact primarily a movement from his side and if the finding that goes with it, the modified *intellegere*, did not take place."[79] Anselm's piety, forged in monastic practice and prayer, did not constitute some arbitrary quirk in a brilliant mind that invented the ontological argument. It enabled him to think. Barth explains:

---

76. Barth, *Anselm: Fides Quarens Intellectum*, trans. Ian Robertson (Richmond, VA: John Knox, 1960).

77. Barth, *Anselm*, 26.

78. Barth, *Anselm*, 27.

79. Barth, *Anselm*, 38–39.

Everything depends not only on the fact that God grants him grace to think correctly about him, but also on the fact that God himself comes within his system as the object of this thinking, that he "shows" himself to the thinker and in so doing modifies "correct" thinking to an *intellegere esse in re* (understanding of to be in itself). Only thus does the grace of Christian knowledge become complete.[80]

As *ens entis*, God foregrounds all being, and therefore foregrounds all knowing. Being precedes knowing; something is before it is known. Barth writes laconically, "Ontic necessity precedes noetic"; and later, "Ontic rationality precedes noetic."[81] This metaphysics, for Barth, underlies medieval theology. Insofar as modernity puts knowing before being, it enables the misbegotten projects of Descartes, Kant, and others.[82] Channeling Barth, Andrew Moore writes: "God's self-revelation is a unique event and so cannot properly be judged or measured by human standards, such as those of critical reason. [. . .] Revelation governs human thought about its object."[83] Barth's theological method insisted on the priority of God's speech over human reflection.

One hundred years after Barth's *Römerbrief*, and in the wake of waves of scholarship on Karl Barth, one can read much of the theology since Barth as either affirming or reacting against his theological realignment. Many scholars have gently but convincingly countered the narrative of Barth's unique genius by pointing out how others had preceded and worked alongside dialectical theology in countering certain norms, and how Barth's narrative of nineteenth-century Protestant liberalism deserves a more careful telling.[84] As Jan Rohls, one of the leading voices in German Protestant theology, has pointed out, the upshot of Barth's method is that theology, as an act of science

---

80. Barth, *Anselm*, 39.
81. Barth, *Anselm*, 50.
82. For this point, and Barth's role in shaping the conversation, see Andrew Moore, "Reason," in *The Oxford Handbook of Systematic Theology*, eds. Kathryn Tanner, Iain Torrance, and John Webster (Oxford: Oxford University Press, 2009), 394–412, esp. 396.
83. Andrew Moore, "Reason," 404.
84. For one extremely helpful and under-cited effort, see Jan Rohls, "Credo ut intelligam. Karl Barths theologisches Programm und sein Kontext," in *Vernunft des Glaubens. Festschrift zum 60. Geburtstag von Wolfhart Pannenberg*, ed. Jan Rohls and Gunther Wenz (Göttingen: Vandenhoeck & Ruprecht, 1988), 406–35. For a wider angle on the problem, see Christine Hemler, *Theology and the End of Doctrine* (Louisville: Westminster John Knox, 2014).

undertaken within an ecclesial context, cannot be measured by reigning scientific standards.[85] On this point one can recall the perspective of Ferdinand Christian Baur, and compare it to Barth. Both worked as professors at prestigious universities. Baur thought he could apply scientific standards, especially those employed by historians, and thereby make faith intelligible and theology scientific. Barth abandoned the old rules and broke new ground, in part through a retrieval of Anselm, to show the intelligibility of belief, and thus make faith itself reasonable on its own terms. This move opened a rift between Barth and his liberal precursors, and also distanced Barth from the older tradition of Reformed Orthodoxy, which had adopted the classical position on the possibility of natural theology. Barth's stance had precursors of course, but any effort to understand the shifting ground of twentieth-century theology must take into account Barth's strong "No" to natural theology and to the default religious epistemology. Barth's position convinced many who theologized after him that the only way to keep the faith was to follow Barth's method, whose dialectic maintained a heightened tension between faith and reason.

CONCLUSION

The attempts to show the rationality of faith in the post–Vatican I Catholic climate, and in post-War Protestantism, are not by any means exhausted by recounting the achievements of the three figures/movements treated in this chapter. Spending time on these figures allows, however, a helpful framework for analyzing the achievement of the leading mid-century theologians treated in chapter 8. In saying this, it is also necessary to keep in mind that what has preceded, and what follows, is not a *history* of the theological discussion of faith and reason. There are too many voices, some of them historically underrepresented and repressed, others simply forgotten, to hope to undertake such a history. This topic, lest the reader become impatient, receives due treatment in chapter 9.

---

85. See Rohls, "Credo ut intelligam," 423.

Chapter 8

Mid-Twentieth-Century Theology

THEOLOGY AFTER BARTH

Although it may seem otherwise, not everyone, and not every Protestant, was a Barthian by 1930. Barth certainly provided an attractive alternative to historicist tendencies, but not every theologian concerned with historicism became a dialectical theologian. One direction against historicism, which overlapped in many ways with dialectical theology, was the "de-mythologizing" project undertaken by Barth's friend, Rudolf Bultmann (1884–1976), who fused dialectical theology with the phenomenology of Martin Heidegger. Bultmann's work describes an unbridgeable gulf between the Christ of faith and the Jesus of history, which necessitates, on the part of the believer, an existential movement of the will (faith) in order to encounter the living Christ. This encounter remains separated from the serious, rational historical work that can only tell us about Jesus of Nazareth, but can never produce a conversion.[1]

The real convergence, for Bultmann, occurs during the process of *demythologization*, which demands that the modern believer disentangle the original witness of supernatural events like miracles from their premodern setting. In Bultmann's interrogation, anything less would involve a sacrifice of the intellect: "Is it possible to expect that we shall make a sacrifice of understanding, *sacrificium intellectus*, in order to accept what we cannot sincerely consider true?"[2] The believer must translate or dymythologize central Christian ideas like redemption and resurrection—whose historicity Bultmann denied—to prevent a

---

1. For this point in particular, see Joseph Ratzinger, *Introduction to Christianity*, trans. J. R. Foster (San Francisco: Ignatius, 1990), 196–202.
2. Rudolf Bultmann, *Jesus Christ and Mythology*, (New York: Scribner, 1958), 17.

bifurcation of faith and intellect. Underneath the mythological husk is a theological kernel that can be preserved in order not to offend modern sensibilities. How, Bultmann wonders, can one use electricity and still think that heaven is up and hell is down? One must demythologize, but how much and to what extent is a matter that Bultmann never fully clarifies.[3]

Despite eschewing aspects of historical-critical research in favor of Heidegger's hermeneutical and phenomenological approach, Bultmann helped initiate a new wave in the "Quest" to find the historical Jesus.[4] He inaugurated the trend among New Testament scholars to use recent hermeneutical theories in order to facilitate fresh readings of the text by applying not just the hard tools of history, but the softer tools of theory to faith.[5] This quest also became internationalized, moving from a largely German phenomenon, as relayed by Albert Schweitzer in *The Quest for the Historical Jesus* (1906), to a trans-continental affair. Aided by textual and archeological investigations, scholars from different confessions and nations combined the best of the secular historical sciences with a faithful desire to understand Jesus, the face of God, more deeply.[6] This effort changed the shape of theological education, as "the historical-critical method" was mainstreamed into seminary curricula across most major confessions. It rejected the hardest edge of Barthianism by presuming that secular methods, stripped of naturalist and materialist presuppositions, can fortify faith and teach future ministers to model *fides quarens intellectum* in their reading of the Bible. Though Bultmann represented perhaps the most radical challenge to neo-orthodoxy, many felt skittish about the project of demythologizing and found less radical ways to apply the fruit of historical scholarship and hermeneutical theory to overcome any distance between the Jesus of history and the Christ of faith.

---

3. Even Ratzinger demythologizes in *Introduction to Christianity* when he considers Jesus' descent into hell: this doctrine "seems to call most of all for 'demythologization,' a process that in this case looks devoid of danger and unlikely to provoke opposition" (Ratzinger, *Introduction to Christianity*, 294).

4. For a reliable overview of the quest and Bultmann's role in it, see Ben Meyer, *The Aims of Jesus* (London: SCM Press, 1979), 25–59, and Walter Kasper, *Jesus the Christ* (Mahwah, NJ: Paulist, 1977), 26–40.

5. Subsequent generations applied the hermeneutical theories of Gadamer, Ricoeur, Derrida, and subsequently feminist, queer, and decolonial theory to biblical studies.

Perhaps the greatest challenge to neo-orthodoxy, and to all theology, came not from certain theories, but from events. Just as the Great War served to focus Barth's theological vision, the Second World War overturned many conventions and academic presuppositions. In the aftermath of the war, and the aftershock of the discovery of concentration camps, an increasing number of theologians felt compelled to craft approaches that could account for the experience and the trauma of those years, and to bring to bear the experience of suffering and loss to the task of reconciling faith and reason. Perhaps no biographical snippet captures this mood better than that of Johann Baptist Metz, who decided to orient his theology around his own traumatic experience. Toward the end of the war, he was conscripted into the German army. He was sent to a neighboring village on an errand, and when he returned, he

> found only the dead, nothing but the dead, overrun by a combined bomber and tank assault. I could see only dead and empty faces, where the day before I had shared childhood fears and youthful laughter. I remember nothing but a wordless cry. [. . .] What would happen if one took this sort of remembrance not to the psychologist but into the Church?[7]

Out of this experience his idea of "dangerous memory," that served as the basis of his political theology, was formed. Metz used this concept of dangerous memory to critique entire centuries of theology that overlooked in their very orientation the real experience of suffering from which so many people see and interpret the world. With a renewed call, theologians like Metz urged their discipline to reimagine how to make faith intelligible to the experiences of those at the margins, on the basis of their income, their environment, their gender, and their sexuality. There was also a new ethical paradigm to consider: the complicity of some theologians and theological constructs in the forces that led to the death of millions of Jews and other marginalized

---

6. For an accessible overview, see Benedict Thomas Viviano, *A Short History of New Testament Studies* (Chicago: New Priory Press, 2016). For a single chapter, see Anthony Thiselton, "Biblical Interpretation," in *The Modern Theologians*, 3rd ed., eds. David Ford and Rachel Muers (Malden, MA: Blackwell, 2005), 287–304.

7. Johann Baptist Metz, *A Passion for God: The Mystical-Political Dimension of Christianity*, trans. J. Matthew Ashley (New York, Paulist, 1998), 1–2.

groups. This situation gave newfound urgency to ecumenical theology and inter-religious dialogue rooted in the feeling that older theological paradigms had failed to meet the crisis that faced it.

PANNENBERG'S RETURN TO REASON

In chapter 9 more will be said about the cacophony of theological voices and the magisterial attempt to re-direct the theological conversation. The rest of the current chapter will take up leading theologians who prioritized the reconciliation of faith and reason in the wake of the ruptures described in the last chapter, and in conversation with other movements animating theology and the churches. This analysis begins with Wolfhart Pannenberg (1928–2014), perhaps the most important twentieth-century Protestant contributor to the dialogue on faith and reason. Pannenberg's birth year places him in the inner orbit of a number of impactful German theologians (Peter Hünermann, Max Seckler, Hans Küng, Johann Baptist Metz, Joseph Ratzinger, and Jürgen Moltmann) born in the late 1920s and early 1930s. They experienced the Second World War as teenagers, which shaped their subsequent theological vocations.

In the case of Pannenberg, he was briefly enlisted as a soldier before spending time in a British POW camp. Having grown up in a secular household, he had a transformative religious encounter in 1945. In his own words: "I had a visionary experience of a great light not only surrounding me, but absorbing me for an indefinite time. I did not hear any words, but it was a metaphysical awakening that prompted me to search for its meaning regarding my life during the following years."[8] He studied theology and philosophy intensely, eventually relocating from behind the Iron Curtain to Karl Barth's seminar in Basel. Although he benefitted tremendously from being in close proximity to Barth when he was writing the middle volumes of the *Church Dogmatics*, Pannenberg grew disillusioned, explaining:

---

8. Wolfhart Pannenberg, "An Intellectual Pilgrimage," *Dialog: A Journal of Theology* 45, no. 2 (2006): 184–91, at 185. For this section I have also relied on Theodore Whapham, *The Unity of Theology: The Contribution of Wolfhart Pannenberg* (Minneapolis: Fortress Press, 2015), and Christoph Schwöbel, "Wolfhart Pannenberg," in *The Modern Theologians*, 3rd ed., 129–46.

> In the course of my stay at Basel I became increasingly weary that Barth's talk about God and revelation lacked the philosophical subtlety and precision I thought to be desirable, and I also came to be critical of his very personal way of using biblical texts, which often seemed to be somewhat arbitrary.[9]

Pannenberg's disillusionment with Barth led him to engage intensively with biblical exegesis. He went to Heidelberg, where he took biblical courses from Gerhard von Rad. In these years, the "quest for the historical Jesus" received new impetus, and Pannenberg became convinced that serious, historical-critical investigation of Jesus could advance Christology.[10] Unlike Baur, whose recourse to history was also connected to a closed, causal system, Pannenberg wanted to take seriously the idea that historical testimony could tell us something about miraculous events, the foremost of which was the resurrection.

Pannenberg's engagement with the cutting edge of historical-critical, that is, secular, biblical scholarship anticipates his lifelong dialogue with secular sciences. In Germany, especially after the war, universities became further detached from their medieval and theological roots. Unlike the United States, where theology at this time was still largely carried out in seminaries and schools of divinity insulated from sharp-elbowed secular discourse, German public universities contained no safe space for theology. Pannenberg felt acutely the need for discussion across the aisle, and engaged in this throughout his career. He brought theology in general into conversation with philosophies of science, and the Christian doctrine of creation with the natural sciences. Referencing what he felt to be the well-intended but incomplete approach of Barth, Pannenberg noted: "[I]t was not sufficient to develop some idea of the human person on the basis of biblical presuppositions; but it seemed necessary to claim the human—reality as it is studied and presented by the secular disciplines and try to show

---

9. Pannenberg, "An Intellectual Pilgrimage," 186–87.

10. Regarding the renewal of the quest, Walter Kasper notes, "In 1953 Ernst Käsemann gave a lecture in Marburg on 'The problem of the historical Jesus,' in which he asked for the old liberal quest for the historical Jesus to be resumed on the changed theological premises of the present age. This proved to be the stimulus of a veritable flood of commentaries" (Kasper, *Jesus the Christ*, 33).

that it is necessarily related to religion and to God."[11] Pannenberg's approach presupposed a compatibility between faith and reason but he distinguished between three main currents in Western philosophical reason, and concluded that only the "historical reasoning" oriented toward the future could form a synthesis with Christian faith.[12] The reconciliation of faith and reason, according to Pannenberg, cannot be achieved through Barth's approach. Instead, theology needs philosophy to explain itself: "Theology will always have to engage with philosophical thinking if it attempts to validate its claims that the one God is the ultimate horizon for the unity of the world and our experience of it."[13]

Pannenberg was hardly alone in his theological orientation. Scores of theologians on a number of continents took similar approaches based on comparable motivations. Still, as perhaps the leading Protestant theologian of the final third of the twentieth century, Pannenberg influenced subsequent generations of theologians to follow a similar course. In Pannenberg, therefore, one can find perhaps the most impactful response to Barth's fideistic tendencies, and the worthiest twentieth-century heir of Philip Melanchthon.

OVERTURNING THE NEO-SCHOLASTIC PARADIGM

From the Catholic side, it is nearly impossible to tell the story of twentieth-century theology without chronicling its response to the neo-scholasticism described in the previous chapter. To comprehend what this has to do with faith and reason, it helps to recall that neo-scholasticism, as practiced and taught in the early twentieth century, saw philosophy as a handmaid in the sense that the correct reading of Aristotle provides the necessary principles to accept the articles of faith that formed the essential content of Catholic teaching. There was much to praise in this approach, but, in the minds of many commentators on the period, it became decadent—more interested in giving answers than asking questions. Of this mentality, Frederick Lawrence notes:

---

11. Pannenberg, "An Intellectual Pilgrimage," 190.
12. Whapham, *The Unity of Theology*, 18.
13. Schwöbel, "Wolfhart Pannenberg," 133.

> Philosophy becomes just an instrument of revelational [sic] truth: a philosophical handmaid that has lost its vital roots in wonder. Philosophy thus diminished becomes estranged from questioning, and more preoccupied with the conceptual expression and logical manipulation of the answers than with genuine inquiry.[14]

As handmaid, philosophy acts only for the sake of her queen, theology. Lawrence here narrates the problematic consequences of this formulation for Catholic philosophy, and thus also hints at the reasons that neo-scholasticism and neo-Thomism failed to live according to the dictum of their own *magna carta*: Leo's *Aeterni Patris*. In the encyclical, Leo declared the need "to expand and perfect the old through the new." Bernard Lonergan once joked of his teachers—embodying a decadent scholasticism—who taught as if "Aquinas carefully studied Suarez or John of St. Thomas."[15]

Two generative modes of theology developed out of this growing dissatisfaction with neo-scholasticism. One sought a better scholasticism, which happened through closer and more contextual readings not just of Aquinas, but of medieval theology as a whole. Through creative applications, this group sought to relate the terms of Christian faith to the language and insights of contemporary philosophy. Theologians like Marie-Dominique Chenu, Pierre Rousselot, Erich Przywara, Karl Rahner, Henri de Lubac, Etienne Gilson, Joseph Maréchal, and Lonergan adopted this approach. The second response jettisoned canonical scholasticism and retrieved the pre-scholastic theology of roughly the first eight centuries of Christianity, along with neglected medieval figures. Hans Urs von Balthasar, Josef Ratzinger, Johann Baptist Metz, Jean Daniélou, and Walter Kasper all inclined toward the second mode.[16]

---

14. Frederick Lawrence, "Athens and Jerusalem: The Contemporary Problematic of Faith and Reason," *Gregorianum* 80, no. 2 (1999): 223–44, at 230.

15. Cited in Lawrence, "Athens and Jerusalem," 237.

16. Karen Kilby makes the same point in comparing Rahner and von Balthasar: "[Rahner] did not, like Balthasar, simply set aside neo-scholasticism in order to do theology in a different way. Instead, Rahner worked to a large extent with the system, probing and questioning it, seeking to bring it into contact with modern philosophy, and to open it up from within to the modern world" (Kilby, "Karl Rahner," in *The Modern Theologians*, 3rd ed., 92–105, at 94).

ERICH PRZYWARA

Though our treatment only limns his work, something must be said about perhaps the greatest Catholic mind of the twentieth century, Erich Przywara (1889–1972). A prolific essayist and theological occasionalist, Przywara did not build a system. His most indelible contribution, *Analogia Entis* (1932), was slim enough that its later editor, von Balthasar, felt compelled to complement the volume with an additional thirteen essays.[17] In this volume, as well as in his life's work, Przywara set out to rethink the very structure of reality through an Ignatian lens, and so to find a single frame within which to understand the different currents: (a) in Western theology, including Judaism, (b) in philosophy, both ancient and modern, and (c) between philosophy and theology. He did so by using the concept of analogy, which had previously been employed as a grammatical and literary tool, to rethink theology.

What resulted was a transformation of analogy into a metaphysics, an "analogy of being," that functioned akin to a unified field theory. This transformation allowed Catholic theology to assess the modern playing field and figure out how it could offer a better ontology than that of Przywara's contemporary, Martin Heidegger, who had published his groundbreaking *Being and Time* five years earlier. The analogy of being opened the way for Przywara to avoid both the neo-Thomist model that turned philosophy into a kept woman, and the Barthian model that eliminated philosophy's ability to speak truthfully about God. In Karl Rahner's words, "Przywara succeeded in transforming *analogia entis* from a narrow scholastic term into being a basic structure of what was 'Catholic.' It contains the summit of his theological project."[18]

---

17. The English translation includes all of the supplemental essays plus two additional ones. See Erich Przywara, *Analogia Entis. Metaphysics: Original Structure and Universal Rhythm*, trans. John Betz and David Bentley Hart (Grand Rapids, MI: Eerdmans, 2014). The translation constitutes a massive undertaking and an important milestone in the reception of *Analogia Entis*.

18. Karl Rahner, "Laudatio auf Erich Przywara," in *Gnade als Freiheit. Kleine theologische Beiträge* (Freiburg: Herder, 1968), 270, cited in Thomas O'Meara, *Erich Przywara, S.J. His Theology and His World* (Notre Dame, IN: University of Notre Dame Press, 2002), 80.

Until its recent renaissance, Przywara's work was considered outside mainstream twentieth-century theology, as evidenced by his almost total absence from the leading surveys of theology, paired with his omission from comprehensive exams and surveys for those studying theology at the graduate level.[19] Devotees of von Balthasar and Barth know Przywara, either as von Balthasar's most important teacher, or as the thorn in the side of Barth's radical dialectic; it was Barth, after all, who wrote, "I regard the *analogia entis* as the invention of the anti-Christ."[20] Barth so dominated the narrative arc of twentieth-century theology that many simply took it for granted that Barth won the debate. On this basis, Przywara was caricatured as a needlessly difficult thinker and author of turgid prose, who attributed to Aquinas the *analogia entis* despite the phrase never appearing in the Angelic Doctor's writings.

Until the past decade, one could have ended the story in this way and been done with Przywara. That one can do so no longer is due mainly to a remarkable Przywara resurgence, especially in North America, over the past ten years.[21] Some credit must be given to a revisiting of the debate between Barth and Przywara, and a weighing of the possibility that Przywara, not Barth, had gotten the upper hand.[22] Barth himself had highlighted what was at stake in the debate.

---

19. See Aidan Nichols, *From Hermes to Benedict XVI*, which says nothing about Przywara. See also Ford, *The Modern Theologians*, 3rd ed., who mentions Przywara only in passing as an influence on Barth. The same goes for Fergus Kerr in *Twentieth-Century Catholic Theologians* (Oxford: Blackwell, 2007). Gerald McCool's oft-cited survey, *The Neo-Thomists* (Milwaukee: Marquette University, 1994), passes over Przywara, as does *Mapping Modern Theology: A Thematic and Historical Introduction*, eds. Kelly Kapic and Bruce McCormack (Grand Rapids, MI: Baker Academic, 2012).

20. Karl Barth, *Church Dogmatics I/1*, 2nd ed., trans. G. W. Bromiley (Edinburgh: T&T Clark, [1936] 1975), xiii. This famous quotation inspired the recent volume *The Analogy of Being: Invention of the Antichrist or the Wisdom of God?*, ed. Thomas Joseph White (Grand Rapids, MI: Eerdmans, 2010).

21. At the center of this renewal is the translation of *Analogia Entis* by John Betz and David Bentley Hart. Besides the translation, which in itself is an astounding accomplishment, the "Editor's Introduction" by John Betz could almost serve as a short monograph to familiarize readers with Przywara. In the past several years, monographs on Przywara by Graham McAleer, John Paul Gonzales, and Aaron Pidel have been published. To these one can add the previously cited edited volume, and the roughly dozen Anglophone dissertations recently completed or in process.

22. See, in particular, John Betz's article, "After Barth: A New Introduction to Erich Przywara's *Analogia Entis*," in *The Analogy of Being*, 35–87.

The previous quotation from Barth continues, "I believe that because of [the analogy of being] it is impossible ever to become a Roman Catholic, all other reasons for not doing so being to my mind short-sighted and trivial."[23]

For our purposes, it will be helpful to show how this analogy helped Przywara to re-imagine the relationship between faith and reason. This catalyzation stands out most clearly in the chapter in *Analogia Entis* titled "Philosophical and Theological Metaphysics."[24] An analogy refers to a comparative relationship that contains both a similarity and a difference, such as the relationship between creation and God. Przywara writes, "the principle of metaphysics as such, understood as a 'creaturely metaphysics,' must be called analogy."[25] If God's existence were identical with creation's, one would have pantheism or panentheism, which would collapse the difference between God and the world. Likewise, a theology that only imagined God's being as transcendent and totally other from creation's would fail the analogical test (and here one can anticipate Przywara's disagreements with Barth and the broader dialectical impulse in Protestantism).[26] Przywara turns this analogical principle into doctrine of creation as well as a metaphysics.

The analogical nature of reality applies to the relation between faith and reason, or, for Przywara, theology and philosophy. Rather than using spatial metaphors of domain or territory, Przywara, trained as he was in music, opts for the musical metaphor of rhythm, which even makes its way into the book's title. Referring to enquiry concerning the relation between God and creation, Przywara writes, "They are questions concerning the innermost rhythmic beat between God and the created, in that they are concerned with the innermost beat

---

23. Barth, *Church Dogmatics* I/1, xiii. Here one can only note in passing the extraordinary movement in North American of Protestant theologians and graduate students being received into the Catholic Church. It is unknown whether more cradle Catholics or converts will constitute the guild in the coming decades.

24. Przywara, *Analogia Entis*, 155–91; unless otherwise noted, subsequent parenthetical citations refer to this text.

25. Przywara, *Analogia Entis*, 191.

26. For a clear articulation of this point, see Przywara's early essay, "Gott in uns oder Gott über uns? Immanenz und Transcenenz im heutigen Geistesleben," *Stimmen der Zeit* 53 (1923): 343–62.

of becoming in the creature."[27] At certain movements in creation's score, God seems more intimate to creation, and at others more distant, as God's similarity and dissimilarity vibrates, almost like particles in the branch of physics called string theory. Through this emphasis on rhythm, Przywara is able to extend a greater generosity to philosophy, for he does not need to yield theological territory to do so. He can also insist more emphatically on theology's unique and necessary melody. There is no need for an artificial compromise "between the semi-theological and the semi-philosophical; rather, a genuine and unanxious theology and a genuine and unanxious philosophy are one in the *one* God of the *one* truth, and for this reason [. . .] the *working out* of their union, as it takes shape, will be equally free of anxiety."[28]

While Przywara's proximate concerns were Heidegger and Barth, he clearly had Hegel in mind as well. Przywara was perhaps the first Christian thinker after Hegel who had both the mastery of the tradition and the panache to attempt something as bold as Hegel had done. As a Jesuit, Przywara wanted to defend the Church's teaching, but he also sought to portray its vision of reality in the best light. Przywara interpreted Hegel as combining theology and philosophy—even worse, collapsing theology into philosophy—by demanding that religion express itself in the pure form of the concept. Przywara explains the problem as follows: "Those modern philosophies that seek to be absolute are in fact theologies emptied of theological content—derived from a theology, to be sure, that had already of itself annulled the differences between God and creature."[29] Przywara's anti-Protestant genealogy accused modern philosophy in general, and Hegel in particular, of failing to think analogically. Without analogy, things get out of balance, and God is either confused with or excluded from the created realm: "And we can take as an example of this the way in which Hegel's philosophy originated from and grows out of theology, and conversely the way in which it leads to the transformation of theology into philosophical dialectic."[30] Przywara's genealogy, it should be noted, was not

27. Przywara, *Analogia Entis*, 158. Parentheticals excluded.
28. Przywara, *Analogia Entis*, 187.
29. Przywara, *Analogia Entis*, 164.
30. Przywara, *Analogia Entis*, 165.

exculpatory of his own tradition; it also assigned Scotus and Suarez as precursors to this separation.

For Przywara, Aquinas's maxim that faith (or grace) does not destroy reason (nature), but instead heals and perfects it, expressed succinctly the Catholic principle of analogy. The same analogical principle explains how this maxim applies to the ordering of reason to faith, and nature to grace. If one applies Aquinas's formula, then theology yields to philosophy like a contracting accordion. Philosophy, meanwhile, sets the stage for the accordion's expansion, which perfects—in the sense of *per-facere*, "to make through"—theology. Przywara adds to this arrangement the statement he discovered in the 1920s from the Fourth Lateran Council, which met in 1215: "For between Creator and creature no similitude can be expressed without implying a greater dissimilitude."[31] This magisterial declaration, to Przywara's mind, underscores why Catholicism had to part ways with Hegel; instead of reducing or translating the mystery of revelation into a concept, he advocated for a *reductio in mysterium*.[32] As "all in all," God is "ever more greatly beyond every grasping and comprehending by way of concepts. Not in the measure that the mystery becomes a concept, but in the measure that the concept is overcome in the mystery."[33] Przywara understands Hegel as following in the tradition of Augustine and Aquinas, but breaking off from them at a critical moment.[34]

Przywara's concern is not simply with Hegel, but with Hegel as representing perhaps the most formidable expression of the logic of modernity. To read modernity in a Catholic way is not to follow the antimodern route that leads to a halfway philosophy stripped of wonder (as elegantly described by Frederick Lawrence in the citation above). Instead, the Catholic way is to liberate philosophy, as love of wisdom, to pursue that wisdom. When done authentically, this pursuit leads the

31. Denzinger, 806.
32. Przywara, *Analogia Entis*, 182.
33. Przywara, *Analogia Entis*, 181.
34. Przywara makes the same point toward the end of the chapter: "The *reductio in mysterium* [. . .] is thus a way into the mystery 'in' the concept and 'beyond' the concept—in response to Hegel's attempt to grasp the mystery 'as' concept (in 'absolute knowledge'), for whom it is primarily the concept which appears 'as' mystery" (Przywara, *Analogia Entis*, 189).

practitioner to accept the need for the counter note that theology as faith provides. In explaining the relationship between faith and reason in this way, Przywara was able to reveal a Catholic vision that "centers on the interplay of divine activity in creation and revelation."[35]

Przywara's way was the "route not taken," despite the influence of his most devoted student, Hans Urs von Balthasar. Przywara carried forward both the scholasticism that dominated during the peak of his own career, as well as the Blondelian conviction about the inner dynamism of the human being, such that philosophy, rather than supplying all of the answers, oriented the lover of wisdom toward a deeper mystery.[36] John Betz makes the case that the best label for Przywara is "creative Thomist," in the sense of using Aquinas as a model for genuine openness to, without obeisance before, modern thought.[37] One can surmise that Przywara understood his own mission to be what Eric Voegelin had called for when he wrote of the challenge presented by modernity: "Obviously it is a task that would require a new Thomas rather than a neo-Thomist."[38] If there was another Thomas in twentieth-century Catholic theology, Przywara was it.

RAHNER AND LONERGAN

Historians often hail Joseph Maréchal (1878–1944) as the founder of "transcendental Thomism," a Thomism that appropriated the Kantian turn to the subject in a way similar to how Aquinas appropriated Aristotle.[39] Gerald McCool describes Maréchal's *magnum opus*, the five-volume *Le Point de Départ de la Métaphysique* as both "a dialogue with Kantian philosophy" and a "face-to-face confrontation between St. Thomas and Kant."[40] In it, he argues that if Kant had followed through in his arguments more consistently, he would have seen how God is

35. O'Meara, *Erich Przywara, S.J.*, 78.

36. Przywara, *Analogia Entis*, 160–61n5.

37. John Betz, "The Humility of God: On a Disputed Question in Trinitarian Theology," *Nova et Vetera* 17, no. 4 (2019): 757–98, at 787n79.

38. Eric Voegelin, *From Enlightenment to Revolution*, ed. John Hallowell (Durham, NC: Duke University Press, 1975), 22. This remark has morphed in the oral tradition into: "We don't need more Thomists, we need another Thomas."

39 See, for instance, Kilby, "Karl Rahner," 93–94.

40. McCool, *Nineteenth-Century Scholasticism*, 256.

the condition for the possibility of speculative reason, and did not need to be relegated to the status of a postulate for practical reason. This conclusion not only echoed Blondel's claims, but also contradicted Kleutgen's thesis that modern thought was doomed to fail because it begins with the subject and never arrives at reality. Maréchal's school of Thomism counted Rahner and Lonergan (although understandable, this was a mistaken judgment)[41] as its greatest inheritors, and incarnated an openness to modern philosophical trends—long forbidden by neo-scholasticism—as its formal mode of *fides quarens intellectum*.

Before taking up the attempts by Rahner and Lonergan to relate faith to reason, it will be helpful to say a few words about them. Both were born and died in the same years (1904–84), and underwent the standard inter-war formation in manualist scholasticism, which they both found wanting. In Rahner's case, this realization came through his participation in Martin Heidegger's seminars in Freiberg in the 1930s. His exposure to Heidegger resulted most directly in an attempt to update scholasticism and respond to the Kantian critique of metaphysics and agnosticism about the knowability of God. Rahner accomplished this in two early works, *Spirit in the World* (1939) and *Hearer of the Word* (1941).[42] For Rahner, Kant's critique of metaphysics exposed the simplicity of intuitionist accounts, popular among neo-scholastics, about the capacity of human reason to conceive of God. Rahner wanted to modify the transcendental method constructed by

41. Associating Lonergan with "transcendental Thomism" dates to Otto Muck's *Die transzendentale Methode in der scholastischen Philosophie der Gegenwart* (Innsbruck: Rauch, 1964); The English translation appeared with a foreword by Rahner in 1968. This association received additional impulse from E. L. Mascall's 1970 Gifford Lectures, "The Transcendental Method," later published as *The Openness of Being: Natural Theology Today* (Philadelphia: Westminster, 1971). For a more recent instantiation, see Christopher Cullen, "Transcendental Thomism: Realism Rejected," in *The Failure of Modernism*, ed. Brendan Sweetman (Mishawaka, IN: American Maritain Association, 1999), 72–86. Although Cullen focuses on Rahner, he adds that the case could be made for Lonergan being "the leading Transcendental Thomist in history" (Cullen, "Transcendental Thomism," 73). Cullen argues that transcendental Thomism rejects realism by turning to the subject, just as Kant had done. One versed in Lonergan would respond that not every turn to the subject accepts the Kantian premise that objective knowledge is by intuition or not at all. For a recent discussion, see Jeremy Wilkins, *Before Truth: Lonergan, Aquinas and the Problem of Wisdom* (Washington, DC: The Catholic University of America Press, 2018), 165–66.

42. Karl Rahner, *Spirit in the World*, trans. William Dych (New York: Herder and Herder, 1968); *Hearer of the Word*, trans. Joseph Donceel (New York: Continuum, 1994).

Kant so as to arrive at Aquinas's ontology.[43] He did this, however, through copious and intensive engagement with Aquinas, and only oblique or indirect reference to Kant.[44]

Whereas for Hegel so much turned on the concept (*Begriff*), Rahner made great hay out of the human being's pre-apprehension (*Vorgriff*), "which is the condition of the possibility of objective knowledge and of our self-subsistence." Through this pre-apprehension, "we continually transcend everything toward pure being." As such, human beings possess an openness that is "the condition of the possibility for every single knowledge."[45] This pre-conceptual knowledge was transcendental rather than categorical, meaning it was the condition for the possibility of knowledge. In other words, God—the ground of being whom we only pre-apprehend—makes it possible to know anything else.[46] By taking this transcendental turn, Rahner parted ways with a neo-scholasticism that turned God into an object, at least if one accepted Kant's critique.[47] In *Spirit in the World*, Rahner fought fire with fire by arguing that his transcendental approach aligned with Aquinas more faithfully than the neo-scholastic tradition he was taught.

Connected with this abstract epistemological point was an anthropological one.[48] In explaining the pre-apprehension that

43. For this point, and for in general the most helpful navigation of Rahner's relationship to Kant, see Francis Fiorenza, "Introduction: Karl Rahner and the Kantian Problematic," in *Spirit in the World*, xix–xlv, at xxxiii. According to Andrew Moore, Rahner's attempt to bring together Aquinas and Kant was "massively sophisticated and technically accomplished" (see Moore, "Reason," 408).

44. See Rahner, "Author's Introduction," in *Spirit in the World*, xlix–lv, esp. lii: "The limited scope of this work did not permit an *explicit*, detailed confrontation of modern philosophy from Kant to Heidegger with Thomas." Rahner goes on to say that, whereas Kant is concerned with the critique of knowledge, he is concerned with "the metaphysics of knowledge," derived from Aquinas (Rahner, *Spirit in the World*, liii).

45. Rahner, *Hearer of the Word*, 53. In Fiorenza's formulation, "the question concerning being presupposes a knowledge of being . . . [and] is a necessary presumption for the objectivity of human knowledge in general" (Fiorenza, "Introduction," xlii–xliii).

46. Rahner writes, "The *Vorgriff* intends God's absolute being in this sense that the absolute being is always and basically co-affirmed by the basically unlimited range of the *Vorgriff*." For this point, see the entire paragraph, to which this quotation is the conclusion, in *Hearer of the Word*, 50–51.

47. Fiorenza, "Introduction," xliiin39.

48. For the best discussion of Rahner's anthropology see the chapter, "Karl Rahner: Transcendental Anthropology," in Stephen J. Duffy, *The Dynamics of Grace: Perspectives in Theological Anthropology* (Collegeville, MN: Liturgical Press, 1993), 261–341.

accompanies enquiry into an individual object or question, something else happens: "In every single act of knowledge it always already reaches beyond the individual object."[49] The human being is oriented toward this beyond which is never experienced as such. This anthropological orientation put Rahner within the Blondelian orbit, but in the scholastic garb of such phraseology as "agent intellect" and "obediential potency."[50] Rahner would come to apply this anthropology to a number of questions and topics. One area of note was the theology of grace, to which Rahner added the idea of the supernatural existential. Another was in the theology of religion through his theory of the "anonymous Christian," whose acceptance of an unnamed grace takes on a Christian form without explicitly naming it such.[51] During the first two decades of his professional career, this approach raised suspicions and put him in the crosshairs of the Magisterium. Opinions about Rahner shifted during the Second Vatican Council, where Rahner played a prominent role as *peritus* (advisor) to Franz König, archbishop of Vienna. The Council's documents reflected a new, post-scholastic approach to theology advocated by Rahner. After the Council, Rahner's theology grew more popular; during those years he continued his torrid pace of publication, both as author and editor, all while forming the outlook of a new generation of students.

Some would call Rahner's optimistic orientation toward modernity naïve. Although he made substantial contributions to twentieth-century understandings of original sin, his epistemology seemed to elide the impact of social and individual sin on the thinking subject. In his theology he presented the human being, even in the face of radical sinfulness, as predisposed to hear the voice of God: "Our philosophy of religion as fundamental theological anthropology establishes a positive human receptivity for revelation, so that this

---

49. Rahner, *Hearer of the Word*, 47.
50. For a helpful comparison of Rahner and Blondel, see Peter Henrici, "Karl Rahners 'Hörer des Wortes' und Maurice Blondels 'L'Action,'" in *Die philosophischen Quellen der Theologie Karl Rahners*, ed. Harald Schöndorf (Freiburg: Herder, 2005), 81–99.
51. These ideas, and their roots in his early work, are clearly distilled in Karen Kilby, "Karl Rahner," in *The Modern Theologians*, 3rd ed., 92–105.

receptivity is not simply the negative dialectical repercussion, not merely the critical judgment pronounced on all that is human and innerworldly."[52] On the basis of his anthropology, one could label Rahner the "anti-Barth" of twentieth-century theologians.[53] His epistemology also explained how reason, associated with humanity's natural capacity, was deeply compatible with faith, even faith conceived as supernatural gift, thus unattainable without grace. Rahner's optimistic account of human receptivity to divine revelation fused traditional scholastic boldness concerning the relationship between faith and reason into a modern philosophical idiom. The irony of this move was that it took place just as postmodern theories began calling into question the modern project, especially as espoused by Kant. When these trends came to the forefront of the discourse in academic theology, a decreasing number of the leading scholars found succor in Rahner's approach.

If one were to fill out a triptych of influential mid-century Catholic theologians who wanted to fight neo-scholastic distortions with a better and deeper reading of Thomas, Bernard Lonergan would occupy, next to Przywara and Rahner, the third panel. Like Rahner, he undertook a sophisticated reading of Aquinas early in his career, and the process of doing so—in Lonergan's words, "reaching up to the mind of Aquinas"[54]—gave him the moxie to depart from the scholastic system and articulate his own theory of cognition. For Lonergan, this happened through two studies—a doctoral dissertation on the theme of operative grace in Aquinas, and in a subsequent project on cognitional theory—both of which first appeared as a series of articles in

52. Rahner, *Hearer of the Word*, 153.

53. Although he did not engage with Barth's work to the degree that Przywara or von Balthasar did, Rahner clearly disagreed with the approach, which would have denied on methodological grounds the step to base theology upon what Rahner thought was a strong metaphysical basis. See *Hearer of the Word*, 18–20. For Rahner as the anti-Barth, see Duffy, *The Dynamics of Grace*, 286; and Moore, "Reason," 408.

54. Bernard Lonergan, *Collected Works of Bernard Lonergan*, eds. Frederick E. Crowe and Robert Doran, vol. 3, *Insight: A Study in Human Understanding* (Toronto: University of Toronto Press, 1992), 769. The full citation reads, "After years of reaching up to the mind of Aquinas, I came to a twofold conclusion. On the one hand, that reaching had changed me profoundly. On the other hand, that change was the essential benefit. For not only did it make me capable of grasping what, in the light of my conclusions, the *vetera* really were, but also it opened challenging vistas on what the *nova* could be."

the Jesuit journal, *Theological Studies*, in the 1940s, and were only much later published as books after Lonergan's profile grew.[55]

Like Rahner, Lonergan reframed Aquinas's account of how human cognition works, and did so by translating scholastic vocabulary into a modern idiom. This meant replacing faculty psychology, focused as it was on the faculties of intellect and will, with what he called intentionality analysis, which describes different levels of consciousness. How all of this works cannot detain us, but it is important to note the overlap between Lonergan and Rahner, which led to the two being mistakenly grouped together as transcendental Thomists. From the outside, the two seemed quite similar, but when one gets into the meat of their arguments, one comes to understand that Lonergan and Rahner had very little in common.

Lonergan's most impactful book was *Insight* (1957), a colossal work best described as an analogue to Newman's *Essay in Aid of a Grammar of Assent*. This work brought Lonergan international acclaim, while displaying a confidence in reason that recalls Anselm and Hegel. His "Epilogue" to *Insight* captures this confidence and suggests how Lonergan saw the project contributing to the theological task of faith seeking understanding. Lonergan declared: "I have written as a humanist, as one dominated by the desire not only to understand but also, through understanding understanding, to reach a grasp of the main lines of all there is to be understood."[56] This project of "understanding understanding" involves a self-appropriation that "begins as cognitional theory, expands into a metaphysics and an ethics, mounts to a conception and an affirmation of God."[57] Like Hegel's *Phenomenology of Spirit*, Lonergan's *Insight* is a book about (almost) everything. After undergoing nearly eight hundred pages of this thought experiment, Lonergan's "Epilogue" reconsiders his project in light of his status as a believer and a professor of dogmatic theology.

This "Epilogue" bemoans both a rationalism that excludes faith, and the fideistic tendencies that exclude reason, both of which have

---

55. The works in question are *Grace and Freedom: Operative Grace in the Thought of Aquinas*, and *Verbum: Word and Idea in Aquinas*. Both are available as volumes 1 and 2 in *Collected Works of Bernard Lonergan* (Toronto: University of Toronto Press, 1992).

56. Lonergan, *Insight*, 753.

57. Lonergan, *Insight*, 753.

taken up too much of modernity's oxygen.[58] Lonergan felt the same urgency that Aquinas and Bonaventure had felt seven centuries earlier: to produce "a synthesis that unites the two orders of truth and to give evidence of a successful symbiosis of two principles of knowledge."[59] Lonergan recognized that modern science has produced a new set of challenges for the believer. The explosion of scientific breakthroughs in fields as varied as physics and Semitic literature have put the believer "in the unenviable position of always arriving on the scene a little breathlessly and a little late."[60] Lonergan wrote *Insight* to give an account of the human process of understanding that explained what was common to reasoning that propelled the natural and the human sciences, including theology. Lonergan sought to make it possible for the believer not arrive so breathless and so late to every conversation.

Though at first glance his program expressed the same mid-century optimism that marked Rahner's project, Lonergan has proved more durable in the face of postmodern discourse.[61] His popularity never reached the level of Rahner's, but enthusiasm for his work has remained steady, while it has clearly declined for Rahner.[62] In the turbulent decades following the Second Vatican Council, both Rahner and Lonergan provided models for robust and zealous encounters with secular thought, which encouraged students and devotees to do the same, hopeful that such encounters would deepen theological understanding. Since the two possessed such an easily discernable balance in perspective and intellectual vigor, they gave the hope that a new synthesis was achievable, or even that it had been achieved in their distinct but parallel intellectual projects.

58. For Lonergan's brief genealogy of modernity, see *Insight*, 550–52. For a more detailed account, see the essays "The Transition from a Classicist World-View to Historical-Mindedness" and "Theology in its New Context," in Bernard Lonergan, *A Second Collection*, eds. Ryan and Tyrrell (Toronto: University of Toronto Press, 1974), 1–9, 55–67.

59. Lonergan, *Insight*, 754–55.

60. Lonergan, *Insight*, 755.

61. For two examples, see Frederick Lawrence, "The Fragility of Consciousness: Lonergan and the Postmodern Concern for the Other," *Theological Studies* 54 (1993): 55–94, and the volume *In Deference to the Other: Lonergan and Contemporary Continental Thought*, eds. Jim Kanaris and Mark Dorley (Albany: SUNY Press, 2004).

62. In the United States alone, there are meetings devoted to Lonergan's thought that take place annually in Boston, Milwaukee, and Los Angeles.

NON-SCHOLASTIC CATHOLIC APPROACHES

The driving forces in twentieth-century Catholic theology were not only "creative Thomists" in the vein of Przywara, Rahner, and Lonergan. Certain figures sidestepped scholasticism almost entirely, either by doing historical work that eschewed neo-scholasticism's framework (Raymond Brown and Marie-Joseph Lagrange, pre-eminently, in biblical studies, and Marie-Dominique Chenu in medieval theology) or inventing an entirely different mode of theology, oftentimes inspired by Blondel. The most obvious figures to fall into this camp are Henri de Lubac (1896–1991) and Hans Urs von Balthasar (1905–88). Both responded to neo-scholasticism's extrinsicism; de Lubac did so by revisiting the nature-grace debate that Jansenism had ignited in the seventeenth century. Balthasar's project was more capacious, and it closely paralleled Barth's *Church Dogmatics*. Balthasar's "trilogy" modeled itself on the transcendentals—beauty, goodness, truth—and took fifteen volumes to complete. Beginning with beauty, von Balthasar initiated a ground-breaking turn toward what he labeled theological aesthetics.

Balthasar called Przywara his greatest teacher and inherited his preoccupation with analogy. Owing to this influence, Balthasar also engaged with Barth well before Catholic theology adopted an ecumenical focus at and following the Second Vatican Council.[63] Here we can briefly recount how von Balthasar imagines the relation between faith and reason, as he lays it out in the first volume of *Glory of the Lord*.[64] By beginning with beauty, von Balthasar initiated a methodological revolution that charted a new trajectory for understanding how faith and reason relate. By beginning with beauty, von Balthasar wanted to compensate for the deleterious effects of centuries-long neglect. He defended putting beauty first (and indeed devoted seven volumes to it before turning to the good and the true) by noting how one could not properly discern the good and the true without it: "In a world that no longer has enough confidence in itself to affirm the beautiful, the proofs

---

63. Balthasar, *Karl Barth: Darstellung und Deutung seiner Theologie* (Cologne: Hegner, 1951).

64. Balthasar, *The Glory of the Lord: A Theological Aesthetics*, trans. Erasmo Leiva-Merikakis, vol. 1, *Seeing the Form* (San Francisco: Ignatius, 1982). Subsequent citations refer to this volume.

of the truth have lost their cogency. In other words, syllogisms may still dutifully clatter away [. . .] but the logic of these answers is itself a mechanism which no longer captivates anyone."[65] Unlike Rahner, who was more directly concerned with the extrinsicism taught in seminaries, von Balthasar's main target was a modern world that had endeavored to sunder the beautiful from the true and the good, and likewise sever philosophy from theology, of which neo-Thomism was more an epiphenomenon than a cause.[66] This diagnosis led von Balthasar to turn not just to Thomas, as Rahner had done, but to the Church Fathers, especially the Eastern Fathers, as modeled by French *ressourcement* Jesuits, Henri de Lubac and Jean Daniélou.[67]

Balthasar's most important insights into the relation between faith and reason come in section II/A, "The Light of Faith,"[68] which opens with a New Testament comparison of Johannine *gnosis* (knowledge) and Pauline *pistis* (faith). Balthasar's critique of modernity's fractious tendency leads him to uphold a unified account of faith and reason, or in this case, *pistis* and *gnosis*. Balthasar does not want the act of faith isolated, as if faith could thereby be purified from anything gnoseological. He finds this integration in Scripture, especially in the Gospel of John. After discussing their connection in Paul, von Balthasar concludes, "In John, faith and knowledge are almost more intimately and inseparably intertwined."[69]

Balthasar flirts with illuminism, and a kind of fideism, even though he swears it off,[70] with his emphasis on "seeing the form." The form is Christ, both as object of faith, and model of subjective faith. On this point of entry, von Balthasar differs most sharply from Rahner. In Rahner's account, grace is always present, and thus uni-

---

65. Balthasar, *The Glory of the Lord*, 19.
66. For this point, see *The Glory of the Lord*, I, 70ff. And, with greater precision, von Balthasar's mini-summa, *Love Alone is Credible*, trans. D. C. Schindler (San Francisco: Ignatius, 2004), 15–30.
67. For the best overview of the *ressourcement* movement, see *Ressourcement: A Movement for Renewal in Twentieth-Century Theology*, eds. Gabriel Flynn and Paul D. Murray (Oxford: Oxford University Press, 2012). Balthasar produced important monographic studies of Maximus the Confessor and Origen of Alexandria.
68. Balthasar, *The Glory of the Lord*, 131–218.
69. Balthasar, *The Glory of the Lord*, 134.
70. Balthasar, *The Glory of the Lord*, 142.

versal. From this universal gift of grace, one understands the particularity of Christ as a historical person who came to embody the fullness of this grace. Balthasar reverses the order by beginning with Christ, who is the form to be seen: "The witness of the Gospels, and John's in particular, has it rather this way: Christ is recognized in his form." He continues, "Just as a natural form—a flower, for instance—can be seen for what it is only when it is perceived and 'received' as the appearance of a certain depth of life, so, too, Jesus' form can be seen for what it is only when it is grasped and accepted as the appearance of a divine depth transcending all worldly nature."[71] Balthasar does not understand form as the other side of content: "The content (*Gehalt*) does not lie behind the form (*Gestalt*) but within it."[72] Jesus is not a sign pointing to something universal or elsewhere; instead, Jesus is the manifestation of truth: "Jesus the Man, in his visibility, is not a sign pointing beyond himself to an invisible 'Christ of faith.'"[73] Once one encounters, or, even more radically, is encountered by the concrete, Christian particularity, one finds a measure to make sense of other things. One experiences this form not as something grasped or attained, but instead as a gift to be received. He explains, "Man's vision of God is like an echo of the antecedent and foundational event of being seen by God [. . .] his vision of God is included in his being seen by God."[74]

By reimagining the shape and starting place of Christian apologetics, von Balthasar makes his most impactful contribution to the relation between faith and reason. For von Balthasar, Christian apologetics does not begin with the claims of Jesus, and then show how these claims clear the bar of rationality set by a scientific standard. In his account:

71. Balthasar, *The Glory of the Lord*, 133–34.
72. Balthasar, *The Glory of the Lord*, 151. As Avery Dulles points out, by refusing to separate content and form, Balthasar undercuts an extrinsicist account that would justify belief on the basis of reading content from the signs. See Avery Dulles, *The Assurance of Things Hoped For: A Theology of Christian Faith* (Oxford: Oxford University Press, 1994), 147–52.
73. Balthasar, *The Glory of the Lord*, 437.
74. Balthasar, *The Glory of the Lord*, 329. See also, 153: "The witness of the Gospels, and John's in particular, has it rather this way: Christ is recognized in his form only when his form has been seen and understood to be the form of the God-man."

> Anyone asking the question in this way has really already forfeited an answer, because he is at once enmeshed in an insoluble dilemma. On the one hand, he can believe on the basis of sufficient rational certainty; but then he is not believing on the basis of divine authority, and his faith is not Christian faith. Or, on the other hand, he can achieve faith by renouncing all rational certainty and believing on the basis of mere probability, but then his faith is not really rational.[75]

Balthasar's warning against the problem of epistemological Pelagianism does not lapse into a fideism that permits no place for reason. Balthasar finds the solution in an aesthetic apologetics and boldly declares that ignoring the need to see Christ's form "has stunted the growth of this branch of theology over the past hundred years."[76] To see the form of Christ is also to be seen by Christ, and thus to grasp the wholeness and unity of God and humanity, soul and body, Father, Son, and Spirit, time and eternity. Failure to see Christ's form results, inevitably, in so many modern divisions—between the Christ of faith and the Jesus of history, between theology and philosophy, beauty and goodness, and, most importantly for our study, between faith and reason. Both Protestant and Catholic theology have failed in this matter: "This tragic dialectic, into which Protestant theology has largely fallen, lacks exactly the same thing as the rationalistic school of Catholic apologetics: namely, the dimension of aesthetic contemplation."[77] Unlike Rahner, von Balthasar does not pursue or call for a synthesis that would translate Aquinas into modern philosophy; von Balthasar's negative diagnosis of modernity requires a sharper-edged approach.

In assessing von Balthasar and in tracing the path of his trajectory, it is important to avoid vertiginous judgments that seem so tempting. Many late-twentieth century academic theologians felt the need to take sides with regard to the conflicting elements between Rahner and

---

75. Balthasar, *The Glory of the Lord*, 173.

76. Balthasar, *The Glory of the Lord*, 173. On this point Aidan Nichols is correct to name Balthasar's account of reason as "aesthetic reason" (Nichols, *From Hermes to Benedict XVI*, 195).

77. Balthasar, *The Glory of the Lord*, 174.

von Balthasar, the former representing a neo-Thomism optimistically oriented toward modernity, and the latter a cautious Augustinianism mistrustful of modernity. Just as modern Protestant theology played out as a dialectic between Schleiermacher and Barth, so did recent Catholic theology unfold as a dialectic between Rahner (the Catholic Schleiermacher) and von Balthasar (the Catholic Barth).[78] Balthasar's direct and impactful critique of Rahner, especially of the idea of "anonymous Christianity,"[79] certainly gives ammunition to those eager to draw the greatest possible contrast between them, especially as they have become proxies for how Catholics should receive the Second Vatican Council.[80] Still, the differences should not be exaggerated. Take, for instance, the following statement by von Balthasar: "The self-revelation of God, who is absolute being, can only be the fulfilment of man's entire philosophical-mythological questioning as well. As such it is an answer to men's questions which comes to us in God's revealing Word."[81] This is a sentence that Rahner could have written, for it echoes Rahner's supernatural existential. Similarly, when von Balthasar defends the idea of natural faith, one should realize that he is probably closer to Rahner than to Barth. Balthasar articulates the idea that natural faith implies that "natural finite reason is directed to an infinite freedom by which created reason knows itself to be posited and before which it must persevere in an attitude of primary obedience that is beyond all demands, longings, and enterprises."[82] Balthasar modifies the Rahnerian (and Blondelian, and Pascalian) position by insisting

78. In Andrew Moore's article on reason in theology, he treats von Balthasar and Barth under the same sub-heading (Moore, "Reason," 403–5).

79. For this critique, see Balthasar, *The Moment of Christian Witness*, trans. Richard Beckley (San Francisco, Ignatius, 1994). His critique was already in gestation as early as 1961 when the first volume of *Glory of the Lord* appeared, and thus Balthasar's opposition should not be read as a post-Vatican II reaction. There he writes, "These [non-Christian religious] constructions are distinct from the Christian reality in the sense that, even though they could be the testimonies of religious persons—even, latently, of believers—they nonetheless cannot be God's immediate self-witness in historical form and, pre-eminently, in Christ, who, *as* a historical form, demands faith for himself" (Balthasar, *The Glory of the Lord*, 168).

80. For this contrast, see Massimo Faggioli, *Vatican II: The Battle for Meaning* (New York: Paulist, 2012), 50–53, 66–90.

81. Balthasar, *The Glory of the Lord*, 145.

82. Balthasar, *The Glory of the Lord*, 451.

on the priority of God's word, through a dramatic approach that sprinkles a Barthian dusting on a traditionally Catholic construction.

One cannot overstate von Balthasar's importance for multiple generations of Catholics who wanted a more practical and relatable way to enter into theology. Though never a university professor—von Balthasar's doctorate was in German literature, not theology—and a nonfactor during the Second Vatican Council—the most important Church event in his lifetime—von Balthasar's *aesthetic* faith and dramatic reason gave Catholic theology a non-scholastic option for relating faith and reason.[83] Indeed, like Barth, he has exercised an impressively trans-confessional reach. One sees this, for instance, in the dissertation that launched the career of the Eastern Orthodox theologian, David Bentley Hart: *The Beauty of the Infinite*.[84] Despite never having been a Catholic, and trained entirely outside of Catholic institutions, Hart's work clearly follows in the wake of von Balthasar and continues the project of "aesthetic apologetics" for which von Balthasar laid the groundwork forty years earlier. Balthasar has also been a fruitful conversation partner for Protestants in part because they do not need to enter the citadel of scholasticism in order to appropriate his work, even as von Balthasar has (rightly) been suspected as a gateway drug to Catholicism.[85]

The discipline of theology has undergone massive changes, often resulting from intense external pressures, over the past two centuries. In many ways, and from many quarters, calls for retreat from the world of academic discourse have been loud, persistent, and persuasive. The theologians profiled in this chapter all found interesting modes for thinking through the intelligibility of faith. These theologians opened up conversations between theology and a variety of discourses ranging from philosophy and the natural sciences, to the social sciences and even the arts. They did so in spite of, and in dia-

83. Balthasar's dramatic notion of reason is helpfully exposited in D. C. Schindler, *The Catholicity of Reason* (Grand Rapids, MI: Eerdmans, 2013), 35–57.

84. David Bentley Hart, *Beauty of the Infinite: The Aesthetics of Christian Truth* (Grand Rapids, MI: Eerdmans, 2004).

85. For a helpful study of the topic, see Rodney Howsare, *Hans Urs von Balthasar and Protestantism: The Ecumenical Implications of His Theological Style* (London: T&T Clark, 2005).

logue with, constituencies within their own denominations that gave intellectual and institutional cover to those who would have preferred to withdraw in one way or another. Rather than withdrawing from their traditions, the theologians treated here found ways to deepen connections, often quite creatively, to these traditions. At the time of their deaths, or even concurrent with the publication of their respective *magna opera*, major changes were afoot, and the modern terrain, which had proven so challenging a place for theology to find its footing, was giving way to a new, postmodern set of challenges.

Chapter 9

Theology after Modernity
The Postmodern Predicament

One way to understand modernity is by examining the "sacred cows" that it challenges, including political and ecclesial authority, theology, and faith itself. Modernity's assault on elements of the Christian worldview often put theology on its heels. By redefining reason, science, and philosophy, Enlightenment modernity presented an unprecedented challenge to Christian faith. The previous two chapters in part III profiled leading mainstream figures and movements in twentieth-century Western Christianity. Truly great minds rose to and met a stiff challenge, only for Christianity to face a new, postmodern challenge. This chapter, the final chapter in the book, describes the key components of postmodern thought before profiling two different categories of theological appropriation of the postmodern idiom. It ends in a manner similar to how part III began: by examining Catholic magisterial interventions into the debate about how best to relate faith and reason.

THE POSTMODERN PREDICAMENT

The phenomenon of *postmodernism* has many names,[1] and its application to diverse fields means different things. Poststructuralism, anti-foundationalism, post-secularism, deconstruction, and critical theory are just some of the terms that signal a postmodern affiliation. Just as modernity or modernism can signal something different in art and literature, as compared to theology, so too with postmodernism. Post-

---

1. Some theologians prefer the substantive *postmodernity* to postmodernism in order to avoid an association with Modernism, understood within Catholic theology as a particular movement condemned by Pius X. Here and below I follow the lead of the authoritative theological surveys that use *postmodernism*, without intending any connection to the Modernism condemned by Pius.

modern theology refers to the theology that repeats or incorporates postmodern critiques of various modern signposts—the autonomous subject, the authority of reason and science, the zeal for the universals as expressed in metanarratives, and the colonialism, racism, and sexism that underlies so much of the modern political project, expressed in the nation-state and its bureaucratic apparatus.

Postmodernism has been a long time in the making. Already in the nineteenth century, figures like Kierkegaard and Nietzsche radically challenged modern understandings of the subject and of truth. In addition, women and non-white men like Mary Wollstonecraft and Frederick Douglass questioned the universality of rights and the purported democratization of power if it did not extend to women and people of color. Thinkers like Hegel inspired Karl Marx to consider how modern capitalism exploited laborers. These considerations launched what became known as Marxist theory, which questioned the logic of markets, consumer choice, and desire. Likewise, Sigmund Freud captured the unconscious as an entire ocean of untapped forces and drives that complicated modern understandings of the subject as an autonomous and rational deliberator. All of these movements inspired and also foretold postmodernism.

Historians often trace the ascendance of postmodernism to 1968, or thereabouts. As *post*, it is after whatever is deemed modern. This lexical convention behooves practitioners and scholars of postmodernism to state when it began. Pinning down the breaks between historical eras is an inexact science. James K. A. Smith explains that postmodernism "is sometimes even linked to particular historical events such as student riots in 1968, the abandonment of the gold standard, the fall of the Berlin Wall [in 1989] or, to be specific, 3:32 pm on July 15, 1972."[2] Others tie the arrival of postmodernism in the United States to the conference sponsored by Johns Hopkins University in 1966. Here Jacques Derrida, Roland Barthes, and Jacques Lacan spoke

---

2. James K. A. Smith, *Who's Afraid of Postmodernism? Taking Derrida, Lyotard, and Foucault to Church* (Grand Rapids, MI: Baker Academic, 2006), 19. The final date indicates the destruction of the Pruitt-Igoe housing project in Saint Louis, which was based on modern architectural ideals of living together but failed spectacularly to do anything but become a symbol of governmental housing mismanagement.

for the first time in the Unites States at the invitation of another French theorist working in the United States, René Girard. The conference caused a decisive turn toward poststructuralism and postmodern theory in the American academy.[3]

For our purposes, it will be helpful to identify the postmodern critique of reason, specifically a critique of the modern understanding of reason, to pave the way for understanding how postmodern theology relates faith to reason, even when it advances the pointlessness of such a venture. The most effective way to pinpoint the postmodern suspicion toward reason is through its critique of metanarrative. In perhaps the most essential text of postmodernism, *The Postmodern Condition*,[4] Jean-François Lyotard (1924–88) lays out his definition of postmodernism as suspicion toward metanarratives or grand narratives (*grand récits*), in favor of more localized and particular narratives (*petit récits*).[5] At first glance, one might associate such grand narratives with epics or big stories like the Bible or Augustine's *City of God*. This is not what makes a *récit* "grand" according to Lyotard. Grand narratives certainly tell a big story, but they also make a claim that theirs is the only story to be told. James Smith explains, "These stories not only tell a grand story but also claim to be able to legitimate or prove the story's claim by an appeal to universal reason."[6]

The best example of a grand narrative is modern science, which in the course of legitimizing itself also insists that it can only be refuted according to the rules it has pre-established. In the face of a global pandemic, one can respond to a fundamentalist or a skeptic by saying, "I believe in science," as if this belief was both clear and rational. But what is one saying? That one trusts scientific experts to be truthful and honest? That one believes in the scientific method? That the natural sciences collectively and exclusively participate in something

---

3. For a delightful account of this conference see Cynthia Haven's "The French Invasion," in *Evolution of Desire: A Life of René Girard* (East Lansing, MI: Michigan State University Press, 2018), 121–46.

4. Jean-François Lyotard, *The Postmodern Condition: A Report on Knowledge*, trans. Bennington and Massumi (Minneapolis: University of Minnesota Press, [1979] 1984).

5. See Lyotard, "Introduction," in *The Postmodern Condition*, helpfully summarized in Smith, *Who's Afraid of Postmodernism?*, 62–65.

6. Smith, *Who's Afraid of Postmodernism?*, 65.

called *science*?[7] Postmodernism raises suspicion toward the kind of presuppositions that go unquestioned, and thereby allow certain modes of discourse to dominate.

The same kind of critique applies to reason. Postmodernism does not suggest we abandon reason, logic, and argument. It calls into question, however, appeals to reason's universality and autonomy, as if reason designated an activity divorced from anything particular, like language, or specific traditions of discourse. It is no coincidence that the modern figure who did the most to shape subsequent understandings of reason—Immanuel Kant—openly admitted a kind of "science envy" in which he expressed a desire that philosophy should strive for the ideal established by the natural sciences. One might respond to Lyotard by suggesting that science really is universal, and universally true. One could appeal to scientific successes like landing on the moon, mapping the human genome, and the improvement of health and longevity. Indeed, the massive improvement in standards of living, especially through the invention of technologies derived from scientific breakthroughs, seems to provide incontrovertible evidence for the power of science and reason. All of this would not just miss the point, but make the point that Lyotard wants us to see. Science as metanarrative, unchecked by any suspicion, allows for belief in adjacent ideas like progress, expansion, colonization, and even eugenics, that seem to follow almost directly from believing in science, or reason. The postmodern thinker *suspects* that these ideas and their after-effects— elimination of native peoples and cultures, environmental destruction, exploitation of labor, and the commodification of human beings— follow so effortlessly precisely because the communities that perpetuate them are incapable or unwilling to suspect reason and science.

Postmodern suspicion also extends into political realities like nations, freedom, secular space, and even binary understandings of sex. From a postmodern perspective, the problem is not that we have, until very recently, divided the species into male and female, but that this division is assumed to be universal, in the sense of being affirmed at all times and places, and thus impervious to a *petit écrit* that would witness

---

7. For a helpful problematizing, or *deconstruction* of science, see Peter Harrison, *The Territories of Science and Religion* (Chicago: University of Chicago Press, 2015).

to a particular community or a group within a community that understand themselves to be outside this norm. At this point one can add to the postmodern cocktail an analysis of power. The political ramification of grand stories means that one should also ask a question about who benefits from the way these grand narratives tell their stories. Friedrich Nietzsche already articulated this when he deconstructed the Bible through a hermeneutic of suspicion.[8] In *The Antichrist*, Nietzsche deconstructs the prophetic Hebraic calls for justice and especially Paul's emphasis on the meaning of the resurrection as nothing more than a priestly ruse for power. Michel Foucault (1926–84) extended this analysis in his histories of different institutions,[9] and postmodern historians of gender and race in his wake encouraged their readers to reassess their approach to history. Doing so results in asking how the writing of history could both whitewash atrocities committed by current power groups, and also normalize the circumstance that, for almost all of modern Western history, power has been vested in white men. Postmodern suspicion encourages greater attention to power and a re-telling of history to incorporate hitherto unheard voices.

At the heart of postmodernism lies a theory of truth that destabilizes modern assumptions. Although much of modern philosophy has been categorized as a "turn to the subject," those most closely associated with this movement, the German Idealists, did so with an aim toward vouchsafing, not abandoning, a grasp of objective reality.[10] Postmodernism questioned objectivity more radically, first through Martin Heidegger's account of pre-understanding (*Vorverständnis*) and then through a host of theorists, most significantly Jacques Derrida. In modernity, truth became inseparable from objectivity.[11] Post-

8. See Friedrich Nietzsche, *The Antichrist*, trans. Anthony Ludovici (Amherst, MA: Prometheus Books, 2000), #s 31, 37, 40, 42, and 45.

9. For Foucault's most direct and sustained engagement with Nietzsche, see his essay, "Nietzsche, Genealogy, History," which is the introductory chapter for *The Archaeology of Knowledge* and is also printed in *The Foucault Reader*, ed. Paul Rabinow (New York: Pantheon, 1984), 76–100.

10. For this point, see Frederick Beiser, *German Idealism: The Struggle against Subjectivism, 1781–1801* (Cambridge, MA: Harvard University Press, 2002).

11. James Smith describes this modern idea of truth as follows: "Something is true only insofar as it is objective—insofar as it can be universally known by all people, at all times, in all places" (Smith, *Who's Afraid of Postmodernism*, 48).

modernism challenges this position by recalling that everyone makes judgments about the truth of things from somewhere, and also from some time. We necessarily see things from a certain perspective, which does not deny, but instead relativizes our judgments. On this basis, critics accuse postmodernists of relativism, a critique not without substance. Most of us, even those who fashion themselves postmodern, do not look out the window and say that the tall green thing with leaves is only a tree from a certain perspective. We think what we perceive as a tree is more than just a social or linguistic convention. The attempt to preserve objectivity becomes more fraught, and the postmodern argument more persuasive when the subject turns to the interpretation of texts, which we do not read from nowhere. We read the latest Zadie Smith story in the *New Yorker*, consciously or not, in light of the last one. We encounter the opinion of one news source through the lens of another we deem more reliable. To watch an old video of a celebrity subsequently cancelled for egregious transgressions is to watch it differently than before. Two people can examine the same grainy video; one viewer sees the police brutality she has recently read about, while the other assumes the exculpatory evidence has been left out of the frame. Postmodernism claims something more and different from mere perspectivalism by accounting not just for space, but also for time. We are, in the spirit of Heidegger's famous book, *beings in time*, and the act of interpretation passes through all facets of human activity. French theorists like Derrida and Girard have taken this postmodern position to biblical texts and offered radical and unsettling accounts of its implications.

Does a denial of objectivity imply a denial of truth? For postmodernism, one can still believe in truth and reality while denying that truth must conform to the modern standards of objectivity and universality. Even the claim, *everything is relative* (or Derrida's variant— *there's nothing outside of the text*), encompasses a kind of absolutism that a consistent and rigorous postmodernity would have to reject. If postmodernism does not result in the oxymoronic absolute relativism, it at least requires pluralism, in the sense of recognizing the contingency of one's own interpretation by merely acknowledging it as interpretation. Put another way, let a thousand *petits récits* bloom.

POSTMODERN THEOLOGY AS LIBERATIONIST
AND COUNTER-TRADITIONALIST

Part of postmodernism's "bad reputation" within theological and Christian circles has to do with the way that these postmodernists position themselves toward modernity. Some theologians bound themselves to modern presuppositions and others proceeded as if postmodern theory did not even exist. If modernity and Christianity could co-exist, why overturn modernity? Those representing this position were inclined to regard postmodernism's anti-modernity as anti-Christianity. Other theologians deemed postmodernism too bound up with modernity, despite its protests, and therefore at odds with the gospel.[12] In his review of the field, Graham Ward writes:

> Postmodernism popularly invokes fears of relativism, nihilism, and linguistic idealism. Liberal postmodern a/theologies do nothing to counter this popular conception. In fact, they have helped create it with their own emphases upon the death of God, an ontology of violence, and the untameable [sic] flux of existence.[13]

Ward expresses frustration with the *a/theology* associated with people like Mark C. Taylor and John Caputo, and attributes the negative reaction to postmodern theory by believing Christians to the conclusions drawn by Taylor, Caputo, and their ilk.[14] A generation earlier, the leading radical theologian of the 1960s, Thomas Altizer, claimed that God was dead. For Ward, these theologies, ranging from the 1960s to the

---

12. James Smith traces much of these arguments in *Who's Afraid of Postmodernism?* Smith, here and elsewhere, concerns himself with the debate as it has been understood in American Evangelical theology. Regarding postmodern apologetics, see James Smith, "Who's Afraid of Postmodernism? A Response to the 'Biola School,'" in *Christianity and the Postmodern Turn: Six Views*, ed. Myron Penner (Grand Rapids, MI: Brazos, 2005), 215–28. For the most piercing theological critique of postmodernism as still too modern, see David Hart, *The Beauty of the Infinite*, 43–125.

13. Graham Ward, "Postmodern Theology," in *The Modern Theologians*, 322–38, at 335.

14. See Ward's subsection, "Liberal Postmodern Theologies," in his article on postmodern theology in *The Modern Theologians*, 325–29. For Taylor, see especially Mark Taylor, *Erring: A Postmodern A/theology* and *Altarity* (Chicago: University of Chicago Press, 1984, 1987).

present, warranted dismissive attitudes toward postmodern theory. This section limns this movement by nodding toward the influence of existentialist and process thought on their ideas.

The aim in reviewing this mode of discourse is to identify its consequences for relating faith and reason. Ward summarizes: "The death of God is the death of a transcendental signifier stabilizing identity and truth. It is the death of identity, *telos*, and therefore meaning in anything but a local and pragmatic sense."[15] This theology unhooks the idea of God from order, thus rejecting John the Evangelist's claim in his prologue: "In the beginning was the *logos* [. . .] and the *logos* was God" (John 1:1). By rejecting the transcendent signifier, postmodernism eliminated any path for relating faith and reason because reason itself was to be jettisoned for its universalizing tendencies. These tendencies were to be subordinated to the level of the local and particular.

Within this framework, any attempt to synthesize faith and reason could be branded as "logocentric." What can be preserved in Christianity are interruptive elements like grace, or revelation understood as gift and received more experientially, antecedent to efforts that would contain these interruptive realities by systematizing them. Faith, as a kind of existential exercise of blind trust in the sense articulated by Luther and Kierkegaard, avoids being subject to deconstruction, provided one does not reduce faith to a list of items to be believed, or a kind of preliminary step to be completed by reason. Remarking on grace, Derrida noted:

> If it's given, let's say, to someone in a way that is absolutely improbable, that is, exceeding any proof, in a unique experience, then deconstruction has no lever on this. [. . .] But once this grace [. . .] is embodied in a discourse [. . .] in a religion, in a theology—that is why the word "theological" is a real problem to me—then deconstruction, a deconstruction, may have something to say.[16]

15. Ward, "Postmodern Theology," in *The Modern Theologians*, 326.
16. See the interview in *Derrida and Religion, Other Testaments*, eds. Yvonne Sherwood and Kevin Hart (New York: Routledge, 2005), 39. I was led to this citation via an abbreviated version of it in Walter Lowe, "Postmodern Theology" in *The Oxford Handbook of Systematic Theology*, 607–33.

Deconstruction, or postmodern theory more broadly, need not require a plunge into irrationalism or fideism, although its application by what Graham Ward calls "liberal" postmodern theologians forecloses any recognizable quest for synthesizing faith and reason.[17]

This brings us to the adjectives used in this subsection: *liberationist* and *counter-traditionalist*. *Counter* signifies a concern that things have been going in the wrong direction, and that they need to run counter to how they have been going. The liberationist discourse, meanwhile, begins by asserting what is hardly postmodern; it claims that the God of the Bible and of Jesus Christ is a God who sets people free. It understands the Exodus narrative as a story onto which other stories of liberation can be grafted. Liberationists also seek to raise Christian consciousness so that believing communities prioritize the social and economic liberation of oppressed peoples in our world today.[18] Liberation theology understood so broadly is bound neither to modern nor to postmodern modes of enquiry; it can find precursors wherever they are, whether it be Gregory of Nyssa, who called for the manumission of all slaves in his homilies from the 380s,[19] or Bartolomé de las Casas (1474-1566), the Spanish Dominican, who protested the mistreatment of native peoples and championed their full humanity.[20]

In the 1960s, the movement out of Central and South America that came to be known as liberation theology began to integrate Marxist social and economic theory into Christian liberationism. This social

17. Ward's overview of the field favors "conservative" postmodern theology. Noteworthy is his reason for so doing: "These [liberal] theologians, in fact, are continuing the crisis of theology characteristic of 'modernism,' where it was believed that a clean break from theology's past was possible and necessary for a new liberation and new humanism" (Ward, "Postmodern Theology," in *The Modern Theologians*, 328).

18. Dwight N. Hopkins summarizes this position in his overview of black liberation theology: "The Exodus of slaves from bondage to freedom obviously becomes an overarching hermeneutical reference frame" (Dwight N. Hopkins, "Black Theology of Liberation," in *The Modern Theologians*, 451-68).

19. See "Fourth Homily," in *Gregory of Nyssa, Homilies on Ecclesiastes*, ed. Stuart George Hall (Berlin: Walter de Gruyter, 1993), 72-84. For an instance of retrieval, see J. Kameron Carter, *Race: A Theological Account* (Oxford: Oxford University Press, 2008), 229-51.

20. For an example of his retrieval, see Gustavo Gutierrez, *Las Casas: In Search of the Poor of Jesus Christ* (Maryknoll, NY: Orbis, 1993).

theory was dissatisfied with a longstanding tendency in moral theology to analyze human problems through the lens of personal sin. The poverty that conditioned so many lives in South and Central America compelled liberation theologians to apply the teachings of Marx theologically. Sin, they argued, manifests itself not just on an individual level, but also penetrates the social, political, and economic realms. The gospel calls Christians to personal piety, but also and perhaps more importantly, to eliminate unjust social structures. Faithfully hearing this call will generate movements to help lift people out of poverty and decrease the exploitation of children. To the extent that mainstream Christianity fails to emphasize the social element of human sin, it fails to hear and live the gospel faithfully. Marx's analysis, and more broadly, the insights generated by the social sciences, illuminates how the systemic causes and cycles of poverty are sinful. When mainstream theology fixes the cause of evil in individual sin, it fails to address the full scope of the problem because it ignores social sin as cause, or at least factor, in individual sin. From a liberationist perspective, individualist modes of theological explanation unwittingly or not, perpetuate evil.

This Marxist critical theory, when appended to feminist and liberationist theology, asks probing questions that can even be turned upon each of the preceding chapters in this book. The historical trajectory offered up to this point has focused almost exclusively on males, most of whom have been European. This approach, regardless of intent, wilts under the gaze of a liberationist hermeneutic that interrogates a narrative of the "mainstream" tradition for stifling the perpetually muffled voices of women and non-European men. Motive matters little because the effect is the same—norming a tradition that perpetuates exclusion. Bryan Massingale crystallizes this critique when he writes, "What makes [the US Catholic Church] 'white' and 'racist' is the pervasive belief that European aesthetics, music, theology, and persons—and only these—are standard, normative, universal, and truly 'Catholic.'"[21] Such a stance combines the ethical imperative of liberationist theology with postmodern hermeneutical suspicion, expounded by not just Marx, but Nietzsche and Freud as well.

---

21. Bryan Massingale, *Racial Justice and the Catholic Church* (Maryknoll, NY: Orbis Books, 2010), 80.

Especially in the current century, scholars have been willing to think, along with Massingale, about how far down this problem goes, as the focus of liberation has shifted from economic to racial and sexual categories.[22] The question emerges: How fundamental are the sinful structures that perpetuate poverty, racism, sexism, and ableism to traditional theological discourse? Two scholars, Margaret Pfeil and Michael Jaycox, speak of epistemological advantages and deficiencies based on one's relationship to "'white' hegemony." Pfeil worries that white scholars may be "epistemologically compromised." For Pfeil this means that an a priori deficiency among white thinkers infects whatever theology follows. Jaycox comes to a similar conclusion: "Catholic ethicists of color [. . .] write with comparatively greater moral epistemological acuity than whites about race and racism."[23] These interrogations raise the question: If the problems go that far down, then is it worth asking how far back they go as well?

The mode of criticism exhibited by Massingale, Pfeil, and Jaycox seems to necessitate a wholesale dismissal of almost any canonical account of Christianity. This implication in itself is nothing new, as at no point in Christian history did all theologians agree about what counted as tradition. Early groups fought over what belonged in the biblical canon, as both sides, the "gnostic" and the "Catholic," knew that the triumphant party would determine what counted as normative. Similarly, as chronicled in chapter 4, Protestant reformers chose to "cancel" the scholastic corpus, partially or *in toto*, as inauthentic developments of Christian tradition. One could imagine a history of Christian theology as a history of what each era and generation has forgotten, for even retrieval movements can abandon as much as

---

22. Rachel Muers, for instance, frames her overview of feminism and theology within the larger project of liberation. See Muers, "Feminism, Gender, and Theology," in *The Modern Theologians*, 431–50, at 432).

23. Both citations are found in Michael Jaycox, "Black Lives Matter and Catholic Whiteness: A Tale of Two Performances," *Horizons* 44 (2017): 306–41, at 332. Jaycox explains the epistemologically compromised status of whites later in the article: "The ethical claim of the intrinsic value of black life simply cannot be reliably known and understood as a natural law claim by white scholars operating in a purely conceptual mode, in consideration of the formative influence of whiteness upon their patterns of thought." Further, white ethicists should "acknowledge the epistemic privilege of black natural law" (Jaycox, "Black Lives Matter and Catholic Whiteness," 337).

they retrieve. Still, the question must be raised: If certain groups can, on the basis of class, ethnicity, or gender, be dismissed as epistemologically insufficient, then must one not say the same of traditions, especially those that tilt heavily toward a certain gender, class, or ethnicity? Scholasticism, for instance, was hatched in an institutional structure that forbade women to teach or study. This feature seems to have sexism baked into it. It would follow that its teachings, not just about gender, but about anything else, would be epistemologically deficient and its conclusions irredeemably flawed. And the same unassailable conclusions would apply to almost all periods of Christian theology.[24]

It is worth considering how this approach reorders the project of reconciling faith and reason. Just as postmodernism asserted that there was something rotten at the very core of modernity, so liberationist postmodernism, at least in certain iterations, argued that Christian theology, as it had been normatively practiced, is at its root problematic. Rachel Muers expresses this point in her overview of feminist theology: "The new event of the twentieth century was the explicit recognition, in the context of the feminist movement, of the ways in which earlier theology had tended systematically to silence women and to lend ideological support to their oppression."[25]

One of the most radical attempts to rethink theology from the perspective of feminist liberationism came from Mary Daly (1928–2010). This work began with *Beyond God the Father* (1973) and continued through her subsequent publications.[26] Daly's liberationist approach attempts to emancipate theology from a Christian tradition rotten at its foundation. This rot is not just institutional, but also extends to theological discourse that identifies God with maleness. By so identifying God, theological discourse has not only limited our speech and imagination about God, but also informs the structure of

24. This logic, against which Charles Camosy registered a strong objection, resulted in a heated debate within the guild of Christian ethicists. See Charles Camosy, "The Crisis of Catholic Moral Theology," *Church Life Journal*, November 15, 2018, https://churchlife-journal.nd.edu/articles/the-crisis-of-catholic-moral-theology/.

25. Muers, "Feminism, Gender, and Theology," 431.

26. Mary Daly, *Beyond God the Father: Toward a Philosophy of Women's Liberation* (Boston: Beacon, 1973).

our speech.[27] The problem, for Daly, is that our language rests upon the same phallocentric logic that makes God male.[28] She explains how a liberationist method addresses this problem:

> The method of liberation, then, involves a *castrating* of language and images that reflect and perpetuate the structures of a sexist world. It castrates precisely in the sense of cutting away the phallocentric value system imposed by patriarchy. [. . .] As aliens in a man's world who are now rising up to name—that is, to create— our own world, women are beginning to recognize that the value system that has been thrust upon us by the various cultural institutions of patriarchy has amounted to a kind of gang rape of minds as well as of bodies.[29]

Although Daly's work represents an extreme, it logically presses the premises of postmodern liberationism to its extreme. Even if Daly's position can still allow a cautious retrieval of tradition, it remains the case that any kind of project that reconciles faith and reason will do so in ways virtually unrecognizable to what has preceded it.[30]

One can trace a similar project within the discourse connecting theology and race. One year before Daly's *Beyond God the Father*, William R. Jones published the provocatively titled, *Is God a White Racist?*[31] A Unitarian Universalist, Jones questioned whether the first wave of black liberation theology, led by James Cone, was sufficiently radical. Cone, not Jones, is considered the ground-breaking pioneer in the field of black theology, but in Jones one sees how certain critical and postmodern lines of enquiry interrogate the deepest interiority of human consciousness. This interrogation results in conclusions, at

27. See the sections on method in Daly, *Beyond God the Father*, 7–12. For a recent appraisal of Daly's contribution to feminist theology, see Jessica Coblenz and Brianne Jacobs, "Mary Daly's The Church and the Second Sex after Fifty Years of U.S. Catholic Feminist Theology," *Theological Studies* 79, no. 3 (2018): 543–65.

28. Daly's position lies at the edge of feminist liberationist theology, but she is hardly alone there. For other examples, see Muers, "Feminism, Gender, and Theology, 436–37.

29. Daly, *Beyond God the Father*, 9.

30. Daly, *Beyond God the Father*, 19.

31. William R. Jones, *Is God a White Racist? A Preamble to Black Theology* (Garden City, NY: Doubleday, 1973).

least in Jones's mind, that undermine attempts to retrieve almost any part of the received tradition.[32]

Alongside Jones one can compare the project of Charles Long, which Dwight Hopkins describes as "deconstructive-reconstructive."[33] Hopkins writes that Long, "feels that both Christianity and theology are imperialistic discourses that embody, in a highly overdetermined manner, hegemonic linguistic power. In other words, one who adopts their language usage and language categories has already acquiesced in a process whose very nature is to oppress people of color or Third World people."[34] This critique logically extends to other oppressive discourses, whether they be sexist, ablest, cis-gendered, or heteronormative. The imperative to retrieve a purer, less oppressive form of religion within Christianity, as opposed, say, to recollecting indigenous African religious practices, loses its urgency once one accepts Long's

---

32. In addition to Jones, one can mention Cecil Cone, Gayraud Wilmore, and Charles Long, all of whom (among them James Cone's own brother!) deemed James Cone too tethered to traditional Christianity. For this point, see Hopkins, "Black Theology of Liberation," 456–57. It should be noted that although Jones and others find James Cone insufficiently radical, Cone's own theology, while remaining focused on the Christian narrative, exhibits an alarming distrust of Christian tradition in his most important book, *God of the Oppressed* (Maryknoll, New York: Orbis Books, [1975] 1997). Like Jaycox, Cone questions the epistemological capacity of whites. On Marx, Cone demurs, "Any analysis that fails to deal with racism, that demon embedded in white folks' being, is inadequate" (Cone, *God of the Oppressed*, 143). He later states, "While recognizing the possibility of overlap in human experience, I contend that black people's experience of liberation as hope for a new heaven and a new earth represents a new mode of perception, different from the experience of white people" (Cone, *God of the Oppressed*, 146). Whites, even those eager to help in the cause, "must be *made* to realize that they are like babies who have barely learned how to walk and talk. Thus they must be told when to speak and what to say" (Cone, *God of the Oppressed*, 222). The theological tradition, when applied to questions like reconciliation, has almost nothing to contribute. As Cone explains, "These theologians cannot tell us what reconciliation means in black-white relations, because their consciousness is defined by the political structures responsible for our humiliation and oppression" (Cone, *God of the Oppressed*, 224). The concern with the particular evil of "white racism" leads Cone not just to focus on how whites have oppressed non-whites, but to refuse to speak of violence perpetuated against other white groups like Jews. The Holocaust, unsurprisingly, receives no mention in Cone's list of egregious historical deeds (Cone, *God of the Oppressed*, 216). It is hard to imagine how the future of this mode of postmodern liberationism will be interested in, let alone capable of defending, any usage of the theological canon.

33. For an extended but not always helpful meditation on Long's project, see Carter, *Race: A Theological Account*, 195–227.

34. Hopkins, "Black Theology of Liberation," 456–57. See Charles Long, *Significations: Signs, Symbols, and Images in the Interpretation of Religion* (Minneapolis: Fortress, 1986).

basic premise. To phrase the crisis as a question: Why not throw out the white baby Jesus with the Christian bathwater?

It needs to be noted, at this point, that most liberationist projects aspire toward some kind of retrieval attained through method, whether it be a feminist or race-critical hermeneutic, in the case of biblical studies, or by choosing to recover forgotten voices from the past in historical theology. Here it helps to distinguish between "tradition" and "traditioning," that is, between the canon of texts and practices that provide a norming function, and the act of reading those texts and interpreting those practices. If one takes this distinction into account, then feminist and liberationist hermeneutic practices and acts of retrieval are involved in their own project of faith seeking moral legitimacy, rather than faith seeking understanding. The postmodern liberationist project prioritizes a faith that can be justified to the extent that it generates solidarity with oppressed groups. This project lies at, or close to, the center of the Christian message, but postmodern liberationist approaches tend to begin by delegitimizing modes of theology *not* engaged in the same process.

This section ends by taking up the work of one of the leading black theologians in the United States, J. Kameron Carter. Carter's 2008 book *Race: A Theological Account* straddles the line between postmodern liberation and retrieval. Carter offers careful readings of such patristic figures as Gregory of Nyssa, Maximus the Confessor, and Irenaeus of Lyons, but, in his own words, "by having [them] speak in relationship to the conditions of a dark reality, by having them speak in relationship to the 'Holy Saturday' conditions of dark flesh in modernity."[35] Carter connects theological anti-Judaism to modern, Western imperialism that made abominations like slave trade possible. "Modernity's racial imagination," for Carter, "has its genesis in the theological problem of Christianity's quest to sever itself from its Jewish roots."[36] Carter's genealogy relies heavily on Foucault's own archeology,[37] and although he centers his critique on stalwarts of modern, Enlightenment thinking like Kant, there is a creeping concern, man-

---

35. Carter, *Race: A Theological Account*, 378.
36. Carter, *Race: A Theological Account*, 4.
37. Carter, *Race: A Theological Account*, 44–77.

ifested in lengthy footnotes, that mainstream, historical Christianity is deeply tainted.[38] This point bubbles to the surface in Carter's reading of canonical figures and their interpreters. For instance, after deploying Aquinas's metaphysical arguments, Carter explains his strategic appropriation of St. Thomas in a footnote:

> For I am acutely aware that any reading of Thomas Aquinas must be done in relationship to the history of Thomism, especially in relationship to the colonialist and racial side of this history. [. . .] The modern vision of the human being as a bearer of race or as marked with racial identity was made possible by fifteenth-century and six-teenth-century Portuguese and Spanish Thomist–Aristotelian intellectuals. Which is to say, modern colonialism and the world born of it arose within a Thomistic discursive space.[39]

Carter's argument cites no text from Aquinas or from his Portuguese or Spanish interpreters. If one accepts Carter's suspicion toward such a broad and capacious intellectual tradition as Thomism, then one can almost effortlessly apply it to other, older traditions, like the Greek patristic theology of Nyssa and Maximus that Carter engages.

Carter's tone seems to shift mid-work, as if suddenly realizing the possibility just mentioned. Of John Milbank, one of his teachers, Carter writes,

> It is a significant shortcoming of Milbank's work that he [. . . does not have] a narrative of his own formation as a British theologian, who is heir to colonialist uses of both theological orthodoxy and liberalism, nor, finally a theological accounting of nineteenth-century and twentieth-century British imperialism as a religious, political, and cultural process (these are gaps that must be filled).[40]

---

38. One finds a similar project underway in one of the more influential books by a North American theologian in the twenty-first century. I refer to Willie James Jennings, *The Christian Imagination: Theology and the Origins of Race* (New Haven, CT: Yale University Press, 2010). Jennings's project interweaves with Carter's and is more rhetorically persuasive but far less philosophically sophisticated.

39. Carter, *Race: A Theological Account*, 431n100.

40. Carter, *Race: A Theological Account*, 388n5. Carter makes a similar but more laconic claim about David Bentley Hart, whose failure to address the question of race "is a profound lacuna in his otherwise important meditation on Gregory [of Nyssa]" (Carter, *Race: A Theological Account*, 435n38). One finds a parallel interrogation of Stanley

Even if Carter is correct, questions remain: Can any element of Christianity's tradition be preserved? Is the faith of most adherents, as expounded by its highest lights, beyond redemption? These questions are notable only because Carter's work itself practices a deep *ressourcement*, but it does so in tension with the postmodern liberationist scythe with which he threshes, sometimes fairly, sometimes not, Western, European theology.

It remains an open question how deep the liberationist critique cuts into Christian theological traditions. Carter's work highlights the tension in using critical theory to uproot traditions that perpetuate the oppression of dark bodies while attempting to find less tainted episodes of Christian discourse. Postmodern liberationism destabilizes the norms and methods that purport objectivity on one hand, while justifying oppression, or silence in the face of oppression, on the other. This discourse increasingly sees the Christian faith, as it has been articulated and practiced throughout most of its recorded history, as likewise perpetuating injustice. Only a faith aligned with the marginal will be worthy of aligning with reason. This faith was in large part the faith of the earliest Christians. Will the long process of showing the rationality of faith start from the beginning, or will it be possible to take what is best from a twenty-century-long tradition of enquiry? As postmodern liberationism continues to gain ascendency, it will need to answer this question.

POSTMODERN RETRIEVAL AND TRADITIONALISM
Alasdair MacIntyre

Alasdair MacIntyre (1929–) has done more than anyone to shape the field of Christian ethics over the past fifty years. MacIntyre has written philosophy since the 1950s, but he did not become *MacIntyre* until the publication of *After Virtue* in 1981, around which time he also became Catholic on the basis of a deep engagement with Thomism.

Hauerwas in a recent article by Kristopher Norris: "Witnessing Whiteness in the Ethics of Hauerwas," *Journal of Religious Ethics* 47, no. 1 (2019): 95–124. Norris argues that Hauerwas's failure to talk more frequently about issues of race casts a pall over his entire theological project.

Later in the decade he wrote two additional books—*Three Rival Versions of Moral Enquiry* and *Whose Justice? Which Rationality?*—which, together with *After Virtue*, form a kind of trilogy that capture MacIntyre's project.[41] His most influential work articulates a robust postmodern understanding of truth, which he uses to provide a tradition-based, narrative account of Christianity.

To understand MacIntyre's postmodern traditionalism it will be helpful to begin with his critique of liberalism. Though it may seem that MacIntyre's critique overlaps with the "postliberal theology" of the Yale School—the work of George Lindbeck and Hans Frei, but carried on in the more recent work of Kathryn Tanner, David Kelsey, and Serene Jones[42]—MacIntyre's project differs substantially. Postliberal theology is best thought of as an extension of Barthianism, and its critique of liberalism is not nearly as radical and as foundational as MacIntyre's.[43] According to MacIntyre, liberalism constitutes "a repudiation of tradition in the name of abstract, universal principles of reason."[44] This kind of thinking is also called modern, and in *After Virtue* MacIntyre associates modern thought with the "Enlightenment project."[45] In both *After Virtue* and *Whose Justice? Which Rationality?*, MacIntyre takes the irresoluble nature of disagreements as an existential challenge, for it constitutes the most serious reason to reject liberalism. By liberalism, MacIntyre means a mode of thinking that aspired to find new paths forward, especially in politics, by shedding old dogmas and traditions. MacIntyre rejects liberalism's premises: "It is an illusion to suppose that there is some neutral standing ground, some locus for rationality as such, which can afford rational resources sufficient for enquiry

---

41. For the purposes of this project, I engage with only two of these: Alasdair MacIntyre, *After Virtue: A Study in Moral Theory* (Notre Dame, IN: University of Notre Dame Press, 1981); and *Whose Justice? Which Rationality?* (Notre Dame, IN: University of Notre Dame Press, 1988).

42. For an overview, see James Fodor, "Postliberal Theology," in *The Modern Theologians*, 229–48.

43. Or for that matter John Milbank's, who seems to have the Yale School in mind when he asks, "Has there really been in this century, at least within Protestantism, *any* post-liberal theology?" (Milbank, "Knowledge," in *Radical Orthodoxy*, 22).

44. MacIntyre, *Whose Justice? Which Rationality?*, 349. Unless otherwise noted, subsequent citations refer to this book.

45. See chapters 4 and 5 in *After Virtue*, 36–61.

independent of all traditions. [. . .] The person outside all traditions lacks sufficient rational resources for enquiry and *a fortiori* for enquiry into what tradition is to be rationally preferred."[46] The optimal cosmopolitan liberal does not reason better on the basis of her rootlessness. MacIntyre's critique is indistinguishable from the standard postmodern critique of modern claims to neutrality and objectivity. MacIntyre (and really all of the thinkers in this subsection) echoes the postmodern critique but rejects its conclusions, which unintentionally mirror to the modernity and liberalism it purports to reject.

The liberal position suspects all traditions of bias and dogmatism, and by contrast understands itself to be free of bias. The postmodern position says that nobody can be free of a perspective, or a subjective stance, and thus considers objectivity just another ruse by those seeking power. MacIntyre affirms this critique by demonstrating how liberalism is a tradition, just like other traditions, even though it claims not to be one: "Liberal theory is best understood, not at all as an attempt to find a rationality independent of tradition, but as itself the articulation of an historically developed and developing set of social institutions and forms of activity, that is, as the voice of a tradition."[47] Like other traditions, liberalism has its own canon of texts, history of disputes, and levels of hierarchy. It is both unable to deliver a universally agreed upon set of rules for reasoning, and untrue to its own description of what it means to be liberal.

If liberalism cannot stand above particular communities, including theological communities, in order to rule definitively on the norms that govern our common life, then postmodern relativism and perspectivalism would seem to prevail. According to the postmodern account, all truth claims are relative to the person or the community making them, and therefore each community or individual sees from its own particular perspective. According to this perspective, X might be licit or good, whereas from another perspective X is not licit or good. At this decisive point, MacIntyre argues that critiques of modern liberalism need not doom themselves to hopeless perspectivalism or relativism. He rejects these conclusions because they share the same

46. MacIntyre, *Whose Justice? Which Rationality?*, 367.
47. MacIntyre, *Whose Justice? Which Rationality?*, 345.

modern, liberal assumptions about rationality and truth: "The pro-
tagonists of post-Enlightenment relativism and perspectivalism claim
that if the Enlightenment conceptions of truth and rationality cannot
be sustained, theirs is the only possible alternative."[48] MacIntyre
instead reconsiders the rationality with which traditions operate, and
enlists Newman to his cause.[49]

Traditions for MacIntyre are not intellectually static, dormant discourses closed to rational critique. They move through stages of development, starting from acceptance of authorities, through an identification of shortcomings, and then concluding with a reformulation or
clarification made in light of this challenge. This progression does not
operate in a manner similar to a natural law of growth; it only happens
through a free, mental operation.[50] Although this form of reasoning
does not rise to the standards of the Cartesian method, or Hegelian dialectical logic, MacIntyre still defends the rational nature of these developments within tradition. The principles developed by that tradition to
determine what is true, or good, or reasonable, are not the "self-justify-
ing epistemological first principles"[51] exalted by modernity, but instead
contingent, particular first principles that a tradition discovers to have
enabled it to preserve and develop its founding truths.

As traditions develop, they almost inevitably undergo what Mac-
Intyre calls an "epistemological crisis."[52] One can recall the fourth-century theological crisis in which Christians had to wrestle with questions
about Jesus's status as divine and human. The formulations that had
been handed down through religious revelation required greater theoretical clarification in the face of disagreements between what became
known as the Arian and Nicene factions. The application of Greek
philosophical traditions, which had long been brought together with
Christian religious revelation, helped Christians reach a temporary solu-

---

48. MacIntyre, *Whose Justice? Which Rationality?*, 353.

49. In a book without footnotes or a bibliography, one should take MacIntyre at his
word when he writes of his "massive debt" toward Newman regarding the rationality of a
tradition (MacIntyre, *Whose Justice? Which Rationality?*, 354). MacIntyre has in mind Newman's essay on doctrinal development and his patrology, specifically the study of the Arian
controversy.

50. MacIntyre, *Whose Justice? Which Rationality?*, 355.

51. MacIntyre, *Whose Justice? Which Rationality?*, 360.

52. MacIntyre, *Whose Justice? Which Rationality?*, 361–69.

tion. By contrast, late medieval physics could not respond to the questions raised by the "new" science of Galileo and Newton, and found, on the basis of its own tradition of reasoning, its account of physics wanting. Thus, traditions can reason through their localized, traditional accounts of reality and also jettison these accounts in favor of something it deems more reasonable. But in neither case do inhabitants of a tradition, or those who inhabit multiple traditions, reason from "some neutral standing ground, some locus for rationality as such."[53] Nor do traditions find themselves unable to undergo a process of translation.

One can without much difficulty imagine how faith relates to reason in MacIntyre's account. Reason, for MacIntyre, needs to be shrunk to its proper size. At the same time, his postmodern traditionalism explains what earlier accounts of faith and reason could not: how Christianity came to seem so unpersuasive to a new generation of secular unbelievers. For MacIntyre, traditions are like languages, which take time and immersion to understand. One cannot put on another tradition like an outfit at a mall, studying Buddhism for a month, and then Islam, and then Christianity in a comparative religions course. Like an anthropologist, an outsider to a tradition must embed herself in the native culture or belief system if she wants to understand it; it needs to be grasped from within. Liberalism gestures toward an open-mindedness, but it tends to devise structures and processes that make real debate and encounter impossible.

Traditional Christianity, on MacIntyre's account, can be far more liberal (in the sense of open-minded) than Enlightenment liberalism. It can do so by being honest about how its rationality is rooted in the particulars of its own history and narrative. As a tradition, Christianity possesses the capacity to exhibit profound rationality while appearing unable to do so in the eyes of today's cultured skeptics. One can accept postmodern discourse, in the sense of recognizing the Enlightenment's failure "to provide neutral, impersonal tradition-independent standards of rational judgment"[54] without extending that position into a fideism. MacIntyre himself concludes that Thomism, which fuses both the Augustinian and the Aristotelian traditions, presents a

53. MacIntyre, *Whose Justice? Which Rationality?*, 367.
54. MacIntyre, *Whose Justice? Which Rationality?*, 395.

robust account of rationality that preserves the good and the true. Yet MacIntyre knows that Aquinas cannot answer questions that he never asked, and one should not expect him to do so. Nevertheless, these questions press urgently upon the modern believer. MacIntyre's post-modern traditionalism makes possible a synthesis between faith and reason, but it will be another, doubtless very different, synthesis.[55]

Radical Orthodoxy

After chapters on Derrida, Lyotard, and Foucault, James Smith's *Who's Afraid of Postmodernism?* concludes by presenting Radical Orthodoxy as a full-fledged, postmodern, "orthodox" Christian appropriation of postmodernism.[56] Radical Orthodoxy has been artfully described as: "That stridently anti-modern, post-postmodern, high-church school of Cambridge Platonists and speculative Augustinians that has sprung up in the intellectual vicinity of John Milbank and that boasts Cathe-rine Pickstock as one of its guiding spirits."[57] The springboard for the movement was the publication of *Theology and Social Theory* by John Milbank in 1990.[58] This book has exercised perhaps more influence than any other work of Christian theology over the past forty years. On the basis of her groundbreaking work of liturgical theology, in addition to the books she has co-authored and co-edited with Mil-bank, Catherine Pickstock must be considered the second-most important expositor of Radical Orthodoxy.[59] It offers a different kind

55. The final phrase intentionally parrots MacIntyre's infamous conclusion to *After Virtue* (MacIntyre, *After Virtue*, 263).

56. Smith, *Who's Afraid of Postmodernism?*, 109–46.

57. David Bentley Hart, "Review Essay of *After Writing*," *Pro Ecclesia* 9, no. 3 (2000): 367–72, at 367. The *Oxford Dictionary of the Christian Church* describes the Cambridge Platonists, a group of seventeenth-century University of Cambridge divines, as asserting a "mystical view of reason," derived from Neoplatonism, with some inflection from Des-cartes, which involved an "indwelling of God in the mind" ("Cambridge Platonists" in *The Oxford Dictionary of the Christian Church*, eds. F. L. Cross and Elizabeth A. Livingstone [Oxford: Oxford University Press, 2005], 225).

58. John Milbank, *Theology and Social Theory: Beyond Secular Reason* (Oxford: Blackwell, 1990).

59. Catherine Pickstock, *After Writing: On the Liturgical Consummation of Philosophy* (Oxford: Blackwell, 1998); see also Catherine Pickstock and John Milbank, *Truth in Aqui-nas* (London: Routledge, 2001), and *Radical Orthodoxy: A New Theology*, eds. John Mil-bank, Catherine Pickstock, and Graham Ward (London: Routledge, 1998).

of postmodern retrieval than MacIntyre's, with significant consequences for relating faith to reason.

One way to tell the history of theology's relating faith to reason is
by recounting its relationship to other sciences, whether they be philosophy, natural sciences, social sciences, or comparatively new
sciences (philology, archeology, and paleography, for instance). Radical Orthodoxy reminds theology that it has played too nicely with
certain disciplines. *Theology and Social Theory* argues that social
sciences, especially sociology and political science, do not operate
neutrally and independently of theology, but instead import their own,
para-theological presuppositions. Modern secularism talks about a
neutral, public space free of any religious or sacred meaning, like a
mall or a marketplace. This is a ruse, however, as Milbank reminds
readers: "Once there was no secular," for "the secular as a domain had
to be instituted or *imagined*, both in theory and in practice."[60] The purported neutrality of secular space had to be created. This artificial creation extends to fields of knowledge, where disciplines feign neutrality
or presuppose neutrality of the fields upon which they depend. These
secular discourses depend upon theological presuppositions or foundations concealed from both the practitioner and the reader of the
social sciences. This situation presents a crisis for Christianity, especially given how complicit most theology has been by capitulating to
the modern order. Milbank explains:

> The pathos of modern theology is its false humility. [. . .] Once the-
> ology surrenders its claims to be a metadiscourse, it cannot any
> longer articulate the word of the creator God, but is bound to turn
> into the oracular voice of some finite idol, such as historical schol-
> arship, humanist psychology, or transcendental philosophy. If the-
> ology no longer seeks to position, qualify or criticize other dis-
> courses, then it is inevitable that these discourses will position
> theology.[61]

Milbank's faith seeks understanding by showing how modern rationality, if left unchecked, will devour theology's claims to knowledge.

60. Milbank, *Theology and Social Theory*, 9.
61. Milbank, *Theology and Social Theory*, 1.

Milbank issues perhaps the strongest call from within academic theology for the discipline to close ranks. It seems as though Milbank echoes the Barthian position, but Milbank and Radical Orthodoxy make it clear that they are moving beyond Barth's neo-orthodoxy to a more radical orthodoxy. They write:

> Barthianism tended to assume a positive autonomy for theology, which rendered philosophical concerns a matter of indifference. Yet this itself was to remain captive to a modern—even liberal—duality of reason and revelation, and ran the risk of allowing worldly knowledge an unquestioned validity within its own sphere.[62]

Milbank rejects the Barthian presupposition that philosophy and theology belong to their own autonomous spheres. Milbank offers in its place a more Platonic understanding of knowledge. In recounting neo-orthodoxy's prioritization of revelation, Milbank notes: "And yet what often remains unclear [in neo-orthodoxy] is the degree to which these theological categories are permitted to disturb a philosophical account of what it is to be, to know and to act, without reference to God."[63] It is not enough for theology to leave philosophy to itself, or to declare that philosophy's natural knowledge is not salvific. The traditional sub-branches of philosophy—ontology and epistemology—must be re-conquered by theology: "The danger here is, as is well exemplified in Barth, that if we fail to redefine being and knowledge theologically, theological difference, the radical otherness of God, will never be *expressible* in any way without idolatrously reducing it to our finite human categories."[64] Milbank's broadside against social science extends to philosophy, whose autonomy theology should not accept. Milbank's argument results in a sweeping criticism of a modernity whose defining features were the creation of a secular space that sought to dislodge academic disciplines from their Christian, theological roots.

Radical Orthodoxy applies postmodern tropes and methods to reimagine Christian theology's place in post-secular discourse. Like

---

62. Milbank, Ward, and Pickstock, "Introduction, Suspending the material: the turn to radical orthodoxy," in *Radical Orthodoxy*, 1–20, at 2.

63. Milbank, "Knowledge," in *Radical Orthodoxy*, 21.

64. Milbank, "Knowledge," in *Radical Orthodoxy*, 22.

MacIntyre, it critiques the leading postmodernists for being too wedded to modernity.[65] For Radical Orthodoxy, if postmodernism accurately undercuts Enlightenment claims to objective methods and universal truths, then theology must reconsider the way it gives reasons for what it believes. For Milbank, this reconsideration takes on a narrative reformulation: "Theology purports [sic] to give an ultimate narrative, to provide some ultimate depth of description, because the situation of oneself within such a continuing narrative is what it means to belong to the Church, to be a Christian. However, the claim is made by faith, not a reason which seeks foundations."[66] Theology need not retreat from the academic or scholarly realm if it insists that the modern, Enlightenment account tells a particular story. Rather than accept modernity's story, Christianity must redouble efforts to tell its own story, which is also the better story.

In an older taxonomy, one might say that Radical Orthodoxy elevates rhetoric over logic. Its exponents might not disagree. Our concern is whether it allows faith to relate to reason, or whether Christian faith is at best to be stood alongside another form of secular faith, in which case the apologetic task seems marginal, rather than central. It may be helpful to home in on Milbank's understanding of narrative: "'Narrating,' therefore turns out to be a more basic category than either explanation or understanding [. . . it is not] concerned with universal laws, nor universal truths of the spirit."[67] Narrative allows for a non-identical repetition, and in Milbank's vision, the Church is doing just this when it retells the story of Christ and God's self-giving love, both in the biblical account and, in later Christian history, through the lives of the saints.[68] Narrative is prior and not

---

65. See, for instance, Pickstock's critique of Heidegger and Derrida in *After Writing*, esp. 101–18, and Milbank's chapter, "Ontological Violence or the Postmodern Problematic," in *Theology and Social Theory*, 278–325. See also the first nine aphorisms in John Milbank, "'Postmodern Critical Augustinianism': A Short *Summa* in Forty-Two Responses to Unasked Questions," *Modern Theology* 7, no. 3 (1991): 225–37. Smith's *Who's Afraid of Postmodernism?* does not sufficiently distinguish Radical Orthodoxy's postmodernism from Lyotard, Derrida, and Foucault's.

66. Milbank, *Theology and Social Theory*, 249.

67. Milbank, *Theology and Social Theory*, 267.

68. Milbank, *Theology and Social Theory*, 387: "Hence the metanarrative is *not* just the story of Jesus, it is the continuing story of the Church, already realized in a finally

subsequent to dogma and understanding. Not just Enlightenment modernity, but even the natural sciences tell stories. Or as Derrida would say, nothing is outside the text. One sees this at the origins of modern science: "The 'new science' was therefore, from the outset, preoccupied with narratives of the transformation of nature."[69] In good postmodern fashion, Milbank uses narrative theory to put all discourses—whether they are social scientific, philosophical, or natural scientific—on the same narrative plane. He does so in the process of explaining why MacIntyre did not go far enough in his account of rival traditions: "MacIntyre, of course, wants to *argue* against this stoic-liberal-nihilist tendency, which is 'secular reason.' But *my* case is rather that it is only a *mythos*, and therefore cannot be refuted, but only out-narrated, if we can *persuade* people [. . .] that Christianity offers a much better story."[70]

Radical Orthodoxy's model for this narrative approach is Augustine's *City of God*, which, among other things, retells the history of Rome from the Christian perspective. Though Augustine uses all the tools of philosophy and dialectic to expose problems with pagan virtues, above all he tells a story of two cities, ordered by two different loves. For Milbank, Augustine prioritizes peace over agonistic strife. As he is quick to clarify: "This principle is firmly anchored in a narrative, a practice, and a dogmatic faith, not in universal reason."[71] The greatest challenge to Augustine's vision is not modern science, or secular theory, but Nietzsche, who tells a different story that makes violence prior to peace; Milbank explains: "*The Genealogy of Morals* is a kind of *Civitas Dei* written back to front."[72] Christianity tells a story

---

exemplary way by Christ, yet still to be realized universally, in harmony with Christ, and yet *differently*, by all generations of Christians."

69. Milbank, *Theology and Social Theory*, 269.

70. Milbank, *Theology and Social Theory*, 330. One finds the same kind of claim in David Bentley Hart, whose intellectual trajectory was shaped by Radical Orthodoxy. See in particular Hart, *Beauty of the Infinite*, esp. 148.

71. Milbank, *Theology and Social Theory*, 390. Elsewhere Milbank highlights Christianity as practice prior to any theory or dogma. See Milbank, "'Postmodern Critical Augustinianism,'" at 226: "Postmodern theology can only proceed by explicating Christian practice. The Christian God can no longer be thought of as a God first seen, but rather as a God first prayed to."

72. Milbank, *Theology and Social Theory*, 389; also, 288.

in which God ushers forth only harmonic peace, from creation to eschaton. All violence is subsequent, from creation to eschaton, unnecessary, privative, and ultimately incoherent without the pacific goodness from which it deviates.

After reducing all competing claims made by philosophy and all secular discourses to the level of rhetoric, Radical Orthodoxy attempts to show the rationality of faith. As already noted, Radical Orthodoxy from the outset fashioned itself as a kind of Augustinianism. In addition, it employs a participatory theory of understanding reminiscent of Platonism.[73] In a surprising twist, Pickstock and Milbank rally Aquinas to their cause.[74] Against typical readings of Aquinas they argue that "reason and faith in Aquinas represent only different degrees of intensity of participation in the divine light of illumination and different measures of absolute vision."[75] To know anything means to know it insofar as it participates in God, since all known reality is created, and therefore exists in a ratio to the creator. This epistemology has profound consequences for any purportedly non-theological modes of knowing: "Were one to attempt to comprehend a finite reality not as created, that is to say, not in relation to God, then no truth for Aquinas could ensue, since finite realities are of themselves nothing and only what is can be true."[76] Their synthesis of faith and reason does not require explaining how the natural meets the supernatural, since faith and reason merely embody two different intensities or grades of participation in what is ultimately the same kind of activity. They write, "the 'light of faith' is for Aquinas simply a strengthening of the *intellectus* by a further degree of participation in the divine light."[77] Aquinas, for Radical Orthodoxy, continues the

73. Pickstock, Milbank, Ward, "Introduction," at 3: "The central theological framework of radical orthodoxy is 'participation' as developed by Plato and reworked by Christianity."

74. See Pickstock and Milbank, *Truth in Aquinas*.

75. Pickstock and Milbank, *Truth in Aquinas*, xiii.

76. Pickstock and Milbank, *Truth in Aquinas*, 20.

77. Pickstock and Milbank, *Truth in Aquinas*, 20. Later in the same subsection they describe their relationship as "successive phases of a single extension" (Pickstock and Milbank, *Truth in Aquinas*, 21), and they subsequently use the same language of successive phases to talk about the relationship between *sacra doctrina* and metaphysical or philosophical theology (Pickstock and Milbank, *Truth in Aquinas*, 31).

neo-Platonic tradition of Augustine that laid out a participatory theory of knowledge.[78]

Radical Orthodoxy imagines a near total identification of faith and reason. Despite its emphasis on practice, it does not simply reissue Pascal's preference for the God of Abraham, Isaac, and Jacob. It instead declares that theology requires no help from other sciences while calling into question whatever conclusions such sciences could reach. Radical Orthodoxy rejects these conclusions through enlisting (not always faithfully) great figures in the tradition.[79] Like MacIntyre, their work has substantially altered the conversation in theology, and Pickstock and Milbank represent perhaps the most sophisticated approximation to and gesture toward fideism (even if their Platonism buffers them from full-fledged fideism) in contemporary academic theology.

French Postmodern Phenomenology: Jean-Luc Marion

Over the past forty years there has emerged a stream of French Catholic philosophers engaged in theology. These philosophers have steadily propelled philosophical and theological conversation. Structural factors help to explain the fecundity of French philosophy: Due to the particular historical circumstances of French *laïcité* that became enshrined in the 1905 separation of church and state, French theology takes place in seminaries among a mostly clerical caste, while lay theology takes place under the cloak of philosophy or history. Just as many Christian analytic philosophers in the United States have prior theological interests, so too many Catholic French intellectuals do theology by another name. This awkward relationship in France has proven fruitful, with such figures as Rémi Brague, Emmanuel Falque,

78. On Aquinas's Platonism, see the many articles of Wayne Hankey, in particular "Aquinas, Plato, and Neoplatonism," in *The Oxford Handbook of Aquinas*, eds. Eleonore Stump and Brian Davies (Oxford: Oxford University Press, 2012), 55–64.

79. Their readings of Aquinas and Scotus have come under particular scrutiny. For essays on these figures and a critical assessment of radical orthodoxy, see *Deconstructing Radical Orthodoxy: Postmodern Theology, Rhetoric and Truth*, eds. Wayne Hankey and Douglas Hedley (New York: Ashgate, 2005). One contributor complains of Pickstock and Milbank's "blatant misreading of Aquinas that ignores the ordinary canons of scholarly enquiry" (*Deconstructing Radical Orthodoxy*, 49).

Michel Henry, and Jean-Luc Marion generating rich conversations and inventing new ways to make faith credible against the backdrop of a postmodern phenomenological horizon. This overview focuses on Marion, who has cast the longest shadow over theology.

Marion's first book appeared in 1977, but he gained acclaim in the Anglophone world through his 1982 text, translated into English in 1991, *God without Being*, which not only challenged Heidegger's critique of onto-theology, but also gave phenomenological readings of icons, the Eucharist, and the importance of the bishop for the practice of theology.[80] In the thirty years since *God Without Being*, over twenty of his books have been translated into English. Marion's recognition has also generated critiques. These have come from different directions, some complaining that his philosophy is really theology in disguise, and others that his theology is too philosophical.[81] The aim here is to investigate how Marion applies postmodern phenomenology to theology in ways that allow for new insights into the relationship between faith and reason.[82]

One element of the postmodern program is anti-foundationalism. The metaphor of a foundation—a solid something upon which one stands, judges, and sees—collapses under the critique of objective universalism. One person's foundation is another's quicksand. The ambition of metaphysics, understood as a foundational, architectonic discipline that would ground subsequent investigations, came under anti-foundational scrutiny, especially from Martin Heidegger. Traditionally understood as the investigation into being *qua* being, meta-

---

80. Jean-Luc Marion, *God Without Being*, trans. Thomas A. Carlson (Chicago: University of Chicago Press, 1991).

81. For a summary of these critiques, see Christina Gschwandtner, "A New 'Apologia': The Relationship between Theology and Philosophy in the Work of Jean-Luc Marion," *Heythrop Journal* 46 (2005): 299–313, at 300. One can also note the fierce reactions to *God Without Being* from Thomists, who took great issue with how Marion treated Aquinas. Marion references these critiques in the "Preface to the English Edition," at xxii. The corresponding footnote lists the major French critiques.

82. For his own thoughts on the relationship, see the essays collected in Jean-Luc Marion, *Believing in Order to See: On the Rationality of Revelation and the Irrationality of Some Believers*, trans. Christina Gschwandtner (New York: Fordham University Press, 2017). His student, Emmanuel Falque, has provided a more focused treatment of the subject in *Crossing the Rubicon: The Borderlands of Philosophy and Theology*, trans. Reuben Shank (New York: Fordham University Press, 2016).

physics deals not only with questions of the soul and the universe, but of ontology. And theology has, in this telling, ridden the tails of metaphysics by understanding God as the "being of being," or the "ground of being." As Robyn Horner summarizes, "It is Heidegger who relentlessly uncovers the fragility and inadequacy of a metaphysical thinking of being as substance, as cause, and as presence. It is he who protests the thinking of God as highest being—most substantial, *causa sui*, most present, ultimate ground."[83] Although many theologians associate Descartes with modern thought and the beginnings of subjectivism, Heidegger regards him as a quintessentially foundationalist thinker in the sense of wanting to establish his investigations on a set of principles that lead to a forgetfulness of being. Descartes did so by equating being with presence or substance, and by imagining God as a kind of producer of being, within the constraints of a metaphysics of presence. By unsettling this foundationalism and the role of God in it, Heidegger was criticizing both modern philosophy and the theological tradition that had accepted a modern metaphysics derived from Descartes, Christian Wolff, and Francisco Suarez.

Marion accepts much of what Heidegger says concerning metaphysics.[84] The intricacies of this critique of onto-theology need not detain us. Marion finds wanting the traditional proofs for God's existence because they yield only the God of the philosophers or, even worse, an idolatrous misunderstanding of God, not the God of religious experience.[85] In his gloss on Heidegger's critique, Marion concludes: "To reach a nonidolatrous thought of God [...] one would have to manage to think God outside the metaphysics insofar as metaphysics infallibly heads, by way of blasphemy (proof) to the twilight of the idols (con-

83. Robyn Horner, *Jean-Luc Marion: A Theo-logical Introduction* (New York: Routledge, 2016), 36.

84. Of the post-metaphysical Heideggerians under which she groups Marion, Judith Wolfe writes that they see "in Heideggerian philosophy the potential—stunted by Heidegger's own rejection of a transcendental horizon—for responding to the call of the divine without turning God into an idol by metaphysical speculation" (Judith Wolfe, *Heidegger and Theology* [London: Bloomsbury: 2014], 169, 193–94).

85. For this point, see Marion, *God without Being*, 29–37. The classical theism of Augustine and Aquinas identifies the God of the philosophers with the God of the Bible. For this argument, see Eleonore Stump's fine essay, *The God of the Bible and the God of the Philosophers* (Milwaukee: Marquette University Press, 2016), esp. 11–40.

ceptual atheism)."[86] Marion wants to think of God free of ontology: "To think God without any conditions, not even that of Being, hence to think God without pretending to inscribe him or to describe him as a being."[87] Marion's avoidance of onto-theology may appease Heideggerians but seems to lead to a dangerous place for a theological tradition based on texts that identify God with being (Ex 3:14—"I am who I am").

Marion's postmodernism, however, does not fall into an extreme apophaticism or a-theism that closes itself off from speaking of God. Instead, Marion liberates philosophy so that it can talk about God in two distinct ways: first, by applying phenomenological method to abiding questions about God and the human quest for meaning, and second, by retrieving aspects and figures of the Christian tradition that make it possible to locate Marion much closer to the liberationist camp than could be done with either Radical Orthodoxy or MacIntyre.

Marion thinks of God without being by elevating the scriptural correlation of God with love, and contemplating the gifted quality of this love.[88] As Marion states, a bit cryptically, "God gives Himself to be known insofar as He gives Himself—according to the horizon of the gift itself."[89] He avoids the accusation of falling into onto-theology not only by refusing to equate God with being, but by making love and goodness prior to being. In perhaps his most controversial turn, Marion criticizes Aquinas for departing from Pseudo-Dionysius, author of *On the Divine Names*, and insisting that being is one of the names of God,[90] a move that earned him the ire of many interlocu-

---

86. Marion, *God without Being*, 37.
87. Marion, *God without Being*, 45.
88. See Marion, *God without Being*, 47, 73–83.
89. Marion, *God without Being*, xxiv. One also finds this metaphysic of gift articulated with remarkable precision in David Bentley Hart, *The Experience of God: Being, Consciousness, Bliss* (New Haven, CT: Yale University Press, 2014), at 150–51. In debating the world's contingency, Hart implores that these questions "should end more or less where they begin: in that moment of wonder, of sheer existential surprise." He calls for "a simple return to that original apprehension of the gratuity of all things," adding that by doing so, the mind "opens up upon the limitless beauty of being, which is to say, upon the beauty of being seen as a gift that comes from beyond all possible beings."
90. Marion, *God without Being*, esp. 73–75. Marion later develops this genealogy to highlight William of Saint-Thierry's prioritization of charity, resulting in a kind of fusion of love with knowledge. See Jean-Luc Marion, *Givenness and Revelation*, trans. Stephen E. Lewis (Oxford: Oxford University Press, 2016), 36–45.

tors, especially Thomists.[91] In doing so, Marion retrieves a line in the tradition, traceable from the New Testament texts, that runs through Pseudo-Dionysius and Bonaventure, in which goodness or love precede being. Channeling these two theologians, Marion writes, "Being [. . .] is only uncovered in being dispensed by a gift; the gift, which Being itself thus requires, is accomplished only in allowing the disclosure in it of the gesture of a giving as much imprescriptible as indescribable, which receives the name, in praise, of goodness."[92] Marion aims to do more than simply prefer one name for God over another; he wants to think and reason about God in a way that affirms God's attribute as "creator of all things visible and invisible." Marion fears a metaphysical attempt to domesticate this God, writing: "One still must show concretely how the God who gives himself as *agape* thus marks his divergence from Being, hence first from the interplay of beings as such."[93]

Marion blends this retrieval with a bold and fearless phenomenological interrogation that addresses not just religious experience, but also supernatural realities like incarnation, transubstantiation, and resurrection.[94] These discussions prompt the question whether Marion has made phenomenology into a new version of natural theology.[95] Marion theorizes about how faith should relate to reason, or, in a different register, how theology should relate to philosophy,[96] but he also performs this relationship by giving phenomenological interpretations of Scripture and offering theories of revelation. This work aims to

91. Marion recounts these critiques in the preface to the English edition of *God without Being* (see esp. xxii–xxiv). Here Marion writes, "Saint Thomas certainly marks a rupture: contrary to most of his predecessors, as well as to several of his successors, he substitutes *esse* for the good as the first divine name" (xxiii). For a sample of critical reviews, see 199–200n5.

92. Marion, *God without Being*, 75.

93. Marion begins doing this in the chapter 3 of *God without Being*, and later offers an extended phenomenological meditation on gift in *Étant Donne. Essai d'une phénoménologie de la donation* (Paris: Presses Universitaires de France, 1997).

94. For an application of Marion's idea of saturated phenomenon, see Brian D. Robinette, *Grammars of Resurrection: A Christian Theology of Presence and Absence* (New York: Crossroad, 2009), 67–115.

95. Matthew Farley notes this claim in, "Introduction," to Falque, *Crossing the Rubicon*, 1–13, at 3.

96. See especially Marion, *Believing in Order to See*, 3–44.

make faith more credible to philosophers and to help theology avoid the pitfalls of bad faith, in the sense of a faith sealed off from reason and thus closed to the fullness of divine revelation.[97] His "postmodern" approach calls for a humbler apologetics that prioritizes, with a heavy phenomenological gloss, love over intellect.[98]

One can fill in Marion's conceptual model by revisiting an instance of Marion performing the relation between faith and reason. In an essay on the Incarnation, Marion meditates on its precise meaning: "The incomprehensible infinite has therefore taken flesh in our reason."[99] Marion's meditation on this encounter recalls Blondelian and Balthasarian notes. He questions whether this event could lead to a rupture or breakdown of rationality, but ultimately denies it. For the incarnate "has laid claim to a name—namely that of the *logos*." Paradoxically, "reason [Christ the *logos*] has taken flesh in our reason." Like Pascal, Marion concludes that reason pushed to the edge comes to recognize its own insufficiency, foretold by the event of the Incarnation: "Our *logos*, including its formal logic, its mathematical computations, its quantifications and models, its hypotheses and even its ideological deliriums, remains haunted by the infinite *logos* within it." Perhaps more than any contemporary figure, Marion feels liberated, on the basis of certain postmodern philosophical breakthroughs, to stake out new terms for negotiating the relation between faith and reason. By doing so he comes closest to realizing, at least within a postmodern horizon, a new kind of synthesis, one upon which a number of phenomenologically minded theologians have built and continue to build.

97. Marion writes, "The most threatening irrationalism comes not from belief but from the failure of belief and confidence—in short, from the lack of faith in rationality itself." And later, "In my own regard, I have experienced that the opposite of faith is not so much doubt, disbelief, or unbelief, but bad faith. [. . .] The opposite of rationality is found neither in irrationality nor in belief but in ideology" (Marion, *Believing in Order to See*, xii).

98. For this point, see Gschwandtner, "A New 'Apologia,'" 308–11.

99. This citation and those below are found in Marion, *Believing in Order to See*, 37.

MAGISTERIAL INTERVENTIONS

John Paul II's *Fides et Ratio*

John Paul II (fl. 1978–2005) and Benedict XVI (fl. 2005–13) decisively shaped the modern understanding of the papacy.[100] Unlike many popes who emerged through the Vatican bureaucracy and Italian ecclesiastical politics, John Paul and Benedict came to occupy the seat of Peter as outsiders: They were non-Italian intellectuals more suited to the professorial life than pastoral responsibilities. Indeed, John Paul was the first non-Italian pope in 455 years! Among their contributions as popes, their discourses on the relationship between faith and reason occupy particular importance. Building on their academic backgrounds—they were fast-rising university professors before being appointed bishops— John Paul and Benedict added significant magisterial heft to the discussion of how to relate faith and reason. John Paul did so in the form of a long encyclical, *Fides et Ratio*, which he promulgated in 1998. Benedict gave a controversial, albeit much shorter speech, colloquially known as the Regensburg Address, at his former university, in 2006. On the basis of their authority, their interventions spurred and encouraged further reflection on the relationship between faith and reason.[101] The aim here is to put these reflections into conversation with what has preceded as a coda on both this chapter and the book as a whole.

Born in Poland in 1920, Karol Wojtyla, the future Pope John Paul II, felt the full force of both Nazism and Soviet Communism during his formative years. After clandestinely entering the seminary in Poland during World War II and subsequently studying in Rome, Wojtyla briefly occupied a teaching position in Lublin before becoming coadjutor bishop of Krakow in 1958. Five years later he became archbishop, as his intellectual and poetic inclinations gave Soviet officials the mistaken impression that he would avoid political maneuvering. John Paul, however, exalted the Western ideals of rights and freedom, especially given their Christian origins, and he came to ver-

---

100. For sake of brevity, I will refer to them henceforth as John Paul and Benedict.

101. Many journal issues, panels, symposia, and edited volumes resulted. One particularly noteworthy volume in response to *Fides et Ratio* is *Reason and the Reasons of Faith*, eds. Paul J. Griffiths and Reinhard Hütter (New York: T & T Clark, 2005).

balize these ideals in a religious, moral appeal against the Soviet dom-
ination of Poland. His efforts to assist the collapse of the Iron Curtain,
which accelerated after he became pope in 1978, finally succeeded in
1989. These biographical details help explain *Fides et Ratio*'s strong
reaction against postmodernism, which will be treated below.

Fides et Ratio is the most sustained magisterial treatment of the
question about how to relate faith and reason. In what follows, certain
key points of the text are revisited with an aim toward showing John
Paul's importance to the discussion before turning to Benedict's
shorter but equally impactful lecture at Regensburg. *Fides et Ratio* is
best understood against the backdrop of not only the Second Vatican
Council, but also the earlier discussions of faith and reason in *Dei
Filius* and *Aeterni Patris*. John Paul updates these texts by taking into
account the new circumstances facing the Catholic faithful at the end
of the second millennium, including not only a crisis of faith, but more
urgently, a crisis of reason. In what follows, four major points will be
made, both summative and evaluative: first, John Paul's reminder of
the Church's continued commitment to synthesizing faith and reason.
Second, although *Fides et Ratio* recommends a version of Thomist
revival stripped of the hostility toward modern thought forms, it still
tells a story of modern decline. Third, *Fides et Ratio* exalts certain
modern figures and by doing so gives the faithful more recent models
to imitate in the task of relating faith and reason. Fourth, the encyclical's openness to elements of modernity is paired with a negative
assessment of postmodernism. These judgments might lead readers
to foreclose the opportunity to engage and build on the postmodern
insights, a practice exemplified in the authors treated in the previous
section, which has proven so fecund in the past several decades.

On the dedication page of *Fides et Ratio*, John Paul provides an
arresting metaphor for the relation between faith and reason. He
writes, "Faith and reason are like two wings on which the human spirit
rises to the contemplation of truth; and God has placed in the human
heart a desire to know the truth."[102] John Paul's point of departure

---

102. Here and below I cite from the following: John Paul II, Encyclical Letter *Fides
et Ratio*, Vatican translation (Boston: Pauline Books & Media, 1998). Subsequent citations
come from this translation, and will be cited by paragraph number.

echoes the opening of Aristotle's *Metaphysics*: all human beings desire
to know. This truth is revealed naturally to us, and does not require
any specific Christian perspective, a point brought home by John
Paul's reference to the oracle at Delphi, which recalls the most fundamental human questions. These questions have been posed by great
religious and speculative thinkers and texts, both Eastern and Western. Just as ancient philosophy chronicled the move from myth and
conventional wisdom to dialectic and theoretical understanding, so
too did Christianity transcend religious mythology to encounter God
as *logos*, or a principle that gives intelligibility to things. For Christians,
the desire to know is not just kindled by this *logos*, but more specifically by the *logos* made flesh, whom we encounter in the person of
Christ. John Paul describes both orders of knowledge—the natural
and the supernatural—as belonging to "a body of knowledge which
may be judged a kind of spiritual heritage of humanity."[103] This hard-
fought knowledge possesses a universal quality and represents a real
achievement to be passed on to later generations. The supernatural
truths are preserved in Christian doctrines, while the natural truths,
though not possessing the quality of divine revelation, still deserve to
be regarded as more than just human convention. These truths are
part of humanity's shared knowledge, and bear the stamp of universal
veracity. John Paul writes, "Once reason successfully intuits and formulates the first universal principles of being and correctly draws from
them conclusions which are coherent both logically and ethically, then
it may be called right reason."[104] This body of knowledge and the habit
of thinking that produces it can also aid Christians toward a deeper
understanding of doctrines and articles of faith.

Writing to an educated audience assailed by movements opposed
to faith, John Paul calls for a renewal to understand the faith: "The
Church reaffirms the need to reflect upon the truth. This is why I have
decided to address you, my venerable brother bishops [. . .] as also
theologians and philosophers whose duty is to explore the different
aspects of truth."[105] The need for this reaffirmation extends to the

103. John Paul II, *Fides et Ratio*, 4.
104. John Paul II, *Fides et Ratio*, 4.
105. John Paul II, *Fides et Ratio*, 6.

seminaries, where the study of philosophy waned following the Second Vatican Council.[106] Although faith and reason, or theology and philosophy, express different notes and use different methods in the search for meaning, they are united in seeking "the ultimate purpose of personal existence."[107] The Bible reflects this conviction about the unity of the two different orders of knowing. Any conflict between the two is illusory and without basis, for "each contains the other, and each has its own scope for action."[108] Both faith and reason need to reach their highest heights to arrive at this truth. In a time when both philosophers and theologians have lost faith in the power of reason to attain the highest truths, *Fides et Ratio* reminds readers that the Catholic Church affirms not only reason's latent capacity, but also the compatibility of these truths with the results of religious illumination.

In calling for a return to the great medieval synthesis, Leo XIII's *Aeterni Patris* embraced a narrative of steep decline. *Fides et Ratio* follows in the tradition of *Aeterni Patris* but presents a kinder, gentler version of Thomistic renewal by softening *Aeterni Patris*'s critique of modern philosophy and theology. *Fides et Ratio* reminds readers that Aquinas's desire for synthesis explains how he embodied doctrinal fidelity while learning from his dialogue "with the Arab and Jewish thought of his time."[109] Desire for truth also breeds an openness to the hitherto unfamiliar. In retrieving Aquinas, therefore, the magisterium is not foreclosing alternative approaches to understanding Christianity or reconciling it with reason. Aquinas does not simply represent a deposit of answers, but an approach to questions. John Paul explains:

> The magisterium's intention has always been to show how St. Thomas is an authentic model for all who seek the truth. In his thinking, the demands of reason and the power of faith found the most elevated synthesis ever attained by human thought, for he could defend the radical newness introduced by revelation without ever demeaning the venture proper to reason.[110]

---

106. John Paul II, *Fides et Ratio*, 61.
107. John Paul II, *Fides et Ratio*, 15.
108. John Paul II, *Fides et Ratio*, 17.
109. John Paul II, *Fides et Ratio*, 43.
110. John Paul II, *Fides et Ratio*, 78.

John Paul's appeal to Aquinas does not signal retreat, but rather the best kind of renewal.

In John Paul's retelling of the decline that followed the medieval synthesis of secular learning with Christian faith he focuses on how the two orders—supernatural and natural, faith and reason, the theological and the philosophical—came to be seen as irreconcilable. The distinctions between these two orders—arising out of the scholastic attempt, including Aquinas's own work, to relate nature and grace—led to a perceived separation. John Paul writes, "From the late medieval period onward, however, the legitimate distinction between the two forms of learning became more and more of a fateful separation. [...] Eventually there emerged a philosophy which was separate from and absolutely independent of the contents of faith."[111] In the wake of this separation, attempts to relate faith and reason reached a stalemate, harmful to both philosophy and theology, "because each without the other is impoverished and enfeebled."[112]

After recalling this separation, John Paul also reminds readers of a number of more recent figures who have not simply pointed to the problem, but who also posed a solution. He remarks: "Even in the philosophical thinking of those who helped drive faith and reason further apart there are found at times precious and seminal insights which, if pursued and developed with mind and heart rightly tuned, can lead to the discovery of truth's way."[113] In contrast to *Aeterni Patris*, *Fides et Ratio* insists that not merely the patristic and medieval periods fruitfully modeled faith seeking understanding; the modern period also produced laudable examples. One can seek a deeper understanding of faith without simply repeating what Aquinas said about the matter. Examples include, "in a Western context, figures such as John Henry Newman, Antonio Rosmini, Jacques Maritain, Etienne Gilson and Edith Stein and, in an Eastern context, eminent scholars such as Vladimir Soloviev, Pavel Florensky, Petr Chaadaev, and Vladimir Lossky."[114] These figures,

---

111. John Paul II, *Fides et Ratio*, 45.
112. John Paul II, *Fides et Ratio*, 48.
113. John Paul II, *Fides et Ratio*, 48.
114. John Paul II, *Fides et Ratio*, 74. Wayne Hankey suggests that the encyclical "may perhaps be an act of reparation in so far as it recommends thinkers condemned or

"offer[s] significant examples of a process of philosophical enquiry which was enriched by engaging the data of faith."[115] By listing so many Eastern Orthodox thinkers, John Paul acknowledges that the Roman Catholic Church does not have a monopoly on these efforts. Likewise, the subsequent reference to Kierkegaard in the context of intellectual humility provides one of the first instances of a Catholic papal document positively referencing a Protestant thinker.[116]

Though not among those explicitly named, Maurice Blondel's thoughts seem to find an echo throughout *Fides et Ratio*.[117] As highlighted in chapter 7, Blondel proposed a method of immanence in order to account for the human subject's inner dynamism, which resulted in the assertion that humanity naturally strives for a knowledge and completion that could only be found in God's freely bestowed and supernaturally endowed gift. *Fides et Ratio* remarks how "philosophy is able to recognize the human being's ceaselessly self-transcendent orientation toward the truth."[118] Stronger Blondelian notes resound when John Paul recounts various non-Thomistic approaches that proved fruitful. One of these approaches "produced a philosophy which, starting with an analysis of immanence, opened the way to the transcendent."[119] Here John Paul does everything but name Blondel. This line, and the style employed by the encyclical more

---

dismissed in the nineteenth-century turn to Neo-Thomism." In particular, the Congregation of the Holy Office placed two books by Rosmini (1797–1855) on the Index, near the end of his life, and then subjected his philosophy to posthumous scrutiny in *Post obitum*, which listed Rosmini's errors (Denzinger, 3201–41). The Hankey citation is found in Nichols, *From Hermes to Benedict XVI*, 214. As head of the Congregation for the Doctrine of the Faith, Joseph Ratzinger, the future Pope Benedict XVI, declared that the concerns expressed in *Post obitum* had been superseded, and no longer apply (see Congregation for the Doctrine of the Faith, "Note on the Force of the Doctrinal Decrees Concerning the Thought and Work of Fr. Antonio Rosmini Serbati," https://www.vatican.va/roman_curia/congregations/cfaith/documents/rc_con_cfaith_doc_20010701_rosmini_en.html).

115. John Paul II, *Fides et Ratio*, 74.

116. John Paul II, *Fides et Ratio*, 76.

117. For this argument, see Peter Henrici, "The One Who Went Unnamed: Maurice Blondel in the Encyclical *Fides et Ratio*," *Communio* 26, no. 3 (1999): 609–21. Henrici goes so far as to say that "Blondel's *Action* can serve as a concrete illustration of what *Fides et Ratio* intended" and "*Fides et Ratio* could be read precisely as a magisterial sanctioning of Blondel's concept of philosophy." (Henrici, "The One Who Went Unnamed," 617).

118. John Paul II, *Fides et Ratio*, 23.

119. John Paul II, *Fides et Ratio*, 59.

generally, abandons scholastic vocabulary and replaces it with a notably modern mode of expression.

Despite the many positive gestures, John Paul also imbues the text with a sense of dismay at what has been lost. This begins when the encyclical identifies metaphysics and ontology as the highest philosophical pursuits. Modern philosophy, unfortunately, lacks the mettle to ask these questions: "Abandoning the investigation of being, modern philosophical research has concentrated instead upon human knowing."[120] This detour by way of epistemology or cognitional theory did not ever lead modern philosophy, upon receiving the necessary clarifications provided by these investigations, back to the nature of being. Instead, this detour, according to *Fides at Ratio*, "has given rise to different forms of agnosticism and relativism which have led philosophical research to lose its way in the shifting sands of widespread skepticism. [. . . Philosophers have] tended to pursue issues—existential, hermeneutical or linguistic—which ignore the radical question of the truth about personal existence, about being and about God."[121] By severing connections to its premodern heritage, modern philosophy risks succumbing to a sundry list of errors: eclecticism, historicism, scientism, pragmatism, and nihilism.[122] *Fides et Ratio* calls nihilism "the common framework of many philosophies which have rejected the meaningfulness of being," and "the denial of all foundations and the negation of all objective truth."[123] Although the encyclical does not call for a return to medieval scholasticism, it employs a narrative of decline seen earlier, most notably in the outlook of the sixteenth-century reformers and in the documents that gave rise to neo-scholasticism.

John Paul's willingness to engage certain forms of modern thought, especially the phenomenology of Max Scheler (the subject of his dissertation), does not extend to postmodernism. The biogra-

120. John Paul II, *Fides et Ratio*, 5.
121. John Paul II, *Fides et Ratio*, 5. It must be mentioned here that the most radical philosopher of the twentieth century, Martin Heidegger, explained how an historicist and hermeneutical approach to philosophy would go a long way toward correcting the modern forgetfulness of being plaguing our technological societies.
122. John Paul II, *Fides et Ratio*, 86–90.
123. John Paul II, *Fides et Ratio*, 90.

phical details noted above might go some way toward explaining this disparity. The major writings of the postmodern theologians were not published until after he became Pope John Paul II, and do not appear to have influenced his thinking about the relationship between faith and reason. The universality ascribed to the classic figures and works at the outset of the encyclical remains an abiding feature of John Paul's description of truth: "Every truth—if it really is truth—presents itself as universal, even if it is not the whole truth. If something is true, then it must be true for all people and at all times."[124] He considers this approach to truth almost existentially necessary: "Whether we admit it or not, there comes for everyone the moment when personal existence must be anchored to a truth recognized as final, a truth which confers a certitude no longer open to doubt."[125] The attribute of certitude was not lacking in premodern thinkers, but as historians like Stephen Toulmin have chronicled, it began taking a larger role in the century of Descartes.[126]

Fides et Ratio deems approaches that stress the centrality of interpretation, or emphasize the historically rooted nature of truth and subjectivity, to run the risk of destabilizing the seeker and pushing her toward skepticism and nihilism. Faith and reason work in a kind of tandem, with faith, or revelation, putting a stamp of certainty on what natural reason can know about God: "Revelation renders this unity [of truth] certain, showing that the God of creation is also the God of salvation history. It is the one and the same God who establishes and guarantees the intelligibility and reasonableness of the natural order of things upon which scientists confidently depend."[127] This framing of questions of truth anticipates John Paul's critique of postmodernism. After noting equivocal meanings of postmodern, he writes:

> According to some [postmodern currents of thought], the time of certainties is irrevocably past, and the human being must now learn to live in a horizon of total absence of meaning, where everything

124. John Paul II, *Fides et Ratio*, 27.
125. John Paul II, *Fides et Ratio*, 27.
126. Toulmin, *Cosmopolis: The Hidden Agenda of Modernity*, cited previously in chapter 5.
127. John Paul II, *Fides et Ratio*, 34.

is provisional and ephemeral. In their destructive critique of every certitude, several authors have [. . .] called into question the certitudes of faith.[128]

The encyclical connects the lack of certitude with a crisis of meaning, which is existential. Insofar as it destabilizes certitude, postmodernism leads directly not just to a relativism, but to a nihilism in which all meaning is lost. To answer the question of James Smith's book, it appears that John Paul *is* afraid of postmodernism. Indeed, *Fides et Ratio*'s negative assessment of postmodern thought creates the need for the very thing that the encyclical accomplished in regard to modernity: an act of reparation between the Church and postmodernism.

Benedict XVI's "Regensburg Address"

Although much shorter than *Fides et Ratio*, Benedict's "Regensburg Address" from 2006 proved to be equally generative of discussion. Unfortunately, most remember the talk for its purportedly anti-Muslim comments. A citation lifted out of context led to a wave of uproar and violence. Adding to this tragedy was the misfortune that the mainstream press ignored Benedict's comments and critique of Western secularism. These comments were made as a prelude to his claim that faith and reason require one another, lest both lose their way without the other's assistance.

The central historical reference point of the address is a fourteenth-century dialogue between a learned emperor from the Christian East, Manuel II Palaeologus, and an anonymous Persian follower of Islam.[129] Manuel II at one point declares, "Not to act reasonably, not to act with *logos*, is contrary to the nature of God." For Benedict, the connection between God and *logos* lies at the center of Christianity. This connection functions as a guiding norm, not only for Christianity, but for all of the major religions and cultures. Upholding this norm

---

128. John Paul II, *Fides et Ratio*, 91.

129. The text can be found at https://www.vatican.va/content/benedict-xvi/en/speeches/2006/september/documents/hf_ben-xvi_spe_20060912_university-regensburg.html. Its proper title is "Faith, Reason, and the University." It contains no paragraph numbers, so when citations to the text are given, no footnote will be added.

is the *sine qua non* for any successful dialogue between or across cultures. Benedict chooses this dialogue on account of its setting: the siege of Constantinople, which took place between 1394 and 1403 and symbolizes how the failure to talk across cultures and religions can lead to war. The prevention of war requires more than simple willingness to dialogue; Benedict adds the necessity of de-coupling violence from one's conception of the divinity, which he relays in the words of Manuel II: "Violence is incompatible with the nature of God." To act violently, and to imbed violence within one's religion, is incompatible with worship of the true God. Manuel II states, "God is not pleased by blood, and not acting reasonably is contrary to God's nature." Benedict employs this anecdote to address the central question of his lecture: the compatibility between faith and reason.

Benedict introduces this topic by asking a question: "Is the conviction that acting unreasonably contradicts God's nature merely a Greek idea, or is it always and intrinsically true?" Benedict then offers a meditation on different biblical texts, most especially the prologue to John's Gospel, where the Evangelist identifies the Word, the *logos*, with God's creative act. Benedict had meditated on this prologue throughout his writings, most notably in the set of lectures given in 1967 that became *Introduction to Christianity*.[130] In the "Preface to the New Edition" to this book, he wrote:

> Ever since the Prologue to the Gospel of John, the concept of *logos* has been at the very center of our Christian faith in God. *Logos* signifies reason, meaning, or even "word"—a meaning, therefore, that is Word, that is relationship, that is creative. The God who is *logos* guarantees the intelligibility of the world, the intelligence of our existence, the aptitude of reason to know God.[131]

John's prologue matters so much to Benedict because it offers the best evidence against the thesis of Hellenization associated with Adolf von Harnack. In this theory, the first generations of Christianity were

---

130. Joseph Cardinal Ratzinger, *Introduction to Christianity*, trans. J. R. Foster (San Francisco: Ignatius Press, 2004), esp. chapter III: "The God of Faith and the God of the Philosophers" (Ratzinger, *Introduction to Christianity*, 137–50).
131. Ratzinger, *Introduction to Christianity*, 26.

mostly untainted by Greek thought; only later, in response to battles with the Gnostics, did the early Jewish Christianity of the first disciples amalgamate Greek thought into its grammar and syntax.[132] "Dehellenization" refers to the effort to retrieve a pure, pre-philosophical Christianity stripped of much of its doctrinal accretion, exemplified in terms from the Creed like "consubstantial" and "begotten."

Benedict locates the encounter of Greek philosophy and Hebrew religion centuries before Harnack supposed this to have taken place. For Benedict, it happened during the fourth century B.C., when the Greek empire annexed Israel. Despite the bitterness and resentment resulting from this occupation, "biblical faith, in the Hellenistic period, encountered the best of Greek thought at a deep level, resulting in mutual enrichment." The most brilliant example of this amalgamation is the Septuagint, a Greek version of the Hebrew Bible. This cultural achievement comprises more than a mere translation according to Benedict: "It is an independent textual witness and a distinct and important step in the history of revelation, one which brought about this encounter in a way that was decisive for the birth and spread of Christianity. A profound encounter of faith and reason is taking place here." Already in the fourth and in subsequent centuries, Judaism underwent important evolutions which allowed for texts like the Book of Wisdom and other Greek language texts to be included in later canons. Without these texts, argues Benedict, the Jewish milieu of the first century could not have received Jesus as it did, and certainly could not have produced the religious texts that it produced, most especially the Gospel of John. Harnack, therefore, has it wrong in presupposing a pure, biblical faith that only later amalgamated Greek thought. Already in the first century, many Jews read their "Bible" in Greek translation and understood their religion, as someone like Philo of Alexandria attests, through a "Greek" interpretive matrix.[133] The project of dehellenization is misbegotten from the outset because Hellenization is in the Christian DNA.

---

132. See Adolph [sic] Harnack, *History of Dogma*, trans. Neil Buchanan, vol. 1 (New York: Dover, [1961] 1900).

133. If this is true, it only begs the question of how "pure" any part of Jewish religious life was, for it was always, at least as far back as the texts go, under some influence, be it Roman, Persian, Babylonian, Sumerian, or Phoenician.

Benedict then pivots to offer a genealogy of modern efforts to dehellenize Christianity. The event that anticipates Benedict's "Three Waves of De-Hellenization" is late medieval nominalism, which he associates with Duns Scotus.[134] This voluntarism "led to the claim that we can only know God's *voluntas ordinata.*" Knowledge of the divine will lies beyond our grasp. This will, the will by which God creates and sustains the sun and the moon and all of the stars, is so exalted, "that our reason, our sense of the true and good, are no longer an authentic mirror of God." In contrast to the voluntarist approach, Benedict insists that our reason can know God, even if this knowledge is only analogous, because God manifests Himself as *logos*. Our worship is not sheer mystery; it is, in the words of Saint Paul, *logike latreia*, "reasonable worship" (Rom 12:1). Critical to any synthesis between faith and reason is the idea that God is not shrouded entirely in mystery, but instead is knowable, albeit analogically. Once one abandons the hope of synthesis, one risks making God arbitrary, which can lead to religious violence.

Benedict identifies three markers in the "program of dehellenization" that has "dominated theological discussions since the beginning of the modern age." The first instance arose with the Reformers, who rejected the scholastic system for a theology done *sola scriptura*. It was "dehellenization" in the sense that it sought to purify theology of scholasticism, which had turned Christian faith into a synthesis of Aristotle and the Bible. This first wave extends all the way to Kant, who cordoned off metaphysics from human reason and thus imported the Reformers' program into modern philosophy, albeit "with a radicalism that the Reformers could never have foreseen." As a consequence, confessional theology no longer needed to integrate natural theology into dogmatic texts, and thus freed itself from the kind of concerns that traditionally animated theologians.

Benedict identifies the "second wave" with Harnack, which was foretold in Pascal's distinction between the God of the philosophers

134. Whatever Benedict's reservations about Scotus, they should be read in concert with the appreciation he indicated in his "Apostolic Letter" to a group of scholars commemorating the seventh centenary of Scotus's death, in 2008. The letter can be found at https://www.vatican.va/content/benedict-xvi/en/apost_letters/documents/hf_ben-xvi_apl_20081028_duns-scoto.html.

and the God of biblical experience. Harnack transformed this aphorism into a program of liberal theology: "Harnack's central idea was to return simply to the man Jesus and to his simple message, underneath the accretions of theology and indeed of Hellenization." Harnack's goal of dehellenization did not result in a hyper-Judaized Jesus; Harnack was known for harboring the anti-Jewish sentiments typical of German liberal Protestantism at the turn of the twentieth-century. Instead, Harnack wanted something like Kant's vision of Christianity reduced to the categorical imperative, and stripped of any theological particularism or supernaturality. Benedict writes: "Harnack's goal was to bring Christianity back into harmony with modern reason." The best way to do this was to follow through on Baur's historicism, outlined above in chapter 6, but absent Baur's philosophical underpinnings. By the standards of the nineteenth-century positivism upon which Harnack based his historical method, non-empirical reality remained off limits. Harnack was willing to accept this demarcation, which meant stripping theology of its capacity to treat supernatural realities or doctrines related to the personhood of God or the divinity of Jesus.

Benedict judges Harnack's method to be an unmitigated disaster in the course of lamenting how these scientific standards inevitably limit what reason can know about the highest and most important truths. Many of the social and human sciences, to Benedict's regret, attend only to the undeniable success of modern sciences while ignoring their obvious methodological limitations. They adopt the methods of natural science toward human fields in order to remain within science's good graces. Like Bonaventure, the lead subject of one of his two dissertations, Benedict worries whether the social and human sciences that operate in this manner can behold the human being in her full glory. The human being is more than a composite of natural and social elements. Recalling Bonaventure's *On the Reduction of the Arts to Theology*, no subject can be understood fully without comprehending its relationship to the God that made it. The purported neutrality of sciences depends on a prior metaphysical claim that its objects of study are exhausted by the natural realm. Bonaventure argued the exact opposite of this, and Benedict continues this line of argument, complaining: "For the specifically human questions about our origin and destiny, the questions raised by religion and ethics, then have no place within the purview of collective reason as defined by 'science,' so understood, and must be relegated to the realm of the subjective." He makes the same complaint as John Paul about reducing reason to the instrumental and empirical realm. He finds wanting any account of reason in which it does not flap its wing in concert with faith's.

Benedict's third stage of dehellenization corresponds to the current age. It states "that the synthesis with Hellenism achieved in the early Church was an initial inculturation which ought not to be binding on other cultures." Like Harnack, the third stage wants to strip Christianity of its Greek accretion, but it does so with the aim of inscribing other cultural forms within it. If there can be a Greek version of Christianity, then why not an African, or a Caribbean, or an Asian version? Benedict's defense of Greek Christianity leads to perhaps the most important utterance of any pope about the relationship between faith and reason: "The fundamental decisions made about the relationship between faith and the use of human reason are part of the faith itself; they are developments consonant with the faith itself."[135] Christian faith, in Benedict's account, is not some prior emotional or affective experience restricted to the domain of the will. Since God is *logos*, faith always contains a rational component. Faith's rationality is not limited to the rational intelligibility of its doctrines: Since the biblical God is *logos*, one must, if one believes in the biblical God, understand that belief to be rational. Otherwise, one risks subjecting religion to a pathology that can lead to violence because it is merely a matter of will or emotion.

Despite modernity's pathologies, Benedict's assessment of modernity is not entirely negative. He writes: "The positive aspects of modernity are to be acknowledged unreservedly." These aspects range from the undeniable improvement in standards of living made possible by modern technology, as well as the modern forms of government that preserve minority rights and alleviate material suffering. Once modernity comes to understand not just the benefits of modern science,

---

135. Here I have slightly amended the text to make it correspond more precisely to the German.

but also its limitations, it becomes clear, at least to the believer, that Christianity and modern science can coexist peacefully, especially in light of the fact that both are animated by the desire for truth, and thus are aligned in a common project. Benedict calls for a new synthesis to unite the modern scientific spirit and Christian faith: "We will succeed in doing so only if reason and faith come together in a new way." One will need to do this to engage in the dialogue of cultures that the age demands. Given how most of the non-Western cultures tend to be religious, it will benefit the West if it learns to "listen to the great experiences and insights of the religious traditions of humanity, and those of the Christian faith in particular." Failure to do so, to be open to the transcendent, would rob reason of its true calling.

This openness toward modernity also accompanies his dialogue with Jürgen Habermas, which can serve as a footnote to the Regensburg Address. To the surprise of many, Habermas, who saw himself as the heir to Max Weber and had admitted being "tone deaf" on the matter of religion, responded to the attacks of September 11, 2001 by calling for secular society to take more seriously the convictions of religious believers.[136] Pope Benedict took up this call for dialogue and takes up the Kantian desire to purify religion with reason. Benedict admits that religion, stripped of reason, can be pathological: "Religion must continually allow itself to be purified and structured by reason."[137] The concern does not run only one way: Reason can also exhibit a pathology born of hubris, exhibited in the development of weapons of mass destruction and other technologies that dehumanize. Reason left to its own devices is not healthy: "This is why reason, too, must be warned to keep within its proper limits, and it must learn a willingness to listen to the great religious traditions."[138] Benedict in this text does not use the metaphor of John Paul's two wings, but makes a similar argument, calling on each mode of thinking to purify

136. For this point, and the backdrop of the dialogue between Habermas and Ratzinger, see Florian Schuller, "Foreword," in Joseph Cardinal Ratzinger and Jürgen Habermas, *Dialectics of Secularization: On Reason and Religion*, ed. Florian Schuller, trans. Brain McNeil (San Francisco: Ignatius Press, 2006), 7–18, at 11.

137. Ratzinger, "That Which Holds the World Together," in *Dialectics of Secularization*, 53–80, at 77.

138. Ratzinger, "That Which Holds the World Together," 78.

the other: "They need each other, and they must acknowledge this mutual need."[139] The mutuality emphasized in the dialogue with Habermas complements the Regensburg Address while bringing his thought into closer orbit with John Paul's.

It is fitting to conclude by noting that for Roman Catholicism, a branch of Christianity most closely associated, even if unfairly, with intolerant authoritarianism, the call for a synthesis between faith and reason has resounded loudly from the first two popes of the current century. And in the broad history of religion, it is worth recalling, especially to the religiously illiterate, that leaders of a two-thousand-year old religion would insist that it be rational. And it is perhaps even more remarkable that so many heard these comments and found them perfectly consistent with an agreement, held for almost two thousand years, to *ask* how faith and reason relate. For the asking is the piety of thinking.

---

139. Ratzinger, "That Which Holds the World Together," 78.

Epilogue

I

Looking back at two millennia of theological history, one has the right to ask: Where is the relationship between faith and reason going? And why has it taken so long to get there? The goal of this essay, as noted in the preface, was neither to develop a theory of how faith and reason relate, nor to devise a synthesis that would bring the two together in some definitive way. Still, I hope the reader has detected, at the very least, an aim or perhaps even a trajectory guiding the narrative. Some of the marks of this trajectory can be traced in these final pages.

II

The most obvious challenge to relating faith to reason is that both faith and reason are moving targets in history. Although most Christians would maintain that the content or deposit of faith is unchanged, faith encompasses more than just this deposit. What it means to believe, and what is entailed in the assent of faith—in short, the faith that permits one to accept the articles of faith—has changed and will continue to change. To assent or to receive the gift of faith depends on a number of factors, not all of which can be enumerated. One reminder suffices to make the point: Everyone who believes learns about the faith *from* someone. To believe what one's parents, or the religious sister who taught one in primary or secondary school, or one's parish priest or minister, tells one to believe requires no heroic act of faith. At least this was true during various eras in Christian history when the vast number of people one encountered believed or claimed to believe these same things.

Under such circumstances belief would have consisted in an infusion of the theological virtue of faith, which is given by God. But to assent to that gift would have struck many recipients as part of the shared cultural inheritance that one learns to accept as an act of belonging to a family, a tribe, a community, a people, and a nation. In such instances, the theological challenge is to show that faith is a gift, a grace, for the truths to which one assents belong to a different order than the truths about a nation's origins or a family's illustrious lineage, fabulous or not. In our late-capitalist culture, on the other hand, faith perhaps comes to the believer in spite of her parents and religious leaders, and in defiance of what respectable people believe. The task in these circumstances is to show the reasonability of the assent, since its gifted, non-obligatory quality is on full display.

Even more so than faith, reason is a moving target in history. If one needs to build a bridge, it helps to know the territory on both sides of a river, or between two islands in a sea. If one imagines two unstable entities, faith and reason, that must be connected, any corresponding bridge must be pliable. To add to the metaphorical complexity, reason moves at a much quicker pace than faith. This means that one cannot find a solution or, better yet, point to an exemplary era, as if the matter of relating faith to reason involved nothing more than repeating a formula for stretching across a body of water to find dry land according to the last bridge one built. One must first know the land on which one stands, and then measure the distance to the far shore. To drop in a ready-made bridge, indifferent to the native water and land, would portend disaster. Lacking a ready-made plan for connecting faith and reason, one's best hope is to look for a pattern (or, to use a musical metaphor, a series of notes that might be brought into a melody) that maps various attempts to relate faith and reason. But there can be no question of definitively solving the relation of faith and reason.

III

Although these conclusions in no way gesture toward a comprehensive catalogue of the points and insights offered in the previous nine chapters, a list of conclusions can be made based on my study.

1. The premodern tradition frequently presumed a participatory notion of human cognition. In this model reason itself was already a graced, supernatural activity in which the human participated in the divine mind. Faith, then, represented only an intensification or an acceleration of that in which illuminated reason already partook. By contrast, modern reason, in

conjunction with the mechanistic metaphors that undergirded so many modern sensibilities about how the natural world works, assumes that reason, philosophy, and any other faculty or activity in the natural realm operates autonomously, without influence or interruption from anything above or outside the mechanistic, natural world. In light of these divergent understandings, the task of showing the reasonability of faith presents a much greater challenge if one adopts, either uncritically or unwittingly, a modern presumption of how reason operates.

2. Institutional structures will continue to shape the course of theology and the task of relating faith to reason. The main theological eras—early, medieval, modern—are best distinguished by the audiences for which they wrote. These institutional structures, often underwritten by secular powers, largely determine who gets to be an authority, a doctor, or a master. Christianity has both anti-institutional and institutional impulses. It pushes at walls to the point of toppling them. It also retains an impressive continuity with the past, often by means of institutions like the monastery, the school, and the university, all of which are sites of learned theology. Christian theologians work within institutional structures and norms (Eriugena, Anselm, Lombard, Melanchthon, Kuhn, Rahner, Pannenberg), and also rebel against these structures (Abelard, Bonaventure, Luther, the Pietists, Kierkegaard, Mary Daly, Milbank) with corresponding effects on the task of showing the rationality of faith. Christian theology has a history of both playing within the institutionally established rules of what counts as discourse, and of, at the same time, challenging these rules.

3. One can, at the end of this study, call into question the metanarrativity of reason. Put another way, one can justly interrogate whether reason can give a full account of itself, on its own terms and with the aid of its own powers. Reason seeks to explain what lies beyond the borders of its ratiocinative capacity. It finds itself wanting to know more than it can deliver. It is not just faith, then, that seeks rational support, but also reason that comes to realize it needs more than reason. In

John Paul's metaphor, reason needs the wing of faith to take flight. So many of the greatest thinkers came to see what Pascal put so laconically: "Reason's last step is the recognition that there are an infinite number of things which are beyond it."[1]

4. The trust in reason displayed by so many leading Christian intellectuals is based on more than a hunch. A chorus of voices in the tradition—Augustine, Aquinas, Pascal, Newman, Blondel, Rahner, Balthasar, John Paul, to name just a few—find different ways of, and justifications for, giving free reign to speculation, confident that any appearance of a reason untethered from faith, or hostile to faith, is only provisional and, in the long run, untrue to reason itself. Yet this trust in reason need not involve a slavish devotion to whatever cultural or intellectual forces understand reason to be. As a living tradition, Christian theology has a better grasp on the evolution of reason than secular intellectuals who refuse to encounter any traditions older than the ones in which they swim. The battle over reason is one that Christianity can win.

5. The final chapter ends with an apparent paradox: two recent popes making appeals to reason. The papacy symbolizes a nearly inexhaustible religious authority, and the office even claims the charism of infallibility in matters of faith and morals. Yet these two popes have made these pronouncements to a purportedly scientific, rational culture, the likes of which world history has never seen. Their calls to return to reason were prophetic, for many forces in the world today either reject the power of reason or truncate it to a domesticated form—what Kant called *Verstand* and what some today call discursive reason. Both John Paul and Benedict made impassioned pleas that believers and non-believers alike embrace reason as means to forestall violence and renew dialogue between cultures and religions. For reason can never be separated from the God who gives the gift of faith so that humanity can be united with that God in both heart and intellect.

---

1. Pascal, *Pensées*, #188 (#267).

Bibliography

Abelard, Peter. *Ethical Writings: His Ethics or "Know Yourself" and His Dialogue between a Philosopher, a Jew, and a Christian*. Translated by Paul Vincent Spade. Indianapolis: Hackett, 1995.

Adler, Mortimer Jerome. *How to Read a Book: The Art of Getting a Liberal Education*. New York: Simon and Schuster, 1940.

Alison, James. *Undergoing God: Dispatches from the Scene of a Break-In*. New York: Continuum, 2006.

Alker, Stefan. "Belief in Miracles as the Gateway to Atheism: Theological-Historical Remarks about Ferdinand Christian Baur's Critique of Miracles." In *Ferdinand Christian Baur and the History of Early Christianity*, edited by Martin Bauspiess, Christof Landmesser, and David Lincicum, 261–86. Translated by Peter Hodgson and Robert Brown. Oxford: Oxford University Press, 2017.

Anselm. *Basic Writings: Proslogium; Monologium; Gaunilon's On Behalf of the Fool; Cur Deus Homo*. Translated by S. N. Deane. 2nd ed. La Salle, IL: Open Court, 1962.

———. *L'oeuvre de S. Anselme de Cantorbéry*. Vol. 1, *Monologion, Proslogion*, edited by Michel Corbin. Paris: Cerf, 1986.

———. *L'oeuvre de S. Anselme de Cantorbéry*. Vol. 3, edited by Michel Corbin and Alain Galonnier. Paris: Cerf, 1988.

Anselm, and Thomas Williams. *Proslogion, with the Replies of Gaunilo and Anselm*. Indianapolis: Hackett, 2001.

Aquino, Frederick. *Communities of Informed Judgment: Newman's Illative Sense and Accounts of Rationality*. Washington DC: The Catholic University of America Press, 2003.

Aristotle. *Aristotle's Metaphysics*. Translated by Hippocrates George Apostle. Grinnell, IA: Peripatetic Press, 1979.

Asselt, Willem J. Van. *Introduction to Reformed Scholasticism*. Grand Rapids, MI: Reformation Heritage Books, 2011.

Athanasius. *On the Incarnation*. Yonkers, NY: St. Vladimir's Seminary Press, 1977.

Aubert, Roger. *Le Problème de L'Acte de Foi*. Troisième Édition. Louvain: E. Warny, 1958.

Augustine. *Augustine: Earlier Writings*. Translated by John H. S. Burleigh. Louisville: Westminster John Knox Press, 2006.

———. *Confessions.* Translated by Henry Chadwick. Oxford: Oxford University Press, 1991.

———. *The Literal Meaning of Genesis.* Vol. 1. Translated by John Hammond Taylor. New York: Paulist, 1982.

———. *On the Trinity.* Translated by Arthur W. Haddan. Peabody, MA: Hendrickson Publishers, 1995.

Balthasar, Hans Urs von. *The Glory of the Lord: A Theological Aesthetics.* Vol. 3., edited by John Riches and Joseph Fessio, SJ. Translated by Andrew Louth et al. San Francisco: Ignatius Press, 1986.

———. *Karl Barth: Darstellung und Deutung seiner Theologie.* Cologne: Hegner, 1951.

———. *Love Alone Is Credible.* Translated by D. C. Schindler. San Francisco: Ignatius, 2004.

———. *The Moment of Christian Witness.* Translated by Richard Beckley. San Francisco: Ignatius, 1994.

———. *The Realm of Metaphysics in the Modern Age.* Translated by Oliver Davies et al. Vol. 5 of *The Glory of the Lord: A Theological Aesthetics.* Edinburgh: T&T Clark, 1991.

———. *Seeing the Form.* Translated by Erasmo Leiva-Merikakis. Vol. 1 of *The Glory of the Lord: A Theological Aesthetics.* San Francisco: Ignatius, 1982.

Barth, Karl. *Anselm: Fides Quarens Intellectum.* Translated by Ian Robertson. Richmond, VA: John Knox, 1960.

———. *Church Dogmatics I/1.* 2nd ed. Translated by G. W. Bromiley. Edinburgh: T&T Clark, 1975.

———. *Der Römerbrief 1922.* Zurich: Theologischer Verlag, 1989.

———. *The Epistle to the Romans.* 2nd ed. Translated by Edwyn Hoskyns. Oxford: Oxford University Press, 1933.

———. "Nachwort." In *Schleiermacher-Auswahl,* edited by Heinz Bolli, 290–312. Hamburg: Siebenstern Taschenbuch, 1988.

Bauerschmidt, Frederick Christian. *Thomas Aquinas: Faith, Reason, and Following Christ.* Oxford: Oxford University Press, 2013.

Baur, Ferdinand Christian. *Church and Theology in the Nineteenth Century,* edited by Peter Hodgson. Translated by Robert Brown and Peter Hodgson. Eugene, OR: Cascade Books, 2018.

———. *The Church History of the First Three Centuries.* Vols. 1–2, edited and translated by Allan Menzies. London: Williams & Norgate, 1878.

———. *Die frühen Briefe (1814–1835)*, edited by Carl Hester. Sigmaringen: Jan Thorbecke, 1993.

———. *Symbolik und Mythologie, oder die Naturreligion des Alterthums. Erster oder Allgemeiner Theil*. Stuttgart: J. B. Metzler, 1824.

Bauspiess, Martin, Christof Landmesser, and David Lincicum, eds. *Ferdinand Christian Baur and the History of Early Christianity*. Translated by Peter Hodgson and Robert Brown. Oxford: Oxford University Press, 2017.

Beckmann, Jan Peter. *Wilhelm von Ockham*. Originalausg. München: C. H. Beck, 1995.

Behr, John. *Origen: On First Principles: A Reader's Edition*. Translated by John Behr. Oxford: Oxford University Press, 2019.

Beiser, Frederick. *German Idealism: The Struggle against Subjectivism, 1781–1801*. Cambridge, MA: Harvard University Press, 2002.

Benedict XVI, Pope. Apostolic letter commemorating the seventh centenary of Scotus's death. https://www.vatican.va/content/benedict-xvi/en/apost_letters/documents/hf_ben-xvi_apl_20081028_duns-scoto.html.

———. "Faith, Reason, and the University." http://www.vatican.va/content/benedict-xvi/en/speeches/2006/september/documents/hf_ben-xvi_spe_20060912_university-regensburg.html.

Benson, Joshua C. "Identifying the Literary Genre of De Reductione Artium Ad Theologiam: Bonaventure's Inaugural Lecture at Paris." *Franciscan Studies* 67 (2009): 149–78.

Betz, John. "After Barth: A New Introduction to Erich Przywara's *Analogia Entis*." In *The Analogy of Being: Invention of the Antichrist or the Wisdom of God*, edited by Thomas Joseph White, 35–87. Grand Rapids, MI: Eerdmans, 2011.

———. "The Humility of God: On a Disputed Question in Trinitarian Theology." *Nova et Vetera* 17, no. 4 (2019): 757–98.

Boehner, Philotheus. *The History of the Franciscan School. Part III: Duns Scotus*. St. Bonaventure, NY: 1945.

Boethius. *The Theological Tractates: The Consolation of Philosophy*. Translated by H. F. Stewart, E. K. Rand, and S. J. Tester. Cambridge, MA: Harvard University Press, 1978.

Boethius, and V. E. Watts. *The Consolation of Philosophy*. Baltimore: Penguin Books, 1969.

Bonaventure. *The Journey of the Mind to God*, edited by Stephen F. Brown. Translated by Philotheus Boehner. Indianapolis: Hackett, 1993.

———. *Saint Bonaventure's Disputed Questions on the Mystery of the Trinity*. Translated by Zachary Hayes. St. Bonaventure, NY: Franciscan Institute Publications, 1979.

———. *St. Bonaventure's on the Reduction of the Arts to Theology*. Translated by Zachary Hayes. St. Bonaventure, NY: Franciscan Institute Publications, 1996.

———. *The Works of Bonaventure V: Collations on the Six Days*. Translated by José de Vinck. St. Anthony Guild Press, 1970.

Brown, Raymond E., Joseph A. Fitzmyer, and Roland E. Murphy, eds. *The New Jerome Biblical Commentary*. Englewood Cliffs, NJ: Prentice-Hall, 1990.

Buckley, Michael J. *At the Origins of Modern Atheism*. New Haven, CT: Yale University Press, 1987.

———. *Denying and Disclosing God: The Ambiguous Progress of Modern Atheism*. New Haven, CT: Yale University Press, 2004.

Bultmann, Rudolf. *Jesus Christ and Mythology*. New York: Scribner, 1958.

Burnett, Amy Nelson. *The Oxford Handbook of Martin Luther's Theology*. Edited by Robert Kolb, Irene Dingel, and Ľubomír Batka. Oxford: Oxford University Press, 2014.

Calvin, John. *The Acts of the Apostles*, edited by David W. Torrance and Thomas F. Torrance. Translated by John W. Fraser and W. J. G. McDonald. Grand Rapids, MI: Eerdmans, 1995.

———. *Institutes of the Christian Religion*, edited by John T. McNeill. Translated by Ford Lewis Battles. Philadelphia: Westminster, 1960.

———. *Theological Treatises*. Translated by J. K. S. Reid. Philadelphia: Westminster Press, 1954.

Camosy, Charles. "The Crisis of Catholic Moral Theology." *Church Life Journal*, November 15, 2018. https://churchlifejournal.nd.edu/articles/the-crisis-of-catholic-moral-theology/.

Carabine, Deirdre. *John Scottus Eriugena*. New York: Oxford University Press, 2000.

Carter, J. Kameron. *Race: A Theological Account*. Oxford: Oxford University Press, 2008.

Cavanaugh, William T. *The Myth of Religious Violence: Secular Ideology and The Roots of Modern Conflict*. Oxford: Oxford University Press, 2009.

Chenu, Marie-Dominique. *Nature, Man, and Society in the Twelfth Century: Essays on New Theological Perspectives in the Latin West*. Translated by Jerome Taylor and Lester K. Little. Chicago: University of Chicago Press, 1968.

Clement of Alexandria. *Stromateis Books One to Three*. Translated by John Ferguson. Washington, DC: The Catholic University of America Press, 1991.

Coakley, Sarah. *God, Sexuality, and the Self: An Essay "on the Trinity."* Cambridge: Cambridge University Press, 2013.

Coakley, Sarah, and Richard Cross, eds. *Oxford Handbook of the Reception of Christian Theology*. Oxford: Oxford University Press, forthcoming.

Coblenz, Jessica and Brianne Jacobs. "Mary Daly's *The Church and the Second Sex* after Fifty Years of U.S. Catholic Feminist Theology." *Theological Studies* 79, no. 3 (2018): 543–65.

Colish, Marcia L. *Peter Lombard*. Vols. 1–2. Leiden: E. J. Brill, 1994.

Cone, James. *God of the Oppressed*. Maryknoll, New York: Orbis Books, 1975.

Congregation for the Doctrine of the Faith. "Note on the Force of the Doctrinal Decrees Concerning the Thought and Work of Fr. Antonio Rosmini Serbati." https://www.vatican.va/roman_curia/congregations/cfaith/documents/rc_con_c faith_doc_20010701_rosmini_en.html.

Cross, F. L. and Elizabeth A. Livingstone. *The Oxford Dictionary of the Christian Church*. Oxford: Oxford University Press, 2005.

Cross, Richard. *Duns Scotus*. Oxford: Oxford University Press, 1999.

Cullen, Christopher. "Transcendental Thomism: Realism Rejected." In *The Failure of Modernism*, edited by Brendan Sweetman, 72–85. Mishawaka, IN: American Maritain Association, 1999.

Dahlke, Benjamin. *Karth Barth, Catholic Renewal*. London: Bloomsbury, 2012.

Daly, Mary. *Beyond God the Father: Toward a Philosophy of Women's Liberation*. Boston: Beacon, 1973.

Descartes, René. *Discourse on Method and Meditations on First Philosophy*. Translated by Donald A. Cress. Indianapolis: Hackett, 1993.

Dieter, Theodor. *Der junge Luther und Aristoteles*. Reprint ed. Berlin: De Gruyter, 2001.

Dietrich, Donald J., and Michael J. Himes, eds. *The Legacy of the Tübingen School: The Relevance of Nineteenth-Century Theology for the Twenty-First Century*. New York: Crossroad, 1997.

Dixon, C. Scott. "The Radicals." In *The Oxford Handbook of the Protestant Reformation*, edited by Ulinka Rublank, 190–213. Oxford: Oxford University Press, 2017.

D'Onofrio, Giulio, ed. *The History of Theology II: The Middle Ages*. Translated by Matthew O'Connell. Annotated ed. Collegeville, MN: Liturgical Press, 2008.

Dragseth, Jennifer Hockenbery. *The Devil's Whore: Reason and Philosophy in the Lutheran Tradition.* "Studies in Lutheran History and Theology." Minneapolis: Fortress Press, 2011.

Dru, Alexander. "Introduction: Historical and Biographical." In Maurice Blondel. *The Letter on Apologetics* and *History and Dogma*, 11–79. Translated by Alexander Dru and Illtyd Trethowan. Grand Rapids, MI: Eerdmans, 1964.

Duffy, Stephen J. *The Dynamics of Grace: Perspectives in Theological Anthropology.* Collegeville, MN: Liturgical Press, 1993.

Dulles, Avery. *The Assurance of Things Hoped For: A Theology of Christian Faith.* Oxford: Oxford University Press, 1994.

Erasmus, Desiderius, and Clarence H. Miller. *The Praise of Folly.* New Haven, CT: Yale University Press, 1979.

Erb, Peter C., ed. *Pietists: Selected Writings.* New York: Paulist Press, 1983.

Eriugena, John Scottus. *Periphyseon: The Division of Nature.* Translated by Inglis Patric Sheldon-Williams and John J. O'Meara. Montreal: Bellarmin/Dumbarton Oaks, 1987.

———. *Treatise on Divine Predestination.* Translated by Mary Brennan. Notre Dame, IN: University of Notre Dame Press, 1998.

Evans, Gillian. "'An Organon More Delicate, Versatile and Elastic': John Henry Newman and Whately's *Logic.*" *The Downside Review* 97 (1979): 151–91.

Faggioli, Massimo. *Vatican II: The Battle for Meaning.* New York: Paulist Press, 2012.

Falque, Emmanuel. *Crossing the Rubicon: The Borderlands of Philosophy and Theology.* Translated by Reuben Shank. New York: Fordham University Press, 2016.

Ferreira, Jamie. "Faith and the Kierkegaardian Leap." In *The Cambridge Companion to Kierkegaard*, edited by Alastair Hannay and Gordon Marino, 207–34. Cambridge: Cambridge University Press, 1998.

———. "Leaps and Circles: Kierkegaard and Newman on Faith and Reason." *Religious Studies* 30, no. 4 (1994).

Fiorenza, Francis Schüssler, and John P. Galvin, eds. *Systematic Theology: Roman Catholic Perspectives.* 2nd ed. Minneapolis: Fortress Press, 2011.

Fitzgerald, Allan, and John C. Cavadini, eds. *Augustine through the Ages: An Encyclopedia.* Grand Rapids, MI: Eerdmans, 1999.

Flynn, Gabriel and Paul D. Murray, eds. *Ressourcement: A Movement for Renewal in Twentieth-Century Theology.* Oxford: Oxford University Press, 2012.

Fodor, James. "Postliberal Theology." In *The Modern Theologians*, 3rd ed., edited by David Ford, 229–48. Malden, MA: Blackwell, 2005.

Fortin, Ernest L. *Classical Christianity and the Political Order: Reflections on the Theologico-Political Problem*, edited by J. Brian Benestad. Lanham, MD: Rowman & Littlefield, 1996.

Foucault, Michel. *The Foucault Reader*, edited by Paul Rabinow. New York: Pantheon, 1984.

French, R. K., and Andrew Cunningham. *Before Science: The Invention of the Friars' Natural Philosophy*. Brookfield, VT: Scolar Press, 1996.

Galilei, Galileo. *The Galileo Affair: A Documentary History*, edited by Maurice A. Finocchiaro. Berkeley: University of California, 1989.

Gay, Peter. *The Enlightenment, an Interpretation: The Rise of Modern Paganism*. New York: Vintage Books, 1968.

Gillespie, Michael Allen. *The Theological Origins of Modernity*. Chicago: University of Chicago Press, 2008.

Gilson, Etienne. *History of Christian Philosophy in the Middle Ages*. New York: Random House, 1955.

———. *John Duns Scotus: Introduction to his Fundamental Positions*. Translated by James G. Colbert. London: T&T Clark, 2019.

———. *Reason and Revelation in the Middle Ages*. New York: Charles Scribner's Sons, 1938.

———. *The Spirit of Mediaeval Philosophy*. Translated by Alfred Howard Campbell Downes. New York: Charles Scribner's Sons, 1940.

Görres, Joseph von. *Athanasius*. Regensburg: G. J. Manz, 1838.

Gouwens, David. "Søren Kierkegaard: Between Skepticism and Faith's Happy Passion." In *The Devil's Whore: Reason and Philosophy in the Lutheran Tradition*, edited by Jennifer Hockenberry Dragseth, 115–22. Minneapolis: Fortress Press, 2011.

Grant, Edward. *God and Reason in the Middle Ages*. Cambridge: Cambridge University Press, 2001.

Grant, Robert M. *Irenaeus of Lyons*. London: Routledge, 1997.

Gregory, Brad S. "Genre, Method, and Assumptions." *The Immanent Frame* (blog), January 21, 2014. https://tif.ssrc.org/2014/01/21/genre-method-and-assumptions/.

———. *The Unintended Reformation: How a Religious Revolution Secularized Society*. Cambridge, MA: Belknap Press of Harvard University Press, 2012.

Gregory of Nyssa. *Homilies on Ecclesiastes*, edited by Stuart George Hall. Translated by Stuart George Hall and Rachel Moriarty. Berlin: Walter de Gruyter, 1993.

Griffiths, Paul and Reinhard Hütter, eds. *Reason and the Reasons of Faith*. New York: T&T Clark, 2005.

Gschwandtner, Christina. "A New 'Apologia': The Relationship between Theology and Philosophy in the Work of Jean-Luc Marion." *Heythrop Journal* 46 (2005): 299–313.

Gutierrez, Gustavo. *Las Casas: In Search of the Poor of Jesus Christ*. Maryknoll, NY: Orbis, 1993.

Gwynn, David M. *Athanasius of Alexandria: Bishop, Theologian, Ascetic, Father*. Oxford: Oxford University Press, 2012.

Hadot, Pierre. *Philosophy as a Way of Life: Spiritual Exercises from Socrates to Foucault*, edited by Arnold I. Davidson and Michael Chase. Oxford: Blackwell, 1995.

Hadot, Pierre, and Michael Chase. *What Is Ancient Philosophy?* Cambridge, MA: Belknap Press of Harvard University Press, 2002.

Hammond, Jay M., J. A. Wayne Hellmann, and Jared Goff, eds. *A Companion to Bonaventure*. Leiden: Brill, 2014.

Hankey, Wayne. "Aquinas, Plato, and Neoplatonism." In *The Oxford Handbook of Aquinas*, edited by Eleonore Stump and Brian Davies, 55–64. Oxford: Oxford University Press, 2012.

Hankey, Wayne and Douglas Hedley, eds. *Deconstructing Radical Orthodoxy: Postmodern Theology, Rhetoric and Truth*. New York: Ashgate, 2005.

Hardy, Daniel W. "Karl Barth." In *The Modern Theologians*, 3rd ed., edited by David Ford, 21–42. Malden, MA: Blackwell, 2005.

Harnack, Adolf von. *History of Dogma*. Vol. 1. Translated by Neil Buchanan. New York: Dover, 1961.

Harris, Horton. *The Tübingen School*. Oxford: Clarendon, 1975.

Harrison, Peter. *The Territories of Science and Religion*. Chicago: University of Chicago Press, 2015.

Hart, David Bentley. *The Beauty of the Infinite: The Aesthetics of Christian Truth*. Grand Rapids, MI: Eerdmans, 2004.

———. *The Experience of God: Being, Consciousness, Bliss*. New Haven, CT: Yale University Press, 2013.

———. "A Gift Exceeding Every Debt: An Eastern Orthodox Appreciation of Anselm's Cur Deus Homo." *Pro Ecclesia* 7, no. 3 (1998): 333–48.

———. "Review Essay of *After Writing*." *Pro Ecclesia* 9, no. 3 (2000): 367–72.

———. *A Splendid Wickedness and Other Essays*. Grand Rapids, MI: Eerdmans, 2016.

Haven, Cynthia. "The French Invasion." In *Evolution of Desire: A Life of René Girard*, 121–46. East Lansing, MI: Michigan State University Press, 2018.

Heine, Heinrich. *Religion and Philosophy in Germany: A Fragment*. Translated by John Snodgrass. London: Trübner, 1882.

Hemler, Christine. *Theology and the End of Doctrine*. Louisville: Westminister John Knox, 2014.

Henrici, Peter. "Karl Rahners 'Hörer des Wortes' und Maurice Blondels 'L'Action.'" In *Die philosophischen Quellen der Theologie Karl Rahners*, edited by Harald Schöndorf, 81–100. Freiburg: Herder, 2005.

———. "The One Who Went Unnamed: Maurice Blondel in the Encyclical *Fides et Ratio*." *Communio* 26, no. 3 (1999): 609–21.

Hermes, Georg. *Einleitung in die christkatholische Theologie. Erster Theil: Philosophische Einleitung*. Münster: Coppenrath, 1819.

Herring, George. *Introduction to the History of Christianity*. Washington Square, NY: New York University Press, 2006.

Hibbs, Thomas. "Habits of the Heart: Pascal and the Ethics of Thought." *International Philosophical Quarterly* 45, no. 2 (June 2005).

Hirsch, Emmanuel. *Geschichte der neuern evangelischen Theologie*. 3rd ed. Gütersloh: G Mohn, 1964.

Hochschild, Joshua. "The Re-Imagined Aristotelianism of John Henry Newman." *Modern Age* 45, no. 5 (Fall 2003): 333–42.

Hodgson, Peter. *The Formation of Historical Theology: A Study of Ferdinand Christian Baur*. New York: Harper & Row, 1966.

Hoitenga, Dewey J. *Faith and Reason from Plato to Plantinga: An Introduction to Reformed Epistemology*. Albany: State University of New York Press, 1991.

Hopkins, Dwight N. "Black Theology of Liberation." In *The Modern Theologians*, 3rd ed., edited by David Ford, 451–68. Malden, MA: Blackwell, 2005.

Horner, Robyn. *Jean-Luc Marion: A Theo-logical Introduction*. New York: Routledge, 2016.

Howard, Thomas Albert. *The Pope and the Professor: Pius IV, Ignaz von Döllinger, and the Quandary of the Modern Age*. Oxford: Oxford University Press, 2017.

Howsare, Rodney. *Hans Urs von Balthasar and Protestantism: The Ecumenical Implications of His Theological Style*. London: T&T Clark, 2005.

Hughes, Kevin. "St. Bonaventure's Collationes in Hexaëmeron: Fractured Sermons and Protreptic Discourse." *Franciscan Studies* 63 (2005): 107–29.

Hugh of St. Victor. *The Didascalicon of Hugh of St. Victor: A Medieval Guide to the Arts*. Translated by Jerome Taylor. New York: Columbia University Press, 1961.

Hume, David. *Dialogues Concerning Natural Religion*. London: Penguin Classics, 1990.

———. *An Enquiry Concerning Human Understanding*, edited by Eric Steinberg. Indianapolis: Hackett, 1977.

Enchiridion Symbolorum: A Compendium of Creeds, Definitions, and Declarations of the Catholic Church. 43rd ed., edited by Peter Hünermann. San Francisco: Ignatius Press, 2012.

Ignatius of Loyola. *Ignatius of Loyola: The Spiritual Exercises and Selected Works*, edited by George E. Ganss. New York: Paulist Press, 1991.

Ingram, Mary Beth. *Scotus for Dunces: An Introduction to the Subtle Doctor*. Saint Bonaventure, NY: Franciscan Institute Publications, 2003.

Irenaeus. *The Scandal of the Incarnation: Irenaeus against the Heresies*, edited by Hans Urs von Balthasar and John Saward. San Francisco: Ignatius Press, 1990.

Israel, Jonathan I. *Enlightenment Contested: Philosophy, Modernity, and the Emancipation of Man, 1670–1752*. Oxford: Oxford University Press, 2006.

———. *Radical Enlightenment: Philosophy and the Making of Modernity 1650–1750*. Oxford: Oxford University Press, 2002.

Jaycox, Michael. "Black Lives Matter and Catholic Whiteness: A Tale of Two Performances." *Horizons* 44 (2017): 306–41.

Jennings, Willie James. *The Christian Imagination: Theology and the Origins of Race*. New Haven, CT: Yale University Press, 2010.

John Paul II, Pope. *Encyclical Letter Fides et Ratio of the Supreme Pontiff John Paul II*. Vatican translation. Boston: Pauline Books & Media, 1998.

Jones, William R. *Is God a White Racist? A Preamble to Black Theology*. Garden City, NY: Doubleday, 1973.

Jordan, Jeff, ed. *Gambling on God: Essays on Pascal's Wager*. Lanham, MD: Rowman & Littlefield, 1994.

Justin Martyr. *Dialogue with Trypho*, edited by Michael Slusser. Translated by Thomas Halls. Washington DC: The Catholic University of America Press, 2003.

———. *The First and Second Apologies.* Translated by L. W. Barnard. New York: Paulist Press, 1997.

Kaminksi, Phyllis. "Seeking Transcendence in the Modern World." In *Catholicism Contending with Modernity,* edited by Darrell Jodock, 117–41. Cambridge: Cambridge University Press, 2000.

Kanaris, Jim and Mark Dorley, eds. *In Deference to the Other: Lonergan and Contemporary Continental Thought.* Albany: SUNY Press, 2004.

Kant, Immanuel. *Critique of Pure Reason.* Translated by Paul Guyer and Allen W. Wood. Cambridge: Cambridge University Press, 1998.

———. *Kants Gesammelte Schriften.* Berlin: G. Reimer, 1902.

Kapic, Kelly and Bruce McCormack, eds. *Mapping Modern Theology: A Thematic and Historical Introduction.* Grand Rapids, MI: Baker Academic, 2012.

Kaplan, Grant. *Answering the Enlightenment: The Catholic Recovery of Historical Revelation.* New York: Crossroad/Herder, 2006.

———. "Revisiting Johannes Eck: The Leipzig Debate as the Beginning of the Reformation." *Logos: A Journal of Catholic Thought and Culture* 24, no. 2 (2021): 73–97.

Kaplan, Grant, and Kevin Vander Schel, eds. *Oxford History of Modern German Theology: Volume 1: 1781–1848.* Oxford: Oxford University Press, forthcoming.

Kasper, Walter. *Jesus the Christ.* New York: Paulist, 1977.

Keen, Ralph. "Philipp Melanchthon." *The Encyclopedia of Protestantism.* New York: Routledge, 2004.

Kerr, Fergus. *Twentieth-Century Catholic Theologians.* Oxford: Blackwell, 2007.

Kierkegaard, Søren. *Concluding Unscientific Postscript to Philosophical Fragments.* Vols. 1–2, edited and translated by Howard and Edna Hong. Princeton: Princeton University Press, 1992.

———. *Fear and Trembling/Repetition,* edited and translated by Howard and Edna Hong. Princeton: Princeton University Press, 1983.

———. *Journals and Papers.* Vol. 1, edited and translated by Howard and Edna Hong. Bloomington, IN: Indiana University Press, 1967.

———. *Kierkegaard's Attack Upon "Christendom" 1854–55.* Translated by Walter Lowrie. Princeton: Princeton University Press, 1944.

Kilby, Karen, "Karl Rahner." In *The Modern Theologians,* 3rd ed., edited by David Ford, 92–105. Malden, MA: Blackwell, 2005.

Kleutgen, Jospeh. *Die Theologie der Vorzeit*. Vols. 1–5. Münster: Theissingschen, 1853–70.

———. *Pre-Modern Philosophy Defended*. Translated by William Marshner. South Bend, IN: St. Augustine's, 2019.

Koerpel, Robert. *Maurice Blondel: Transforming Catholic Tradition*. Notre Dame: University of Notre Dame Press, 2019.

Kolb, Robert. "Luther on the Theology of the Cross." *Lutheran Quarterly* 16, no. 4 (2002): 443–66.

Koritensky, Andreas. "The Early John Henry Newman on Faith and Reason." *Newman Studies Journal* 14, no. 1 (2017).

Kuhn, Johannes Evangelist von. *Philosophie und Theologie; Eine Streitschrift*. Tübingen: Laupp'schen, 1860.

———. "Princip Und Methode Der Speculativen Theologie." *Theologische Quartalschrift* 23 (1840): 1–80.

———. "Ueber Den Begriff Und Das Wesen Der Speculativen Theologie Oder Christlichen Philosophie." *Theologische Quartalschrift* 14 (1832): 253–304.

Kuhn, Johannes von, and Grant Kaplan. *Faithfully Seeking Understanding: Selected Writings of Johannes Kuhn*. Washington, DC: The Catholic University of America Press, 2009.

Kusukawa, Sachiko. *The Transformation of Natural Philosophy: The Case of Philip Melanchthon*. Cambridge: Cambridge University Press, 1995.

Lash, Nicholas. *Believing Three Ways in One God: A Reading of the Apostles' Creed*. Notre Dame, IN: University of Notre Dame Press, 1993.

Lawrence, Frederick G. "Athens and Jerusalem: The Contemporary Problematic of Faith and Reason." *Gregorianum* 80, no. 2 (1999): 223–44.

———. "The Fragility of Consciousness: Lonergan and the Postmodern Concern for the Other." *Theological Studies* 54 (1993): 55–94.

Legaspi, Michael C. *The Death of Scripture and the Rise of Biblical Studies*. Oxford: Oxford University Press, 2010.

Lehner, Ulrich L. *The Catholic Enlightenment: The Forgotten History of a Global Movement*. Oxford: Oxford University Press, 2016.

Leo XIII. "Encyclical Letter of Pope Leo XIII." In *The Summa Theologica of St. Thomas Aquinas*. Translated by Fathers of the English Dominican Province. Vol. 1. Allen, TX: Christian Classics, 1948.

Lessing, Gotthold Ephraim. *Lessing's Theological Writings: Selections in Translation.* Translated by Henry Chadwick. London: Adam & Charles Black, 1956.

———. *Philosophical and Theological Writings.* Translated by H. B. Nisbet. Cambridge: Cambridge University Press, 2005.

Livingston, James, Francis Schüssler Fiorenza, Sarah Coakley, and James H. Evans. *The Twentieth Century.* Vol. 2 of *Modern Christian Thought.* 2nd ed. Minneapolis: Fortress Press, 2006.

Locke, John. *An Essay Concerning Human Understanding,* edited by Alexander Fraser. New York: Dover, 1959.

Lombard, Peter. *The Sentences.* Translated by Giulio Silano. Toronto: Pontifical Institute of Mediaeval Studies, 2007.

Lonergan, Bernard J. F. *Collected Works of Bernard Lonergan.* Vols. 1–25. Toronto: University of Toronto Press, 1992–2019.

———. *Collection: Papers by Bernard J. F. Lonergan,* edited by Frederick E. Crowe. New York: Herder and Herder, 1967.

———. *Insight: A Study in Human Understanding,* edited by Frederick Crowe and Robert Doran. Vol. 3 of *Collected Works of Bernard Lonergan.* Toronto: University of Toronto Press, 1992.

———. *A Second Collection,* edited by Robert Doran and John Dadosky. Vol. 13 of *Collected Works of Bernard Lonergan.* Toronto: University of Toronto Press, 2016.

Long, Charles. *Significations: Signs, Symbols, and Images in the Interpretation of Religion.* Minneapolis: Fortress, 1986.

Lowe, Walter. "Postmodern Theology." In *The Oxford Handbook of Systematic Theology,* edited by Kathryn Tanner, John Webster, and Iain Torrence, 617–33. Oxford: Oxford University Press, 2009.

Luther, Martin. *Early Theological Works.* Translated by James Atkinson. Louisville: Westminster John Knox Press, 1962.

———. *Lectures on Romans.* Translated by Wilhelm Pauck. Louisville: Westminster John Knox Press, 1961.

———. *Luther's Works.* Vol. 34, edited by Lewis Spitz. Philadelphia: Muhlenberg, 1960.

———. *Selections from His Writings.* Translated by John Dillenberger. Garden City, NY: Doubleday, 1961.

Lyotard, Jean-François. *The Postmodern Condition: A Report on Knowledge.* Translated by Geoff Bennington and Brian Massumi. Minneapolis: University of Minnesota Press, 1984.

MacIntyre, Alasdair. *After Virtue. A Study in Moral Theory.* Notre Dame, IN: University of Notre Dame Press, 1981.

———. *Whose Justice? Which Rationality?.* Notre Dame, IN: University of Notre Dame Press, 1988.

Marenbon, John. *Boethius.* Oxford: Oxford University Press, 2003.

Marion, Jean-Luc. *Believing in Order to See: On the Rationality of Revelation and the Irrationality of Some Believers.* Translated by Christina Gschwandtner. New York: Fordham University Press, 2017.

———. *Étant Donne. Essai d'une phénoménologie de la donation.* Paris: Presses Universitaires de France, 1997.

———. *Givenness and Revelation.* Translated by Stephen E. Lewis. Oxford: Oxford University Press, 2016.

———. *God without Being.* Translated by Thomas Carlson. Chicago: University of Chicago Press, 1995.

Marmion, Declan, and Mary E. Hines, eds. *The Cambridge Companion to Karl Rahner.* Cambridge: Cambridge University Press, 2005.

Martens, Peter W. "Embodiment, Heresy, and the Hellenization of Christianity: The Descent of the Soul in Plato and Origen." *Harvard Theological Review* 108, no. 4 (October 2015): 594–620. https://doi.org/10.1017/S0017816015000401.

———. *Origen and Scripture: The Contours of the Exegetical Life.* New York: Oxford University Press, 2012.

Mascall, E. L. *The Openness of Being: Natural Theology Today.* Philadelphia: Westminster, 1971.

Massingale, Bryan. *Racial Justice and the Catholic Church.* Maryknoll, NY: Orbis Books, 2010.

Mattes, Karl Joseph. *Die Kontroverse zwischen Johannes v. Kuhn under Constantin v. Schäzler über das Verhältnis von Natur und Gnade.* Freiburg: Universitätsverlag Freiburg, 1968.

McCool, Gerald. *The Neo-Thomists.* Milwaukee: Marquette University, 1994.

———. *Nineteenth-Century Scholasticism: The Search for a Unitary Method.* New York: Fordham University Press, 1977.

McIntosh, Mark. "Go as First Truth, the Will's Good and Faith's Cause: The Theology of Faith and Newman's *University Sermons*." *International Journal of Systematic Theology* 15 (2013): 416–36.

McKim, Donald K., ed. *The Cambridge Companion to John Calvin*. Cambridge: Cambridge University Press, 2004.

McMahon, Darrin. *Enemies of Enlightenment: The French Counter-Enlightenment and the Making of Modernity*. Oxford: Oxford University Press, 2001.

McMullin, Ernan. "Galileo on Science and Scripture." In *The Cambridge Companion to Galileo*, edited by Peter K. Machamer, 271–347. Cambridge: Cambridge University Press, 1998.

Meconi, David Vincent, ed. *The Cambridge Companion to Augustine*. 2nd ed. Cambridge: Cambridge University Press, 2014.

Melanchthon, Philipp. *Melanchthon on Christian Doctrine: Loci Communes, 1555*. Translated by Clyde Leonard Manschreck. Oxford: Oxford University Press, 1965.

———. *Orations on Philosophy and Education*, edited by Sachiko Kusukawa. Translated by Christine F. Salazar. Cambridge, UK: New York: Cambridge University Press, 1999.

Metz, Johann Baptist. *A Passion for God: The Mystical-Political Dimension of Christianity*. Translated by J. Matthew Ashley. New York, Paulist, 1998.

Meyer, Ben. *The Aims of Jesus*. London: SCM Press, 1979.

Milbank, John. "'Postmodern Critical Augustinianism': A Short *Summa* in Forty-Two Responses to Unasked Questions." *Modern Theology* 7, no. 3 (1991): 225–37.

———. *Theology and Social Theory: Beyond Secular Reason*. Oxford: Blackwell, 1990.

Milbank, John and Catherine Pickstock. *Truth in Aquinas*. London: Routledge, 2001.

Milbank, John, Catherine Pickstock, and Graham Ward, eds. *Radical Orthodoxy: A New Theology*. London: Routledge, 1998.

Mongrain, Kevin. *The Systematic Thought of Hans Urs von Balthasar: An Irenaean Retrieval*. New York: Crossroad, 2002.

Moore, Andrew. "Reason." In *The Oxford Handbook of Systematic Theology*, edited by Kathyn Tanner, John Webster, and Iain Torrence, 394–412. Oxford: Oxford University Press, 2009.

Moreland, Anna Bonta. *Known by Nature: Thomas Aquinas on Natural Knowledge of God*. New York: Crossroad, 2010.

Muck, Otto. *Die tranzendentale Methode in der scholastichen Philosophie der Gegenwart*. Innsbruck: Rauch, 1964.

Mueller, Gustav. "The Hegel Legend of Thesis-Antithesis-Synthesis." *Journal of the History of Ideas* 19, no. 3 (1958): 411–14.

Muers, Rachel. "Feminism, Gender, and Theology." In *The Modern Theologians*, 3rd ed., edited by David Ford, 431–50. Malden, MA: Blackwell, 2005.

Murphy, Francesca Aran, Balázs M. Mezei, and Kenneth Oakes. *Illuminating Faith: An Invitation to Theology*. New York: Bloomsbury Academic, 2015.

Nédoncelle, Maurice. "Le Drame de la Loi et de la Raison dans les Sermons Universitaires de J. H. Newman." *Études* 247 (1945): 66–83.

Newman, John Henry. *Apologia Pro Vita Sua*, edited by William Oddie. London: Dent: 1993.

———. *The Controversy with Gladstone: January 1874 to December 1875*. Vol. 27 of *The Letters and Diaries of John Henry Newman*, edited by Charles Dessain and Thomas Gornall. Oxford: Oxford University Press, 1975.

———. *An Essay in Aid of a Grammar of Assent*. Notre Dame: University of Notre Dame Press, 1979.

———. *Fifteen Sermons Preached before the University of Oxford between A.D. 1826 and 1843*. Notre Dame: University of Notre Dame Press, 1996.

———. *The Quotable Newman*. Vols. 1–2, edited by Dave Armstrong. Self-published, 2013.

———. *Theological Papers of John Henry Newman on Faith and Certainty*. Oxford: Clarendon, 1976.

Nichols, Aidan. *The Conversation of Faith and Reason: Modern Catholic Thought from Hermes to Benedict XVI*. Mundelein, IL: Hillenbrand Books, 2011.

———. *From Hermes to Benedict XVI: Faith and Reason in Modern Catholic Thought*. Leominster, UK: Gracewing, 2009.

Nietzsche, Friedrich. *The Anti-Christ, Ecce Homo, Twilight of the Idols, and Other Writings*, edited by Aaron Ridley. Cambridge: Cambridge University Press, 2005.

Norris, Kristopher. "Witnessing Whiteness in the Ethics of Hauerwas." *Journal of Religious Ethics* 47, no. 1 (2019): 95–124.

O'Connor, Flannery. *The Habit of Being: Letters*, edited by Sally Fitzgerald. New York: Farrar, Straus, Giroux, 1979.

O'Malley, John W. *Four Cultures of the West*. Cambridge, MA: Belknap Press of Harvard University Press, 2004.

———. *The Jesuits: A History from Ignatius to the Present*. Lanham, MD: Rowman & Littlefield, 2014.

———. *Trent and All That: Renaming Catholicism in the Early Modern Era*. Cambridge, MA: Harvard University Press, 2000.

O'Meara, Thomas. *Erich Pryzwara, S. J.: His Theology and His World.* Notre Dame: University of Notre Dame Press, 2002.

Ong, Walter J. *Orality and Literacy.* New York: Routledge, (1982) 2002.

O'Regan, Cyril. *Gnostic Return in Modernity.* Albany: State University of New York Press, 2001.

Origen. *Contra Celsum.* Translated by Henry Chadwick. Cambridge: Cambridge University Press, 1953.

———. *On First Principles.* Translated by G. W. Butterworth. New York: Harper & Row, 1966.

Padberg, John, ed. *The Constitutions of the Society of Jesus and Their Complementary Norms: A Complete English Translation of the Official Latin Texts.* St. Louis: Institute of Jesuit Sources, 1996.

Pannenberg, Wolfhart. "An Intellectual Pilgrimage." *Dialog: A Journal of Theology* 45, no. 2 (2006): 184–91.

Pascal, Blaise. *Pensées.* Translated by A. J. Krailsheimer. New York: Penguin, (1966) 1995.

Pauck, Wilhelm, Philipp Melanchthon, and Martin Bucer. *Melanchthon and Bucer.* Philadelphia: Westminster Press, 1969.

Pelikan, Jaroslav. *From Luther to Kierkegaard: A Study in the History of Theology.* 2nd ed. St. Louis: Concordia, 1963.

Pickstock, Catherine. *After Writing: On the Liturgical Consummation of Philosophy.* Oxford: Blackwell, 1998.

Pieper, Josef. *Scholasticism: Personalities and Problems of Medieval Philosophy.* Translated by Richard and Clara Winston. South Bend, IN: St. Augustine's Press, 2001.

Piketty, Thomas, and Arthur Goldhammer. *Capital in the Twenty-First Century.* Cambridge, MA: The Belknap Press of Harvard University Press, 2014.

Plantinga, Alvin. *The Ontological Argument, from St. Anselm to Contemporary Philosophers.* Garden City, NY: Anchor Books, 1965.

Pottmeyer, Hermann Josef. *Der Glaube Vor Dem Anspruch Der Wissenschaft: Die Konstitution Über Den Katholischen Glauben, Dei Filius Des1. Vatikanischen Konzils Und Der Unveröffentlichten Theologischen Voten Der Vorbereitenden Kommission.* Freiburg: Herder, 1968.

Preus, Daniel. "Luther and Erasmus: Scholastic Humanism and the Reformation." *Concordia Theological Quarterly* 46, no. 2–3 (April 1982): 219–30.

Przywara, Erich. *Analogia Entis, Metaphysics: Original Structure and Universal Rhythm*. Translated by John Betz and David Bentley Hart. Grand Rapids, MI: Eerdmans, 2014.

———. "Die Problematik der Neuscholastik." *Kant Studien* 33 (1928): 73–98.

———. "Gott in uns oder Gott über uns? Immanenz und Transcenenz im heutigen Geistesleben." *Stimmen der Zeit* 53 (1923): 343–62.

Pseudo-Dionysius. *The Complete Works*. Translated by Colm Luibhéid and Paul Rorem. New York: Paulist Press, 1987.

Purvis, Zachary. *Theology and the University in Nineteenth-Century Germany*. Oxford: Oxford University Press, 2016.

Rahner, Karl. *Hearer of the Word*. Translated by Joseph Donceel. New York: Contiuum, 1994.

———. "Laudatio auf Erich Przywara." In *Gnade als Freiheit: Kleine theologische Beiträge*, 266–73. Freiburg: Herder, 1968.

———. *Spirit of the World*. Translated by William Dych. New York: Herder and Herder, 1968.

Ratzinger, Joseph. *Introduction to Christianity*. Translated by J. R. Foster. San Francisco: Ignatius, 1990.

Ratzinger, Joseph and Habermas, Jürgen. *Dialectics of Secularization: On Reason and Religion*, edited by Florian Schuller. Translated by Brain McNeil. San Francisco: Ignatius Press, 2006.

Reimarus, Hermann. *Fragments*. Translated by Ralph Fraser. Cambridge: SCM-Canterbury, 1970.

Reinhardt, Rudolf. "Die katholish-theologische Fakultät Tübingen im ersten Jahrhundert ihres Bestehens." In *Tübinger Theologie und ihre Theologie*, edited by Rudolf Reinhardt, 1–42. Tübingen: J. C. B. Mohr, 1977.

Richardson, Cyril C. *Early Christian Fathers*. New York: Simon and Schuster, 1995.

Ridder-Symoens, Hilde de, ed. *A History of the University in Europe. Volume I: Universities in the Middle Ages*. Cambridge: Cambridge University Press, 1992.

Roberts, Alexander, and James Donaldson, eds. *Ante-Nicene Fathers: The Writings of the Fathers Down to A.D. 325*. Vol. 3. Peabody, MA: Hendrickson Publishers, 1994.

Robinette, Brian D. *Grammars of Resurrection: A Christian Theology of Presence and Absence*. New York: Crossroad, 2009.

Rohls, Jan. "Credo ut intelligam. Karl Barths theologisches Programm und sein Kontext." In *Vernunft des Glaubens. Festschrift zum 60. Geburtstag von Wolfhart Pannenberg*, edited by Jan Rohls and Gunther Wenz, 406–35. Göttingen: Vandenhoeck & Ruprecht, 1988.

Rosemann, Philipp W. *Peter Lombard*. Oxford: Oxford University Press, 2004.

Rosenberg, Randall. *The Givenness of Desire: Concrete Subjectivity and the Natural Desire to See God*. Toronto: University of Toronto Press, 2017.

Rummel, Erika. *The Humanist-Scholastic Debate in the Renaissance & Reformation*. Cambridge, MA: Harvard University Press, 1995.

Sadler, Gregory. *Reason Fulfilled by Revelation: The 1930s Christian Philosophy Debates in France*. Washington, DC: The Catholic University of America Press, 2011.

Sauer, Joseph. "Desiderius Erasmus." *The Catholic Encyclopedia*. New York: Robert Appleton Company, 1909.

Scharlemann, Robert. "Theology in Church and University: The Post-Reformation Development." *Church History*, no. 1 (1964): 23.

Scheible, Hans. "Philipp Melanchthon." In *The Oxford Encyclopedia of the Reformation*, 41–45. Oxford: Oxford University Press, 1996.

Schindler, D. C. *The Catholicity of Reason*. Grand Rapids, MI: Eerdmans, 2013.

Schleiermacher, Friedrich. *The Christian Faith*, edited by H. R. Mackintosh and James S. Stewart. Edinburgh: T & T Clark, 1948.

Schwöbel, Christoph. "Wolfhart Pannenberg." In *The Modern Theologians*, 3rd ed., edited by David Ford, 129–46. Malden, MA: Blackwell, 2005.

Scottus, John Duns. *Prologue de l'Ordinatio*, edited and translated by Gérard Sondag. Paris: Presses Universitaires de France, 1999.

Shea, C. Michael. "Faith, Reason, and Ecclesiastical Authority in Giovanni Perrone's Praelectiones Theologicae." *Gregorianum* 95, no. 1 (2014): 159–77.

———. *Newman's Early Roman Catholic Legacy, 1845–1854*. Oxford: Oxford University Press, 2017.

Sherwood, Yvonne and Kevin Hart, eds. *Derrida and Religion: Other Testaments*. New York: Routledge, 2005.

Skaggs, Rebecca. "The Role of Reason in Faith in St. Thomas Aquinas and Kierkegaard." *Heythrop Journal* 58 (2017): 612–25.

Smith, James K. A. "Who's Afraid of Postmodernism? A Response to the 'Biola School." In *Christianity and the Postmodern Turn: Six Views*, edited by Myron Penner, 215–28. Grand Rapids, MI: Brazos, 2005.

————. *Who's Afraid of Postmodernism? Taking Derrida, Lyotard, and Foucault to Church.* Grand Rapids, MI: Baker Academic, 2006.

Sorkin, David Jan. *The Religious Enlightenment: Protestants, Jews, and Catholics from London to Vienna.* Princeton: Princeton University Press, 2008.

Spade, Paul Vincent, ed. *The Cambridge Companion to Ockham.* Cambridge: Cambridge University Press, 1999.

Spinoza, Benedictus de. *Theological-Political Treatise.* Translated by Samuel Shirley. Indianapolis: Hackett, 1998.

Stump, Eleonore. *The God of the Bible and the God of the Philosophers.* Milwaukee: Marquette University Press, 2016.

Taylor, Charles. *A Secular Age.* Cambridge, MA: Belknap Press of Harvard University Press, 2007.

————. *The Sources of the Self: The Making of Modern Identity.* Cambridge, MA: Harvard University Press, 1989.

Taylor, Mark. *Altarity.* Chicago: University of Chicago Press, 1987.

————. *Erring: A Postmodern A/theology.* Chicago: University of Chicago Press, 1984.

Thiessen, Matthew. *Paul and the Gentile Problem.* Oxford: Oxford University Press, 2016.

Thiselton, Anthony. "Biblical Interpretation." In *The Modern Theologians*, 3rd ed., edited by David Ford, 287–304. Malden, MA: Blackwell, 2005.

Thomas Aquinas. *On Faith and Reason*, edited by Stephen F. Brown. Indianapolis: Hackett, 1999.

————. *On the Truth of the Catholic Faith: Summa Contra Gentiles.* Translated by Anton C. Pegis. Garden City, NY: Hanover House, 1955.

Toulmin, Stephen. *Cosmopolis: The Hidden Agenda of Modernity.* New York: Free Press, 1990.

Turner, Denys. *Faith, Reason, and the Existence of God.* Cambridge: Cambridge University Press, 2004.

————. *Thomas Aquinas: A Portrait.* New Haven, CT: Yale University Press, 2013.

Turner, Frank. *John Henry Newman: The Challenge to Evangelical Religion.* New Haven, CT: Yale University Press, 2002.

Van Nieuwenhove, Rik. *An Introduction to Medieval Theology.* Cambridge: Cambridge University Press, 2012.

Viviano, Benedict Thomas. *A Short History of New Testament Studies*. Chicago: New Priority Press, 2016.

Voegelin, Eric. *From Enlightenment to Revolution*, edited by John Hallowell. Durham. NC: Duke University Press, 1975.

Ward, Graham. "Postmodern Theology." In *The Modern Theologians*, 3rd ed., edited by David Ford, 322–38. Malden, MA: Blackwell, 2005.

Waugh, B. G. "Reason Within the Limits of Revelation Alone: John Calvin's Understanding of Human Reason." *Westminster Theological Journal*, 2010.

Wesley, John. *The Heart of John Wesley's Journal*, edited by Percy Livingstone Parker. Peabody, MA: Hendrickson, 2008.

Westphal, Merold. "Kierkegaard on Faith, Reason, and Passion." *Faith and Philosophy* 28, no. 1 (2011): 82–92.

Whapham, Theodore. *The Unity of Theology: The Contribution of Wolfhart Pannenberg*. Minneapolis: Fortress Press, 2015.

White, Carolinne, ed. *Early Christian Lives*. New York: Penguin, 1998.

Whitford, David M., ed. *T&T Clark Companion to Reformation Theology*. London: T & T Clark, 2012.

Wilken, Robert Louis. *The Spirit of Early Christian Thought: Seeking the Face of God*. New Haven, CT: Yale University Press, 2003.

Wilkens, Steve and Alan Padgett. *Faith & Reason in the 19th Century*. Vol. 2 of *Christianity and Western Thought*. Downers Grove, IL: InterVarsity, 2000.

Wilkins, Jeremy. *Before Truth: Lonergan, Aquinas and the Problem of Wisdom*. Washington, DC: The Catholic University of America Press, 2018.

Williams, George Huntston. *The Radical Reformation*. 3rd ed. Kirksville, MO: Sixteenth Century Journal Publishers, 1992.

Wilson, Peter H. *Heart of Europe: A History of the Holy Roman Empire*. Cambridge, MA: Belknap Press of Harvard University Press, 2016.

Wolfe, Judith. *Heidegger and Theology*. London: Bloomsbury, 2014.

Index

Abelard, Peter, 41n8, 54–66, 97, 217, 333
Anselm of Canterbury, 3, 39, 48–55, 65,
 82, 89n65, 93, 103, 107, 134, 155–57,
 182, 191, 215, 250–53, 272, 333
Aquinas, Thomas, xivn8, xv, 179, 334; the
 Angelic Doctor, 73–86; and Aristotle,
 207; and Bonaventure, 69, 71, 86, 89,
 93, 96, 132; and early modernity, 154–
 55; and Kierkegaard, 218n112,
 220n118; and Kuhn, 189–92, 195; and
 Lombard, 40, 63; in mid-twentieth-
 century theology, 261, 263, 266–69,
 271–73, 277; and Ockham, 97–98,
 103–4; and postmodern theology, 296,
 302, 307–11, 317–18; and the Reformation, 107, 112, 121n49, 134, 145;
 and Scotus, 96–101, 103–4. *See also*
 neo-Thomism/neo-Thomist
Aristotle: and the Bible, 325; and Calvin,
 139; and the *Constitutions of the Society of Jesus*, 145; and early medieval
 theology, 40, 42, 57; and early modernity, 152; and the High Middle Ages,
 71–74, 76–77, 80–81, 87, 90–91, 93,
 95–98, 100–103; and humanism, 107–
 9, 111–14; and Kierkegaard, 220; and
 Luther, 116, 121; and Melanchthon,
 122–26, 132; *Metaphysics*, 316; and
 neo-scholasticism, 260; and Newman,
 196–97, 199, 204–7; *Nicomachean
 Ethics*, 32, 206. *See also* Aristotelean
Aristotelean, 235, 238, 296, 301. *See also*
 Aristotle
Athanasius of Alexandria, 24–29, 95
Augustine of Hippo, 14n25, 29–37, 39,
 148–51, 179, 251, 266, 334; and Abelard, 57; and Anselm, 50, 52; and Aristotle, 73; and Boethius, 42; and Bonaventure, 88, 91–92, 95; and Calvin,
 134; and Erasmus, 112–13; and Eriugena, 46–47; and Hugh of St. Victor,
 59–59; and the Jansenists, 171; and
 Kuhn, 189, 191–92; and Lombard, 63–
 64; and Luther, 120; and Melanchthon,
 125; and the Pietists, 165; and postmodernity, 283, 306–8, 310n85; and

Scotus, 99, 102; and Spinoza, 160. *See
 also* Augustinian/Augustinianism
Augustinian/Augustinianism, 46–47, 92,
 99, 115, 134n85, 173n66, 278, 301–2,
 305–7
Averroes. *See* Ibn Rushd

Balthasar, Hans Urs von, 14–16, 18, 110,
 174n66, 245, 250n74, 261–63, 267,
 271n53, 274–79, 313, 334
Barth, Karl, 120n42, 227–28, 245–53,
 255–60, 262–65, 271, 274, 278–79,
 298, 304
Baur, Ferdinand Christian, 177, 209–16,
 227, 229, 245, 253, 259, 326
Benedict XVI, x, xv, 187–88, 232n15,
 244n52, 263n19, 277n76, 314–15,
 319n114, 322–28, 334
Bernard of Clairvaux, 55, 57, 59, 89n65
Blondel, Maurice, 93, 227, 236–45, 267–
 68, 270, 274, 278, 313, 319
Boethius, Anicius Manlius Severinus, 41–
 44, 48, 62, 71, 75, 107
Bologna (university), 70
Bonaventure, 69, 71, 74, 86–100, 124,
 132–33, 157, 234, 238, 273, 312, 326,
 333
Buddhism, 182, 301
Bultmann, Rudolf, 120n42, 255–56

Calvin, John/Calvinist, 128n67, 133–41,
 143, 174
Carter, J. Kameron, 289n19, 294–97
Catholic Worker, 73
Chenu, Marie-Dominique, 54–55, 261,
 274
Clement of Alexandria, 11, 189
Copernicus, Nicolaus, 147, 150, 181
Corinth/Corinthians, 4–6, 8, 22, 33, 37,
 139

Day, Dorothy, 73
de Lubac, Henri, 18, 110, 227, 242, 261,
 274–75
Derrida, Jacques, 256n5, 282, 286, 288,
 302, 305–6